Planet Cosplay

Planet Cosplay
Costume Play, Identity and Global Fandom

Paul Mountfort, Anne Peirson-Smith and Adam Geczy

intellect Bristol, UK / Chicago, USA

Published in the UK in 2019 by
Intellect, The Mill, Parnall Road, Fishponds, Bristol, BS16 3JG, UK

Published in the USA in 2019 by
Intellect, The University of Chicago Press, 1427 E. 60th Street,
Chicago, IL 60637, USA

A catalogue record for this book is available from the
British Library.

Copy-editor: MPS Technologies
Cover designer: Aleksandra Szumlas
Cover image: *Sentinel of Atlantis* by Marko Stamatovic.
Adobe Stock image no. 94559032.
Production manager: Matthew Floyd and Faith Newcombe
Typesetting: Contentra Technologies

Print ISBN: 978-1-78938-151-1
ePDF ISBN: 978-1-78320-958-3
ePUB ISBN: 978-1-78320-957-6

Contents

Acknowledgements

The authors would like to thank Mark Lewis, James Campbell, Matthew Floyd and Faith Newcombe at Intellect Books for their invaluable support throughout the development of this book.

We would also like to thank all of the cosplayers who were interviewed and photographed during our many visits to Planet Cosplay, as it has allowed us to share their story with a wider community.

Introduction

Cosplay, a portmanteau term derived from 'costume + play', is both a highly contemporary phenomenon and also part of something quite venerable. Dressing up is fundamental to interpersonal relations, communication and socialization. In a sense, dressing is always dressing up, as it is central to the social performance of self. Nonetheless, dressing up in the specific context of cosplay is different from its historical, costumed precursors. It has its roots in the mid to late twentieth century cross-pollination between American and Japanese popular culture, and has gone global with twenty-first-century media convergence. Cosplay today reflects contemporary fandoms' unprecedented modes of mass cultural engagement, on and offline.

While San Diego's Comic-Con and Tokyo's Comiket are famous, flagship cosplay events, with hundreds of thousands of 'cosers' dressed up for the occasion, cosplay runs the gambit of venue and convention spaces. A typical example of the niche cosplaying events that are proliferating globally has been recent Seattle Sakura-Cons, modest sized manga/anime conventions that see the streets, cafés and foyers of boutique hotels around the Washington State Convention Centre spilling over with masked participants in a surreal spectacle. Inside the halls, delegates are treated to exhibitions, merchandise, screenings and, of course, cosplay competitions. Outside, the hanging gardens of Freeway Park provide spaces that fans appropriate for displaying their costumes, meeting and greeting, staging more-or-less impromptu celebrations of popular cosplay characters, and setting up photo shoots against the Brutalist sculptural backdrop of this unique urban oasis. A visitor from another planet—or from some far-flung part of this one where cosplay is unknown—might wonder what kind of strange and wondrous species humanity is, so rich and diverse in its garb and many shades of costumed embodiment.

While cosplayers may be readily identifiable at habitual sites of performance such as fan conventions, cosplay is a deceptively complex practice that defies neat description and ready categorization. An uncontroversial definition would be that cosplay refers to people dressing up and performing as characters from popular media, including comics, animated or live action films, television, games and other pop culture sources such as music videos. A particular indebtedness to the science fiction and the superhero genres, along with Japanese sources such as manga, anime, gaming, *otaku* and idol culture is often stressed. However, even this broad definition conceals tensions and shifts that have taken place among cosplay scholars—and cosers—over time. Early commentators such as Theresa Winge linked cosplay specifically to the Japanese otaku (hardcore nerd, geek) practice of wearing 'detailed makeup and elaborate costumes modelled after their favourite anime, manga and related video game characters.'[1] When occurring outside of Japan, cosplay was consequently seen as the assumption of character personae from Japanese source media[2] or an opportunity for 'fans to dress up for playing their favourite characters from sources such as animation, mangas, video games, science fiction stories, and fantasy.'[3] Despite recognition that cosplay today has become a truly global phenomenon it is still commonly claimed to have started in Japan, largely because the term was coined there in 1983.[4]

In fact, the backstory of cosplay provided in this book shows how cosplay's immediate progenitor, costuming, started in the United States, which had at least equal influence alongside Japan during the formative phase of its development from the late 1960s through to the 1990s. Media texts from these countries, two of the world's largest cultural producers, still dominate cosplay culture two decades into the twenty-first century, but today, anything is fair game from music videos to Internet memes. Many scholars consequently opt for broader definitions, referring to the more general 'practice of adopting the appearance of fictional characters from popular culture'[5] or 'dressing up and posing in a visually recognizable way as characters from popular media.'[6] Instead of revolving around Japan alone, cosplay is widely acknowledged as part of a 'global practice of building costumes and performing as characters' from popular media sources 'whose narratives have produced characters that have developed a fan base.'[7]

Fans dressing up for dedicated events in fantastical garb from popular media may at first sight appear to be a relatively straightforward phenomenon. However, as this book will demonstrate, this surface impression conceals many subtleties that need to be approached from multiple perspectives in order to be progressively unmasked. These range from the material, including the physical construction of costumes, to the aesthetic, such as the affective responses they provoke.[8] Critical issues implicated in cosplay include the citation of specific source texts, photographic practices circulating around (and shaping) their costumed embodiment, and the performative intersection of these textual and visual dimensions at cosplay events. There is the particular form of play alluded to in cosplay to be considered, the mapping of cosplaying sites, physical and virtual, and the creative element of this community of practice beyond 'mere' technical craft. Resonances with past performance arts involving mask and masquerade abound, along with considerable bending of gender and identity, (real or projected) associations with the erotic and—provocatively— the pornographic. Cosplay is an affect-laden practice, but one whose psychology is only truly activated in the social sphere. Philosophically, it chimes with our posthuman, virtual and networked selves. Correspondingly, the title of this book refers both to cosplay as a global practice and the fact that it constitutes a world of its own, referred to below as the 'cosphere,'[9] in which fans forge and contest identity.

For cosplay is, above all, the acting out of a hybridized identity that has been described as 'akin to performance art, taking on the habitus of a particular character through costume, accessories, gesture and attitude; it is therefore not simply "dressing up" but rather inhabiting the role of a character both physically and mentally.'[10] In the words of Matthew Hale, the term

4

describes a performative action in which one dons a costume and/or accessories and manipulates his or her posture, gesture and language in order to generate meaningful correspondences between a given body and set of texts from which it is modelled and made to relate.[11]

A performance requires an audience, and as Ellen Kirkpatrick notes of the role of spectators, cosplay is 'a simultaneous performance—as source character and as member of the cosplaying community'.[12] This community is itself a double-edged sword that can mete out approval or condemnation, not to mention the wider audience of online commentators and self-appointed opinion makers. Like all performers, cosplayers find themselves in a hall of specular gazes, not all of them welcome.

What perhaps above all distinguishes cosplay from earlier performance practices, such as carnivals, masques, masquerades and theatrical forms, both eastern and western, is its dependence on source texts from popular new media. Given that these were non-existent prior to the twentieth and twenty-first centuries, it must inevitably be seen as a product of modernity, postmodernity and even what has been dubbed the posthuman. The birth of comic superheroes and popularization of science fiction coincide with a period that was only beginning to recover from the Depression, and which faced the very real threats of both fascism and Stalinism. Created in the year that the Nazis came to power in 1933, Superman first appeared in *Action Comics #1* in June 1938, Batman a year later (*Detective Comics #27*, May 1939). As if anticipating historical events, Captain America was born in March 1941 and would be 'every boy's' nationalist hero once the United States entered the Second World War in the wake of Japan's attack on Pearl Harbor eight months later in early December. Wonder Woman debuted in *All Star Comics #8* in October of that same eventful year, her depiction drawing inspiration from early feminists and Amazonian mythology, though all wrapped up, of course, in the Stars and Stripes (Diana Prince, after all, worked for the Justice Society of America). As symbolic defensive avatars of Cold War peril, Spiderman arrived, ironically again, just three months before the Cuban Missile Crisis in October 1962, followed by the troubled crusaders, Hulk and Thor, and then Iron Man the following year. These would eventually incarnate into action figures and media identities, but not before G.I. Joe, who appeared on the market in 1964.

Cosplay's immediate precursor, in the practice known as costuming, is evidenced in Worldcon sci-fi conventions from as early as 1939 and gained a foothold in the cons of the 1940s and 1950s with some notable costume makers, performers and competitions. However, it did not fully take off until several decades later. Given the many constraints and the turmoil of the Depression (including Prohibition), and that comics were still young, along with the rigours imposed by a second world war, it is entirely understandable that the popularization of dressing up in science fictional garb or as superheroes, not yet called cosplay, only gained real impetus from the late 1960s on. It was one of many indications of the great economic surge that the United States enjoyed at the time, with transformations in the media economy and the rise of what we would now identify as modern fandoms and associated fan practices. The influence of comics culture (such as independent comic stands that would become independent stores) and the introduction of colour television would see a widening fan base that would dress up as Batman, Wonder Woman or their favourite characters from *Star Trek* (1966–69) and other classic sci-fi series in the late 1960s and into the 1970s. Fanzines had existed since the early 1930s, but suddenly fan appropriation really began to gain wings via the often subversive practices of fanfiction writing. The advent of mega-conventions cemented in place the older craze of costuming, in which fans embodied their chosen characters in fantastical garb, often of their own construction. It will be argued that this popularity and visibility of dressing up in North America helped provide Japanese fans the impetus in the 1970s and 1980s to dress as their preferred heroes, derived from manga, anime and Japanese popular culture more generally.[13]

Ironically, for those who insist on Japanese origins, the word cosplay was promoted and popularized by Nobuyuki Takahashi after attending the Los Angeles Worldcon in 1984. Although some costuming was already taking place in Japan, as founder of the anime publishing company Studio Hard, Takahashi was impressed by the number of people dressed up and the quality of their costumes, which indicated that they were in collegial competition with one another. He took this experience back to Japan and encouraged his readers to do the same—to realize popular Japanese media characters with their own costumed selves. The coinage of the word cosplay was necessitated by the nuanced meaning of the Japanese equivalent of the word 'masquerade,' which literally connoted the less than appropriate notion of an 'aristocratic costume party.' To surmount this problem he coined his own phrase, 'costume play,' which was quickly truncated to 'cosplay' or *kosupure*, following the common habit of appropriating *gairaigo* (foreign language) terms into Japanese. Practitioners were by extension 'cosplayers.'[14] Japanese fans were referred to as otaku, a slur levelled at a subculture of extreme geeks with affective attachments to a range of niche cultural products—though the otaku identity has since gained some degree of cultural cache. By this time, manga and anime had already begun to have a considerable effect on North American markets, and some fans adopted the term as a badge of subcultural belonging. Just as western media and related fan practices, such as sci-fi and comics conventions, influenced Japanese popular culture, so Japanese media in turn began to cross-pollinate western popular culture.

Since the 1980s, the fan convention has been organized much like major conferences in academe, except oriented towards popular culture. It has focus activities, panels, ordinary attendees and special 'delegates' who are usually the celebrities that played a character or did the voice-over in a popular franchise, with video rooms for screenings and organized performances. Unlike academia, prizes are often offered for the best costumes, on the basis of masquerades or competitions sometimes staged on catwalk runways, and there are numerous stands selling pop cultural merchandise. It is also an appropriate market for launching upcoming films, televisions series, computer games, and of course spills over into promotional websites and related online platforms. Fan conventions are now highly structured gatherings that have become a significant means by which cosplayers communicate with one another and form affinity groups. They are literally sites for action and exchange in which the participants share a common language and common goals. They are a way of giving material locus to what exists simultaneously on a virtual scale online.

Hence cosplay is a complex marriage of the immaterial and material, the virtual and the actual. It gives the imaginary embodiment. In parallel with its momentum in virtual space, an important aspect to have emerged is the way in which costumes are designed and crafted. While costumes of varying levels of quality can be bought in shops or online, dedicated cosplayers tend to lavish enormous amounts of attention on making their own costumes, or overseeing their making. Theresa Winge's comments of a decade ago still pertain today, though 3D printing is beginning to make inroads into their manufacture:

> Cosplayers exist at various places along a cosplay continuum, which is based on their level of commitment. At one end are cosplayers content with dressing (e.g., wig, makeup, and costume) as their chosen character and attending conventions and events for socializing and having fun. At the other end are those cosplayers obsessed with a given character, re-creating that character with meticulous attention to detail and performing as that character as often as time and money will allow. Between these two extremes there are cosplayers who research, study, and practice their characters and participate in cosplay events, such as masquerade and karaoke. Regardless of his or her place on the cosplay continuum, each cosplayer has an extraordinary level of dedication and commitment to the depiction of the chosen character, based on individual objectives that may include, but are not limited to, the following criteria: humor, accurate depiction, and casual participation.[15]

From this we can conclude that cosplay is not your typical play, but rather a subcultural activity of a very unusual and distinctive bent that sits at the intersection of multiple fandoms, which for some people are a way of life, of being in the world.

It is also metonymic of wider shifts in an age of pervasive new and social media whereby identity is increasingly framed not simply by literal bodies in physical space but digital avatars. The proliferation of these virtual selves has helped radically overturn older, common-sense notions of who we are and what we can be. At this point it may be useful to dispense with the presumption that there is a real identity behind the constructed one, a vestigial human truth behind the mask. Rather, identity in our posthuman society lies in a series of transformations through which the self becomes the self. The self is performance, or a set of performances. While this has arguably always been the case, virtual identities have made this a normal form of social and psychological conditioning. As is so often commented, the selves that exist on social media sites such as Instagram and Tumblr are particular projections of a self that the individual deems desirable, and reflects the kinds of personalities and types they wish to attract. They present wish-worlds that have escaped from workaday reality.

One of the important lessons of media theorists such as Walter Benjamin, Marshall McLuhan and Jean Baudrillard is to try to break the habitual perception that we are somehow outside of media, and that we have a perceptual power and control that is independent of the media we use. Rather, media inhabits us and is coterminous with our cognitive functions. To embrace this is also to understand the lifeworlds of most of us who, to differing degrees, exist not only distributed across messenger apps, micro-blogs and other social media platforms but express ourselves in cartoonish likes and dislikes, emojis and avatars. We have devices that need 'customization' wherein we make choices that reflect who we are (read: who we want to be). We constantly curate our online profiles. Consider these prophetic words by McLuhan in his essay on photography:

> Even the inner life of feelings and emotions began to be structured and ordered and analyzed according to separate pictorial landscapes [...]. Photography, by carrying the pictorial delineation of natural objects much further than paint or language could do, had the *reverse* effect. By conferring a means of self-delineation of objects, of 'statement without syntax,' photography gave the impetus to a delineation of the inner world.[16]

Two points can be made here. The first is the way in which the medium insinuates itself into consciousness and creates a different order of thought and different way of organizing the world. The second is an extrapolation of this point: social media and multiple moving image formats mean we exist in several places and in several guises at once. We no longer think it magical to see images from the other side of the world unfold before us, nor do we think twice when we are given a raft of choices to customize our action character or our racing vehicle in our Xbox or PlayStation game. We are not simply 'made to believe' that we have a character or thing unique to us, these are our avatars—they are us.

Approaches

While doing appropriate justice to the cosplay phenomenon requires multiple disciplinary approaches, one affordance is that the history of academic investigation into the subject stretches back a mere decade. Despite subcultural studies dating to the formative 1970s, before 2005, commentary on cosplay was limited to general and non-scholarly sources, essentially newspapers, magazines and online articles. Comparatively short, non-academic works such as Michael Bruno's pieces for *Glitz and Glitter Newsletter* in 2002, and books like Takako Aoyama and Jennifer Cahill's *Cosplay Girls: Japan's Live Animation Heroines* (2003) and Robert Holzek's *Cosplay: The New Main Attraction* (2004), are still quoted in journal articles due to the relative dearth of material in this pre-theoretical phase.[17] However, the 1990s and early 2000s saw the groundwork laid in the arenas of subcultural, gender and performance studies for an appreciation of cosplay. Intersections around gender as a performance inscribed on the physical bodies of social actors, and its queering, have proved especially well suited.[18] At the same time, related practices such as fanfiction were being reframed by Henry Jenkins' famous formulation of fans as 'textual poachers,'[19] while discourses around gaming, narrative and identity foregrounded the 'ludic' (or rule-based play) as both a performative and, potentially, critical practice.[20]

Parallel with these developments, manga, anime and associated fandoms in Japanese otaku culture had become fashionable topics in the 1990s. The millennial milestone was marked by Susan Napier's frequently quoted *Anime from Akira to Princess Mononoke* (2001), later reissued as *Anime from Akira to Howl's Moving Castle* (2005).[21] The following year, 2006, saw the launch of *Mechademia*, an international peer-reviewed academic journal oriented around Japanese popular culture studies edited by Frenchy Lunning. The inaugural issue was subtitled 'Emerging Worlds of Anime and Manga,' and the journal has since helped establish Japanese popular culture as a major site of critical theory, alongside a range of other journals, books and related publications.[22] *Mechademia*'s first issue contained a pivotal article, Theresa Winge's 'Costuming the Imagination: Origins of Manga and Anime,' which offered one of the first theoretical accounts of cosplay. Fans' performance of their chosen characters was based on research and study into a source text, leading to an 'interpretation that takes place by reading and watching.'[23] This was the same year Jenkins famously argued in *Convergence Culture* (2006) that, far from being cultural dupes to corporate franchises, fans were critical readers and (re)writers of cultural texts.

Articles rapidly followed on cosplay's relationship to gaming and conventions, the motif of the doll, and site-specific studies in the United States as well as Taiwan, with the first published photographic monograph, Elena Dorfman's *Fandomania*, appearing in 2007.[24] The horses were out of the stable, so to speak, and there has been since then a rising drumbeat of critical and theoretical response to this dynamic popular cultural practice. The text-to-performance continuum has remained a notable focus. Nicolle Lamerichs, for instance, has explored cosplay in relation to allied fan practices such as fanfiction, fan videos and fan art. She concludes it involves both textual interpretation and performativity, in reference to Judith Butler's notion of gender as a socially predetermined performance.[25] Matthew Hale evokes intertextuality to describe how cosplay replicates, revises and modulates mass-mediated public texts.[26] Some have honed in on particular canons of source or 'parent' texts, such as Maria Patrice Amon's discussion on innocence and deviance in Disney cosplay, Kane Anderson's autoethnographic investigation of 'becoming Batman' at San Diego's Comic-Con, and Ellen Kirkpatrick on the particular relevance of the superhero genre, both as source material and a metonym of cosplay itself (as for caped crusaders, so for fans: Peter Parker by day, Spiderman by night).[27]

However, others have been critical of overly textual approaches, stressing the bodily and embodied dimensions of the practice. Gender, queer and 'crossplay' have been frequently constellated. For Alexis Hieu Truong cosplayers negotiate bodily and subjective experience, including that of gender, through play, with implications teased out in terms of Harold Garfinkel's conception of gender as a '"doing" rather than a "being."'[28] Larissa Hjorth has looked at how, through cosplay, her Melbourne-based female gaming subjects re-imagined Japanese markers of gender.[29] Similarly, Patrick W. Galbraith has considered cosplay and Lolita in relation to gender in both Japanese and Australian convention culture contexts, while Kinko Ito and Paul A. Crutcher have triangulated cosplay with manga and pachinko in Japanese role playing and gender-bending.[30] Lunning's original study of crossplay in light of cross-dressing and gender-shifting characters in source texts has proved to be a useful point of departure, extended by Emerald King, for example, to female cosplayers playing male characters from *yaoi*, also known as BL (Boys Love) anime.[31] For Joel Gn the ambiguous appearance of cosplayer's bodies is a 'queer simulation' that challenges essentialist notions of gender in their quintessential artificiality.[32] Indeed, few authors have ignored gender as it is fundamental to so many aspects of cosplay.

Cosplay is clearly a performance form that radically problematizes identity. Lamerichs has looked elsewhere at ways in which the creating and wearing of costumes in cosplaying circles are both a subcultural practice and performance that go beyond the 'remit of the theatre,' while Anne Peirson-Smith has used social interaction theory to frame cosplay in the South East Asian context as the fashioning of a fantastical self via themed costumes.[33] Ethnography and autoethnography have been pivotal to the emerging theorization of cosplay, and some scholars are part of the cosplaying community. Where Rie Matsuura and Daisuke Okabe's participant observation frames cosplay in the Japanese context as a female DIY (do-it-yourself) culture of doing-and-making that is the collective achievement of a peer-based fan culture, Osmud Rahman, Liu Wing-sun and Brittany Hei-man Cheung deploy 'quasi-ethnography' to examine Hong Kong's cosplay culture experientially in terms of the motivations of cosplayers, with profound implications for authenticity, affective attachment and the 'extended self.'[34] Craig Norris and Jason Bainbridge challenge the romanticizing of cosplay as a grassroots practice with their situated model of industry interaction, in contrast to Suzanne Scott who is critical of the gendering and exploitation of female labour in the commercialized context of the Syfy Channel's widely loathed reality TV show, *Heroes of Cosplay* (2013–14).[35]

This reminds us that still and moving images are central both as sources and expressions of cosplay. Cosplay lends itself most willingly to the medium of the photo essay, as proved by Eron Rauch in co-publications with Christopher Bolton and Maranatha Wilson, with an emphasis on networks of desire (including those of researchers) in cosplay observation and participation.[36] Matthew Ogonoski has analysed cosplay in terms of the ontological characteristics of manga and anime, concluding that it is materially and conceptually allied to the phenomenon of the anime database, and thus static image iconicity.[37] Sebastian Domsch has likened this iconicity to the *tableaux vivants* (living pictures) of the nineteenth century, when set poses replicating famous scenes were the order of the day.[38] New media, such as cosplay music videos (CMVs), where fans remediate the convention cosplay performance in online video mash-ups on YouTube, are coming to light. Future directions have been suggested by Paul Booth's 2015 chapter 'Digital Cosplay,' where he discusses the mechanics of corporate-funded sites such as Polyvore where users 'dress' avatars from popular media shows in clothes that can be purchased via conveniently positioned links, mixing 'the nostalgia inherent in fan pastiche and the novelty implied in media parody.'[39] Finally, not to be forgotten are the non-academic and often on-demand or indie-published 'how to' guides for costume making and cosplay practice that continue to find a ready market among dedicated fans.[40] However, to date the field has not occasioned sustained, book-length scholarly reference works and there is a glaring lack of integration among the diverse disciplinary approaches to cosplay.

Planet Cosplay

Planet Cosplay aims to address the current dearth of scholarly monographs on cosplay by providing as rounded an account of these multiple dimensions of the practice as possible. While acknowledging that there can be no one 'critical theory of cosplay' it does nonetheless offer three major avenues of approach within the broader domain of popular culture studies. Of course, these are not discrete and there are multiple overlaps, but they do serve to define some key modes of investigation into the subject.

The first, presented in Part I: Critical Practice, builds on literary and critical theory around intertextualities, photographic practices and their points of intersection. Chapter 1, 'Cosplay as Citation' frames cosplay as a contemporary fan practice via the ways in which cosplayers' reference their chosen source texts. Cosplay itself thus becomes a critical practice—a form of citation by which players' bodies are transformed into texts that make reference to other, publically available texts. This way of relating to popular media sits alongside the emergence of modern fan cultures and parallel practices of 'textual poaching' such as fanfiction. A brief genealogy of some founding texts is provided, starting with *Star Trek* (1967–69) and other sci-fi and comics media from the 1960s and 1970s. Japan is where the term 'cosplay' arose, yet this chapter argues that the evidence clearly points to its emergence from a circulation of cultural practices between the United States and Japan. Ultimately, the performance of cosplay is seen to generate alternate states of mind and ways of being in the world. Equally, amid the spectacle of the convention, a tableau of predominantly static images is produced for spectators, paving the way for the discussion of cosphotography in the next chapter.

Chapter 2, 'Cosphotography and Fan Capital' investigates photographic practices at cosplaying sites. Cosplay's direct antecedent, costuming, is evidenced from as early as New York's Worldcon of 1939, prefiguring the emergence of three formative genres of cosplay photography: the fashion-shoot, studio portrait and 'hallway' snapshot. Today, cosphotography is a site of tension between fan-directed and commercial cosplay, the heterotopian and hegemonic control of cosplaying spaces. For cosers, photographs and video can serve as tokens of exchange within an economy of desire that values subcultural capital or hipness rather than raw dollar value. However, commercial conscription and other regressive social forces constantly threaten the heterotopian (or anti-hegemonic) spaces of cosplay. The reality TV shows *Heroes of Cosplay* (2013–14) and its follow up *Cosplay Melee* (2017–)[41] have been vilified as prime culprits in repositioning cosplay from a collective endeavour into a competitive sport. This chapter concludes, however, that for the moment static images remain the privileged product of fan-directed cosphotography, retaining considerable currency within the cosphere and even preconditioning elements of cosplay performance, both in and beyond convention spaces.

Chapter 3, 'Cosplay at Armageddon,' brings these textual and visual dimensions together in a photo-essay and commentary framing five years of cosplay practice at an Australasian-based fan convention, Armageddon Expo. This popular 'con' exhibits a glittering array of cosplayed characters from a global collection of media texts, including sci-fi shows such as *Doctor Who* (1963–), space fantasies like *Star Wars* (1977–), fantasy works such as *Game of Thrones* (2011–), as well as a wide variety of manga, anime, gaming and other media sources. The half-decade between 2012 and 2016 that the fifty photographs document is sufficient to reveal some micro-trends, including the spiking of certain cosplay memes. They represent a complex mixture of the new laced with older, legacy media texts that continue to be recycled in cosplaying circles. The photographic approach here largely eschews the cultural dominants of cosphotography discussed in Chapter 2 to present, instead, a candid style aligned to street photography. The rationale for this is discussed in terms of a documentary purpose that highlights the unscripted juxtaposition of fantastic bodies—in the Bakhtinian sense—within the often quotidian locations of conference halls and adjacent spaces. The ethos is that of the 'civil contract' model of public photography, which is itself a critical practice.

Part II: Ethnographies charts cosplay in a globalized context informed by observation and interview material that has a significant, but not exclusive, East Asian focus. Located in a variety of scapes—ethno, techno, media, finance and ideoscapes[42]—it gravitates towards the more situated, sociological approach associated with the French, Frankfurt, Chicago and Birmingham schools (and beyond). Chapter 4, 'Cos/play' locates accounts by cosplayers of their activity within the discourses and dualities of play theory. Such dualities include the formal versus informal, rule-based versus non-rule based, bounded versus non-bounded cosplay. Central to these is the construction of performed individual identity as validated by the audience gaze. This chapter explains cosplay as an imaginative escapade derived from childhood mimicry founded on socialization and learning, through to lived adult experiences that are hedonic yet purposeful. In other words, cosplay is a form of play that occurs in its own physical, cognitive and social domain that expresses an extraordinary otherness through spectacular costumed performance. It occurs metaphorically in a dynamic playworld, an interactive membrane or 'magic circle' whereby cosplayers traverse and transgress the realities of everyday life, seeking solace in a like-minded community of practice based on endless interpretations of how to play within the rules of the game.

Chapter 5, 'Cosplay Sites,' tracks cosplay as a global practice that is nonetheless characterized by specific transnational culture flows between—and radiating out from—dominant cultural centres. This chapter demonstrates how these multiple mobilities underpin cosplay practice, largely arcing out from the world's top two media production centres, North America and East Asia. Some commentators have seen transnational flows in terms of a borderless world that has constantly reduced difference, thereby suppressing local differences. Others emphasize the dynamic hybridity of localized cultural forms and practices. Cosplay can be explained in terms of these situated dualities, which help frame the substantial body of participant observation and interviews underpinning this chapter. It will also suggest that regional divergences in the degree of agency afforded to cosers in cosplay activity are subject to the prevailing contexts—political, economic and cultural—in which cosplayers find themselves.

Bringing together the previously discussed factors of the playworld and multiple sites in which cosplay is performed, Chapter 6, 'Cos/creation,' situates cosplay within both capital flows and the cultural economies to which it often has an ambivalent relationship. The practice has evolved in concert with shifting definitions of creativity that have progressively repositioned the latter from being seen in terms of the aesthetic achievements of the individual artist to a social practice owing at least as much to the collective efforts of cultural intermediaries. Consequently, the main argument centres on how cosplay exemplifies creativity-in-action through a range of acts by individuals operating within a cultural field. Creativity in this domain occurs, as the coser testimonies related here suggest, as expressions of individual agency within a wider collaborative effort. It is a form of resistance to, and perhaps accommodation with, the everyday practices of living and being, based on cultural appropriation, the re-creation of fictional characters and reification of the imaginary.

As its title suggests, Part III: Provocations invites readers to consider cosplay from some provocative positions, both philosophical and performative, and acts as a call for further reflection. Where Parts I and II elide between close textual and situated ethnographic analysis, here acquaintance with cosplay is assumed in order to explore its points of intersection with, and divergence from, historical festive and attendant theatricalisms, performances of gender and queer, and the vexed arena of 'cosporn.' Chapter 7, 'Proto-Cosplay,' provides a foil to contemporary cosplay by distinguishing it from its precursors in a predominantly western cultural historical context, though parallels are drawn with Asian antecedents. Self-conscious play is seen as a modern practice that begins with Renaissance masque and finds an important watershed in the *commedia dell'arte* from the sixteenth century onwards. Like cosplay subjects, its stock characters such as Harlequin and Scaramouche were recognizable popular cultural figures in their day, though arising out of festive life, masque and the carnivalesque. Their non-western counterparts, in Japan and East Asia more generally, have their own historical forms of masked performance including Kabuki theatre and Noh. This chapter also discusses the influence of Orientalism on western costuming and fashion practices prior to the twentieth century.

Chapter 8, 'Cosgender/Cosqueer,' goes beyond the usual discussion of 'crossplay' (where cosers perform characters of an opposing gender) to suggest that gender representation in cosplay is inherently queered. The analysis draws on a range of founding concepts, including the queer theory of Judith Butler, Teresa de Lauretis' 'technologies of gender,' Donna Harraway's evocation of the cyborg as a way out of the gender binary bind, and LGBTQIA (lesbian, gay, bisexual, transgender, queer, intersex and asexual) studies more generally. It is not only that many cosplayers crossplay, but that cosplay itself is analogous to drag in that it denaturalizes gender and recasts it as performance. *Kawaii* ('cute') elements in Japanese cosplay challenge humanist ideals, meshing human, hyper- and extra-human characteristics to provoke strong affective responses. Moreover, this chapter argues that animation collapses distinctions between biological and artificial bodies. One metonym for this is the doll, alluding to the posthuman—a cultural condition predicated on the collapse of the dualistic human subject of western philosophy, which happened to coincide with the crystallization of cosplay in the 1990s. In summation, cosplay can be viewed as a form of posthumanist drag.

Chapter 9, 'Cosporn,' is perhaps most provocative of all in arguing that, while it is under no circumstances to be conflated with pornography per se, cosplay nevertheless shares certain affinities with porn. Arguably, pornography is dialectically relevant to cosplay in the body's extraction from the real life-world and the everyday. It objectifies bodies, and identifies the body as a system of parts. Cosplay and pornography are both located at the shared site of the 'natrificial' body, for cosplay is in many ways a process of sublimation, in particular in asserting and expressing desire through identification, and entering into a certain character and the narratives associated with it. The chapter concludes with an account of a cosporn performer, Marie-Claude Bourbonnais, who combines her aptitudes as a costume maker, model and fashion designer with cosplay/porn, as literalizing this abstract crossover. This begs wider questions about female labour and cosplay as it is commodified and marketed online by such well-known figures as Yaya Han, Jessica Nigiri and Katyuska Moonfox. In doing so, Part III's final chapter brings full circle the prior discussions of performance, gender and gender as performance.

Finally, the conclusion, 'Cosplay Futures,' asks how cosplayers think about the future and what the future of cosplay may look like in light of disruptive new technological developments and social practices, against a backdrop of global political and environmental crisis. It is the culmination of a diverse range of approaches that explore the contemporary phenomenon and practice of cosplay from multiple perspectives—those of critical practice, ethnographic research and philosophical enquiry. Spanning the textual and visual, social, economic and political, festive, gendered and psycho-sexual, this book aims to take readers on a journey through the many realms of practice and play, performance and identity, costumed self and collective endeavour that constitute *Planet Cosplay*.

Notes

1 Theresa Winge, 'Costuming the Imagination: Origins of Manga and Anime,' *Mechademia 1, Emerging Worlds of Anime and Manga* (2006), 65.
2 Anne Peirson-Smith, 'Fashioning the Fantastical Self: An Examination of the Cosplay Dress-Up Phenomenon in Southeast Asia,' *Fashion Theory* 17, no. 1 (2013), 77.
3 Jin-Shiow Chen, 'A Study of Fan Culture: Adolescent Experiences with Animé/Manga Doujinshi and Cosplay Taiwan,' *Visual Arts Research* 33, no. 1 (2007), 15.
4 See Patrick W. Galbraith, 'Cosplay, Lolita and Gender in Australia and Japan: An Introduction,' *Intersections: Gender and Sexuality in Asia and the Pacific* 32 (2013), para. 1; Brian Ashcraft and Luke Plunkett, *Cosplay World* (London: Prestel, 2014), 20.

5   Kane Anderson, 'Becoming Batman: Cosplay, Performance, and Ludic Transformations at Comic-Con', in *Play, Performance and Identity: How Institutions Structure Spaces*, eds. Matt Omasta and Drew Chappell (New York: Routledge, 2015), 106.

6   Sebastian Domsch, 'Staging Icons, Performing Storyworlds—From Mystery Play to Cosplay', *Acta Universitatis Sapientiae, Film and Media Studies* 9 (2014), 125.

7   Frenchy Lunning, 'Cosplay', in *Berg Encyclopedia of Dress and Fashion, Vol. 10—Global Perspectives*, ed. Joanna B. Eicher (2011), n.pag., accessed 1 January 2018, http://www.bergfashionlibrary.com/view/bewdf/BEWDF-v10/EDch10024.xml.

8   See Matthew Ogonoski, 'Cosplaying the Mix: Examining Japan's Media Environment, Its Static Norms, and Its Influence on Cosplay', *Transformative Works and Cultures* 16, Materiality and Object-oriented Fandom (2014), para. 1.1; Nicolle Lamerichs, 'Stranger than Fiction: Fan Identity in Cosplay', *Transformative Works and Cultures* 7 (2011), para. 1.2; Nicole Lamerichs, 'Costuming as Subculture: The Multiple Bodies of Cosplay', *Scene* 1, no. 1&2 (2014), 113; Rie Matsuura and Daisuke Okabe, 'Collective Achievement of Making in Cosplay Culture', *Proceedings COINs* 15 (2015), n.pag.

9   Paul Mountfort, 'Cosplay, Photography and Fan Capital', Plenary, 6th *Annual European Popular Culture Association Conference* (London University of Arts, June 2017).

10 Craig Norris and Jason Bainbridge, 'Selling *Otaku*? Mapping the Relationship between Industry and Fandom in the Australian Cosplay Scene', *Intersections: Gender and Sexuality in Asia and the Pacific* 20 (2009), para. 1. See also Joel Gn, 'Queer Simulation: The Practice, Performance and Pleasure of Cosplay', *Continuum: Journal of Media and Cultural Studies* 25, no. 4 (2011), 583.

11 Matthew Hale, 'Cosplay: Intertextuality, Public Texts, and the Body Fantastic', *Western Folklore* 73, no. 1 (2014), 8.

12 Ellen Kirkpatrick, 'Towards New Horizons: Cosplay (Re)imagined through the Superhero Genre, Authenticity and Transformation', *Transformative Works and Cultures* 18, Praxis (2015), para. 0.1.

13 Winge, 'Costuming the Imagination', 66. See also M. Bruno, 'Cosplay: The Illegitimate Child of S F Masquerades', *Glitz and Glitter Newsletter*, Millennium Costume Guild, October 2002, accessed 1 January 2018, http://millenniumcg.tripod.com/glitzglitter/1002articles.html.

14 Winge, 'Costuming the Imagination', 66–67.

15 Ibid., 68.

16 Marshall McLuhan, *The Language of Media: The Extensions of Man* (London and New York: Routledge, 2001; 1964), 218–19, original emphasis.

17 Michael Bruno, 'Cosplay: The Illegitimate Child of SF Masquerades', *Glitz and Glitter Newsletter* (Millennium Costume Guild, October 2002), accessed 1 January 2018, http://millenniumcg.tripod.com/glitzglitter/1002articles.html; 'Costuming a World Apart: Cosplay in America and Japan', *Glitz and Glitter Newsletter* (Millennium Costume Guild, October 2002), accessed 1 January 2018, http://millenniumcg.tripod.com/glitzglitter/1002articles.html; Takako Aoyama and Jennifer Cahill, *Cosplay Girls: Japan's Live Animation Heroines* (Tokyo: DH, 2003); Robert Holzek, *Cosplay: The New Main Attraction*, accessed 1 January 2018, http://www.jivemagazine.com/article.php?pid=1953. Citations include Winge 'Costuming the Imagination', 76 and Lamerichs 'Stranger than Fiction', para. 8.

18 See Judith Butler, *Gender Trouble: Feminism and the Subversion of Identity* (New York: Routledge, 1990), *Bodies That Matter: On the Discursive Limits of 'Sex'* (New York: Routledge, 1993), 'Bodily Inscriptions, Performative Subversions,' in *The Judith Butler Reader*, ed. Sara Salih with Judith Butler (Malden: Blackwell, 2004), 90–119; Stuart Hall, 'Who Needs "Identity"?' in *Identity: A Reader*, eds. Paul DuGay, Jessica Evans, and Peter Redman (Thousand Oaks: Sage, 2000), 15–30; Paul Hodkinson, *Goth: Identity, Style and Subculture* (Oxford: Berg, 2002).

19 Henry Jenkins, *Textual Poachers: Television Fans and Participatory Culture* (New York: Routledge, 1992); *Convergence Culture: Where Old and New Media Collide* (New York: NYU Press, 2006), 169–205; Francesca Coppa, 'Writing Bodies in Space: Media Fan Fiction as Theatrical Performance,' in *Fan Fiction and Fan Communities in the Age of the Internet: New Essays*, eds. Karen Hellekson and Kristina Busse (Jefferson: McFarland, 2006), 225–44.

20 See Henry Bial, 'What is Performance?' in *The Performance Studies Reader*, ed. Henry Bial (New York: Routledge, 2004), 57–59; Jos de Mul, 'The Game of Life: Narrative and Ludic Identity Formation in Computer Games,' in *Handbook of Computer Game Studies*, eds. Joost Raessens and Jeffrey Goldstein (Cambridge: MIT Press, 2005), 251–66; James Newman, 'Playing (with) Videogames,' *Convergence: The International Journal of Research into New Media Technologies* 11 (2005), 48–67; Sharon Pugh, *The Democratic Genre: Fan Fiction in a Literary Context* (Bridgend, Wales: Seren, 2005); James Paul Gee, *What Video Games Have to Teach Us about Learning and Literacy, Revised Edition* (New York: Palgrave Macmillan, 2007); Celia Pearce, *Communities of Play: Emergent Cultures in Multiplayer Games and Virtual Worlds* (Cambridge: The MIT Press, 2009).

21 Susan Napier, *Anime from Akira to Howl's Moving Castle* (London: St. Martin's Press, 2005).

22 Sharon Kinsella, 'Amateur Manga Subculture and the Otaku Panic,' *Journal of Japanese Studies* 24, no. 2 (1998), 289–316; Masami Toku, 'What Is Manga? The Influence of Pop Culture in Adolescent Art,' *Art Education* 54, no. 2 (2001), 11–17; Matt Hills, 'Transcultural "Otaku": Japanese Representations of Fandom and Representations of Japan in Anime/Manga Fan Cultures,' (2002), accessed 1 January 2018, http://web.mit.edu/cms/Events/mit2/Abstracts/MattHillspaper.pdf.); Jin-Shiow Chen, 'The Comic/Animé Fan Culture in Taiwan: With a Focus on Adolescent Experiences,' *Journal of Social Theory in Art Education* 23 (2003), 89–103; Fred Patten, *Watching Anime, Reading Manga: 25 Years of Essays and Reviews* (Berkeley: Stone Bridge Press, 2004); Isaac Gagné, 'Urban Princesses: Performance and "Women's Language" in Japan's Gothic/Lolita Subculture,' *Journal of Linguistic Anthropology* 18, no. 1 (2007), 130–50.

23 Winge, 'Costuming the Imagination,' 65, 68.

24 See Patrick R. Benesh-Lui, 'Anime Cosplay in America,' *Ornament* 31, no. 1 (2007), 44–49; Paula Brehm-Heeger, Ann Conway, and Carrie Vale, 'Cosplay, Gaming, and Conventions: The Amazing and Unexpected Places an Anime Club Can Lead Unsuspecting Librarians,' *Young Adult Library Services* 5, no. 2 (2007), 14–16; Chen, 'A Study of Fan Culture,' 12–24; Mari Kotani and Thomas LaMarre, 'Doll Beauties and Cosplay,' *Mechademia* 2, Networks of Desire (2007), 49–62; Elena Dorfman, *Fandomania: Characters & Cosplay* (McCormack, New York: Aperture, 2007).

25 Nicolle Lamerichs, 'Stranger than Fiction,' para. 1–8.

26 Hale, 'Cosplay,' 5–37.

27 Maria Patrice Amon, 'Performances of Innocence and Deviance in Disney Cosplaying,' *Transformative Works and Cultures* 17 (2014), para. 1.1–6; Anderson, 'Becoming Batman,' 105–80; Kirkpatrick, 'Towards New Horizons,' para. 0.1–8.

28 Alexis Hieu Truong, 'Framing Cosplay: How "Layers" Negotiate Body and Subjective Experience through Play,' *Intersections: Gender and Sexuality in Asia and the Pacific*, 32 (2013), para. 1.

29 Larissa Hjorth, 'Game Girl: Re-imagining Japanese Gender and Gaming via Melbourne Female Cosplayers,' *Intersections: Gender and Sexuality in Asia and the Pacific*, 20 (2009), para. 26–29.

30 Galbraith, 'Cosplay, Lolita and Gender,' 1–27; Kinko Ito and Paul A. Crutcher, 'Popular Mass Entertainment in Japan: Manga, Pachinko, and Cosplay,' *Society* 51 (2014), 44–48.

31 Lunning, 'Cosplay,' n.pag.; Emerald King, 'Girls Who Are Boys Who Like Girls To Be Boys: BL and the Australian Cosplay Community,' *Intersections: Gender and Sexuality in Asia and the Pacific* 32 (2013), para. 1–29. BL is also known as *shōnen ai* or *yaoi*.

32 Gn, 'Queer Simulation.'

33 Lamerichs, 'Costuming as Subculture,' 113–25; Peirson-Smith, 'Fantastical Self,' 77–111.

34 Osmud Rahman, Liu Wing-Sun, and Brittany Hei-man Cheung, '"Cosplay": Imagining Self and Performing Identity,' *Fashion Theory* 16, no. 3 (2012), 317–42.

35 *Heroes of Cosplay*, created by Lauren Brady, Dave Caplin and Mark Cronin (New York: Syfy, 2013–), TV series.

36 Eron Rauch and Christopher Bolton, 'A Cosplay Photography Sampler,' *Mechademia* 5, Fanthropologies (2010), 180.

37 Ogonoski, 'Cosplaying,' para. 3.1.

38 Domsch, 'Staging Icons, Performing Storyworlds.'

39 Paul Booth, *Playing Fans: Negotiating Fandom and Media in the Digital Age* (Iowa City: University of Iowa Press, 2015), 150.

40 Recent examples include Kristie Good, *Epic Cosplay Costumes* (Winterset: Fons and Porter, 2016), Svetlana Quindt, *The Costume Making Guide: Creating Armor and Props for Cosplay* (Oakland: Impact Books, 2016), Miyuu Takahara, *Cosplay: the Beginner's Masterclass* (Scoots Valley: CreateSpace Publishing, 2015), Shawn Thorsson, *Make: Props and Costume Armor* (Sebastopol: Maker Media, 2016).

41 *Cosplay Melee*, created by Jay Peterson and Todd Lubin (New York: Syfy, 2017), TV series.

42 See Arjun Appadurai, 'Disjuncture and Difference in the Global Cultural Economy,' *Theory Culture Society* 7 (1990), 297–99.

Part I

Critical Practice

Chapter 1

Cosplay as Citation

osplay commentators universally agree that cosplay involves fans donning costumes and performing as characters from popular media texts, such as comics, animated or live action films and television, games and other popular cultural media including music videos. As seen in the Introduction, particular indebtedness to Japanese popular culture sources such as manga, anime, gaming, *otaku* and idol culture is often stressed, though western source texts are equally common and cosplayers mix and sometimes mash-up their influences.[1] This chapter is concerned with cosplay as a contemporary fan practice via the ways in which cosplayers commonly reference their chosen source texts. In this particular respect, cosplay can be regarded as a form of citation, with cosplayers collectively involved in performing myriad 'citational acts.' This somewhat abstract concept is easily made concrete if we picture walking through a convention space where cosplayers are in action. The thousands of costumes and accoutrements, such as weapons and other props, are, on one level, like trees in a forest of citation that link the cosplay back to the source text ('ah, look, there's San from *Princess Mononoke*. Do you think she made that dagger?'). The 'act' is in how the player embodies and performs their chosen character ('that Naruto's posing in Sage Mode!').[2]

It may seem strange to use the term citation in this context, as it is typically employed in scholarly settings to describe how academic texts reference each other.[3] Some commentators are critical of the textual metaphor due to the highly visual and performance-orientated nature of cosplay. This occurs against a backdrop of alleged 'textual bias'[4] in discussions of cosplay, which risks downplaying other, performative dimensions at work in the practice. However, a type of referentiality similar to text-based citation occurs in other media, and is widespread in popular culture. Quentin Tarantino's movies, for instance, are full of references to earlier films and film genres, from spaghetti westerns to Samurai classics, which they pay homage to, cheerfully parody and otherwise pillage. In the present context, it is the cosplayer's costumed body that becomes the text or site that references another text—that is, the specific source media that the cosplayer chooses to perform. This embodiment includes not just costume but theatricalism, including pose and gesture. While there may be limitations to analogies between cosplay and citation, investigating the practice, on one level, as a system of reference between texts helps us differentiate it from other forms of dressing up and acting-out. After all, where cosplay differs from dressing up more generally—including fashion subcultures that are sometimes part of the milieu but not strictly cosplay, such as steampunk and Lolita—is in its specific indebtedness to source media on which it is heavily reliant. Cosplay also differs from dramatic performances for the theatre or screen in that cosplayers do not seek to realize an entire script in a sustained performance but smaller or 'parcellized' portions of an original, seldom longer than short skits. Due to these complex factors, descriptions of the ways in which cosplayers cite their source materials veer between textual and more performance-orientated metaphors. Commonly employed terms include modelling, textual performance, translation, transportation, actualization, identification, intertextual or transmedial process and, indeed, 'embodied citational acts'.[5]

It is also important to recognize the political dimension to cosplay's citational practices. A term that is useful in unpacking cosplay from this perspective is *détournement*.[6] Associated with the Paris-based social revolutionary group of intellectuals and artists of the 1950s known as the Situationist International, it remains in use in critical theory today and resonates well with cosplay.[7] Détournement literally means 'to reroute' or 'to hijack' and for the Situationists was linked to the 'ludic,' or purposive play. Unsurprisingly, many commentators have framed cosplay in terms of the ludic,[8] but the Situationist détournement goes beyond mere playfulness to encompass the subversive, and included pranks designed to undermine authority and social hierarchy, political and aesthetic. Crucially, it involved a type of deliberate plagiarism whereby authoritative books, maps and other texts were cut and pasted along polemical and aesthetic lines. Détournement is useful for framing cosplay as not simply a form of fandom, but as a critical practice. Of course, for cosplay to work successfully for both player and audience, the minimum quotient of fandom, familiarity with the source text or at least its storyworld, is a required passport for entry to this play community. But while most cosplayers are fans, this does not mean they lack a critical faculty in relation to the franchises they choose to reference, or are necessarily cheerleaders for the characters they dress up as. Material and social concerns such as a player's body type, the cost of garments, and their collaborative role within a cosplay group may be just as important. Cosplayers also frequently mess with their source material, employing 'parody, pastiche, satire, burlesque, and caricature'.[9] Thus cosplay's particular form of détournement is a 're-contextualization'[10] of sources which aligns it with other mixing and mashing practices, such as fanfiction and the making of anime music videos (AMVs) rather than simply dressing up or acting out a part. Cosplay also often subverts gender, as 'crossplay'—where female fans dress as male characters and vice versa—demonstrates, and the representation of race is often fluid, too.

However exactly we frame its particular form of referentiality, cosplay citation is, in the first instance, inherent in the choice and subsequent appropriation of a source. When a cosplayer executes the intention to dress up as a particular character, citation of that source text is implicitly taking place, if in no one else's eyes but the coser's own, as they adjust garments and put the finishing touches on in front of the mirror. However, it is one thing to wear a lightsabre on your belt and another to come out with it swinging. In other words, it is possible to be in costume but not 'in part,' to be dressed up but not acting out the character role, as when we glimpse 'Batman' in a convention cafeteria incongruously stuffing his mouth with a hotdog. By contrast, when cosplayers perform their character role on the social stage of the competition catwalk, collaborate on a skit or pose in the convention hall or adjacent studio spaces for a photograph, they will play their chosen part in specific ways, especially through pose and gesture. It is thus only situationally that the performed identity is actualized in the eyes of an audience, where the reference becomes a performance, or, in the present terminology, the citation a citational act (pun intended). Such categories are of course fluid and readily flow into one another. Cosplayers can snap into or out of character in an instant, especially when cameras appear. Furthermore, invisible to the spectator are the moments of internal transformation of the cosplayer, the powerful and uncanny affect by which desire transports us into our fantasy selves, at least for an instant. Frenchy Lunning has framed this in terms of Félix Guattari's notion of a traversal moment or 'display of multiple identity eruptions.'[11] Cosplayers often express this internal transubstantiation as one that thrills or, conversely, brings a sense of calm or empowerment, even as a zone to which one is transported. What takes place over a sustained period of cosplaying, then, is a constant elision between alternating states of mind and ways of being in the world.

Source media: Texts and pretexts

There is some debate about whether cosplay originated in the United States, in which, as the next chapter discusses, fannish 'costuming' goes back to the early twentieth century, or Japan, where the portmanteau term was first used in 1983. However, this chapter locates cosplay's origins more contextually in the emergence of media and fan cultures in the latter half of the twentieth century. While dressing up in fantastical garb is evidenced in science fiction conventions from the 1940s and 1950s, it was the late 1960s when cosplay's contemporary shape began to form. Arguably, what distinguishes cosplay, even if it was not yet named as such, from the earlier craze for costuming discussed in Chapter 2 is not so much a matter of kind than of context. That context involved what Fredric Jameson referred to in *Postmodernism, or, The Cultural Logic of Late Capitalism* (1991) as the post–Second World War 'psychic break' with wartime shortages and a cultural, as opposed to merely economic, turn in late capitalist sensibilities.[12] Following new media interrelationships and forms of business organization from around the mid-century mark came the crystallization of what Raymond Williams called a new 'cultural structure of feeling'[13] with its 'reshuffling of canonical feelings and values'[14] in the 1960s and 1970s. While sci-fi and superhero figures had been subjects for public masquerade well before this time, these were the decades in which new media began to coalesce across once discrete boundaries and modern (or, rather, postmodern) fandoms formed. In terms of popular culture, this was predicated on 'the penetration of culture itself by [...] the culture industry, and of which the media itself is only a part.'[15] By the same token, the iconoclastic tenor of the period meant that such fandoms often took up irreverent postures in relation to their source materials, laying the foundation for what would later be recognized as a range of fan-based critical practices. By the late 1970s and early 1980s cosplay was partaking in the cultural circulation between North America and Japan. These decades, characterized by Jameson in terms of the 'conquest of the discursive hegemony' by Thatcherism and Reaganism's economic dogmas,[16] set the stage for cosplay's increasing globalization in the 1990s. From the turn of the twenty-first century, it has undergone increasing massification and now draws on multiple media sources at the various converging streams of transmedia storytelling.

It is sometimes hard to distinguish fact from anecdote in cosplay's early phase of formation (recalling the jibe that if you remember the Sixties you weren't there)[17] but one pivotal moment occurred when 'the Trekkies discovered Worldcon'[18] in 1967, with at least seven attendees reportedly costumed as Mr Spock. *Star Trek: The Original Series* (1966–69) was a trailblazer in the emergence of modern fan practices.[19] The first dedicated Star Trek Convention, as distinct from more general sci-fi conventions, was held in 1972,[20] and trekkies have remained a staple of cons ever since. The show essentially spawned the genre of 'media fanzines,'[21] with *Spockanalia* from September 1967 marking a milestone in the development of modern fanfiction, a practice whereby fans conscript (or 'détourner') existing media content in the creation of new, non-canonical narratives. Fanfiction can be viewed as a writerly parallel to the embodied practice of cosplay and can range from anodyne homage to the aggressively disruptive. An example of the latter is the slash genre, named after the forward slash (/) that appears between the initials of characters paired in this way.[22] K/S fanfiction, in which the ostensibly straight characters of Kirk and Spock are brought together in homoerotic fashion, debuted soon after the show first aired[23] and is reckoned by Henry Jenkins to be the earliest example of the genre. As we will see, related forms of such double deviancy—in which intellectual property is not only summarily appropriated but fundamentally subverted—occurs in cosplay as well, especially in relation to gender and race.

Cosplay is often associated in the popular imagination with comic book superheroes, who certainly populate cons globally in large numbers to this day. An early recorded instance occurred in 1969 when Kathy Bushman (née Sanders) performed the character Vampirella from the eponymous comics album at the World Science Fiction Convention (Worldcon) in St Louis.[24] Superhero comics provide a kind of implicit model for cosplay, in that like Clark Kent and Diana Prince cosplayers don costumes and transform into their (albeit imagined) caped crusader avatars.[25] However, while such popular comics date approximately to the Second World War—*Superman* and *Wonder Woman*, for example, debuted in 1938 and 1941 respectively—the rise of costumed heroes at cons only really seems to have taken off following the success of screen adaptations.[26] Photographic evidence suggests the cosplaying of Superman as early as the 1940s but it is commonplace by 1974, 'by which time Worldcon "masquerades" had grown to more than 100 participants per year.'[27] Wonder Woman was in evidence by at least 1977, closely tracking with the rise of popular television and movie adaptations.[28] As the venues at which these events took place suggest, the period also saw the birth of a new type of mass comics convention, as distinct from the older dedicated sci-fi conventions, with Comic-Con inaugurating in San Diego in 1970. This subject is discussed in more depth in the next chapter, but in brief cons of this kind would proliferate globally in the decades that followed to provide what James Paul Gee calls 'affinity spaces' for cosplayers to congregate, and where their performances are normalized in relation to their subcultural communities of practice or taste cultures.[29]

The 1975 release of the film adaptation of the musical stage production, *The Rocky Horror Picture Show*, is also sometimes seen as a milestone in the rise of what would soon be tagged cosplay.[30] A parodying tribute to B-grade movies of the times, its titular reference to the horror genre evokes the film's camping up not only of the atmosphere but sets and props from Hammer Film Productions, famous for their 'Hammer Horror' films of the 1950s–1970s. Attendees of the original midnight-movie screening were asked to don suitable costumes, with Tim Curry's character Dr Frank N. Furter rapidly becoming an iconic instance of drag and establishing an early genetic link between cosplay and the gender-bending practice of crossplay, if not indeed the notion of cosqueer discussed in Chapter 8. However, in the mid-1970s sci-fi continued to enjoy pride of place in convention culture, with the original *Star Wars* (1977)[31] providing wildly popular material, as did television shows developed from sci-fi films, such as *Logan's Run* (1976; 1977–78).[32] Moving into the 1980s, *Star Trek: TOS* continued to be a popular source as were *Star Wars* sequels *The Empire Strikes Back* (1980) and *Return of the Jedi* (1983),[33] with wizened Yodas and bikini-clad 'Slave Leahs' much in evidence.[34] In synopsis, then, modern fandom, including fanfiction and bustling cons, grew out of the mass audience spectatorship that crystalized around popular television shows and movies in the 1960s and 1970s, especially science fiction and superhero genres. Cosplay evolved in tandem with these general developments as a related expression of popular fandom in the age of transmediation.

There are also accounts of attendees costumed as characters from imported Japanese anime in the United States by the late 1970s. Anime first arrived in the west in the form of *Astro Boy (Tetsuwon Atomu)* (1963–66),[35] which premiered in 1964 and continued to be re-run in fan circles such as the 1978 Worldcon in Phoenix.[36] This exposure remained, of course, incredibly niche. Craig Norris and Jason Bainbridge claim that for 'many westerners—in the U.S., the U.K. and Australia—their first exposure to the possibility of cosplay would be a diegetic (textual) one: in the late 1970s anime series *Science Ninja Team Gatchaman* (better known as *G-Force* or *Battle of the Planets* in the West).'[37] Given the history of costuming at western cons and the fact that the term 'cosplay' had not yet been invented, this conflation of the practice with Japanese popular media is dubious. However, they would contribute an important element. By the legendary 1979 Comic-Con 'several anime characters in the Masquerade'[38] from the series *Star Blazers* (1979), an American adaptation of *Space Battleship Yamoto I–III (Uchū Senkan Yamato)* (1974–75), and *Space Pirate Captain Harlock (Uchū Kaizoku Kyaputen Hārokku)* (1977–79)[39] had escaped page and screen to take to the convention floor. Patrick W. Galbraith notes that, meanwhile, in Japan 'cosplay had become a part of sci-fi and fanzine events from the mid-1970s. During this decade, sci-fi fandom in Japan overlapped with the fandoms surrounding anime, which was coming into its own as a challenging medium worthy of attention.'[40] Indeed, some have claimed cosplay originated 'with a parodic performance'[41] of a manga or anime character played by Mari Kotani in Japan in 1978, then a fan and later a notable critic and author, though by other accounts it appeared earlier, in the inaugural 1975 Comic Market (Comiket) founded by Yoshihiro Yonezawa.[42]

While the practice may have been gestating for some years on both sides of the Pacific, there is no question that the term 'cosplay' itself crystalized in Japan following the June 1983 issue of *My Anime*, where an article on the subject by Nobuyuki Takahashi, translated in English as 'Hero Costume Operation,' refers to both *kosuchuumu purei* (costume play) and *kosupure* (cosplay).[43] In the same year the Worldcon in Baltimore featured 22 cosplayers costumed as anime characters for a photo shoot, while by July 1990 Project-A-Kon had a huge anime cosplaying constituency and AnimeCon (Aug–Sept 1991) is reckoned by Lunning to be the first western con to be exclusively devoted to anime.[44] By the 1990s, then, cosplay sat squarely at the intersection of North American and Japanese popular culture flows. Pop music videos and computer games rapidly followed television and films as sources for cosplayers to mine, and by the dawn of the twenty-first century a convergence culture in which various media overlap and distribute characters and their storyworlds across once discrete boundaries was in full swing. The source material for cosplay today is astoundingly diverse. The literally thousands of characters who are commonly cosplayed means that to identify the 'trees' in the forest of citations that comprise even a medium-sized convention would be a compendious task, beyond the capacity of even the most pop culturally literate nerd or geek. Further, twenty-first century transmedia storytelling means the roots are frequently tangled and interweave comics, television, films, games and other pop cultural elements in a vast inter-referential network of storyworlds.

Citation and citational acts

The postmodern 'death of the author' as the true controller of textual meaning and birth of the reader—or viewer-user-player (VUP)—as its arbiter has elevated fans to a central position in this network in contemporary critical theory. Jenkins, for example, has made analogies between certain fan practices and academic work, aimed in part at undermining the perception of fans as the 'cultural dupes, social misfits, and mindless consumers that they have been labelled.'[45] In a chapter from *Convergence Culture* (2006), 'Why Heather can write,' he argued that the 13-year-old of the title undertook a range of activities as editor of a fictional online newspaper, *The Daily Hogwarts*, equivalent in many ways to his own labours as editor-in-chief of an academic journal.[46] This included vetting contributions, sourcing reviewers and working with collaborators to organize content. In the same year, one of the most formative early articles on cosplay, Theresa Winge's 'Costuming the imagination: Origins of Manga and Anime,' praised cosplay in similarly glowing terms. For Winge, a cosplayer references the character their costumes are 'modelled after' based on research and study into a source text, leading to an 'interpretation that takes place by reading and watching.'[47] This is what cultural critics would call a close reading. Other commentators in this epistemological approach have discussed cosplay in terms of Kurt Lancaster's notion of the 'textual performer' whereby the particular viewing of the story with 'critical distance' can lead to disruptive practices through which cultural givens (such as gender) can be 'critiqued, negotiated and explored.'[48] If this sounds like critics reformulating cosplay after their own image, Eron Rauch and Christopher Bolton have gone so far as to reverse the arc of influence suggesting that 'professional critics have lately learned to read more like fans' and that like 'fan fiction and *dōjinshi* parodies, cosplay is part of the feedback loop that allows fans to enter into a text and transform it, turning readers into authors and blurring the distinction between fan and critic, as well as reader and text.'[49] They note that cosplay is not only about citing materials from the original source, but also about 'editing' and 'co-creating,' which could prompt us to view cosplay as a form of creative, or disruptive, citation. At the very least, through such détournment fans 'bring something of their own' to a dynamic relationship in which the original protagonist is turned into an enabling character through 'interpretation of the narrative.'[50] It may be thanks to 'modification through wit or sexual play'[51] that such texts are 'interpreted or reconstructed'[52] or 'the desire to make tangible, to give bodily, three-dimensional presence to a storyworld.'[53]

Not everyone has embraced the 'text-centred perspective' associated particularly with Jenkins through which fans 'were conceptualized as critical readers, writers, and "textual poachers" (Jenkins 1992) and their communities were defined by their relationships with, interpretations of, and mobilizations of a variety of publicly available texts.'[54] Matthew Hale argues in a pivotal 2014 article that fan studies has traditionally privileged textual forms such as fanfiction precisely because they can be analysed textually, while performative acts like cosplay have been comparatively ignored because 'they fall outside the purview of textual analysis.'[55] Hale is not, however, suggesting that cosplay cannot be understood, at least on one level, as a textual practice:

> Textuality is not of course absent from this process, as these embodied repertoires are carefully honed through close and critical re-readings of a given source-text (Jenson 1992: 67–69) [...]. A cosplayer's embodied citational acts are both engendered and circumscribed by a specific character or text, its history, and the audience that recognizes that form as a conventional, repeatable configuration of signs (Derrida 1977: 147).[56]

Rather, Hale advocates an understanding of cosplay as a 'somatic, material *and* textual practice,'[57] somatic meaning bodily. The notion of 'embodied citational acts' is a key one for this chapter. Jacques Derrida's 'repeatable configuration of signs,' which Hale references from 'Signature, Event, Context' (1977), is also known as *iterability* or, sometimes, *citationality*, whereby the reiteration of a repeatable form can lead to a copy or counterfeit. For Derrida iterability is not simply referential but a re-performance, as when an actor says 'I do' in a marriage scene, which precisely repeats the original performative utterance but does not result in an actual betrothal.

It is worth further teasing out a distinction between the citation of source texts as an a priori condition that provides a pretext to cosplay and the many 'citational acts' that are involved in going on to actually perform the relevant character, although the two remain intimately entwined. If we look at the first part of the equation, citation, it is obvious that cosplay requires what has variously been described as a source, reference or 'parent text.'[58] We have seen that such 'extant media texts'[59] are frequently 'publicly available' or 'mass-mediated texts,'[60] meaning that they are common property, at least from the point of view of fans (IP rights holders might not agree). Also noted was the fact that the citational pool of media for cosplay is vast, including television, films, anime, manga and related video game as well as pop idol characters—indeed, virtually all contemporary media. Specific genres often cited include science fiction, fantasy, horror, mythology and fetish,[61] with mention in the Japanese context of *tokusatsu* (special-effect movies or television shows) and sub-genres such as mecha, cyborg, furry and Lolita. Superhero movies and Hollywood franchises, such as *Star Wars, Harry Potter, The Matrix* and *Lord of the Rings,* remain staples along with big ticket anime, like *Pokémon, Sailor Moon, Gundam, Digimon* and *Dragon Ball.*[62] Most if not all of these mega-franchises, of course, have game versions, and many games have not only crossed over into cosplay but other media via the widespread 'transmedial process'[63] of adaptation. Cosplaying VUP's may, therefore, hold in mind multiple character iterations across media. Then there is creative reinterpretation or mixing in the form of textual mash-ups from different twenty-first century transmedia storytelling franchises, frequently to humorous effect, producing 'Hello Kitty Darth Vaders, steampunk Bobba Fetts, and zombie Jedis.'[64]

Unsurprisingly, commentators have used a variety of terms to try to pin down the precise type of citation of these sources that is going on in cosplay, in a lexicon that reveals considerable slippage between the a priori textual dimension on the one hand, and the embodied, performative dimension on the other. Winge's reference to costumes being 'modelled after' an original text sits at this intersection, as modelling can take place in written language, where one text can model another, but also of course in theatrical performances, from the stage to the catwalk. Norris and Bainbridge deploy Lancaster's ideal of the 'textual performer,'[65] itself an elaboration on Jenkins' celebration of fans as textual poachers who reappropriate the private property of corporate franchises to a creative commons. This has echoes in Joel Gn's description of the process by which the cosplayer 'emancipates the player from the narrative of the text,'[66] though he is more specifically concerned with how they are moved from one plane of visual embodiment (anime) to another (cosplay). Nicolle Lamerichs defends the analogy to fanfiction in the way fan appropriation 'transforms, performs and actualizes an existing story in close connection to the fan's own identity,' meaning that cosplay 'leans on identification with narrative content.'[67] Fans taking on other genders and ethnicities from their biologically assigned ones is an example of this kind of appropriation.

A complication arises here, however, in that while the sources cited in cosplay generally can be classified as narrative texts—ones that tell stories—the primary content being mined tends to be visually iconic rather than being related to plot. Of course, narrative texts are not limited to the written: cinema can employ visual storytelling and comics use both text and images in ways that usually relate a series of events sequentially. Games are also an increasingly dominant source media for cosplay, so how cosplayers reference them has to be part of any interpretive model of cosplay as citation. There has been considerable debate about whether video games should be classified as narrative media—it depends in part on the game and the form is probably best understood as hybrid.[68] However, even games that are not primarily concerned with storytelling tend to have elements of narrativity. Narration occurs at some level, if in nothing more than an unfolding sequence of events. Gaming also typically revolves around avatars, and the relationship between gamers and their avatars and cosplayers' chosen characters is not only close but in some cases overlapping. Cons are stacked with Kasumis, Links and Marios, to name only a few gaming characters.[69] The question remains, however, of the extent to which the narrative of the original text—whether comic, movie, television show or game—survives adaptation to the somatic medium of cosplay, and thus whether the terminology of narratology, the study of narrative texts, is of any relevance.

Narratology evolved out of Russian formalism and the work of scholars such as Vladimir Propp who, in *The Morphology of the Folktale* (1928), claimed to have articulated a basic grammar of narrative events and repertoire of character types out of which all narratives are fashioned.[70] Mieke Bal provides a synopsis of the formalist lexicon used to analyse narratives:

A *narrative text* is a text in which an agent relates ('tells') a story in a particular medium, such as language, imagery, sounds, buildings or a combination thereof. A *story* is a fabula that is presented in a certain manner. A *fabula* is a series of logically and chronologically related events that are caused or experienced by actors. An *event* is a transition from one state to another state. *Actors* are the agents that perform events. They are not necessarily human.[71]

In relation to cosplay we would identify the *narrative text* as the particular story-based media text that a cosplayer appropriates. The *actor* is the character of one kind or another that the cosplayer decides to cosplay. As Bal points out, it does not have to be human, as the many daleks, droids and aliens whirring around popular cons attest. What distinguishes a *story* from a *fabula* is how it is told (clearly one can narrate a sequence of *events* in entirely different ways to different effects, as anyone who has watched a movie remake will appreciate).

Post-structuralists have problematized the terms used in structuralist schemas such as Bal's, suggesting that narrative meaning is 'a more cognitive construct, or mental image, built by the interpreter in response to the text.'[72] Marie-Laure Ryan, for example, argues in *Narratives across Media: The Languages of Storytelling* (2004) for more fluid, socially situated definitions of narrative texts.

1. A narrative text must create a world and populate it with characters and objects. Logically speaking, this condition means that the narrative text is based on propositions asserting the existence of individuals and of propositions ascribing properties to these existents.[73]

This first point, about creating a world and populating it with characters, is particularly germane to cosplay, because the kinds of texts that appeal are often, if not always, as much concerned with world building as with storytelling. The phrase 'characters and objects' is also useful, because popular culture figures who are typically cosplayed have a variety of accoutrements, such as swords, guns, baskets, wands and other paraphernalia, which are more than mere props: they are extensions and expressions of character-identity. However, how cosplayers actually act out the source text soon begins to depart from classical western narrative concerns, which are highly plot-driven (where Japanese anime and manga are widely regarded as more character-driven). Thus the following—temporal and psychological—dimensions of narrative texts are far less obviously relevant to cosplay:

2. The world referred to by the text must undergo changes of state that are caused by non-habitual physical events: either accidents ('happenings') or deliberate human actions. These changes create a temporal dimension and place the narrative in the flux of history.
3. The text must allow the reconstruction of an interpretive network of goals, plans, causal relations, and psychological motivations around the narrated events. This implicit network gives coherence and intelligibility to the physical events and turns them into a plot.[74]

The temporal dimensions of the plot are seldom a central part of cosplay, except perhaps in fragmentary form in the skits performed at some conventions in the west but rarely in Japan, where purely static displays are favoured.[75] Characters' psychological motivations are barely acted out at all, having been replaced by the cosplayer's own desires.

Cosplay's referencing of source texts can also be understood in terms of translation and adaptation. Ellen Kirkpatrick's concept of 'embodied translation' nicely extends the notion of embodied citational acts: 'Through embodied translation, cosplayers embody source characters from a textual realm into a material one. Consequently, in so doing they subject super or fantastical characters to the laws and limitations of the real world, of real bodies.'[76] Both translation studies and adaptation studies have moved away from the expectation of isomorphism (one-to-one correspondence) between a source text and the target text that characterized their pre-theoretical phase. Translation used to be governed by ideas of 'faithfulness' to the source, with each phrase and even word bearing the burden of respecting the literary original. However, this model was radically challenged by structuralist and post-structuralist concerns with the *skopos* or function of a text, so that gradually the focus shifted from faithfulness to an original to 'fidelity' to the target audience and our needs.[77]

A similar shift has occurred in adaptation studies, which has had to deal with the added dimension of translation across media. Film, for example, is a very different medium from a novel or even a play, despite all three being broadly narrative based. Contemporary theory around film adaptation, therefore, asserts that it should not be slavishly faithful to the original—though this is still how readerly audiences watching literary adaptations often pass judgement—but instead show fidelity to cinema and its spectators.[78] Where cosplay is concerned, cosplayers and audiences alike can be very concerned with faithfulness on the level of concrete representation, both visual (costume, make-up, props) and performative (expressions, poses, gestures, and in the case of skits, voice, movement and other character traits). At the same time, 'cosers' can be intensely aware of the politics of cosplay in relation to issues of ethnicity, gender or the (im)perfect body. Faithfulness to the original text may take a backseat to fidelity to the needs of a diverse, contemporary cosplaying community. Indeed, in this respect the source text may be deliberately and provocatively 'détourned.' Either way, however, what barely figures is keeping faith with the narrative. In cosplay, as indeed is typically the case for manga and anime, character trumps narrative. Story elements are largely lost in translation.

We are left with the paradox that while cosplay depends on citation of a source narrative text for its very *raison d'être*, in performing the citational act cosplayers generally strip characters of their framing narrative content. Gn summarizes this eloquently:

The art of cosplay radically complicates the paradigm of the fan as an active producer or manipulator of the canonical text. On the one hand it is the physical imitation of the image that emancipates the character from the narrative of the text [...]. On the other, the practice of cosplay [...] implies a consumption of the image beyond the site of difference.[79]

Gn is talking, in particular, about the imitation of an 'animated body' and how thereby 'the image of the character is detached from the narrative of the text,'[80] which provides a direct contrast with conventional stage performance. Osmud Rahman, Lui Wing-Sun and Brittany Hei-man Cheung make a similar point, namely that cosplay involves 'converting the two-dimensional (2D) image/fantasy from a page of *manga*, a screen of *anime*, or any 2D character to a three-dimensional (3D) living character in real time.'[81] Maria Amon echoes this in her description of cosplay as 'transposing animated characters onto corporal bodies.'[82] This point can be extended well beyond manga and anime to popular media more generally. For Lamerichs the persistent analogy with fanfiction is found in the fact that cosplay is a form of 'fan appropriation that transforms, performs, and actualizes an existing story in close connection to the fan's own identity.'[83] However, she admits that while 'the audience can judge a costume and behavior, and their resemblance to the source text, they cannot compare the character with the player.'[84] In her view there is a consequent 'actualization' of the narrative, where the character concerned is brought to life, and a fictionalization of everyday life, through which the cosplayer enters into a fictional identity. Story elements subsist, though subordinated to the fan's actualization of that story in the flesh. But while they may be implicit in the source text that the cosplayer cites, do story elements really survive the citational act, in which the chosen character is somatically acted out, bodily performed? If so, how?

Hale highlights the role of the audience or spectator in the process, whereby 'each individual cosplayer's body is "read" through and in relation to the receiver's prior experiences with a given source text.'[85] He distinguishes between 'direct imitation' and 'textual transformations.' The former foregrounds the intertextual relationship with the parent text, which the cosplay is meant to faithfully represent. This is contrasted with transformative acts that are less concerned with being true than promoting 'critical ironic distance.'[86] You could say that the former is concerned with faithfulness, the latter fidelity. Contingencies bearing on this may come down to the particular genre or even franchise being performed. Amon has argued, for instance, that Disney's dogmatic control over the representation of characters from their franchises circumscribes fans' freedom to play with the originals,[87] fuelling concerns about corporate policing of intellectual property, as is the case in many areas of fan appropriation. Equally, audiences may have internalized these conventions. Of course, all this presumes that spectators have at least some familiarity with the original and can thus decode a cosplayer's coding or recoding of the source text. This may well be the case with Disney, Marvel, DC, together with major anime such as *Naruto* and *Pokémon*, and similar big ticket franchises. Even in cosplaying circles, however, the degree of recognition will obviously differ, depending on the choice of character and the knowledge bank of spectators. Cosers of more obscure content probably assume, nonetheless, that at least some members of a convention crowd will identify their chosen character, and such recognition may be credited with subcultural capital or hipness.[88] Moreover, not everyone in the audience has to recognize every get-up for there to be the sense of a collective pool of cultural reference based on the shared consumption of pop culture. In other words, the storyworlds cosplayers are citing are part of the gestalt.

A useful analogy has been proposed by Sebastian Domsch, who frames cosplay in relation to medieval Mystery Plays and the later photographic genre of *tableaux vivants* (living pictures). The characters in Mystery Plays were generally recognizable to an audience in the Middle Ages so appreciation of the performance presupposed a kind of shared cultural mythology. The translation of such archetypal figures onto actual bodies becomes a kind of transubstantiation, in that Domsch suggests that 'the "thing" that can be transported from one medium to another' is the 'mental construct that we call a narrative storyworld and its existents.'[89] The shared desire by cosplayers and audience to give characters from the source storyworld material form elevates them to their own 'ontological level of existence that is equal or even higher than the actual world.'[90] Domsch uses the Japanese concept of *moe* as an analogy here in its particular sense of attaching intensities of feeling to fictional characters, leading to a desire to transcend mere reading and watching, the desire to give a tangible, bodily 'presence to a storyworld and its existents *beyond* its original source text or image.'[91] The cited text, player and audience are all triangulated in the process.

Central to cosplay is the fact that the 'text' that cites, translates or adapts the source text is the cosplayer's body. In cosplay, citational acts are chiefly somatic or bodily ones. As Kane

Anderson puts it, 'cosplayers [...] write these characters and their narratives onto their own bodies.'[92] But while it is possible to cite a character's appearance with one's costumed body, and to act out discrete aspects of the character, inscribing an actual narrative onto—or, better, with—your body is effectively impossible, especially when the source narrative may be hundreds of episodes long and have been adapted across multiple media. What is tangibly cosplayed, again, is precisely what remains after the stripping away of narrative elements, even if these survive more intangibly in the minds of spectators. While talking specifically about anime and related media in otaku culture, Matthew Ogonoski places cosplay within a wider cultural shift away from narrative significance towards 'database consumption' of moe-elements. This reflects a turn in Japanese society away from the metanarratives of the modernist period to the 'small narratives' of the present, often consisting of discrete elements such as 'uniforms, poses, gestures, or situations.'[93] Cosplayers 'perform' just these kinds of parcellized fragments when they costume up and pose for the camera, while their spectators consume a succession of 'superflat structures' rather than a conventional narrative sequence.

That this popular consumption practice is part of the cultural logical of late capitalism is reinforced by direct parallels with animators' use of a commercial database, known as an anime CEL bank, which is a commercial reservoir of images comprising, particularly, a variety of dynamic body poses from various angles. Both manifest what Ogonoski calls 'static image iconicity.'[94] This shift does not apply only to Japan, and reminds us of the adage that in some respects the postmodern resembles the premodern more than the modern. Domsch argues that cosplay, like its medieval European precursors, is a form of 'static live-performance adaptation of the iconographic qualities of well-known narrative existents,'[95] suggesting again the importance of the pooled audience knowledge of what is being cited: in the Middle Ages, Christian and folk mythology, today, pop culture source texts. And yet the subversiveness of cosplay, both inherent and in potentia, suggests something more profound and more political is taking place than the mere consumption of late capitalist pop culture in embodied form. For cosplay is simultaneously a détournement, a requisitioning of prefabricated materials in order to fashion new identities, even if this largely takes place in culturally marginal locations and on the interior plane of self-actualization rather than in the traditional body politic.

Interiorizing the citation

In certain respects, cosplay's form of citationality has analogies with referencing, as with the endnotes in this book, which can be understood as precursors to the hypertextual 'jump.' The familiarity of a cosplay audience with the original storyworlds whose existents are being acted out may prompt audience members to make a mental jump back to the source narrative, especially when spurred by cosers acting 'in part.' Citational acts of this kind that triangulate a text, performer and audience are reminiscent of literary theoretical ideals and hypermedia theory around texts as nodes within networks of meaning, Roland Barthes' 'galaxy of signifiers,'[96] Ted Nelson's notion of literature as 'a system of interconnected writings' so that western culture itself becomes 'a great procession of writings, all with links implicit and explicit between them.'[97] However, the costumed body is a crucial mediating factor in cosplay not present, for example, in related textual and inter-referential practices such as fanfiction. Cosplay requires, in the first instance, physical bodies in actual spaces, whether of the conventional hall, on the competition stage, urban locales such as the once mighty coser site of Jingu Bashi (Harajuku Bridge), or more recently the floor of a *kosupure karaoke* party—though, as the conclusion to *Planet Cosplay* suggests, that could all change with the rise of mixed (virtual and augmented) reality technologies.

At this point, the citational act fractures, in a sense, into two main nodes: the exterior expression of character identity (costumed bodies) and the interiority of experience (interior actualization). The usual disclaimers are, of course, necessary, in that both these elements are in a state of constant interaction. As Jacques Lacan argued, subjectivity is always located within a system of perception and dialogue with the social world.[98] Cosplay, as a performance, depends on an audience, who simultaneously consume and help construct a constantly reiterated database of images, quite literally and materially in the case of cosplay photography. Simultaneously, the cosplayer's realization of a fantastical self manifests on an experiential plane that is in Domsch's words 'higher than the actual world' and which depends on spectatorship to bolster the fictional or symbolic transubstantiation. People seldom cosplay alone: it is an intensely social activity. The next chapter will focus on spectatorship and the visuality of performance, particularly in the context of photography and the ways in which the visual snapshots that cosers generate while posing in costume produce image banks for circulation and consumption, most notably online. This chapter concludes with a consideration of the more subjective dimension of cosplay as an experiential territory in its own right. This can be described as an interiorization of citation, the flipside of the succession of material images that are produced through its externalization as visual spectacle, especially as mediated by photography.

Bainbridge and Norris cite Kurt Lancaster in identifying cosplay with wider fan cultures where fans 'try to capture—through participation and immersion—the original cathartic moment felt during the first viewing of the story.'[99] The player not only inhabits the character physically but in some way mentally, in a fluid space where age, race and gender can be played with. Gender, as noted, is especially fluid in cosplay, even when it has nothing to do with drag in a conventional sense. Given the predominance of young women in cosplay, especially in Asia,[100] this often means females dressing as male characters, though it is also not uncommon to see men dressed as female avatars. Race is also commonly challenged by western fans playing anime characters, and conversely Asian fans playing western comic heroes or villains. Indeed, Larissa Hjorth has documented how for some Australian cosplayers performing anime characters allowed them to 'feel Japanese' and express their affiliation with a range of other cultural identities and practices.[101] Identification with a specific character who is being performed is often seen as, however vicariously, transcending race. As Hjorth's subject 'Rachel,' for example, responded, the idea of dressing up as a character and "being them" (to a degree) for a day appealed to me because it's a chance to do some acting, try out a different personality (for example a shy person cosplaying as an extroverted character has to be extroverted for the day) and dress cutely without people thinking you're a freak![102]

'Michelle' similarly referred to the 'coolness of being that character.' Gn has described this dimension of cosplay as mediated fantasy, arguing that like 'the simulated world in a video game, the ability to mimic an animated body becomes a form of "psychological transportation."'[103]

This transportation can be described as an *affect*, the term referring here not just to the feelings provoked by cosplay but an intense corporeal response. A passage from Giles Deleuze and Félix Guattari (1998) illustrates this: '[Affect] is a prepersonal intensity corresponding to the passage from one experiential state of the body to another and implying an augmentation or diminution of the body's capacity to act.'[104] In his *Ethics*, Spinoza famously associated affect with desire, pleasure, pain and sorrow, within which are contained a whole plethora of states. It is present in Classical ideals of catharsis achieved through dramatic enactment and the Romantic sense of the sublime. Above all, it is located in the body and not just the mind. In hypermodern culture, we tend to regard notions such as the sublime and even catharsis with inherent scepticism. Few would claim that cosplayers seriously believe themselves to sacramentally transform into their staged identities. As discussed, cosplayers' relationships with the source text and the role playing of popular media avatars are often complex and parodic. Arguably cosplay, like other contemporary fan practices such as fanfiction, is performed within an encompassing meta-irony that popular culture nerds and geeks tacitly acknowledge, however seriously they may take certain aspects of cosplay, such as craft construction. It is a conscious suspension of disbelief, not some chthonic state of *participation mystique*.[105] However, there is a powerful longing at work in the desire to give a tangible, bodily presence to a storyworld and its existents, and considerable pleasure in symbolically morphing in this way, however vicarious or fleeting it may be.

Online and offline discussions among cosers tend to suggest that the most frequent feelings that cosplay evokes are ones of empowerment, inclusion, feeling 'hot' or 'cool,' in the obvious senses of being sexually attractive and hip, respectively, and of a strong sense of identification with the character. A Buzzfeed page associated with the 2016 Hype JapanCon, for instance, asked cosplayers from around the world to describe in a word or phrase how cosplaying made them feel. Responses included such affirmations of self as 'marvellous,' 'empowered,' 'included,' 'hot,' 'awesome,' 'cool,' 'sassy' and 'super-cute,' but also 'Like a Death-god!' (Grell from *Black Butler* [*Kuroshitsuji*][106] and 'Like a Pokémon' [Umbreon from *Pokémon*] for example).[107] This might be, as Lamerichs has suggested, quoting Judith Butler on drag and gender performativity, part of a 'complex identity play'[108] or as Lunning put it an 'escape from mundane life.'[109] Social roles and culturally prescribed identities can be fatally constricting; cosplay offers an opportunity to inhabit other fantastical selves from exotic storyworlds in symbolic form.

Another description has been proposed by Anne Peirson-Smith, who discusses cosplay in terms of a duality of meaning. Employing Dick Hebdige's notion of 'documented subcultural narratives,' she has noted how the public costumed self corresponds to a 'parallel universe' in which a change in appearance allows for the expression of new individual and collective identities and ideologies:

> This corporeal duality is a consistent theme as the Cosplayer is both integrated into an imaginary world, and is separated from an everyday reality, whereby the players co-create fantasy worlds by putting on costumes as the ultimate expression of their collective and individual creative imaginations.[110]

Kane Anderson goes a step further in observing how Comic-Con fans, among whom he conducted auto-ethnographic research, 'saw themselves as contributing to the narratives of the fictional worlds of their costumed identities—that is, *they saw themselves as part of the character's stories.*'[111] This offers us one route back to the narrative text, albeit not necessarily the *source text* as such. In the citational acts of cosplay, the original citation of sources as a stable referent is, in a sense, erased and overlaid. The visual component is stripped from the source and cited as faithfully, or subversively, as possible through costumes and related elements inscribed on, and by, the cosplayer's body-as-text. Narrative elements are left behind or referenced only fleetingly in a series of parcellized gestures or in the fragmentary form of skits. What is ostensibly performed and consumed is a series of visual frames from the database. This performance/consumption nexus is less akin to theatre and more to Mystery Plays and *tableaux vivants,* with their static iconicity, especially given that, as the next chapter argues, the still image tends to dominate the economy of cosplay's fan capital despite the emergence of moving image media such as cosplay music videos (CMVs).

Where narrativity re-emerges is in a fantastic sphere—Lacan's Imaginary—suspended somewhere between the fantasy life of the individual and the wider popular cultural matrix of narratives within which cosplay takes place. Whether for the purpose of homage or parody, in cosplay the character has been temporarily made flesh. The audience recognizes the cosplayer as both herself and not herself. She or he has, briefly, opened a kind of gate between worlds: the storyworld of the source text and the everyday world. The event is, of course, ludic and symbolic: a form of play. There is little of the liturgical religiosity of a medieval Mystery Play at work, except perhaps for those who identify themselves on census forms as Jedi. However, in the simultaneous internalization (as psychological event) and exteriorization (as spectacle) of the citation in the citational act, a new, parcellized storyworld is born in which the cosplayer takes on an extended, hybridized identity, in the eyes of both the audience and herself. This transubstantiated self moves within a new narrative matrix: the parallel multiverse of the cosphere, a vast conurbation of spaces globally and digitally distributed in which once discrete texts and media are being brought together in a constant cacophony of inter-referentiality and citation.

Notes

1   See, for example, such character amalgams as 'Popeye the Sailor Moon,' 'Princess Ariel/ Leia' and 'Captain Jake Sparrow.' Anon, 'Cosplay Mashups,' accessed 1 January 2018, http:// www.dorkly.com/post/71689/why-dress-up-as-just-one-thing-mashup-cosplays-baybee/ page:2.

2   *Princess Mononoke* (*Mononoke Hime*), directed by Hayao Miyazaki (Tokyo: Studio Ghibli, 1997), Anime film; *Naruto*, directed by Masashi Kishimoto (Tokyo: Shōnen Jump, 1999– 2014), Anime TV series; *Naruto*, directed by Hayato Date (Tokyo: TV Tokyo, 2002–07), Anime TV series; *Naruto Shippuden*, directed by Hayato Date (Tokyo: TV Tokyo, 2007–), Anime TV series.

3   For a description of the particular processes in the humanities, see Ken Hyland, 'Academic Attribution: Citation and the Construction of Disciplinary Knowledge,' *Applied Linguist* 20, no. 3 (1999), 341–67.

4   Jonathan Gray, *Watching with the Simpsons: Television, Parody and Intertextuality* (New York: Routledge, 2006), 6.

5   Matthew Hale, 'Cosplay: Intertextuality, Public Texts, and the Body Fantastic,' *Western Folklore* 73, no. 1 (2014), 8.

6   Ken Knabb, trans., 'Definitions,' *Internationale Situationniste #1* (June 1958), ed. Guy Debord, accessed 1 January 2018, http://www.cddc.vt.edu/sionline///si/definitions.html.

7   Situationist ideas underwent renovation in the 1990s and remain in play, recently being applied, for example, to digital capitalism and social media. See Marco Briziarelli and Emiliana Armano, eds, *The Spectacle 2.0: Reading Debord in the Context of Digital Capitalism* (London: University of Westminster Press, 2017).

8   E.g. Kane Anderson, 'Becoming Batman: Cosplay, Performance, and Ludic Transformations at Comic-Con,' in *Play, Performance and Identity: How Institutions Structure Spaces*, eds. Matt Omasta and Drew Chappell (New York: Routledge, 2015); Nicolle Lamerichs, 'Stranger than Fiction: Fan Identity in Cosplay,' *Transformative Works and Cultures* 7 (2011), para. 1–8; Nicolle Lamerichs, 'The Remediation of the Fan Convention: Understanding the Emerging Genre of Cosplay Music Videos,' *Transformative Works and Cultures* 18, Performance and Performativity in Fandom (2015), para. 1–8; Susan Scott, '"Cosplay Is Serious Business": Gendering Material Fan Labor on *Heroes of Cosplay*,' *Cinema Journal* 54, no. 3 (2015), 146– 54.

9   Hale, 'Cosplay,' 20.

10 See Norman Fairclough, *Analysing Discourse: Textual Analysis for Social Research* (New York: Routledge, 2003), 51.

11 Frenchy Lunning, *Fetish Style* (London: Bloomsbury, 2013), 137.

12 Fredric Jameson, *Postmodernism or the Cultural Logic of Late Capitalism* (Durham: Duke University Press, 1991), xix.

13 Cited in Ibid.

14 Ibid., xiii.

15 Fredric Jameson, 'Periodizing the 60s,' *Social Text* 9, no.10 (1984), 207.

16 Ibid.

17 As Hale notes, 'Con culture has been under researched and under theorized and, by extension, so have the material and corporeal qualities of many fandoms,' 'Cosplay,' 73. By consequence many of the references in this section are to online archival sources that are often amateur or fan-based by scholarly standards but which nonetheless have validity as accounts by participants often supported by photographic resources.

18 Mike Resnick, …Always a Fan: True Stories from a Life in Science Fiction (Rockville: Wildside Press, 2009), 109.

19 Star Trek: The Original Series, created by Gene Roddenberry (Los Angeles: CBS Television Distribution, 1966–69), TV Series.

20 Frenchy Lunning, 'Cosplay,' in Berg Encyclopedia of Dress and Fashion, Vol. 10—Global Perspectives, ed. Joanna B. Eicher (2011), accessed 1 January 2018, http://www.bergfashionlibrary.com/view/bewdf/BEWDF-v10/EDch10024.xml.

21 Joan Marie Verba, Boldly Writing: A Trekker Fan & Zine History 1967–1987, 2nd ed. (Minnetonka: FTL Publications, 2003), 42.

22 Henry Jenkins, Textual Poachers: Television Fans and Participatory Culture (London: Routledge, 1992), 191–92.

23 Elizabeth Woledge, 'Decoding Desire: From Kirk and Spock to K/S,' Social Semiotics 15, no.2 (2005), 235–50.

24 Vampirella, created by Forrest J. Ackerman and Trina Robbins (Philadelphia: 1969–), Comics series. See Anon., 'The Models of Kathy Bushman,' accessed 1 January 2018, www.vampilore.co.uk/models/bushman_kathy.html.

25 See Ellen Kirkpatrick, 'Towards New Horizons: Coplay (re)imagined through Superhero Genre, Authenticity and Transformation,' Transformative Works and Cultures 18, Performance and Performativity in Fandom (2015), para. 0.1–21.

26 While too numerous to list here, it is worth noting that aside from the Superman movie of 1941 and a television series in 1952, it was the 1970s and 1980s that saw cinematic adaptions centred around the Man of Steel with the Christopher Reeves star vehicle movies of 1978, 1980, 1983, 1984 and 1987. Wonder Woman was the subject of a television movie, series and contemporary remake: Wonder Woman, directed by Vincent McEveety (New York: Warner Brothers, 1974), TV Movie; Wonder Woman, created by Douglas S. Cramer and Stanley Ralph Ross (Burbank: Warner Brothers Television Distribution), TV series; Wonder Woman, directed by Patty Jenkins (New York: Warner Brothers, 2017), Film.

27 Anon., '75 Years of Capes and Facepaint: A History of Cosplay' (25 July 2014), accessed 1 January 2018, www.yahoo.com/movies/75-years-of-capes-and-face-paint-a-history-of-cosplay-92666923267.html.

28 Ron Miller, 'Cosplay 1977 Part 2,' (3 March, 2012), accessed 1 January 2018, http://io9.gizmodo.com/5897864/cosplay-1977-part-2.

29 See Herbert Gans, Popular Culture and High Culture: An Analysis and Evaluation of Taste, Revised and Updated (1999, New York: Basic Books, 2008), quoted in Hale, 'Cosplay,' 6.

30 The Rocky Horror Picture Show, directed by Jim Sharman (Century City: 20th Century Fox, 1975), Film. See Frenchy Lunning, 'Cosplay,' accessed 1 January 2018, http://www.bergfashionlibrary.com/view/bewdf/BEWDF-v10/EDch10024.xml.

31   See Ron Miller, 'A Treasure Trove of Cosplay from the Swinging 1970s' (3 March, 2012), accessed 1 January 2018, http://io9.gizmodo.com/5895773/a-treasure-trove-of-cosplay-from-the-swinging-1970s-nsfw.

32   *Logan's Run*, directed by Michael Anderson (Beverly Hills: Metro-Goldwyn-Meyer, 1976); *Logan's Run*, cr. William F. Nolan and George Clayton Johnson (Beverly Hills: MGM Television, 1977–78).

33   *Star Wars IV: A New Hope*, directed by George Lucas (Century City: 20th Century Fox, 1977), Film; *Star Wars V: The Empire Strikes Back*, directed by Irvin Kershner (Century City: 20th Century Fox, 1980), Film; *Star Wars VI: Return of the Jedi*, directed by Richard Marquand (Century City: 20th Century Fox, 1983), Film.

34   See Dik Daniels, 'Dik Daniels Photos: 1980s Westercon,' (7 January 2012), accessed 1 January 2018, www.vintag.es/2012/01/photos-from-1980s-sci-fi-convention.html.

35   *Astro Boy (Tetsuwan Atomu)*, directed by Osuma Tezuka (1965–66; Tokyo: Mushi Production, 1965–71), Anime TV series.

36   Brian Ashcraft and Luke Plunkett, *Cosplay World* (London: Prestel, 2014), 17.

37   *Science Ninja Team Gatchaman (Kagaku Ninjatai Gatchaman)*, directed by Hisayuki Torumi (Tokyo: Fuji TV), Anime TV series. See Craig Norris and Jason Bainbridge, 'Selling *Otaku*? Mapping the Relationship between Industry and Fandom in the Australian Cosplay Scene,' *Intersections: Gender and Sexuality in Asia and the Pacific* 20 (2009), para. 9.

38   Ashcraft and Plunkett, 'Cosplay World,' 16.

39   *Star Blazers* (Baltimore: Claster Television, 1979–84), Anime TV series; *Space Battleship Yamoto I–III (Uchū Senkan Yamato)*, directed by Leiji Matsumoto (Kansai, Japan: Yomiuri TV, 1974–75), Anime TV series; *Space Pirate Captain Harlock (Uchū Kaizoku Kyaputen Hārokku)*, directed by Leiji Matsumoto (Tokyo: Toei Animation, 1977–79), Anime TV series.

40   Galbraith, 'Cosplay, Lolita and Gender,' para. 1.

41   Frenchy Lunning, 'Cosplay and the Performance of Identity,' *Quodilbetica* 6, no. 1 (2012), quoted in Jason Bainbridge and Craig Norris, 'Posthuman Drag: Understanding Cosplay as Social Networking in a Material Culture,' *Intersections: Gender and Sexuality in Asia and the Pacific* 32 (2013), para. 4.

42   Ashcraft and Plunkett, 'Cosplay World,' 19.

43   Ibid., 19.

44   Lunning, 'Cosplay,' n.pag.

45   Jenkins, *Textual Poachers*, 24. For a discussion in relation to cosplay, see Jin-Shiow Chen, 'A Study of Fan Culture: Adolescent Experiences with Animé/manga Doujinshi and Cosplay Taiwan,' *Visual Arts Research* 33, no.1 (2007), 14.

46   Henry Jenkins, *Convergence Culture: Where Old and New Media Collide* (New York: NYU Press, 2006), 169–205.

47   Winge, 'Costuming the Imagination,' 65, 68.

48   Norris and Bainbridge, 'Selling *Otaku*?,' 11.0.

49   Rauch and Bolton, 'A Cosplay Photography Sampler,' 117, original emphasis.

50   Lamerichs, 'Stranger than Fiction: Fan Identity in Cosplay,' para. 5.1, 5.3.

51   Bainbridge and Norris, 'Posthuman Drag,' para. 8.0.

52   Amon, 'Performances of Innocence,' para. 2.3.

53   Sabastian Domsch, 'Staging Icons, Performing Storyworlds—From Mystery Play to Cosplay,' *Acta Univ. Spientiae, Film and Media Studies* 9 (2014), 130.

54   Hale, 'Cosplay,' 6.

55   Ibid.

56   Ibid., 8.

57   Ibid., emphasis added.

58   See Amon, 'Performances,' para. 2.1; Hale 8, 14 and 17 respectively.

59   Ellen Kirkpatrick, 'Towards New Horizons: Cosplay (Re)Imagined through the Superhero Genre, Authenticity and Transformation,' *Transformative Works and Cultures* 18, Performance and Performativity in Fandom (2015), para. 3.2.

60   Hale, 'Cosplay,' 6, 11.

61   Winge, 'Costuming the Imagination,' 65, 70.

62   *Star Wars I: The Phantom Menace,* directed by George Lucas (Century City: 20th Century Fox, 1999), Film; *Star Wars II: Attack of the Clones,* directed by George Lucas (Century City: 20th Century Fox, 2002), Film; *Star Wars III: Revenge of the Sith,* directed by George Lucas (Century City: 20th Century Fox, 2005), Film; *Star Wars IV: A New Hope,* directed by George Lucas (Century City: 20th Century Fox, 1977), Film; *Star Wars V: The Empire Strikes Back,* directed by Irvin Kershner (Century City: 20th Century Fox, 1980), Film; *Star Wars VI: Return of the Jedi,* directed by Richard Marquand (Century City: 20th Century Fox, 1983), Film; *Star Wars: The Clone Wars,* prod. created by George Lucas (US: Disney/ABC, 2015), Film; *Star Wars: The Force Awakens,* directed by J. J. Abrams (Century City: 20th Century Fox, 2015), Film; *Harry Potter and the Philosopher's Stone,* directed by Chris Columbus (New York: Warner Brothers, 2001), Film; *Harry Potter and the Chamber of Secrets,* directed by Chris Columbus (New York: Warner Brothers, 2002), Film; *Harry Potter and the Prisoner of Azkaban,* directed by Alfonso Cuarón (New York: Warner Brothers, 2004), Film; *Harry Potter and the Goblet of Fire,* directed by Mike Newell (New York: Warner Brothers, 2005), Film; *Harry Potter and the Order of the Phoenix,* directed by David Yates (New York: Warner Brothers, 2007), Film; *Harry Potter and the Half-Blood Prince,* directed by David Yates (New York: Warner Brothers, 2009), Film; *Harry Potter and the Deathly Hallows—Part 1,* directed by Mike Newell (New York: Warner Brothers, 2010), Film; *Harry Potter and the Deathly Hallows—Part 2,* directed by Mike Newell (New York: Warner Brothers, 2011), Film; *The Matrix,* directed by The Wachowski Brothers (Burbank: Warner Brothers, 1999), Film; *The Lord of the Rings: The Fellowship of the Ring,* directed by Peter Jackson (Wellington, New Zealand: Wingnut Films, 2001), Film; *The Lord of the Rings: The Return of the King,* directed by Peter Jackson (Wellington, New Zealand: Wingnut Films, 2003), Film; *The Lord of the Rings: The Two Towers,* directed by Peter Jackson (Wellington, New Zealand: Wingnut Films, 2002), Film; *Pokémon,* directed by Kunihiko Yuama et al. (Tokyo: The Pokémon Company International, 1997–), Anime TV series; *Sailor Moon (Bishōjo Senshi Sērā Mūn),* directed by Junichi Sato (Tokyo: Toei Animation, 1992–92), Anime TV series; *Gundam,* created by Yoshiyuki Tomino (Tokyo: Sunrise, 1979–), Anime TV series; *Digimon (Dejitaru Monsutā),* Akiyoshi Hongo (Tokyo:

Toei Animation, 1997), Anime TV series; *Dragonball Z (Doragon Bōru Zetto)*, directed by Daisuke Nishio et al. (Tokyo: Fuji TV, 1989–), Anime TV series. See Peirson-Smith, 'Fashioning the Fantastical Self,' 82.

63   Lamerichs, 'Remediation,' para. 1.4.

64   Hale, 'Cosplay,' 23.

65   Norris and Bainbridge, 'Selling *Otaku*?,' para. 4.0. See also Kurt Lancaster, *Warlocks and Warpdrive: Contemporary Fantasy Entertainments with Interactive and Virtual Environments* (Jefferson: MacFarland and Co., 1999).

66   Gn, 'Queer Simulation,' 584.

67   Lamerichs, 'Stranger than Fiction,' para. 1.2. and 5.2.

68   See Ken Perlin, 'Can there be a Form between a Game and a Story,' in *First person: New Media as Story, Performance, and Game*, ed. Noah Wardrip-Fruin and Pat Harrigan (Cambridge: The MIT Press, 2004), 12–16.

69   From, respectively, *Dead or Alive (Deddo oa Araibu)*, directed by Takashi Miike (Tokyo: Daiei Film, 1999), Anime film; 'Dead or Alive,' created by Tomonobu Itagaki (Tokyo: Koei Tecmo, 1996–), Game; *The Legend of Zelda (Zeruda no Densetsu)*, created by Shigeru Miyamoto and Takashi Tezuka (Tokyo: Nintendo, 1997–), Game; *Mario Bros (Mario Burazāzu)*, created by Shigeru Miyamoto and Gunpei Yokoi (Tokyo: Nintendo, 1983–), Game.

70   See Vladimir Propp, *Morphology of the Folk Tale*, 2nd ed., trans. Laurence Scott (1968; Austin: University of Texas Press, 2003).

71   Mieke Bal, *Narratology*, 2nd ed. (1985; Toronto, Canada: Toronto University Press, 1997), 5, original emphasis.

72   Marie-Laure Ryan, *Narrative across Media: The Languages of Storytelling* (Lincoln: University of Nebraska Press, 2004), 8.

73   Ibid., 8–9.

74   Ibid.

75   Winge, 'Costuming the Imagination,' 73.

76   Kirkpatrick, 'Towards New Horizons,' para. 4.9.

77   See Hans Vermeer, *Towards a General Theory of Translational Action: Skopos Theory Explained* (1984; New York: Routledge, 2013).

78   Patrick Cattrysse, *Descriptive Adaptation Studies: Epistemological and Methodological Issues* (Antwerp, Belgium: Garant, 2014), 21–27.

79   Gn, 'Queer Simulation,' 584.

80   Ibid., 589.

81   Osmud Rahman, Liu Wing-Sun, and Brittany Hei-man Cheung, '"Cosplay": Imagining Self and Performing Identity,' *Fashion Theory* 16, no. 3 (2012), 321.

82   Amon, 'Performances,' para. 1.1.

83   Lamerichs, 'Stranger than Fiction,' para. 1.2.

84   Lamerichs, 'Stranger than Fiction,' para. 5.2.

85   Hale, 'Cosplay,' 12.

86   Ibid., 19.

87   Amon, 'Performances,' para. 2.2.

88 Hale, 'Cosplay,' 9.

89 Domsch, 'Staging Icons,' 129.

90 Ibid.

91 Ibid., 130, original emphasis.

92 Anderson, 'Becoming Batman,' 108.

93 Thomas Lamarre, *The Anime Machine: A Media Theory of Animation* (Minneapolis: University of Minnesota Press, 2009), 258, quoted in Matthew Ogonoski, 'Cosplaying the Mix: Examining Japan's Media Environment, Its Static Forms, and Its Influence on Cosplay,' *Material Fan Culture* 16, Materiality and Object-oriented Fandom (2014), para. 2.3.

94 Ogonoski, 'Cosplaying,' para. 3.1.

95 Domsch, 'Staging Icons,' 125.

96 Roland Barthes, *S/Z, trans.* Richard Miller (New York: Hill & Wang, 1974), 5–6.

97 Ted Nelson, *Literary Machines* (Sausalito: Mindful Press, 1980), 2/9 ff.

98 See Jacques Lacan, 'Symbol and Language,' in *The Language of the Self* (Baltimore: The Johns Hopkins University Press, 1956).

99 Quoted in Norris and Bainbridge, 'Selling *Otaku*?,' para. 4.0.

100 For example, in Japan up to 90 per cent female, mostly in their twenties. Galbraith, 'Cosplay, Lolita and Gender,' para. 6.0.

101 Hjorth, 'Game Girl,' para. 26–29.

102 Hjorth, 'Game Girl,' 29.

103 Gn, 'Queer simulation,' 588.

104 Giles Deleuze and Félix Guattari, *A Thousand Plateaus: Capitalism and Schizophrenia (Mille plateaux)* (London: The Athlone Press, 1998), xvi, quoted in Gn 587.

105 Use of this term is strongly coloured by its conscription by C. G. Jung who wrote that 'PARTICIPATION MYSTIQUE is a term derived from Lévy-Bruhl. It denotes a peculiar kind of psychological connection with objects, and consists in the fact that the subject cannot clearly distinguish himself from the object but is bound to it by a direct relationship which amounts to partial identity.' C. G. Jung, *Psychological Types, Collected Works Vol. 6* (1921; Princeton: Princeton University Press, 1971), para. 781. See Lucian Lévy-Bruhl, *How Natives Think*, trans. Lilian A. Clare (1926; Eastford: Martino Fine Books, 2015).

106 *Black Butler (Kuroshitsuji),* directed by Toshiya Shinohara (Tokyo: Square Enix, 2008–2009), TV series.

107 Ailbhe Malone and Matthew Tucker, '16 Cosplayer's Describe How Wearing Their Costumes Makes Them Feel,' (26 July 2014), accessed 1 January 2018, www.buzzfeed.com/ailbhemalone/cosplayers-costumes?utm_term=.wrKq5XyWl#.sunV8bPjW

108 Lamerichs, 'Stranger than Fiction,' para. 5.6.

109 Lunning, 'Cosplay,' n.pag.

110 Peirson-Smith, 'Fantastical Self,' 81–82.

111 Anderson, 'Becoming Batman,' 108, emphasis added.

Chapter 2

Cosphotography and Fan Capital

Photography plays a crucial role in contemporary cosplay. Just as, historically, fan conventions have shaped the development of particular genres of 'cosphotography,' so photographs and video have gone on to not merely reflect but act as shaping agents in how cosplay is performed. Assembling a costume, applying make-up, hair product and even prosthetics, practicing poses and other gestures, and undertaking the pilgrimage to a cosplay convention or related venue require considerable time and often coin. Consequently, cosplayers may reasonably hope to get back some form of capital in return. Being photographed and videoed, as long as it is not of the invasive variety, can thus provide cosers not only with tokens of private value but fan capital that circulates within wider, largely online networks of exchange operating in the cosphere. Understanding the photograph as a token of 'subcultural or fan capital' or hipness[1] allows us to better scrutinize this economy of desire, and frame some of the polarizing issues that surround cosphotography. These include the tensions between fan-directed and commercial cosplay, heterotopian versus hegemonic control of cosplaying spaces, and supportive audience responses versus the exploitative— including the vicious flaming and body-shaming of cosers that can create an ugly atmosphere, especially on web forums. While online galleries are still the dominant visual discourse of cosphotography, books, prints, coscards and emerging genres of moving image media are increasingly important, from fan-directed cosplay music videos (CMVs) and indie documentaries to network-based reality television shows.

The previous chapter introduced the term *détournement* to refer to the way in which cosplay conscripts and subverts existing media materials, both inherently and in some very particular ways, such as mash-ups and other forms of parody. This is key to understanding cosplay not just as fan-based consumerism but also as a critical practice. There is another term associated with the Situationist International, however, which refers to détournement's archenemesis, *récupération*, which is relevant to a critical understanding of how cosplay can, in turn, itself be conscripted and subverted. Récupération refers to the co-opting of radical, even revolutionary ideas by mainstream culture.[2] In the context of cosplay, this would include the proliferation of prefabricated costumes marketed online, hyper-commercialism of many cons and the media sensationalization and public trivialization of fan cultures so decried by many committed cosplayers. Perhaps the most egregious example is the Syfy reality TV series *Heroes of Cosplay* (2013–14), which followed cast members competing in cosplay events across the United States and beyond, and its prize money fuelled offspring, *Cosplay Melee* (2017–).[3] Widely panned by cosers and critics alike for its Idol-style format, *Heroes* misrepresented cosplay as being all about winning, body-shamed less fit contestants, and depicted female players as dependent on its male cast, who do most of the physical labour, when in reality cosplay is primarily a product of female DIY (do-it-yourself) culture.[4] *Heroes* is an in-your-face form of récupération that strips cosplay of its subversive potential and reappropriates it to commodification culture, while sending viewers distorted messages concerning what cosplay is about (competition, body fitness, prizes and winning). However, cosphotography more generally offers considerable scope for both détournement and récupération, from the conventional hall to the circulation of photos and videos online.

Costuming and photography

Photographing people engaged in the costumed play of media characters predates cosplay proper, not only in the older fan convention practice known as costuming but as evidenced in even earlier accounts of members of the public dressing up as outlandish characters. Perhaps the earliest instance is a craze documented in the United States from around 1908, when William Fell of Cincinnati attended a masquerade ball held at a skating rink in Ohio dressed as Mr. Skygack, the titular lead from one of the earliest science fiction strip cartoons, A. D. Condo's *Mr. Skygack, from Mars* (1907–17),[5] while his wife appeared as Miss Dillpickles (also syndicated from the *Chicago Daybook*). Strangely, though less fortuitously, the confluence of costumed masquerade and ice rinks had a postscript, as reported two years after:

> Later, in 1910, a young woman in Tacoma, Washington created a Skygack costume to wear to a masquerade ball (where she won first prize). A male friend later borrowed the outfit to advertise a skating rink. As he paraded up and down a main street of the city, the Tacoma police arrested him for violating an ordinance prohibiting masquerading on public streets. He was released on $10 bail.[6]

Not only does this provide an early precedent for female fan labour being rewarded at a masquerade ball, but the fact that Skygack impersonation was so quickly co-opted for advertising by a rink owner[7] suggests that récupération was seldom far behind (even if arrest was to follow for the perpetrator). The illegality of wearing a mask in public is also worthy of mention in relation to prankish détournements.[8] In New York, draconian public order laws of this kind date back to 1865; although updated in 1965, they were applied in recent years to harass Occupy protesters, demonstrating that citizens donning masks still possess the power to unnerve authorities.[9]

The Skygack craze was not easily extinguished. Ron Miller relates how in 1912 a Washington man was honoured in a brief caption accompanying his photo in a local newspaper (Figure 1):

> *Times* Readers don't need to ask who in the dickens this is. Sure, it's Skygack from Mars, one of the *Times'* humorous characters. August Olson of Monroe, Wash., contributed the picture. He made up as Skygack and 'copped' the first prize at the masked ball in Monroe.[10]

Wins First Prize As "Skygack"

Times readers don't need to ask who the dickens this is. Sure, it's Skygack from Mars, one of the Times' humorous characters. August Olson of Monroe, Wash., contributed the picture. He "made up" as Skygack and "copped" the first prize at a masked ball at Monroe.

Figure 1: August Olson made up as Mr Skygack, Monroe, Washington, 1912.

In 'contributing the picture', you could say that Olson was perhaps the unwitting progenitor of the now common practice of photo-sharing one's costumed self using the new-fangled media of the day. It was not until the end of the 1930s, however, that we see the first glimmerings of a wider culture of adults costumed in fantastic garb from fictional and imaginative sources. This came courtesy of the inaugural Worldcon in New York, 2–4 July 1939, held in parallel with the first New York World's Fair (30 April 1939–October 1941). Where the World's Fair offered tantalizing visions of 'The World of Tomorrow', with futuristic domes, transportation and scale models of tomorrow's cities, a smattering of Worldcon's 200-odd participants dressed and posed for photographs in futuristic looking costumes made of the most up-to-date materials, including rayon.

Costuming often differed from modern cosplay, in that many of the outfits its practitioners crafted were imaginative projections of future fashions and trends, rather than specific media references. The first Worldcon's surrounding context of the World Fair suggests an atmosphere of technological positivism. Specific source texts were drawn upon, but they tended to be literary prototypes—science fiction novels and short stories—as often as movies, providing considerable scope for interpreting how a character might conceivably look and carry themselves. Modern cosplay, by contrast, is almost wholly based on characters that exist in highly visual and multi-media source texts. This means visual appearance and behaviour can be modelled quite precisely, a dimension tied to the points made in the last chapter about cosplay being reliant on new media and new media inter-relationships, including, in particular, adaptations to film and television. There is also, of course, the mediation of Japanese manga, anime, games and popular culture threaded in from the 1970s onward—something unimaginable in America circa 1940.

However, right from the start some costuming practices were virtually indistinguishable from modern cosplay. At Worldcon 1939, famous costuming pair Forrest J. Ackerman, financier of Ray Bradbury's *Future Fantasia* zine, and Myrtle R. Jones (later Douglas) appeared in matching 'futuristicostumes' of her construction based on the feature film *H.G. Wells' Things to Come* (1936), anticipating the predominance of female labour and moving image media adaptation that underpins cosplay today.[11] Sci-fi writer Frederick Pohl, while describing them both as 'dressed stylishly in the fashions of the Twenty-fifth Century and turning heads in every cafeteria they entered,'[12] worried, somewhat prophetically, that they may have started a trend. Jones, known in costuming circles as Morojo, remained active

in LASFS [Los Angeles Science Fiction Society] in the late 1930s [...]. 'Morojo,' dressed in supposed twenty-fifth century fashion, made a big impression on New York fans at the First World Science Fiction Convention in 1939 [...]. 'Morojo' was famous enough to be asked to write about 'The Woman in Science-Fiction' for the June, 1940 issue of *Science Fiction* (p. 55). She explained why she liked science fiction and said 'undoubtedly' other women would soon be writing in to give their own reasons.[13]

Morojo was to continue to appear in sci-fi fanzines through the 1940s and 1950s,[14] with the congruence of zines and costuming among practitioners such as her and Ackerman anticipating the ongoing affinity between fanfiction and cosplay, forms of popular cultural appropriation that have cast cosers as textual poachers.[15]

Indeed, early Worldcon costuming provided important models that cosplay would come to adopt almost universally, with costumes being showcased in two major convention settings. First, formally staged costume competitions that originated in an annual Masquerade and second, in more informal convention spaces, leading to the term 'hallway costumes.'[16] By Mike Resnick's account the annual Masquerade—originally a kind of fancy dress ball—was inaugurated at the 1940 Chicago conference,[17] while casual shots are in evidence from 1939 (see Figures 2 and 3). These formal and informal convention settings facilitated the emergence of two distinct photographic genres: the more-or-less staged competition shoot on the masquerade 'runway' and the hallway snapshot. It is not recorded what cameras were used to photograph participants at Worldcon 1939, but the resulting monochromatic photographs are testament to social practices resulting from developments in camera technology, and in particular affordable, mass-market models. Early small format

Figures 2 and 3: Forrest J. Ackerman and Myrtle R. Jones performing characters from *Things to Come* (1936) at Worldcon 1939.

(35mm) handhelds date to the eve of the First World War with the Tourist Multiple in 1913 and the Simplex in 1914. Following the war years, which interrupted development, Leitz began commercializing 35mm cameras from 1925 with the Leica I. Kodak released the Retina I in 1934; the price point of such cameras came within reach of the masses for the first time with the introduction of the Argus A in 1936 and Argus C3 in 1939.[18] By the 1940s camera ownership was becoming ubiquitous.

The Civention (Cincinatti Worldcon) of 1949 is preserved for posterity in granular shots of photographers with flashbulbs seated at the front of the auditorium, while a model, Lois Miles, poses on stage as Miss Science Fiction in a Leopard-spotted swimsuit that made the papers (Figure 4).[19] Black-and-white photography was soon augmented by Polaroids during the 1950s and instamatics from the 1960s. By the 1970s a third photographic genre, that of the studio portrait, had become prominent, though the staging of such shots was generally performed in convention settings rather than actual photographic studios. One star of the genre was New Yorker Angelique Trouvere, who appears in a variety of vampish costumes in the 1970s, playing such characters as Red Sonja, Satana and Vampirella (see Figure 5).[20] Many of these carefully modelled shots resemble fashion studio photographs more than runway and hallway snapshots, though such presentation of the costumed self

51

Figure 4: Lois Miles as Miss Science, Civention (Cinci-natti Worldcon), 1949.

Figure 5: Angelique Trouvere as *Vampirella* (1969), early 1970s.

in a consciously staged manner in ad hoc settings could be regarded as fusion of the two. In such early examples, portraits were largely staged with only minimal props, such as white fabric backdrops, against which costumers posed.[21] Similar settings are still utilized at cons, though the portrait has increasingly spilled over into professional photographic studios, props, blue-screens and all.

Cons and cosplay

Before the term's coinage in Japan in 1983, all western 'cosplay' was technically costuming, with its development into what we understand by the term today being incremental. As the last chapter argues, it is not so much the precise year or exact nomenclature that counts but the wider context of transformations in the media landscape. In the 1970s, for example, an original creation like Judith Miller's Captain Judikah could rub shoulders with more-or-less faithful re-creations of Linda Carter's *Wonder Woman* (1975–79).[22] Miller both harks back to early Worldcons in her futuristic costume and anticipates the genre of contemporary cosplay in which cosers dress-up as original avatars from niche—and often personal—fanfiction.[23] Wonder Woman is an obvious example of the now widespread use of publically available mass-mediated texts present from the earliest cons but massively scaled up by a growing culture of transmediation (in this case, from comics to television).[24] At first sight, Kathryn Mayer's 1980s re-creation of the character Gwendolyn Novak from Robert Heinlein's science fiction novel *The Cat Who Walks Through Walls* (1985) recalls early costuming in her adaptation of a literary source, but closer inspection suggests the importance of reproducing visual media. In fact, her costume replicates in loving detail the 1985 cover illustration of Novak from the Ace edition of Heinlein's novel (Figure 6).[25]

The reference to Wonder Woman is a reminder that the next stage in the evolution of the fan convention came via comics and manga cons: San Diego's Comic-Con, from 1970, and its Japanese equivalent, Comiket, from 1975. These mega-conventions would help inspire a multitude of affiliated and independent cons, large and small, in cities across the United States, Japan and around the globe. Worldcon remains a fixture to this day, not just in science/speculative fiction (SF) circles but for fan cultures more generally, though it has been usurped in sheer scale by the San Diego Comic-Con (not to be confused with New York Comic-Con and a host of other 'comic-cons' globally). Comic-Con was founded in San Diego as the Golden State Comic Book Convention, later called the San Diego Comic Book Convention, and is now properly known as Comic-Con International: San Diego. The attendance in 2017 was around 170,000, classifying it as a mega-event by anyone's standards: it was recently described by *Publisher's Weekly* as 'the largest show in North America.'[26] As such, in the words of Kane Anderson, 'Comic-Con operates on the scale

Figure 6: Kathryn Mayer posing in costume as Gwendolyn Novak from the cover of Robert Heinlein's *The Cat Who Walks Through Walls* (1985).

of the carnivalesque as "an occasion for festive transgression."[27] From humble origins as a forum for largely independent comics marketing, Comic-Con has evolved into a mega fan convention catering to all tastes, from specific genres such as science fiction and fantasy to gaming media. Along with dedicated exhibitions, seminars, panels and workshops, there are film and game previews, portfolio review sessions and award ceremonies, including an annual costume masquerade harking back to Worldcon. While anecdotal estimates suggest that only around 15 per cent of attendees are in costume, cosplay is highly visible with cosers milling around the full gamut of convention spaces over the four-day event schedule. Comic-Con is both a giddying spectacle and big business, with an estimated annual economic benefit of around US $180 million for host city, San Diego.[28]

Mention is due regarding the prominence of competitions and commerce at Comic-Con and other cons, given earlier remarks about its commercial récupération as a competitive practice. Although a competition is by definition competitive, this fixture of early cons was generally playful and tempered by a prankish spirit: there is testimony as early as 1952 at Worldcon of the first nude 'costuming,' a practice that would resurface at Comic-Con in 1971 and become a dominant feature in the louche 1970s. By 1963 there are also accounts of costumers in drag, with a clean-shaven Poul Anderson notably masquerading as 'Gertrude the Bird Woman.'[29] Such elements suggest that costuming was often more than a fancy dress competition: it challenged societal norms and in doing so went hand in hand with social progressivism. This is important to note in relation to contemporary mass media récupérations, such as *Heroes of Cosplay* and *Cosplay Melee*, which treat cosplay as quintessentially competitive in nature. The point is not that cosplay ever lacked a competitive element, and this has indeed affected photographic practices inasmuch as the runway, in particular, lends itself to spectacle and produces effective promotional images. The bone of contention is over all the other dimensions that are lost when the spotlight is exclusively on competitive practice.

Comic-Con today is, inevitably, the site of complex political considerations in terms of identity, gender, sexuality, commodification, fan labour, capital and the politics of representation. The sheer scale of merchandizing could lead sceptics to view the 'con' as, on some levels, exactly that: a vast orgy of commodity fetishism, which for Marx occurs when a system of relations between things, such as consumer goods, becomes reified in value and usurps relations between people.[30] While there has been much discussion of Comic-Con's in-your-face product releases, Melanie Kohnen has suggested that in 'behind the scenes' industry panels, producers cynically feign identification with fans as 'geek consumers' for marketing purposes. Moreover, they do so in ways that privilege 'fan-boys' over female participants and solicit the input of both into their business strategies as a form of free labour.[31] As discussed below, similar issues surround cosphotography, which frequently hypersexualizes women and could be considered, uncharitably, as a form of free advertising for the franchises whose characters and storyworlds are being performed, perhaps reinforcing suggestions by some that cosplay should be retitled 'cost-play.'[32]

The United States has not, of course, been the only player in the story of cosplay, with Japan in particular having a vital role. Jason Bainbridge and Craig Norris have argued that its emergence in the west from the 1970s in connection with manga and anime was strongly correlated with 'the appearance of *shōjo manga* in the U.S.,'[33] and it is hard to imagine cosplay today without the mediation of Japanese popular culture (see Figure 7). Equally, however, its rise, even in Japan itself, owes a considerable debt to western media and fan practices, and in the early twenty-first century is defined not just by the influence of Japanese manga, anime and games but the centrality of hyper-visual media, multimedia platforms, transmedia storytelling and, ultimately, the globalized culture flows discussed in Chapter 6.

The sci-fi conventions staged in Japan from the 1960s were themselves partly in emulation of the American model, but it was against the backdrop of the Comic-Market (popularly known as Comiket or Comi-ke), launched in 1975 as a forum for the promotion of *dōjinshi* (self-published manga), that the term cosplay emerged. Fans began to practice *kasou* (dressing up) in character-costumes from at least the late 1970s,[34] though it was not until 1983 that Nobuyuki Takahashi coined the term *kosupure* (cosplay) from *kosuchuumu purei* (costume-play). By the time of his famous article on the subject in *My Anime*, fans were already attending

Figure 7: Attendees costumed as characters from *Uchū Senkan Yamato (Space Battleship Yamoto I–III)* (1978–87), Baltimore Worldcon 1983.

Comiket dressed as a 'mix of superheroes, robots and sexy characters'[35] from popular anime franchises such as *Techno Police 21C (Tekunoporisu Nijūisseki), Lupin III (Rupan Sansei), Star Blazers* and *Urusei Yatsura*.[36] Takahashi's article carried a special feature on crossplaying female cosplayers, suggesting that, as in the west, cosplay challenged gender and other social norms from its inception in Japan. Comiket is now most likely the largest fan gathering in the world with some 35,000 artists featuring their work in what Aida Miho and Patrick W. Galbraith describe as a 'space of self-affirmation'[37] with a staggering half-million annual visitors.[38] That said, space is considerably more policed in Japan than in western countries. At Comiket the designated 'cosplay area' is separate from the exhibition spaces, company booths and conference rooms.[39] This segregation has traditionally included special changing rooms for getting dressed up, and strictures about wearing costumes outside of sanctioned areas, let alone the surrounding streets. Spaces for legitimately photographing cosers is similarly prescribed, though some (predominantly older, male) photographers put this to the test.

While avowedly driven by concern for female cosers' safety, itself a paternalistic approach critiqued below, Takahashi has complained that if 'you were to leave the convention in costume and venture forth to a restaurant, you would not be served.'[40] Indeed, he has suggested that Japan could learn from the comparative openness of western cosplay culture. As Bainbridge and Norris comment, ironically 'cosplay is more acceptable in the western world than it is in Japan, due to negative stereotyping of *otaku*,'[41] though by way of compensation there are urban sites where cosplay culture is tolerated and even celebrated. These include specific districts in Tokyo: historically, Harajuku, Akihabara, Ikebukaro and Nakano, though the bright star that was Harajuku Bridge (Jingu Bashi) has long since waned. 'Microsites' for cosplay practice include the intimate spaces of karaoke booths; Maid cafés, Butler cafés and Miss Dandy bars; large-scale venues include Tokyo Fashion Town, Toshimaen amusement park and the annual World Cosplay Summit. The Nagoya-based Summit, founded in 2003, now has teams from over 30 countries, with the main events being a massive parade and Grand Championship incorporating rounds of stage performances. The cosplay diaspora is now huge and has been characterized by Nicole Lamerichs as 'a particularly global hobby,'[42] even if practices vary from place to place and cosplay is most established in North America and the Asia-Pacific region.

In parallel with these developments come major new modes of photographic production, circulation and audience reception. While cosphotography has its roots in the photographic practices that circulated around costuming, cultural shifts and technological innovation have radically reconfigured the role of the photograph. It is a story told in a procession of vivid images, from the black-and-white 35mm shots of the 1940s, to Polaroids and instamatics of the 1950s, 1960s and 1970s, to SLRs and digicams of the 1980s and 1990s, to—from the turn of the century—DSLRs, point and shoots, smartphone cameras and a range of high-definition video capture devices. Indeed, one could say that the emergence of cosplay and cosphotography are mutually complicit. Most recently implicated is the rise of online digital archives circulating within social media and the current ease of video production and sharing in the age of 4K smartphones and GoPros.

Cameras and gazes

Lamerichs identifies four elements as central to cosplay globally: the source narrative/s, a set of clothing, play or performance before spectators, and the subject or coser herself. To her list we can add a fifth element, photography. Photography is not only shaped by but helps shape cosplay, both at and beyond conventions. If the cosplay performance is fleeting and ephemeral, for better or worse the photographic image is semi-permanent. Still images and videos have acquired huge value as personal tokens, promotional media and documentary recordings. Furthermore, an audience is required for a costume to become transmuted into 'a cultural product that can be admired at the convention, and therefore spectators also play a role in guaranteeing authenticity.'[43] As Bainbridge and Norris comment:

> Authenticity is a key component. Appreciation of the costume by spectators (evaluation, photography, etc.) is a key part of the cosplay; therefore spectators also play a role in guaranteeing authenticity. Photography—posing for photos and having photos taken—is therefore a compliment and comment on the authenticity of the cosplay.[44]

Photography, ubiquitous at cons, feeds into multiple media streams for subsequent circulation, consumption and recirculation. Matthew Hale's comments on Dragon*Con could apply to almost any cosplay convention, though the current social media platforms of the month are Deviantart, Instagram, Tumblr and dedicated pages like Cure WorldCosplay and Cosplayers Global:

> Con attendees document cosplay performances using camcorders, smartphones, and DSLR cameras and distribute this content through various social media like Dragon*Con's unofficial fan photo gallery, Flickr, and Facebook. As these images and videos circulate through various online social networks, they generate interest in particular cosplayers' costumes and performances within Dragon*Con, but also in cosplaying communities throughout the United States and abroad.[45]

Thus, while intimately bound up in the moment, cosphotography transcends its immediate settings, and feeds into a larger economy of desire: to be seen and acknowledged within the cosphere that is constituted by a vast assemblage of physical and virtual spaces. Subsequently, for fans and researchers alike, photographs and videos of cosplay can fulfil a documentary function, acting as 'fanthropology.'[46] Whether reading through a lavish photographic study such as Brian Ashcraft and Luke Plunkett's *Cosplay World* (2015) or filtering through the hundreds if not thousands of dedicated sites online, one is struck both by the succession of images from the mid-twentieth century to the present day and the global distribution of the phenomenon.

In order to articulate a provisional taxonomy for the diverse range of cosphotography practices and genres, it is, nonetheless, necessary to take a situated approach and look at the particular settings around which cosphotographers cluster. Noting that cosplaying at cons is 'partly institutionalized through and motivated by specific events,' Lamerichs goes on to describe how today the 'most common of these are fashion shows, photography sessions and cosplay acts.'[47] The fashion shows are

> organized much as they are in mainstream fashion culture and are usually held on a catwalk or stage where cosplayers can show their costumes from various angles. At fashion shows, the costume is central. Because fans make the outfits themselves, they can earn praise for their sewing skills here. Fashion shows are also entwined with the narrative the costume is based on. Through their choice of the music that plays as they present their work and their body language, cosplayers can express their chosen characters.[48]

The fashion show is a formal venue where fan labour is showcased, and, as Lamerichs notes, involves not just showing off costumes but a performance that is 'in-character' in the theatrical sense. While the seated audience are the immediate spectators, cameras are out in force, as with regular fashion shows. Organized photography sessions may take place during or after the show, and are likely to result in one variant or another of studio portraiture, whether individual or group based.

Frenchy Lunning has pointed out that fashion photography at cosplay events is part of a kind of bilateral trade, and divides the 'convention performance' of cosplay into the *masquerade*, the *hall performance*, and the *impromptu photo session*.'[49] The shots these photographic settings facilitate provide cosplayers with important acknowledgement and, potentially, something to take away, in what can be understood as a reciprocal arrangement with photographers. As Lamerichs notes:

> The fans function as models for the photographers, but they can also use the photographs themselves to promote their costume activities. Fans who specialize in photography usually initiate the shoots, sometimes at specific times that the convention has arranged. Though many of the photographers are fans who want a snapshot of a cosplayer—or rather, a character—they love, some may want to develop their photography skills further. Most cosplayers see getting their picture taken not just as something to be expected, but as a compliment.[50]

Often the rights to photograph during a fashion show or staged cosplay acts—which may be held in a darkened auditorium where flashes are unwelcome—are policed by convention staff. Permission to take shots of cosplayers following such sessions is usually negotiated between the photographer and cosplayers, often formally via a verbal exchange, sometimes more informally through quite paired down gestures (the inflection of an eyebrow may be answered by a faint nod or cosers simply snapping into pose instinctively as the camera is raised, perhaps followed by a preview on an LCD screen and an exchange of contact or online posting details). The resulting images may go nowhere, but equally they offer potential exposure to a global audience of millions, within and beyond the cosphere.

As observed, cosplay competition parades simulate fashion show practices, with the use of catwalks favouring fast shutters, zoom lenses and repetitive shooting. As Eron Rauch and Christopher Bolton comment: 'Cosplay photography clearly borrows some of its visual logic from high fashion photography—both its formal features and its underlying assumption that the clothes exist to be photographed as much as to be worn.'[51] However, while the catwalk or stage may afford moments of poise that provide for striking images, and may become sources of pride or provide promotional material, it is the more deliberately staged 'studio' shots produced during dedicated photo sessions that tend to be privileged in cosplay circles. Unlike models who are clotheshorses for a seasonal collection, cosplayers are showcasing their own labour, and the level of accomplishment demonstrated in the detailing of garments and props is of particular importance. Many spaces within conventions provide studio-like settings, such as plain white walls, interesting architectural niches and, in some cases, purpose-built props that provide strong visual backdrops. Photographers located somewhere along the continuum between professionals and 'prosumers'—used in photographic circles to refer to consumers with professional-level gear or aspirations—may turn up with tripods, flashes, umbrellas and a range of lenses to best exploit these convention spaces.[52] The surrounding locale may also furnish sets where such equipment is deployed; sometimes there are specifically designated areas.

An example is Sakura-Con in Seattle, the 'oldest and most well attended anime conference in the Pacific Northwest.'[53] The 2016 con, for instance, attracted over 23,000 attendees and comprised 100,000 square feet of indoor space at the Washington State Convention Center. Cosplay is one of its main attractions, alongside anime theatres, gaming, cultural panels, concerts, art contests and industry guests. The Center had a number of dedicated indoor spaces where photographers were allowed to set up (space was tightly policed by security staff). At the same time, the con's location adjacent to Freeway Park provided more heterotopian outdoor spaces—Foucault's notion of heterotopia being essentially defined by a lack of controlling authority—including the picturesque gardens, an undercroft and Brutalist sculptural installation, allowing for more impromptu photo sessions. Some of the photographers were clearly professionals who had some serious and costly rigs, though prosumers and amateurs can also invest in expensive kit with DSLRs or mirrorless camera gear. Attendees with smartphones and point-and-shoot cameras sometimes took 'side' photos of the more staged shoots as they were in progress. Though held in an outdoor setting, the style of shooting in these spaces, at least from the professional through to prosumer photographers, was similar to that of studio-based photographic practice: somewhere on the continuum between posed portraiture and staged fashion photography (see Figures 8–13).

At the other end of Sakura-con's cosphotography spectrum are the less staged and more spontaneous 'hallway' snapshots taken by a vast array of shooters, comprising consumer-level DSLRs, point-and-shoots and smartphones, which do not involve specific setting up in terms of lighting and backdrops. The focus is on the costume and performers

Figures 8–13: *Clockwise from the upper left*: (8) cosplayers wait to be photographed indoors, (9) cosplayer reviews shots with a photographer, (10) photographer shoots cosplayer outdoors, (11) photography in the Freeway Park undercroft, (12) cosplayers pose for photographs against a sculpture park backdrop, (13) outdoor photo shoot set-up 2016. © Paul Mountfort.

themselves rather than the aesthetic integrity of the whole ensemble, and both still and video photography occurred throughout the various levels of convention space, as it does at most cons. That does not mean that such photos are not consciously posed, as cosplayers generally see posing in-character as a key part of their performance that they wish to have captured. Critical theory has in any case exposed the apparent naturalism of the snapshot as a cultural construct. In *Photography: A Middle-brow Art (Un art moyen: Essai sur les usages sociaux de la photographie)* (1965) Pierre Bourdieu described how, even when snapped, people ordinarily face the camera instinctively, striking a respectful pose.[54] Although Bourdieu's limited examples have led to accusations of a Eurocentric bias,[55] it remains true that when photographed in groups, as with family photo albums, subjects cluster in ways that emphasize cohesion, implicitly reinforcing dominant social structures such as the nuclear family (or extended family, or team, and so on).

Where cosplay groups are concerned, when a camera is raised the whole 'troupe' may spontaneously shift into mode, posing in forms that can resemble posters promoting a Marvel movie or anime show. Thus even impromptu shots may illicit an ensemble 'reminiscent of scenes from a fashion show or more accurately from the heritage of creating a veritable *tableau vivant* or a living picture frozen in time.'[56] In the nineteenth-century photographic genre of the *tableau vivant*, subjects aimed to replicate a pre-existent scene in considerable detail, thus attempting in Sebastian Domsch's words 'to merge the media of the stage with those of painting or photography.'[57] He argues that modern cosplay photography has effectively resurrected the tableau as a twenty-first-century idiom. Thus, there is more of a continuum than sharp distinction operating between staged and 'spontaneous' cosphotography. That said, high-definition phone cameras and 4K video have made the comparatively spontaneous hallway shot both easy to shoot and share, and so hallway photography remains the most ubiquitous form, if perhaps lacking the cache of runway and studio styles.

Audience expectation, then, is a huge factor in shaping cosplay, with the camera playing a central part. As Domsch suggests, the 'photographer's presence points to the performer's awareness that what he or she engages in is a staged representation.'[58] Cosplayers and cosplaying troupes are constantly being asked—or respond spontaneously to spectator desire—to pose for photos, and con attendees sometimes ask to have their pictures taken with cosplayers as if they were celebrities. Children, especially, may like to pose with their favourite anime characters, stormtroopers, Captain America or other pop cultural icons. Again, conventions are overflowing with cameras, though there are implicit codes of conduct (invasive practices are decidedly unwelcome; voyeuristic 'hover handing' and upskirt outlawed). The ubiquitous selfie—often styled by cosplayers as a 'selca,' derived from the Korean term for selfie—is of course common at cons, and Instagram is stacked with cosplay selfie galleries. However, the selfie does not seem to be a privileged genre of cosphotography, perhaps because cosers generally hope to be stopped for a snap, providing them with a form of tribute or payment, or to have aesthetically staged images in circulation. A directed Google search around the subject of 'cosplay selfies' suggests that the top results are shots of cosers taken while they are standing alone, or with a friend, in bathrooms, bedrooms and other private spaces. There are some hall and street shots, but relatively fewer appear to have been taken in crowded convention spaces. At a con it is far more hip to wield a mythical sword or other prop from a popular storyworld, have someone complement you on it and take your shot, than to stool around toting a selfie stick.

Despite the rise of video, as discussed in Chapter 1, static image iconicity is a particular attribute of the cosplay 'database' of imagery, a virtual archive that bears a resemblance to the commercial CEL bank of images used by animators. In Asian, and particularly Japanese, contexts the host cultures have often traditionally privileged visuality and aesthetics based on visual regimes that differ from those in the west. For instance, Japanese *ukiyo-e* woodblock prints and kabuki theatre have been identified as influences on anime,[59] with Kabuki's highly theatrical poses creating *ukiyo-e*-like visual frames that are 'animated' by the actor's motions, while Noh theatre employs highly abstract masks that are visual glyphs for stock types of characters.[60] Specific genres, such as *shōjo* (literally 'girl's') manga, have their own particular aesthetics, with shōjo style, for instance, being based 'around fashion illustration with many creators also being fashion illustrators' as 'part of a larger lifestyle package' that 'opened the way for young women to participate in fan culture, given cosplay's emphasis on fashion and clothing, particularly in design and performance.'[61]

Japan has been the world's second largest cultural producer after the United States for decades,[62] and despite recent challengers, such as Korea's Hallyu (cultural wave), is likely still the top dog in Asia. Upwards of half of all its cinema and television are animated, putting it on an even footing with live action.[63] The complex aesthetics of manga and anime can feed back into the composition of photographs—at both the studio and snapshot ends of the spectrum, bringing photographic composition into dialogue with adjacent visual media. As Rauch and Bolton observe:

> Some photographers try to erase difference by creating photographs that reproduce the visual qualities of the animated frame or the manga page. Others intrude literally or figuratively into the frame, forcing us to consider the social contexts in which these images are produced and consumed. Some allow fans to emerge from underneath their costumes or try to pry them violently out of character, while many question the sometimes facile divisions and fraught power relationships these kinds of operations assume.[64]

Dynamic poses recall comic book graphics, while Rauch and Bolton's reference to violence in visual representation and their underlying power relationships remind us that, inevitably where spectatorship is a key dimension of a performance, the issue of the politics of the gaze comes into play.

Cosplayers may actively solicit attention but the gaze comes in many forms, not all of them welcome. Cosplay scholar Kane Anderson has provided an auto-ethnographic account of cosplaying Captain America at Comic-Con along with its highs and lows. Framing cosplay as a practice that weaponizes visuality to challenge mainstream hierarchies, he describes attracting considerable attention from 'fans wanting pictures with me in heroic poses and journalists hoping to deploy my image.'[65] Of particular interest is his discussion of the gazes that are levelled at cosers performing Batman at Comic-Con. On the one hand, 'cosplayers enjoy the validating gaze of other attendees.'[66] On the other, they are frequently subject to a variety of alienating gazes. Referring to John Urry's notion of the 'tourist gaze,' he talks of an ever growing but less specifically fan-based demographic of gazers who may construct

Comic-Con 'as an alien environment filled with people of questionable status,' meaning cosplayers in particular. Conflated in the popular imagination with fetish and 'other kinky behaviors,'[67] cosplayers, especially female, are also frequently objectified by the male gaze, reducing the multivalency of cosplay performance to a clutch of normative clichés about girls in sexy outfits.

However, while noting that the 'myth of cosplay as sexual practice seems ingrained,'[68] Anderson does admit that some players, a notable example being the professional cosplayer Yaya Han, may embrace the overtly sexualized elements of their comic book, manga or anime originals. Yet he suggests that it is the source content rather than cosplay itself that is hypersexual: 'What audiences really confront in her portrayals is not sexualization via cosplay; rather, the attendees who comment in this way tokenize, exoticize, and objectify female cosplayers because they expect to see only their idealized characters represented with as much faithfulness as possible.'[69] One of the problems here is that, as suggested above, like western comic books, manga and anime characters are not depicted 'realistically' and may be not just hypersexualized to the point of caricature but extra-human. Caricature, in other words, is part and parcel of the media, and not just in relation to gender and sex. Questions arise, then, about the extent to which one can faithfully represent characters not derived from a visual lexicon of representational realism, or the extent to which such representations should be judged by its standards. Joel Gn has argued that animated bodies, as visual figures who are also embedded in narrative-texts, have an inherent artificiality and so are to be read as falling 'inside quotation marks.'[70] Paradoxically, while hypersexualized they may also be freed from the deterministic gender constraints of biological bodies to become entirely aesthetic and affective vehicles. Gn uses Steven Shaviro's notion of the cinematic body, whereby the 'viewer's gaze or "voyeuristic behavior" is thus not one of detachment or mastery over the object, but an intense manipulation of the senses by the object itself.'[71]

Similar questions are raised in Chapters 8 and 9, but we can note here that it is problematic to cast (particularly female) cosplayers in the role of passive subjects of the unwelcome, sexualizing and objectifying male gaze, as Galbraith suggests in his comparative study of cosplay and Lolita practices in Japan and Australia. The issue is particularly acute in Japan where the cosplay demographic is overwhelmingly young and gendered, with 90 per cent of participants being female cosers in their twenties.[72] In addition to cons, weekly 'hall events' are held in Tokyo and other Japanese cities where *reiyás* (cosplayers, literally from 'layers,' referring to their costumes) are photographed by mostly male *kameko* (camera kids).[73] Referencing prior research by Daisuke Okabe, Galbraith notes how many Japanese cosplayers carry *meishi* (name cards) with photographs of themselves in order to build social networks.[74] While some reiyás are described as *toreareta* (from *toraretai*, meaning 'I want to have my picture taken') they may still be concerned about where such images may end up, and thus permission to photograph may be limited to an inner circle of trusted contacts. Further, there is a social ritual involved in seeking permission to photograph that is far more formal than in the west. As Domsch summarizes:

- the photographer approaches the cosplayer and asks for their permission to take a picture;
- the cosplayer agrees and starts to strike a number of characteristic poses or gestures;
- the photographer takes one or several images;
- both participants thank each other (and I don't think this is just Japanese politeness, it is an acknowledgement that both have performed their function);
- in a more intimate context than the large conventions, the photographer will often later give prints or copies of the images to the cosplayer.[75]

This ritual is partly designed to guard against the 'hentai lech [who] may be looking for cute girls'[76] (hentai means 'pervert' and also refers to pornographic manga and anime). Takahashi has suggested that the designation of specific cosplay areas at Japanese cons has been effective in curtailing this menace,[77] though—problematically—at the cost of female cosplayers' freedom of movement.

Many toreareta report that they are more interested in responses from other women, and thus from outside the abiding constructs of cuteness and feminine sexuality in Japanese society; for Okabe, they are staging a rejection of the male heterosexual gaze to be celebrated as a form of control over their own bodies.[78] In this context, calls by figures like Masaru Umemoto to save innocent girls from predatory adults at conventions have been critiqued as a patronizing stance that 'denies the subjectivity and sexuality of these cosplayers.'[79] As Galbraith notes, while online galleries posted by agencies such as Tokyo Otaku Mode use taglines such as 'Cosplay Babes From Japan' as clickbait, many reiyás upload their own photos to such sites, as 'posting photos on Tokyo Otaku Mode is productive of subcultural or fan capital'[80] and may gain them a fan following internationally, including in the west. That said, Matthew Hale comments with regard to hypersexualization that:

Many female cosplayers explained that they crossplayed because it enabled them to take control of or avert episodes of harassment wherein they were subjected to the 'male gaze' of an overly aggressive photographer who took their photo without permission or inappropriate convention attendees who tried to touch their costume or body.[81]

Similarly, Anne Peirson-Smith has described how, while many female cosplayers in East Asia enjoyed being looked at and photographed, insecurities about personal appearance and the public 'presentation of their sexualized self' led them to avoid appearing in costume outside of designated spaces, especially alone.[82]

Objectification is not the only risk when displaying oneself in sometimes revealing costumes in publically accessible spaces. As Anderson relates from personal experience, 'not all photographers actually want to celebrate cosplayers. Many spectators surreptitiously diminish cosplayers with their gazes even while the costumed performers enjoy the attention.'[83] His observation is based not only on informal semi-structured interviews—where he found 10 per cent of non-costumed attendees later 'post their photographs online so as to mock those players'[84]—but being himself subject to 'the condemning gaze' of a blogger named Avant who bragged that 'the "personal highlight" of his Comic-Con visit included "taking pictures of people in ridiculous costumes who didn't really seem to be enjoying themselves."'[85] Social media flaming is one of the darker sides of the cosphere that threatens to poison its socially inclusive, heterotopian ethos with the kind of profound incivility that characterizes many online forums, infested as they are with trolls emboldened by anonymity.

Fat-shaming is a particular meme with many (often, though not always) male commentators holding forth on the fitness of female fans to play particular characters. This can spill over into attitudes in mainstream media. Anderson has in his sights *LA Times* writer Geoff Boucher whose 2008 article 'Comic-Con is Bursting at the Seams' made much (word) play of the fact that both the conference and many attendees were literally 'bulging at the seams.'[86] Along with body-shaming come other forms of flaming, including frankly racist remarks on the appropriateness of non-whites playing white characters; at the borderlands of both are websites castigating non-Asian western women for being too plump to fit into manga and anime character costumes. In addition to the continuum of fan-directed versus commercialized cosplay, therefore, must be added a continuum of social progressivism versus regressivism, from both within and outside of the cosphere.

Beyond the con

While the convention and associated spaces are the primary sites of cosphotography, they are by no means the only ones. Already mentioned are the weekly 'hall events' in Tokyo that simulate the more studio-like spaces found at many conventions. Conversely, just as studio-based fashion photography, in particular, has colonized the convention, cosphotography is increasingly making itself at home in photographic studios. As Alexis Truong has noted in the Japanese context, another space in which cosphotography is flourishing is the professional (or quasi-professional) photographic studio:

> These studio events operate on a somewhat similar logic as the hall events, and though they are much smaller in size and cost more, they usually provide layers with the optimal conditions and equipment to take pictures. A gathering in a studio can be organised and held by a small group of friends, or advertised by a third party seeking to recruit other layers for the day. Because these events are generally limited in size, layers usually make reservations with close cosplay partners (*pātonā* or *aikata*) or a group of layers they know and often do group cosplay with (*awase*).[87]

After the necessary social networking rituals have been performed, those who have gathered can focus on photographic activities in 'a calmer and more intimate context for [cosplayers] to enjoy their time together.'[88] Similar practices are taking root in the west where an emerging class of photographers—often cosplayers themselves—is specializing in photographing cosplay, though such sessions tend to be less structured than their Japanese equivalents.

Another difference between the west and Japan is that western countries do not tend to offer specific precincts, such as Tokyo's Harajuku, Akihabara and Ikebukuro dedicated to cosplay culture. Jingu Bashi (Harajuku Bridge) was once to cosplayers and Lolitas across the globe what London's Piccadilly Circus was to punk rockers of the late 1970s: a public space associated with their subculture where they show off their costumes, accoutrements and hang out. However, as with the Piccadilly Circus punk scene by the late 1980s and early 1990s, the Harajuku's scene is largely but a memory, with tourists in general and photographers in particular blamed as primary culprits. Prior to its disappearance, visitors complained, somewhat ironically, about gawking tourists outnumbering cosplayers by a large factor. Reiyás tended to cluster defensively, avoiding the array of cameras directed in their direction unless carefully approached for photographs. That said, the neighbouring Harajuku area retains some subcultural chic for its largely teenage and twenties constituency, though reiyás costuming up and hanging out in nearby Yoyogi Park as they did in the early 2010s[89] is increasingly rare. Akihabara is Tokyo's otaku ground zero and sanctuary, with its bladerunneresque mix of manga and anime outlets, high-tech stores, legacy tech shops and Maid cafés.[90] Maid cafés are venues where a largely male otaku crowd can simulate interaction with their idols in the guise of young women dressed in outfits from manga, anime and Japanese pop culture. The encounter is highly ritualized and centres around being poured tea and polite conversation conducted in an archaic idiom full of respect forms for the clientele. The female focused equivalents are Butler cafés, where women are served by *bishōnen* (beautiful, youthful boys), while the maids in some cafés may be cross-dressers and in Miss Dandy bars women are served by other women in costumes. *Kos-kayaba* (cosplay clubs) are the hostess bar equivalent of Maid cafés.[91] Ikebukuro and Nakano are also known for their manga and anime subcultures. Recently, similar bars and cafés have begun to open throughout Asia and internationally. Notably, in Japan photography is discouraged in these locales without permission: Akihabara maids touting for business shield themselves from the camera by turning away or crossing their hands in front of their faces.

The online spaces in which cosplay images are circulated are worthy of a study in their own right. It is worth stressing that blogs, fan directed websites, those of cosplay photographers and commercial sites associated with cons or similar associations have for some time functioned as the main platforms for the publication and distribution of cosphotography. While today this might appear to be a statement of the obvious, Rachel Leng writing in 2013 suggests their defining role over the last decade:

The internet plays a significant role in the cultivation of many fan communities, particularly for fans of Japanese popular culture (Azuma, 2009). As Landzelius notes in her ethnography, *Native on the Net* (2006), the internet 'defeats distance' so that fans can connect instantly through websites, forums, and communities.[92]

Online environments such as micro-blogging apps and other web forums provide young people, especially, with affinity spaces where they can cluster in taste cultures or techno tribes.[93] As Osmud Rahman, Lui Wing-Sun and Brittany Hei-man Cheung observe:

> Many cosplay enthusiasts tend to form their own communal group(s) or tribe(s) through friends, events, and the Internet/viral communities. Cova (1996: 19) stated that the members of this postmodern community or tribe '[...] can be held together through shared emotions, styles of life, new moral beliefs and consumption practices. They exist in no other form but the symbolically and ritually manifested commitment of their members.'[94]

Sites commonly hosting cosplay galleries include DeviantArt, Tumblr, Instagram and Cosplay.com's forums, while old school social networking apps such as Facebook continue to play a role.[95] The main provisos in relation to this cybertopian vision are the points previously raised about shaming, flaming and other regressive elements that can create a negative din around cosplay, drowning out its generally progressive ethos.

While the main engine for the circulation of photographic images is, of course, the Internet, with hundreds if not thousands of dedicated cosplay websites, the scale of the cosplay phenomenon has inevitably produced dedicated photographic studies. Two examples exemplifying wildly divergent approaches are Elena Dorfman's *Fandomania: Characters and Cosplay* (2007) and Ashcraft and Plunkett's *Cosplay World* (2015).[96] The former is an unnerving series of portraits that isolates its subjects against jet-black backgrounds. They do not always flatter, and despite the stated aim of 'making icons out of icons' it is, indeed, a kind of anti-fashion-photographic shoot that 'suggests the layers of representation in cosplay photography and the ways these layers can be peeled apart (or collapsed together) to shed light on how fandom is viewed and displayed.'[97] What is displayed is, in many cases, what Julia Kristeva described as the 'abject body' discussed in the following chapter. Many of the images are confronting and quite opposite in intent to the professional or prosumer photographers whose work is showcased in *Cosplay World*, with its glossy images from studio settings, outdoors and against blue-screens with fantastical, photoshopped backdrops. While primarily comprising cameos by a variety of cosplayers from the United States, Asia and beyond, *Cosplay World* also provides biopics on historians, entrepreneurs, writers and academics along with those behind the camera, including Andrew Michael Philips, Darrell Ardita, Darshelle Stevens, Judith Stephens, Jay Tablante, Benjamin 'Beethy' Koelewijn, Cynthia Veekens, Eric Ng, Anna Fischer and website owner and photographer Kyle Johnson.

This chapter is focused on contextualizing photographic practices rather than on individual photographers. Conducting such a survey would, in any case, prove to be a Herculean task. Rauch and Bolton point out that photo-sharing sites 'host millions of pictures by hundreds of thousands of photographers, making it impossible to give an overview of this genre, much less a who's who of photographers.'[98] However, for those interested, they provide a rundown on established figures who epitomize various styles of cosplay photography, such as the 'prolific online fan documentarian' Eurobeat King; up and coming technical wizard Alain Caporiva; less documentary, more artistically focused Erich Hober; 'Zan,' known for Sailor Moon self-portraits; Steve Scofield for work photographing British fans in America; Elena Dorfman; and Rauch himself, along with the wider genre of subculture fashion photography.[99] In an article titled 'Bridges of the Unknown: Visual Desires and Small Apocalypses,'[100] Rauch provides one of the few journalized autoethnographic accounts of a cosphotographer working at the intersection of art, fanthropology and desire:

> An awareness of one's own desires seems to be the most difficult choice for the critical artist or academic. It seems to be that to experience the 'transcendence' of the fan, we must sacrifice history and critical discourse. But can we go on lusting to fuck that girl in the Rikku costume or the boy looking lost in his Cloud cosplay? (or pass on both and buy a new set of DVDs), after the fleeting intrusion of an anxiety about the hidden gravities inherent in our 'participation'?[101]

So far this discussion has largely focused on still rather than moving image cosphotography. Filmed material comes in a variety of forms, from smartphone and digital camera video taken at conventions by fans and convention organizers, to more ambitious online documentary projects—of which YouTube has a plethora, with titles like *Leaving Mundania, Perfection Zero, Cosplayers; The Movie, True Otaku, The Art of Cosplay* and so on—along with myriad CMVs. Lamerichs has argued that CMVs constitute 'an emerging genre through which fans document and extend the cosplay performance,' and that:

> Today, the ludic culture of cosplay is increasingly moving away from the convention space to new online environments and creative practices, such as music videos, tutorials on prominent websites (e.g., Cosplay.com), and video blogs about craftsmanship, such as Kamui Cosplay (http://www.kamuicosplay.com). Whereas fictional dress up is intimately associated with modeling and photography, we now see a development of different uses and mediations of the costume.[102]

It may be premature to announce the demise of 'fictional dress' and the associated culture of modelling and photography in favour of moving image production and consumption, but this is certainly a space to watch.

Less watchable, for many fans, has been Syfy channel's ill-fated foray into cosplay culture, *Heroes of Cosplay* (2013–14), which, while acknowledged for taking an interest in a neglected subculture, was, as Lamerichs notes 'also heavily criticized for its style and intent.'[103] Susan Scott has framed the show against a backdrop of bloggers who are 'increasingly engaging the identity politics of convention culture for cosplayers' while 'the labor and materiality of cosplay as a mode of fan production, as well as how that labor is gendered, is rarely addressed.'[104] Cosplay may court commercialism in many of its guises and run the constant risk of récupération by the forces of both commodification and regressivism, but few media portals can compete in this respect with *Heroes of Cosplay*, which

> constructs an aspirational vision of cosplay that tends to ignore its ludic roots entirely, presenting cosplay as a strategic exercise in postfeminist self-branding rather than a form of identity play. The controversial injection of cash prizes into convention competitions featured on the show reinforces this skewed portrait of cosplay as driven by capital and competition rather than creativity or community.[105]

One of its most famous participants is Yaya Han, mentioned above in relation to cosphotography, and who appears in *Cosplay World* as a cosplayer who 'now plays professionally.'[106] While Han worked her way up by hard fan labour, sewing her own garments and constructing costumes, the show has, as mentioned, been criticized for demeaning female labour, reinforcing 'the centrality of men within those scenes, ultimately [helping to] reify the presumed place of the female cosplayers on the show as objects of the male gaze.'[107] In this Kardashians-meet-cosplay exercise, Han comes to sit on a panel of judges who often disparage players on the basis of their physical fitness, in a discursive configuration that, as Lamerichs points out, aligns cosplay with competitive sport rather than the camaraderie of fandom.[108] Syfy has made some attempt to address the distinct lack of coser enthusiasm over *Heroes of Cosplay* with the 2017 release *Cosplay Melee*, though this show nonetheless revolves around elimination rounds and the award of a $10,000 prize to the weekly winner. Losers are progressively voted off, *Survivor* style.

For the moment, at least, still photography remains the *sine qua non* of the economy of images circulating around cosplay, in part because the still complements cosplay's source media's static image iconography. The visually rich but, in terms of narrative content, superflat structures, discussed in the previous chapter, which cosplaying generates are experienced as an immediate spectacle at conventions, but can be consumed at leisure in an infinite number of more-or-less staged visual frames in the vast online archives constituted by the thousands of websites that host cosphotography. Runway still photography and video have a definite presence, especially on promotional websites or pages curated by fans who have been favoured on the competition stage. However, the dominant visual genres that evolved out of convention spaces are those of studio-based fashion photography (whether actually taken indoor or out, against physical props or blue-screens) and the snapshot, a genre that is also staged in Bourdieu's sense but less deliberate in its composition, more focused on cosers and costumes than an aesthetic whole. Visual framing borrows on comic book and anime aesthetic regimes, and the whole project of cosphotography is implicated in competing discourses around gender, identity and how the labour of fans is converted into capital, of one kind or another. Who owns the database? Who benefits? Who pays?

A heterotopian vision of the cosphere is one of a socially progressive/transgressive space where fans enact a kind of collective détournement in the mass requisitioning of intellectual property from their legal rights holders and make it their own. In creating and curating images of their cosplay performances that go on to circulate more widely, fans become not just passive consumers but active culture producers. However, right from the beginning in its distant origins in costuming, the forces of récupération have been ever waiting in the wings. Less than utopian are the commercialism, sexism and racism that threaten to reappropriate cosplay, repudiating its ludic roots and press-ganging it into the service of regressive forces. Commodification and incorporation into *Heroes*-style late capitalist fairy tales of individual success are an obvious menace, even if such shows allow a few lucky members of cosplay royalty to take up their crowns. Linked to this are the politics of representation in terms of gender and race in a sphere that, inevitably, suffers from the incivility of our polarized political climate, especially in online discussion threads and via mainstream media. These tensions are likely to be ongoing in the cosphere, where visual tokens of cosplay performances remain the central, if fraught, currency of fan capital, circulation and exchange.

Notes

1   See, respectively, Patrick W. Galbraith, 'Cosplay, Lolita and Gender in Australia and Japan: An Introduction', *Intersections: Gender and Sexuality in Asia and the Pacific* 32 (July 2013), para. 10; Matthew Hale, 'Cosplay: Intertextuality, Public Texts, and the Body Fantastic', *Western Folklore* 73, no. 1 (Winter, 2014), 9.

2   'Definitions', in *Internationale Situationniste #1* (June 1958), ed. Guy Debord and trans. Ken Knabb, accessed 1 January 2018, http://www.cddc.vt.edu/sionline///si/definitions. html.

3   *Heroes of Cosplay*, created by Lauren Brady, Dave Caplin and Mark Cronin (New York: Syfy, 2013), TV series; *Cosplay Melee*, created by Jay Peterson and Todd Lubin (New York: Syfy, 2017), TV series.

4   Rie Matsuura and Daisuke Okabe, 'Collective Achievement of Making in Cosplay Culture', *Proceedings COINs* 15 (2015).

5   A. D. Condo, *Mr. Skygack, from Mars* (Chicago: Chicago Day Book, 1907–17).

6   Ron Miller, 'Was Mr. Skygack the First Alien Character in Comics', *Gizmodo*, 19 September 2013, accessed 1 January 2018, https://io9.gizmodo.com/was-mr-skygack-the-first-alien-character-in-comics-453576089?IR=T. See also Brian Ashcraft and Luke Plunkett, *Cosplay World* (London: Prestel, 2014), 6.

7   Ibid.

8   Zaid Jilana, 'New York City Police Use 150-Year-Old Law against Wearing Masks to Arrest Wall Street Demonstrators', in *Think Progress* (22 September 2011), accessed 1 January 2018, https://thinkprogress.org/new-york-city-police-use-150-year-old-law-against-wearing-masks-to-arrest-wall-street-demonstrators-641e42aafd67#.ve15ajfub.

9   Ibid.

10 Miller, 'Mr. Skygack.' See also Ashcraft and Plunkett, *Cosplay World*, 6.

11 Ray Bradbury, *Future Fantasia* (New York: Self-published, 1939–40).

12 Frederik Pohl, *The Way the Future Was: A Memoir* (London: Ballantine Books, 1978), 96.

13 Eric Leif Davin, *Partners in Wonder: Women and the Birth of Science Fiction 1926–1965* (New York: Lexington Books, 2006), 86.

14 Anon., 'Get to Know Morojo,' in *Geekquality* (5 Dec. 2011), accessed 1 January 2018, http://geekquality.tumblr.com/post/13795875674/get-to-know-morojo.

15 Henry Jenkins, *Textual Poachers: Television fans and Participatory Culture* (New York: Routledge, 1992).

16 Nicole Lamerichs, 'Costuming as Subculture: The Multiple Bodies of Cosplay,' *Scene* 1, no. 1&2 (2014), 114.

17 Mike Resnick, *...Always a Fan: True Stories from a Life in Science Fiction* (Rockville: Wildside Press, 2009), 106.

18 Robin Lenman and Angela Nicholson, *The Oxford Companion to the Photograph* (London: Oxford University Press), accessed 1 January 2018, http://www.oxfordreference.com.ezproxy.aut.ac.nz/view/10.1093/acref/9780198662716.001.0001/acref-9780198662716.

19 Mark Rich, *C.M. Kornbluth: The Life and Works of a Science Fiction Visionary* (Jefferson: McFarland & Company, Inc., 2010), 155.

20 See Anon., 'Angelique Trouvere,' accessed 1 January 2018, http://www.vampilore.co.uk/sandbox/models/angelique-trouvere.php

21 See Ashcraft and Plunkett, *Cosplay World*, 10–15.

22 *Wonder Woman*, Douglas S. Cramer and Stanley Ralph Ross (Burbank: Warner Brothers Television Distribution, 1975–79). See Ashcraft and Plunkett, *Cosplay World*, 12.

23 Quoted in Hale, 'Cosplay,' 14.

24 Ibid., 6, 11.

25 Robert A. Heinlein, *The Cat Who Walks Through Walls* (New York: Ace, 1985). See Ashcraft and Plunkett, *Cosplay World*, 10.

26 Heidi MacDonald, 'What are the Biggest Comic-Cons in North America,' *Publisher Weekly* (19 June 2013), accessed 1 January 2018, http://blogs.publishersweekly.com/blogs/PWxyz/2013/06/19/what-are-the-biggest-comic-cons-in-north-america/.

27 Kane Anderson, 'Becoming Batman: Cosplay, Performance, and Ludic Transformations at Comic-Con,' in *Play, Performance and Identity: How Institutions Structure Spaces*, eds Matt Omasta and Drew Chappell (New York: Routledge, 2015).

28 Peter Rowe, 'Beer is Big, Bubbly Business in SD, New Study Confirms,' *The San Diego Herald Tribune* (22 April 2013), accessed 1 January 2018, http://www.sandiegouniontribune.com/entertainment/beer/sdut-beer-big-new-study-confirms-2013apr22-story.html.

29 Resnick, *Always a Fan*, 106–108.

30 Karl Marx, *Capital Vol I: Critique of Political Economy* (1867; London: Penguin, 1990), 81.

31 Melanie Kohnen, 'The Power of Geek: Fandom as gendered Commodity at Comic-Con,' *Creative Industries Journal* 7, no. 1 (2014), 75–76.

32 Osmud Rahman, Liu Wing-Sun, and Brittany Hei-man Cheung, '"Cosplay": Imagining Self and Performing Identity,' *Fashion Theory* 16, no. 3 (2012), 322.

33   Jason Bainbridge and Craig Norris, 'Posthuman Drag: Understanding Cosplay as Social Networking in a Material Culture,' *Intersections: Gender and Sexuality in Asia and the Pacific* 32 (2013), para. 5.

34   Bainbridge and Norris, 'Posthuman Drag,' para. 3.

35   Ashcraft and Plunkett, *Cosplay World*, 20.

36   *Techno Police 21C*, directed by Masashi Matsumoto (Tokyo: Toho, 1982); *Lupin III (Rupan Sansei)*, Monkey Punch (Tokyo: Futabasha/Chuokoron-Shinsha/Tokyo Pop, 1967–67); *Lupin III—World's Most Wanted (Rupan Sansei)* (Tokyo: Futabasha/Tokyo Pop, 1977–81). Note: the manga was followed by a variety of film and television productions from 1969–2016); *Star Blazers* (Baltimore, MD: Claster Television, 1979–84); *Space Battleship Yamoto I–III (Uchū Senkan Yamato)* directed by Leiji Matsumoto (Kansai, Japan: Yomiuri TV, 1974–75); *Lum (Urusei Yatsura)*, directed by Rumiko Takahashi (Tokyo: ShogaKukan, 1978–87).

37   Aida Miho and Patrick W. Galbraith, 'The Contemporary Comic Market: A Study of Subculture,' *The Journal of Fandom Studies* 4, no. 1 (2016), 55.

38   Michael Bruno, 'Cosplay: The Illegitimate Chile of SF Masquerades,' *Glitz and Glitter Newsletter* (Millennium Costume Guild, October 2002), accessed 1 January 2018, http://millenniumcg.tripod.com/glitzglitter/1002articles.html.

39   Fan-Yi Lam, 'Comic Market: How the World's Biggest Amateur Comic Fair Shaped Japanese Dōjinshi Culture,' *Mechademia* 5, Fanthropologies (2010), 232, 233, 246.

40   Michael Bruno, 'Costuming a World Apart: Cosplay in America and Japan,' *Glitz and Glitter Newsletter* (Millennium Costume Guild, October 2002), accessed 1 January 2018, http://millenniumcg.tripod.com/glitzglitter/1002articles.html.

41   Bainbridge and Norris, 'Posthuman Drag,' para. 6.

42   Lamerichs, 'Costuming,' 114.

43   Nicolle Lamerichs, 'Stranger than Fiction: Fan Identity in Cosplay,' *Transformative Works and Cultures* 7 (2011), para. 2.

44   Bainbridge and Norris, 'Posthuman Drag,' para. 10.

45   Hale, 'Cosplay,' 9–10.

46   Eron Rauch and Christopher Bolton, 'A Cosplay Photography Sampler,' *Mechademia* 5: *Fanthropologies* (2010), 176.

47   Lamerichs, 'Stranger than Fiction,' para. 2.3.

48   Ibid.

49   Frenchy Lunning, 'Cosplay,' in *Berg Encyclopedia of Dress and Fashion, Vol. 10—Global Perspectives*, ed. Joanna B. Eicher (2011), accessed 1 January 2018, http://www.bergfashionlibrary.com/view/bewdf/BEWDF-v10/EDch10024.xml., original emphasis.

50   Lamerichs, 'Stranger than Fiction,' para. 2.4.

51   Rauch and Bolton, 'A Cosplay Photography Sampler,' 180.

52   Daniel Chandler and Rod Munday, 'Prosumer,' in *A Dictionary of Social Media* (Oxford: Oxford University Press 2016), accessed 1 January 2018, http://www.oxfordreference.com.ezproxy.aut.ac.nz/view/10.1093/acref/9780191803093.001.0001/acref-9780191803093-e-1161.

53   Anon., 'About Us,' *Sakura-Con*, accessed 1 January 2018, http://sakuracon.org/about-us/

54 Pierre Bourdieu, *Photography: A Middle-brow Art (Un art moyen: Essai sur les usages sociaux de la photographie)*, trans. Shaun Whiteside (1965; Redwood City: Standford University Press,1990), 80–81.

55 Jacques Derrida, 'The Death of Roland Barthes', in *Psyche: Inventions of the Other Volume 1*, eds. Peggy Kamuf and Elizabeth G. Rottenberg (Stanford: Stanford University Press, 2007), 272.

56 Anne Peirson-Smith, 'Fashioning the Fantastical Self: An Examination of the Cosplay Dress-up Phenomenon in Southeast Asia', *Fashion Theory* 17, no. 1 (2013), 85.

57 Sebastian Domsch, 'Staging Icons, Performing Storyworlds—From Mystery Play to Cosplay', *Acta Univ. Spientiae, Film and Media Studies* 9 (2014), 127.

58 Domsch, 'Staging Icons', 136.

59 Susan Napier, *Anime from Akira to Howl's Moving* Castle (London: St. Martin's Press, 2005), 4.

60 Gian Carlo Carlza, *Japan Style* (London: Phaidon, 2007), 93–100.

61 Bainbridge and Norris, 'Posthuman Drag', para. 5.

62 Nassim Kadosh Otmazgin, 'Contesting Soft Power: Japanese Popular Culture in East and South East Asia', *International Relations of the Asia Pacific* 8 (2007), 78.

63 Napier, *Anime*, 16.

64 Rauch and Bolton, 'Photography Sampler', 177.

65 Anderson, 'Becoming Batman', 105.

66 Ibid., 108.

67 Ibid., 110.

68 Ibid., 112.

69 Ibid., 113.

70 Joel Gn, 'Queer Simulation: The Practice, Performance and Pleasure of Cosplay', *Continuum: Journal of Media and Cultural Studies* 25, no. 4 (2011), 585.

71 Ibid., 48–9.

72 Galbraith, 'Cosplay', para.6.

73 Alexis Hieu Truong, 'Framing Cosplay: How "Layers" Negotiate Body and Subjective Experience through Play', *Intersections: Gender and Sexuality in Asia and the Pacific* 32 (2013), para. 14.

74 Galbraith, 'Cosplay', para. 4.

75 Domsch, 'Staging Icons', 136.

76 Rauch and Bolton, 'Photography Sampler', 179, original emphasis.

77 Bruno, 'Costuming', n.pag.

78 Galbraith, 'Cosplay', para. 6.

79 Ibid., para. 8.

80 Ibid., para. 10.

81 Hale, 'Cosplay', 22–23.

82 Peirson-Smith, 'Fashioning the Fantastical Self', 95–96.

83 Anderson, 'Becoming Batman', 111.

84 Ibid.

85 Ibid., 113.

86 Geoff Boucher, 'Comic-Con is Bursting at the Seams' (24 July 2008), *LA Times,* accessed 1 January 2018, http://beta.latimes.com/local/la-et-comiccon23-2008jul23-story.html.
87 Truong, 'Framing Cosplay,' 15, original emphasis.
88 Ibid.
89 See Yuniya Kawamura, *Fashioning Japanese Subcultures* (New York: Berg, 2012), 65–75.
90 Ibid., 76–84.
91 Lunning, 'Cosplay,' n.pag.
92 Rachel Leng, 'Gender, Sexuality and Cosplay: A Case Study of Male to Female Crossplay,' in *The Phoenix Papers: First Edition* (2013), 92–93, accessed 1 January 2018, http://fansconf.a-kon.com/dRuZ33A/?p=269.
93 See Herbert Gans, *Popular Culture and High Culture: An Analysis and Evaluation of Taste* (Revised and Updated) (1999; New York: Basic Books, 2008).
94 Rahman, Wing-Sun, and Cheung, '"Cosplay",' 319–20.
95 Emerald King, 'Girls Who Are Boys Who like Girls to be Boys: BL and the Australian Cosplay Community,' *Intersections: Gender and Sexuality in Asia and the Pacific* 32 (2013), para. 3.0.
96 See Ashcraft and Plunkett, *Cosplay World*; Elena Dorfman, *Fandomania: Characters and Cosplay* (New York: Aperture, 2007).
97 Rauch and Bolton, 'Photography Sampler,' 176.
98 Ibid., 177.
99 Ibid., 178–88.
100 Eron Rauch and Marantha Wilson, 'Bridges of the Unknown: Visual Desires and Small Apocalypses,' *Mechademia* 2, Networks of Desire (2007), 143–54.
101 Ibid., 147.
102 Nicolle Lamerichs, 'The Remediation of the Fan Convention: Understanding the Emerging Genre of Cosplay Music Videos,' *Transformative Works and Cultures* 18, Praxis (2015), para. 1.3.
103 Ibid., para. 1.2.
104 Susan Scott, '"Cosplay is Serious Business": Gendering Material Fan Labor on *Heroes of Cosplay,' Cinema Journal* 54, no.3 (2015), 146.
105 Ibid., 146, 148.
106 Ashcraft and Plunkett, *Cosplay World,* 48.
107 Scott, 'Cosplay,' 149.
108 Lamerichs, 'Remediation,' para. 1.3.

Chapter 3

Cosplay at Armageddon

osplay, as the previous two chapters suggest, is a performance medium in which embodied textual citation and photographic practices come together and sometimes collide. Moreover, photography both documents and preconditions elements of the cosplay performance, via visual genres typically spanning those of the fashion runway, studio and 'hallway' shoots. This chapter brings these textual and visual analyses together to present a situated photo-essay shot in the candid style. It documents five years of an Australasian-based fan convention that celebrated its twentieth anniversary in 2015, the Auckland Armageddon Expo. In doing so it offers a snapshot, as it were, of a half decade of 'glocalized' cosplay practice. The term 'glocalization' refers to twin processes at work in late capital. Firstly, capital and regulatory frameworks elide from the national upwards to the global scale and reciprocally downwards to the scale of the local. Secondly, economic activities and networks between business entities become simultaneously more localized, regionalized and transnational.[1] This model has been widely applied to the sphere of cultural capital and is of particular relevance to cosplay, which tends to grow by osmosis out of local conditions but owes its provenance to wider networks of cultural production and associated fandoms.

Armageddon is an instance of the organic way in which glocalized conventions develop and proliferate. It began as a comics and trading card event in Auckland, New Zealand, in 1995 with follow-ups in 1997, and within a few short years had spread to the capital city, Wellington (1998), and on to Melbourne, Australia (1999).[2] Starting off in small community venues, progressing to more major urban events centres, and on to large-scale convention spaces, the Expo has evolved into a major regional sci-fi, comics and gaming convention with over 80 events to date, some 70,000 annual visitors in its home city and 130,000 across its Australasian diaspora. In aggregate, it is, therefore, close in scale to San Diego's annual Comic-Con and exhibits a similar mix of cultural and industry practices. While the Auckland Expo has some factors that are specific to its geographic location, genealogy as a gaming and fan con, specifics of the main site and its mix of events, the photos in this chapter could have been taken at almost any con in the western world, both in terms of the diversity of participants and the franchises, storyworlds and other source media texts represented in the costumes on display. The first part of the commentary which follows discusses the range of sources being cited—the individual trees amid the forest of citations, to quote from the first chapter—along with some identifiable trends in the 50 photographs that comprise this selection. The second part provides a more theoretical rationale in discussing the candid photographic approach as a critical practice, along with some of the political, aesthetic and ethical issues it entails.

A cosphoto-essay

With the identity of the cosplayers included in this chapter being anonymous, the focus of discussion here is on the characters and source texts identifiable in the sample of photos on display, and the popular cultural milieu out of which they have arisen. Many of the sources being mined here are comparatively 'timeless,' harking back decades to milestones in their respective media, such as the 2014 San cosplay and crossplay (Figures 23 and 40) inspired by Studio Ghibli's *Princess Mononoke (Mononoke Hime)* (1997).[3] Half a decade is long enough, however, for micro-historical forces to operate in fan cultures, wherein recent movies, games and media elements enjoy rapid waves of meme-like popularity. Of course, even the most up-to-the-minute sources being cosplayed may spring from long-lived media franchises. For instance, Marvel or DC's blockbuster transmedia storyworlds have comic book precursors going back to the 1930s and 1940s. However, particular movie or game adaptions are often very specific: for example, a 2012 costume of The Joker (Figure 2) is not any old joker but identifiably Heath Ledger's Joker from Christopher Nolan's *The Dark Knight* (2008). Similarly, the 2016 release of the movie *Suicide Squad* (2016), set in the DC Comics universe, indelibly marked the portrayal of Harley Quinn in that year.[4] Nor do new waves of influence always overwhelm old favourites: stormtroopers and even sets from the original *Star Wars* (1977–83) trilogy jostle alongside Sith and other characters from the more recent prequels and sequels (Figures 25, 35 and 36).[5]

Chapter 2 noted that identifying the 'trees' in the forest of citations that comprise even a medium-size convention would prove a challenging, if not impossible, task for even the most pop culturally literate geek or *otaku*. This is because, as we have seen, cosplay draws on multiple media sources: comics, movies, manga, anime, games, pop idols and other media identities, as well as online memes. Most, though not all, of the costumes in this essay proved readily identifiable.[6] However, others were more elusive, with some cosplay, being, in any case, modelled after what Matthew Hale terms a generic (as opposed to discrete) character type[7] or fashion style rather than a titular protagonist—though these two dimensions (character type and style) often go hand in hand. Common western character types include vampires, zombies and other genera of the undead, who shuffle convention spaces alongside Japanese-inspired samurai, ninjas, *shōnen* (boys) and *shōjo* (girls), including sub-types such as *bishōnen* (beautiful boys) and *mahō shōjo* (magical girls). Among the most important generic styles—which may comprise not just fashion tastes but lifestyles—are Lolita and steampunk. These styles have often inflected source media, such as anime and manga. Furthermore, crossovers and mash-ups abound, especially at larger cons with more established coser communities who have the confidence to push cosplaying boundaries. This said, superhero action franchises, sci-fi and fantasy television shows, multi-season anime series and protagonists from popular gameworlds tend to be the dominant flora and fauna at most cosplay cons.

There are identifiable cultural fashions within cosplay, and one of the affordances of an extended photographic study is that we are able to see how the portrayals of certain characters, or iterations of certain characters, spike in relation to recent film, game and other media releases. Photos from Armageddon taken between 2012 and 2016 document a number of character iterations from Marvel and DC. Both are deep-rooted comics franchises from the early twentieth century that have had many adaptations and spin-offs over the decades, and which are now the subject of multiple big movie and television series versions. Marvel exerts a particularly powerful gravitational pull on western cosplay today, with *Avenger's* franchise characters such as Captain America (Figure 32) much in evidence in the wake of the *Captain America: The First Avenger* (2011), *The Winter Soldier* (2014) and *Civil War* (2016) instalments.[8] The interconnected nature of the Marvel universe, where the storylines of characters from discrete shows intersect at various junctures, rewarding fans focused on the detailed timelines and backstories, provides the perfect template for the kind of vast inter-referential networks that operate within the cosphere.

In recent years DC has made serious moves to mimic Marvel's integrated storyworlds in an attempt to establish its own universe, though with mixed success. As mentioned, 'Heath Ledger's' Joker (Figure 2) was cited at Armageddon in 2012, four years after the release of DC's *The Dark Knight* (2008). Ledger's Joker attained iconic status not just through his riveting performance and the relative critical acclaim of Nolan's *Batman* trilogy[9] but also due to the actor's tragic death in the same year as the movie's release, which cemented his cult following in popular culture and ensured both actor and character iteration a viral afterlife. Nolan's trilogy restored a cachet to the *Batman* storyworld notably lacking for DC in the pantheon of contemporary popular culture, including cosplay circles. Hence characters such as the Scarecrow (Figure 25),[10] who was the only villain of genuine vintage to star in the entire rebooted *Batman* trilogy (2005–12), Bane and Harley Quinn (Figure 5) showing up in cosplaying circles following the 2012 release of *The Dark Knight Rises* (2012), even though Quinn does not appear in this particular trilogy. She has had many iterations and her popularity spiked in 2016's Armageddon in response to *Suicide Squad's* fishnet stockings and baseball bat toting version (Figure 39, 50), even though the movie itself was ambivalently received. Superman and Wonder Woman undergo periodic revivals, with 2016's Armageddon showcasing both female and crossplaying versions (Figure 48) in anticipation of *Wonder Woman's* 2017 Warner Brothers' reboot directed by Patty Jenkins, while the Green Arrow (Figure 44) from DC's *The Arrow* (2012–) television series reboot also put in a guest appearance.[11]

While some character iterations clearly follow more or less ephemerally on the heels of a movie or other media release, others enjoy relative longevity. For example, at Armageddon 2014 stormtroopers from the first *Star Wars* (1977) movie (Figure 25), a Ringwraith (Figure 21) and Quidditch player (Figure 20) were in evidence despite the original *Star Wars* trilogy dating back to 1977–83, *Lord of the Rings* from 2001–13 and *Harry Potter* from 2001–11.[12] Of course, like the DC and Marvel storyworlds, these cinematic works have deep and massive roots in popular culture, functioning practically as cultural mythologies in the west, and continue to have currency courtesy of the follow up *Star Wars* prequels, sequels and spinoffs (1999–), *The Hobbit* movie adaptation (2013–14) and *Harry Potter* prequel (2016).[13]

The troupe of stormtroopers who posed in 2014 against a lovingly re-created backdrop from the original Death Star returned in 2015 to find themselves joined by a red guard (Figure 35) from *Star Wars II: Attack of the Clones* 2002 and a scruffy 'sandtrooper' from the extended *Star Wars* universe (Figure 36). Characters from the wider *Star Wars* universe may also make cameos, such as the Twi'lek woman from Armageddon 2014 (Figure 27). Although not an identifiable character from the canon, such as Aayla Secura, she is clearly a member of the alien species that figure in the television series *Star Wars: The Clone Wars* (2008–15). Creative adaptations from the storyworld are fairly common in cosplay, and could be described as fan-driven spinoffs, akin to fanfiction's world building.

Legacy movies that are not part of a larger franchise or storyworld can also provide cosplayers with material, especially where the imagery is iconic or has proved to 'have legs' in popular culture. Examples include the ubiquitous *V For Vendetta* (2006) masks that reference not only the film, but the Occupy movement, the cyber-insurgent group Anonymous and, more recently, NBC-Universal hacktivist drama *Mr. Robot* (2015–), in a feedback loop of popular cultural inter-referentiality (Figure 29).[14] Of course, anonymous masks may also be a cheap and easy way to simulate cosplay while retaining an aura of subcultural capital that other mass-produced masks do not convey. A movie's cult status may ensure the relative immortality of its characters in the cosphere, such as the appearance of the eponymous heroine (Figure 37) from Tim Burton's *Corpse Bride* (2005) coming back to life in 2015.[15] Long running movie series spread out over years mean that the distinction between legacy and current characters is often fluid. *Pirates of the Caribbean's* (2003–)[16] Jack Sparrow is the source of numerous memes and has been widely cosplayed, there even being a professional cosplayer in Italy who has based his career on cosplaying Sparrow. 'Jack's' appearance at Armageddon in 2016 could be a back reference to instalments 1–4 of the seemingly endless *Pirates* movie franchise mill, or may have anticipated 2017's much dreaded *Dead Men Tell No Tales*.

There are character iterations, and then there are regenerations (when dealing with a certain 2822-year-old Timelord). Among the many television shows that jostle for attention with characters from live action movies, the long-running British sci-fi series *Doctor Who* (1963–) is a particularly popular media source. Contemporary characters (e.g. Madame Vastra, Figure 18) rub shoulders with both 'classic' and more recent iterations of the Doctor, as do the Daleks and newer menaces such as the Weeping Angels, the Master in 'his' gender bending guise of Missy and The Ood (Figure 26). Along with sci-fi shows, quasi-historical series such as *Spartacus* (2010–13), represented by a slave gang (Figure 38) and, particularly, fantasy TV shows have massive constituencies, with *Game of Thrones* (2011–) being a major source of cosplay performance.[17] Occasionally, characters from popular novels that are not transmediated, such as the titular hero (Figure 24) from *Skulduggery Pleasant* (2007–), are cosplayed, ostensibly based on book cover and fan art.[18]

Western animation is sometimes adapted for cosplay, notable examples being *Avatar: The Last Airbender* (2005–8) and *The Legend of Korra* (2012–14) (Figure 7).[19] However, Japanese visual media comprise the twin lodestar, along with western live action films and television, around which contemporary cosplay gravitates globally. This is doubtless due to the sheer profusion of visual riches and the subcultural cachet afforded by Japanese manga, anime and gaming. As with live action, characters from classic anime staples continue to appear, such as the face-painted, dagger-wielding San (Figures 23 and 40) from *Princess Mononoke (Mononoke Hime)* (1997), along with many other Studio Ghibli characters and those from other anime studios, such as Toei Animation, Sunrise, Production I.G., Madhouse, Manglobe, Studio Pierrot, PA Works, Kyoto Animation and Bones. Characters from anime TV series spotted at Armageddon include Menma (Figure 9) from A-1 Picture's *Anohana: The Flower We Saw That Day (Ano Hi Mita Hana no Namae o Bokutachi wa Mada Shiranai)* (2011), Q (Figure 1) from *[C] The Money of Soul and Possibility Control* (2011), Mami Tomo (Figure 42) from *Puella Magi Madoka Magica (Mahō Shōjo Madoka Magika)* (2011), along with abundant fauna from big ticket franchises such as *One Piece (Wan Pīsu)* (1997–), *Bleach (Burīchi)* (2001–) and *Naruto* (1999–) (Figure 10).[20]

Game characters are a widely represented—and perhaps the fastest growing—fictional demographic at cosplay cons, doubtless due to the massively increased penetration of gaming platforms into people's homes in the early twenty-first century. Among the many examples of stand-alone game series characters in 2016, for example, was Shay Patrick Cormac (Figure 49) from *Assassin's Creed* (2007–).[21] However, games are widely transmediated and evince complex relations with other media. There are, of course, the manga/anime/trading game tie-ins, resulting in cons being stacked with endless *Pokémon* (1995–)[22] characters along with identities from other systems such as Yami (Figure 30) from *Yu–Gi–Oh! (Yū Gi–Ōh)* (1996–).[23] These franchises are truly gargantuan, with *Pokémon* alone having grossed close to US $50 billion prior to the release in 2015 of the short-lived augmented reality (AR) craze for Pokémon GO.[24] Their reach and formative influence on Millennials and Generation Z make it unsurprising that they constitute a major source for cosplay performance. Many characters and storyworlds migrate from manga to anime and onto gaming platforms, such as *Naruto* and *One Piece*. Indeed, the anime/games crossover is a huge subject that could easily comprise a book in itself.

Quite apart from trading games, there is a broad distinction between games that have evolved out of manga/anime source-texts and those that were games first but have subsequently been made into movies or television series. Thus, for example, the Colossal Titan (Figure 15) from *Attack on Titan (Shingeki no Kyojin)* (2009–) references an acclaimed series that has also spawned official and unofficial games, while Namine and Roxas (Figure 8) are avatars from *Kingdom Hearts (Kingudamu Hātsu)* (2002–), a role-playing action game in the crossover genre—in this case Japanese studio Square Enix's characters occupying a setting from the Disney universe.[25] *Final Fantasy (Fainaru Fantajī)* (1987–) is a long-running gaming franchise that was transmediated from the original games into films, while *Tomb Raider* (1996–) started as a game and was adapted to comics and into movies.[26] Lara Crofts of various iterations remain a convention favourite throughout the west (Figure 41), though she is not unknown in Asia. Some game characters riff off anime genres, such as the magical girl anime style of Monimi Usami (Figure 45) from *Danganronpa 2: Goodbye Despair (Sūpā Danganronpa Tsū: Sayonara Zetsubō Gakuen)* (2012),[27] despite, or perhaps because of, the game itself being *shōnon* (young male). Indeed, the abstracted look of many avatars and certain generic conventions in the depiction of costuming and weapons both here and in some anime can make identification of such cosplay sources difficult. For example, some Samurai cosplay (Figure 13) and fantasy figures (Figure 28) can be hard to distinguish from the general type. Similarly, it is difficult without asking to tell at first glance if a particular player is *Game of Thrones'* Jon Snow or *The Hobbit's* (2012–14) Thor Okenshield (Figure 7). There are whole books devoted to making Japanese kimono-inspired costumes, 'because doing so requires specialized dressmaking skills that are different from western dress-making techniques'[28] and the resulting kimono and *yukata* cosplay (Figures 33 and 34) make it hard to distinguish specific character references from the generic type.

In Japan, characters from transmedia storytelling franchises are sometimes also pop cultural idol (*aidoru*) figures who may embody, or are embodied by, real-life avatars, from media celebrities to café 'maids' and 'butlers.' Some also may be stand-alone complexes, so to speak. The Hatsune Miku cosplay (Figure 43) at Armageddon 2016 comes from a digital avatar used in a synthesizer application Hatsune Miku (2007–) by Crypton Future Media.[29] As a further complication, there are the previously mentioned generic character types such as zombies (Figure 31) and fashion subcultures, such as Lolita and steampunk (Figure 7) that may or may not allude to films and games in which specific Lolis and steampunk characters figure. In some cases one might initially mistake the sackcloth and noose tooting costume from 2014 that was DC's Scarecrow (Figure 22) as a repurposed Halloween mask. Increasingly prevalent is meme cosplay, which is hard to identify for those not in on the joke, and which tends to have a fairly rapid turnover, though less so perhaps in coser circles than more generally. Examples of this include the Onision 'I'm a Banana' (Figure 12) meme from 2009 and zipper-face (Figure 14) and zombie nurse (Figure 31) memes observed at Armageddon 2013 and 2014, respectively (the former meme dates back to at least 2011). More generic garb, such as the not-uncommon 'horse head' masks (Figure 17), may be adopted as an easy way to come costumed to a convention and to create dramatic effect on the cheap. Finally, where the current gallery of photographs is concerned, there are shots that document typical kinds of convention activity from milling around outside the convention (Figure 4) to common commercial features of the covered exhibition halls. These include the promotional application of prosthetics (Figure 3), themed mannequins (Figure 6) and sale of merchandise, such as mood-reflecting *nekomimi* (cat ears) sold at booths on the convention floor (Figure 11). These 'costplay' zones await further documentation within the archives of cosphotography, as do many other domains, both physical and virtual, of the ever-expanding cosphere.

Critical practice

Beyond the project of documenting the coming together of source texts and the visual presentation of the costumed self at a convention, some discussion is necessary about the cosphotography essay itself as a form of critical practice. In particular, employing candid photography in relation to cosplay raises questions of ethos. As discussed in the previous chapter, the dominants of cosplay photography are runway style photo shoots, studio-style portraits and hallway snapshots, though the ubiquitous selfie also commonly figures in online platforms and social media apps. While representing diverse photographic genres, the common denominator of all these styles is that they are more or less staged, or at least posed, and can therefore be contrasted with the less deliberate approach of candid photography. Candid photography itself spans several subgenres, from the journalistic to street photographic. While the former, in particular, qualifies as reportage, even street photography that privileges the aesthetic over social realist concerns can be understood as a documentary form, in that it contributes to the collation of situated moments into a kind of cultural record or archive. The dominant setting for the cosphoto essay presented in this chapter is essentially the convention 'hallway' (the term includes adjacent convention spaces), but one of its aims is to augment the ubiquity of posed if informal portraits with the capture of more unscripted moments.

The genre of candid photography to which it most closely aligns is 'slice of life', in its foregrounding of the spontaneous, un-posed and quotidian—though in the context of cosphotography the mundane is indelibly flecked through with shades of the extraordinary. It was noted in the previous chapter how even apparently spontaneous hallway snapshots often lack genuine candidness. Pierre Bourdieu argued that, even when snapped, people ordinarily face the camera instinctively, striking a respectful pose. Moreover, we commonly do so in ways that emphasize cohesion, implicitly inscribing dominant social structures such as the nuclear family (or extended family, team and so on), thus reinforcing dominant visual regimes. Bourdieu argues that the 'convergence of looks and the arrangement of individuals collectively testifies to the cohesion of the group,'[30] and as Stephen Bull writes: 'In this way each individual snapshot performs in microcosm the role of snapshots en masse: the representation and reproduction of social integration.'[31] In the case of cosplay this inevitably involves cosers snapping into a prefabricated character mode or a group pose, with corresponding expressions.

Of course, attempting to circumvent this fixture of the cosplay convention, as some of the photographs here do, raises issues of ethics, especially in a context where cosphotographic practices have in-group etiquettes, and the threat of invasive pointing and shooting elides into topical issues of consent. As noted, female cosers, in particular, are often wary of voyeurs and may find, to their disgust, that some 'hentai lech' with a camera has posted candid pics of the very worst—sexualizing, demeaning—kind online. Unfortunately, there is a risk that any kind of candid photography can be seen as invasive, in that voyeurism is, to some extent, implicit in the genre. In fact, the very nature of photography, in creating not just an image but a record or archive, threatens intrusion and quasi-permanent capture. In *Camera Lucida* (1980; 1981) Roland Barthes notes that 'the age of Photography corresponds precisely with the explosion of the private into the public,'[32] and this pressure helped spur the modern concern with privacy. Simon Baker sees our current culture of full-spectrum surveillance as existing on a historical continuum with the street scenes, captured unbeknown to their ghostly subjects, of the earliest Parisian daguerreotypes, writing that:

> There is a long and complex history of clandestine image making within which photographers working in urban environments have been forced to think carefully and strategically about their relationship to their subjects [...] some of the most important and celebrated photographers have engaged in processes that either deliberately or inadvertently result in capturing their subjects without their knowledge, or in unguarded moments.[33]

Unguarded moments are, of course, precisely what reporters, documentary makers and street photographers seek out. How to balance the competing need for candour and privacy?

In *Right of Inspection (Droit de regards)* (1993) Jacques Derrida teased out some of the implications of who controls the gaze in relation to public and private space in terms of

> what links the juridicial, or the juridico-political, to seeing, to vision, but also the capture of images, their use. It remains a question as to who, in the end, is authorized to appear but above all authorized to show, edit, store, interpret, and exploit images.[34]

This question is quite pressing in relation to the needs for maintaining reportage in a wider cultural context in which public photography is often demonized, ironically by a citizenry that is constantly and clandestinely surveilled by the state—governmental and corporate— via pervasive CCTV and facial recognition regimes. The capture of candid images for this chapter is, of course, not only legal but sanctioned by laws that protect the making and publication of photographs taken in public spaces.[35] However, in terms of the court of popular opinion, the following summation is probably a widely held position:

> People photographed covertly may also feel their privacy is invaded because the shot is candid rather than posed [...]. Unposed photographs seem to look behind normal social masks. However, a person's expression may not accurately portray their mood. Someone may simply let their face go slack when unobserved, rather than being actually unhappy. Because it is natural for people to smile for photographs, a candid shot seems invasive. People cannot conduct themselves in public as if every moment is under observation. It is, therefore, natural for individuals to feel that photographs taken without their consent amount to an invasion of privacy.[36]

The increasing hypersensitivity to being photographed without permission may appear quite reasonable. However, where reportage is concerned it threatens an older 'civil contract' model of public photography that functions as a form of civil action to be accorded corresponding trust,[37] not to mention freedom of artistic expression.

A number of commentators have noted a troubling shift in perception by which 'photography's unprecedented ubiquity, fostered by the proliferation of mobile phones and digital cameras and the ease of online circulation, has sparked anxieties that have been fuelled by a range of particularly volatile social and political issues.'[38] These include fears of terrorism, crimes against children and loss of privacy that coupled with potential uncontrolled circulation online conspire to 'turn photography into a threat.'[39] In this febrile atmosphere, the trend towards people assuming moral ownership of images of themselves taken in public places threatens to become not so much a form of personal empowerment but a move towards the privatization of the public self, arguably owing more to late capitalist conceptions of self-branding than social progressivism.

This chapter attempts to walk a fine line in deploying a candid approach to its subjects that is revealing in ways that staged portraits, runway shoots and even hallway photographs are not, while respecting the cosers involved as part of an implicit ethics of representation within the civil contract. Photographer Valérie Jardin's defence of street shooting can be applied to publically accessible spaces more generally, including convention centres where cosplay takes place:

> It's fine to photograph people in the street as long as it doesn't harm them (as in ridiculing them, giving away trade secrets, etc.) [...]. I make a point to *never* photograph people in embarrassing or vulnerable situations and I only use my street images for fine art or editorial purposes. I do not sell images to stock agencies.[40]

One might add that it is vital that present and future scholarly studies are able to present and draw upon documentary records of the popular cultural practices of our times in ways that are not purely staged and circumscribed by the current culture of self-curation. As Anne Marsh, Melissa Miles and Daniel Palmer comment in *The Culture of Photography in Public Space* (2015), the imperative of combatting the 'potential loss of our future historical record' is an important ethical consideration in its own right; what is at stake is the maintenance of photography 'as a tool for the formation and reformation of public life.'[41] Correspondingly, the shots in this photo-essay are as candid as possible; when subjects do appear to pose for the camera this has been spontaneous rather than solicited, along with some 'cross' shots staged for the benefit of other photographers who were soliciting portraits or group poses. Of particular interest here are the unselfconscious moments of reverie or transportation discussed in Chapter 1 as the intangible yet very real interiorization of the citational act.

Finally, it is also worth pointing out that there is a longstanding discourse around the carnivalesque body as a collective possession of the people, its exhumation in critical theory having begun with Mikhail Bakhtin's re-readings of Rabelais. Bakhtin regarded the body in its Classical and medieval festive incarnations as representing a fluid boundary between self and world. Though imbricated in the grotesque, this 'ever regenerating body of the people'[42] erased the boundaries between self and other resulting in collective renewal. While this older conception of the 'grotesque body' was largely abandoned in the shift to modernity, for Bakhtin it survived, at least textually, in the literary genre of grotesque realism, with its 'language of artistic images,'[43] as epitomized by Rabelais' mid-sixteenth century *The Life of Gargantua and Pantagruel (La vie de Gargantua et de Pantagruel)*. Features include the profanation of the scared—its 'debasement' or bringing down to earth and the level of body—bodily transformations, reversals, symbolic death and rebirth.

While cosplay differs from older forms of mask and masquerade discussed in Chapter 7, its representation of bodies in space constitutes an allied language of artistic images. Some photographers, such as the Elena Dorfman, as discussed in Chapter 2, veer towards not merely the grotesque but what Julia Kristeva called the 'abject body.' Such abjection provokes disgust, confronting us not only with our corporeality but mortality.[44] Alternative terms to those of the grotesque/abject body are the 'fantastic body' or 'body fantastic,' phrases applied specifically to cosplay by Hale.[45] It is the cosplay convention's juxtaposition of mundane backdrops and the body fantastic—both in its contemporary sense of something wonderful and the older one of something uncanny, even unsettling—that the current photo essay aims to capture and celebrate. For as Linda Bradley writes of the cinematic body, in terms that are also redolent for cosplay: 'The body is terrifying, the body is fantastic.'[46]

Figure 1: Q from *[C] The Money of Soul and Possibility Control* (2011), contest event, Auckland Armageddon Expo 2012. © Paul Mountfort.

Figure 2: 'Heath Ledger's' Joker from *The Dark Knight* (2008), Auckland Armageddon Expo 2012. © Paul Mountfort.

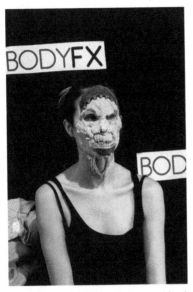

Figure 3: Applying prosthetics, Auckland Armageddon Expo 2012. © Paul Mountfort.

Figure 4: Scene outside the convention space, Auckland Armageddon Expo 2013. © Paul Mountfort.

Figure 5: Bane from *The Dark Knight Rises* (2012) and Harley Quinn from DC universe, Auckland Armageddon Expo 2013. © Paul Mountfort.

Figure 6: Display mannequin, Auckland Armageddon Expo 2013. © Paul Mountfort.

Figure 7: Thorin Oakenshield (*left*) from *The Hobbit* (2012–14) and steampunk cosplayer and (*right*), Auckland Armageddon Expo 2013. © Paul Mountfort.

Figure 8: Namine and Roxas (*left* and *centre*) from *Kingdom Hearts* (2002–), with Korra (*right, background*) from *Legend of Korra* (2012–14), Auckland Armageddon Expo 2013. © Paul Mountfort.

Figure 9: Menma from *Anohana* (2011), Auckland Armageddon Expo 2013. © Paul Mountfort.

Figure 10: Naruto from *Naruto Shippuden* (2007–17), Auckland Armageddon Expo 2013. © Paul Mountfort.

Figure 11: Vendor with mood-reading *nekomimi* (cat ears), Auckland Armageddon Expo 2013. © Paul Mountfort.

Figure 12: Onision 'I'm a banana' meme cosplay, Auckland Armageddon Expo 2013. © Paul Mountfort.

Figure 13: Samurai cosplay, Auckland Armageddon Expo 2013. © Paul Mountfort.

Figure 14: Zipper face nurse meme cosplay, Auckland Armageddon Expo 2013. © Paul Mountfort.

Figure 15: Colossal Titan (*centre, fore-ground*) from *Attack on Titan* (2009–), Auckland Armageddon Expo 2014. © Paul Mountfort.

Figure 16: Armoured anime cosplay, Auckland Armageddon Expo 2014. © Paul Mountfort.

Figure 17: Horse mask meme cosplay, Auckland Armageddon Expo 2014. © Paul Mountfort.

Figure 18: Madame Vastra from *Doctor Who* Series 6 (2011), Auckland Armageddon Expo 2014. © Paul Mountfort.

Figure 19: Cosplayer with police jacket, Cloud from *Final Fantasy* (1988) left shoulder plate, and convention merchandise, Auckland Armageddon Expo 2014. © Paul Mountfort.

Figure 20: Quidditch player from the *Harry Potter* (2001–11) franchise, Auckland Armageddon Expo 2014. © Paul Mountfort.

Figure 21: Ring wraith from *The Lord of the Rings* (2001–2003) movie trilogy, Auckland Armageddon Expo 2014. © Paul Mountfort.

Figure 22: Titular character from DC Comics' *Scarecrow* (1941–), Auckland Armageddon Expo 2014. © Paul Mountfort.

Figure 23: San from *Princess Mononoke* (1997), Auckland Armageddon Expo 2014. © Paul Mountfort.

Figure 24: Titular character from *Sculduggery Pleasant* (2007–), Auckland Armageddon Expo 2014. © Paul Mountfort.

Figure 25: Stormtroopers with fan-constructed backdrop from *Star Wars IV: A New Hope* (1977), Auckland Armageddon Expo 2014. © Paul Mountfort.

Figure 26: An Ood from *Doctor Who* Series 4 (2006), Auckland Armageddon Expo 2014. © Paul Mountfort.

Figure 27: Twi'lek woman from *Star Wars: The Clone Wars* (2008–15), Auckland Armageddon Expo 2014. © Paul Mountfort.

Figure 28: Fantasy figure, Auckland Armageddon Expo 2014. © Paul Mountfort.

Figure 29: *V for Vendetta* (2006) mask, Auckland Armageddon Expo 2014. © Paul Mountfort.

Figure 30: Yami from the *Yu-Gi-Oh* franchise (1998–), Auckland Armageddon Expo 2014. © Paul Mountfort.

Figure 31: Zombie nurses cosplay meme, Auckland Armageddon Expo 2014. © Paul Mountfort.

Figure 32: *Captain America* (2011–), Auckland Armageddon Expo 2015. © Paul Mountfort.

Figure 33: Yukata and kimono cosplaying pair, Auckland Armageddon Expo 2015. © Paul Mountfort.

Figure 34: Sakura kimono cosplay, Auckland Armageddon Expo 2015. © Paul Mountfort.

Figure 35: Red Guard from *Star Wars II: Attack of the Clones* (2002), Auckland Armageddon Expo 2015. © Paul Mountfort.

Figure 36: Sandtrooper, from the *Star Wars* universe, Auckland Armageddon Expo 2015. © Paul Mountfort.

Figure 37: Titular character from *Corpse Bride* (2005), Auckland Armageddon Expo 2015. © Paul Mountfort.

Figure 38: Slave gang cosplay from *Spartacus* (2010–13), Auckland Armageddon Expo 2015. © Paul Mountfort.

Figure 39: Harley Quinn, *Suicide Squad* (2016) iteration, Auckland Armageddon Expo 2016. © Paul Mountfort.

Figure 40: San crossplay from *Princess Mononoke* (1997), Auckland Armageddon Expo 2016. © Paul Mountfort.

Figure 41: Lara Croft from the *Tomb Raider* (1997–) franchise, Auckland Armageddon Expo 2016. © Paul Mountfort.

Figure 42: Mami Tomo from *Puella Magi Madoka Magica* (2011), Auckland Armageddon Expo 2016. © Paul Mountfort.

Figure 43: Hatsune Miku, digital character from *Hatsune Miku V4X Bundle* (2007) synthesizer application, Auckland Armageddon Expo 2016. © Paul Mountfort.

Figure 44: The Green Arrow from DC's *The Arrow* (2012–) television series reboot, Auckland Armageddon Expo 2016. © Paul Mountfort.

Figure 45: Monimi Usami from *Danganronpa 2: Goodbye Despair* (2012), Auckland Armageddon Expo 2016. © Paul Mountfort.

Figure 46: Unidentified cosplay, Auckland Armageddon Expo 2016. © Paul Mountfort.

Figure 47: Captain Jack Sparrow from *The Pirates of the Caribbean* (2003–) movie franchise, Auckland Armageddon Expo 2016. © Paul Mountfort.

Figure 48: Eponymous heroes from the long-running *Superman* (1938–) franchise and *Wonder Woman* (2017) reboot (*left* and *right*), Auckland Armageddon Expo 2016. © Paul Mountfort.

Figure 49: Shay Patrick Cormack from the *Assassin's Creed* (2007–) video game series, Auckland Armageddon Expo 2016. © Paul Mountfort.

Figure 50: Another Harley Quinn from *Suicide Squad* (2016), Auckland Armageddon Expo 2016. © Paul Mountfort.

Notes

Note: Many comic, film, television and game series have multiple directors and are the result of collaboration between several studios, production houses and distributors. For the sake of brevity, the following references limit credit to the main one or two directors, with additional directors noted by et al. Author's names appearing before titles refer to comics or literary works. Production credit is generally given to the distributor, often a dominant partner in the production, due to many works being the result of collaborations with multiple studios. Readers who wish to know more about the specific commercial and artistic collaborations that give rise to specific productions can find detailed information online.

1 See Erik Swyngedouw, 'Globalisation or "Glocalisation"? Networks, Territories and Rescaling,' *Cambridge Review of International Affairs* 17, no. 1 (April 2004).

2 See Anon., 'General-Info/History,' accessed 1 January 2018, https://www.armageddonexpo.com/General-Info/History/.

3 *Princess Mononoke (Mononoke Hime)*, directed by Hayao Miyazaki (Tokyo: Studio Ghibli, 1997), Anime film.

4 *Suicide Squad*, directed by David Ayer (New York: Warner Brothers, 2016), Film.

5 *Star Wars I: The Phantom Menace*, directed by George Lucas (Century City: 20th Century Fox, 1999), Film; *Star Wars II: Attack of the Clones*, directed by George Lucas (Century City: 20th Century Fox, 2002), Film; *Star Wars III: Revenge of the Sith*, directed by George Lucas (Century City: 20th Century Fox, 2005), Film; *Star Wars IV: A New Hope*, directed by George Lucas (Century City: 20th Century Fox, 1977), Film; *Star Wars V: The Empire Strikes Back*, directed by Irvin Kershner (Century City: 20th Century Fox, 1980), Film; *Star Wars VI: Return of the Jedi*, directed by Richard Marquand (Century City: 20th Century Fox, 1983), Film; *Star Wars: The Clone Wars*, produced by Dave Filoni (USA: Disney and ABC, 2008-15), Film; *Star Wars VII: The Force Awakens*, directed by J. J. Abrams (Century City: 20th Century Fox, 2015), Film.

6 Grateful thanks to Jasmin Darnell, Fin Mountfort, Felix Mountfort and to Sye Johnson and his cosplaying circle, for assistance provided to the authors in the identification of cosplay characters and other storyworld, gameworld and media content for this chapter.

7 Matthew Hale, 'Cosplay: Intertextuality, Public Texts, and the Body Fantastic,' *Western Folklore* 73, no. 1 (2014), 10–14.

8 *Captain America: The First Avenger*, directed by Joe Johnston (Hollywood: Paramount Pictures, 2011), Film; *Captain America: The Winter Soldier*, directed by Antonio Russo and Joe Russo (Burbank: Walt Disney Studios, 2014), Film; *The Avengers*, directed by Antonio Russo and Joe Russo (Burbank: Walt Disney Studios, 2014), Film; *Captain America: Civil War*, directed by Antonio Russo and Joe Russo (Burbank: Walt Disney Studios, 2016), Film.

9 *Batman Begins*, directed by Christopher Nolan (New York: Warner Brothers, 2005), Film; *The Dark Knight*, directed by Christopher Nolan (New York: Warner Brothers, 2008), Film; *The Dark Knight Rises*, directed by Christopher Nolan (New York: Warner Brothers, 2012), Film.

10 *Scarecrow*, Bob Kane and Bill Finger, et al. (Burbank: DC Comics, 1941), Comic book.

11 *Superman*, Jerry Siegel and Joe Shudter, et al. (Burbank: DC Comics, 1938–), Film; *Wonder Woman*, directed by Patty Jenkins (New York: Warner Brothers, 2017), Film; *The Arrow*, Greg Berlanti, Marc Guggenheim, and Andrew Kreisberg (New York: Warner Brothers, 2012), Film.

12 *The Lord of the Rings: The Fellowship of the Ring*, directed by Peter Jackson (Wellington, New Zealand: Wingnut Films, 2001), Film; *The Lord of the Rings: The Return of the King*, directed by Peter Jackson (Wellington, New Zealand: Wingnut Films, 2003), Film; *The Lord of the Rings: The Two Towers*, directed by Peter Jackson (Wellington, New Zealand: Wingnut Films, 2002), Film; *Harry Potter and the Philosopher's Stone*, directed by Chris Columbus (New York: Warner Brothers, 2001), Film; *Harry Potter and the Chamber of Secrets*, directed by Chris Columbus (New York: Warner Brothers, 2002), Film; *Harry Potter and the Prisoner of Azkaban*, directed by Alfonso Cuarón (New York: Warner Brothers, 2004), Film; *Harry Potter and the Goblet of Fire*, directed by Mike Newell (New York: Warner Brothers, 2005), Film; *Harry Potter and the Order of the Phoenix*, directed by David Yates (New York: Warner Brothers, 2007), Film; *Harry Potter and the Half-Blood Prince*, directed by David Yates (New York: Warner Brothers, 2009), Film; *Harry Potter and the Deathly Hallows—Part 1*, directed by Mike Newell (New York: Warner Brothers, 2010), Film; *Harry Potter and the Deathly Hallows—Part 2*, directed by Mike Newell (New York: Warner Brothers, 2011), Film.

13 *The Hobbit: An Unexpected Journey*, directed by Peter Jackson (New York: Warner Brothers, 2012), Film; *The Hobbit: The Desolation of Smaug*, directed by Peter Jackson (New York: Warner Brothers, 2013), Film; *The Hobbit*: The Battle of the Five Armies, directed by Peter Jackson (New York: Warner Brothers, 2014), Film.

14 *V For Vendetta*, directed by James McTeigue (New York: Warner Brothers, 2006), Film; *Mr. Robot*, Sam Esmail (US: NBC/Universal Television, 2015), TV series.

15 *Corpse Bride*, directed by Tim Burton (New York: Warner Brothers, 2005), Film.

16 *Pirates of the Caribbean: The Curse of the Black Pearl*, directed by Gore Verbinski (Burbank: Walt Disney Studios, 2003), Film; *Pirates of the Caribbean: Dead Man's Chest*, directed by Gore Verbinski (Burbank: Walt Disney Studios, 2006), Film; *Pirates of the Caribbean: At World's End*, directed by Gore Verbinski (Burbank: Walt Disney Studios, 2007), Film; *Pirates of the Caribbean: On Stranger Tides*, directed by Rob Marshall (Burbank: Walt Disney Studios, 2011), Film.

17 *Doctor Who*, created by Sydney Newman, C. E. Webber and Donald Wilson (London: BBC, 1963–), TV series; *Spartacus*, created by Steven S. DeKnight (Meridian: Starz, 2010–13), TV series; *Game of Thrones*, directed by David Benioff and D. B. Weiss (New York: HBO, 2011–), TV series.

18 Derek Landy, *Skulduggery Pleasant* (London: Harper Collins, 2007).

19 *Avatar: The Last Airbender*, created by Micheal Dante DiMartino and Bryan Konietzko (US: Nickelodeon, 2005–8), Animated TV series; *The Legend of Korra*, Michael Dante DiMartino and Bryan Konietzko (US: Nickelodeon, 2012–14), Animated TV series.

20 *Anohana: The Flower We Saw That Day (Ano Hi Mita Hana no Namae o Bokutachi wa Mada Shiranai)*, directed by Tatsuyuki Nagai (Tokyo: A1 Pictures, 2011), Anime film; *[C] The Money of Soul and Possibility Control*, directed by Kenji Nakamura (Tokyo: Fuji TV, 2011), Anime TV series; *Puella Magi Madoka Magica (Mahō Shōjo Madoka Magika)*,

directed by Akiyuki Shinbo (Tokyo: Shaft, 2011), Anime TV series; *One Piece: Defeat Him! The Pirate Ganzack! (Wan Pīsu: Taose! Kaizoku Gyanzakku)*, directed by Gorō Taniguchi (Tokyo: Fuji TV, 1988), Anime TV film; Eiichiro Oda, *One Piece (Wan Pīsu)* (Tokyo: Jump Comics, 1997), Manga; *One Piece (WanPīsu)*, directed by Kōnosuke Uda et al. (Tokyo: Jump Comics, 2003), Anime TV series; *One Piece: Romance Drawn Story! (One Piece: Romansu Dōn Stori)*, directed by Katsumi Tokoro (Tokyo: Toei Animation, 2003), Anime film; Tite Kubo, *Bleach (Burīchi)* (Tokyo: Jump Comics, 2001), Manga; *Bleach (Burīchi)*, directed by Noriyuki Abe (Tokyo: TV Tokyo, 2004–12), Anime TV series; *Bleach Nintendo Home Console* (Sega, 2005), Console game; Masashi Kishimoto, *Naruto* (Tokyo: Shōnen Jump, 1999–2014), Manga; *Naruto*, directed by Hayato Date (Tokyo: TV Tokyo, 2002–7), Anime TV series; *Naruto Shippuden*, directed by Hayato Date (Tokyo: TV Tokyo, 2007–17), Anime TV series.

21 *Assassin's Creed* (Carentoir, France: Ubisoft Entertainment SA, 2007–), Computer game.

22 *Pokémon*, directed by Kunihiko Yuama et al. (Tokyo: The Pokémon Company International, 1997–), Anime TV series.

23 Kazuki Takahashi, *Yu-Gi-Oh! (Yū Gi-Ōh!)* (Tokyo: Weekly Shōnen Jump, 1996–2004), Manga; *Yu-Gi-Oh (Yū Gi-Ōh!)* directed by Hiroyuki Kakudō (Tokyo: Toei Animation, 1998), Anime TV series; *Yu-Gi-Oh Duel Monsters (Yūgiō Dyueru Monsutāzu)*, directed by Kunihisa Sugishima (Tokyo: TV Tokyo, 2000–4), Anime TV series.

24 'Pokémon,' accessed 1 January 2018, http://vgsales.wikia.com/wiki/Pok%C3%A9mon.

25 *Attack on Titan (Shingeki no Kyojin)*, directed by Hajime Isayama (Tokyo: Bessatsu Shōnen Magazine, 2009), Anime TV series; *Kingdom Hearts (Kingudamu Hātsu)*, created by Tetsuya Nomura and Shinji Hashimoto (Tokyo: Nintendo Entertainment System, 2002), Anime TV series.

26 *Final Fantasy (Fainaru Fantajī)*, created by Hironobu Sakaguchi (Tokyo: Nintendo Entertainment System, 1987), Console game; *Tomb Raider* (London: Eidos Interactive, 2001–), Console game; *Tomb Raider* (Los Angeles: Top Crow, 1997); *Tomb Raider*, directed by Simon West (Hollywood: Paramount Pictures, 2001), Film.

27 *Danganronpa 2: Goodbye Despair (Sūpā Danganronpa Tsū: Sayonara Zetsubō Gakuen)* (Tokyo: Spike Chunsoft, 2012), Computer game.

28 Yuniya Kawamura, *Fashioning Japanese Subcultures* (London: Berg, 2012), 79.

29 *Hatsune Miku V4X Bundle* (Chūōku, SPK, Japan: Crypton Future Media, 2007–), Computer game.

30 Pierre Bourdieu, *Photography: A Middle-brow Art (Un art moyen: Essai sur les usages sociaux de la photographie)*, trans. Shaun Whiteside (1965; Redwood City: Stanford University Press, 1990), 81.

31 Stephen Bull, 'Pierre Bourdieu (1930–2002)' in *Fifty Key Writers on Photography*, ed. Mark Durden (London: Routledge, 2013), 53.

32 Roland Barthes, *Camera Lucinda: Reflections on Photography*, trans. R. Howard (1980; New York: Farrar, Strauss and Giroux, 1981), 98.

33 Simon Baker, 'Up Periscope! Photography and the Surreptitious Image,' in *Exposed: Voyeurism, Surveillance, and the Camera Since 1870*, ed. Sandra S. Philips (New Haven: Yale University Press, 2010), 205.

34 *Right of Inspection (Droit de regards)*, trans. David Wills (New York: Monacelli Press, 1999), 34.

35 See Elspeth Knewstubb, *Photography in Public Places and the Privacy of the Individual*, Master's thesis (Dunedin, New Zealand: University of Otago, 2007); Anon., 'What Are the Rules around Taking Photos or Filming in a Public Place?', accessed 1 January 2018, http://www.police.govt. nz/faq/what-are-the-rules-around-taking-photos-or-filming-in-a-public-place.

36 Knewstubb, *Photography in Public Places,* 8.

37 Ariella Azoulay, *The Civil Contract of Photography* (New York: Zone Books, 2008, 137–86).

38 Anne Marsh, Melissa Miles, and Daniel Palmer, *The Culture of Photography in Public Space* (Bristol: Intellect Books, 2015), 9.

39 Ibid.

40 Valérie Jardin, 'About Street Photography and Privacy Laws (2013),' accessed 1 January 2018, http://valeriejardinphotography.com/blog/2013/8/17/question-4-about-street-photography-privacy-laws.

41 Marsh et al., *Photography in Public Space*, 13, 14.

42 Mikhail Bakhtin, *Rabelais and His World (Tvorčestvo Fransua Rable i narodnaja kul'tura srednevekov'ja i Renessansa)*, trans. Helene Iswolsky (1965; Bloomington: Indiana University Press,1984), 226.

43 Mikhail Bakhtin, *Problems of Dostoevsky's Poetics (Problemy poetiki Dostoyevskogo)*, ed. and trans. Caryl Emerson (1972; Minneapolis: University of Minnesota Press, 1999), 122.

44 See Julia Kristeva, *Powers of Horror: An Essay on Abjection (Pouvoirs de l'horreur. Essai sur l'abjection)*, trans. Leon S. Roudiez (1980; New York: Columbia University Press, 1982).

45 Hale, 'Cosplay,' 5–36.

46 Linda Bradley, *Film, Horror and the Body Fantastic* (Westport: Greenwood Press, 1995), 28.

Part II

Ethnographies

Chapter 4

Cos/play

The notion of play is at the core of the cosplay phenomenon, as signalled in the contraction of the words 'costume' and 'play'. Associating any activity with play might suggest a superficial form of light-hearted engagement. Yet as the accounts by cosplayers provided in this chapter suggest, play can be a profoundly serious concern that reflects the complexities of human behaviour and multiple motivations driving us to act and present ourselves in particular ways. This chapter locates cosplay within the discourses of play theory. We will explore cosplay as a form of fantasy and play, both formal and informal, rule-based and non-rule-based, and in terms of theories of play and performativity: in particular, its ramifications for the construction of identity, the audience gaze and fan participation. This approach builds on Johan Huizinga's foundational notion from the mid-1950s of play existing both within and outside of the play zone or 'magic circle', Roger Caillois' categorizations of rule-based play from the late 1950s, Jürgen Habermas' communicative action as non-rule-based play in the 1980s, and Brian Sutton Smith's more recent thesis on the ambiguity of play. Gregory Bateson's idea of play as exploratory behaviour that tests out the boundaries of existence and non-existence provides an additional point of reference.

Within these theoretical frameworks of play theory, cosplay can be seen as a specific form of re-creation that occurs in its own physical domain, whatever the exact nomenclature used to refer to this circle or zone. Its motivators include escaping the realities of everyday life and seeking solace in a like-minded community of practice based on play that, however impermanent it may be, shares an understanding of the rules of the game that are often expected in the organized and improvised play space.[1]

What is play?

The notion of play has occupied the attention of scholars from a range of academic disciplines with varying interpretations over the past 80 years. As a cultural phenomenon, cosplay can be usefully analysed from different perspectives offered by multiple play theories across the various disciplines of play. As Sutton-Smith observes, 'each discipline had its own notions about play'[2] from the more structured 'ludic' form of play to the more open style of 'paida' play. Between these poles different commentators have divided and taxonomized play in various ways. Sutton-Smith has identified various levels and types of play, including seven culturally derived rhetorics based on intrinsic ambiguities (fate, power, frivolity, identity, progress, self and imaginary).[3] From an anthropological perspective, play is present in all cultures and the logic of play generally informs cultural expression.[4] As such, play is seen as being essential to culture, not an insignificant or meaningless by-product of it. In psychological terms, play is also underpinned in most cultures by a make-believe focus,[5] from childhood adventure play patterns in superhero play[6] through various phases of childhood development.[7] It is a way of sense-making, mastering control or a route to mastering or evading reality.[8] In addition to imparting learning experiences, play can also enable alternative and innovative fantasies that can give rise to, and inspire, new and creative cultural forms in what we might call 'playful forms of play.'[9]

Historically speaking, from the Romantic period (c.1800–50) on, childhood became associated with an innocent nostalgia, often represented in art and literature as a formative, safe, enchanted existence. In morality tales of the period, childhood, which was supposedly grounded in nature, is contrasted with the bleak, alienated, unnatural world of adulthood.[10] In late modern western society childhood make-believe, often involving dressing-up activities, has been further naturalized as a required imaginative pursuit. Childhood playtime is steeped in mythic storylines and references, with the donning of fantasy costumes of literary characters institutionalized, for example, in forms such as the Book Weeks in the British school curriculum. Reflecting on the improvisatory but necessary childhood superhero amity, Michael Chabon describes this common rite of passage:

> You only had to tie a towel around your shoulders to feel the strange vibratory pulse of light stirring in the red sun of your heart [...]. I had imagined the streak of my passage like a red-and-blue smear on the windowpane of vision. I had been Batman too, and like the Mighty Thor. I had stood cloaked in the existential agonies of the Vision, son of a robot and grandson of a lord of the ants [...]. It was not about escape [...] [i]t was about *transformation*.[11]

This association with a mythic, imagined world inhabited by humanoid archetypes which the child is encouraged to replicate in costume helps legitimize the world of make-believe.

Of course, play can be a hedonistic end in itself since games in their most engrossing form, as Erving Goffman states, 'can be fun to play, and fun alone is the approved reason for playing them.'[12] Sutton-Smith has also noted that when 'most scholars talked about play they fundamentally presupposed it to be either a form of progress, an exercise in power, a reliance on fate, a claim for identity, a form of frivolity, an issue of the imagination, or a manifestation of personal experience.'[13] In view of this subtle assessment of play, a basic starting point might be to usefully define it in terms of action and behaviour, a range of voluntary, intrinsically motivated activities usually founded on recreational pleasure and enjoyment.[14] Far from being limited to childhood, it continues to occur across the duration of life, as something we actively choose to do. It has even been contended that play transcends culture and human society itself in its meta-communicative form, operating beyond the psychological and physiological. Huizinga argues that it 'goes beyond the confines of purely physical or purely biological activity. It is a *significant* function—that is to say, there is some sense to it. In play there is something "at play" which transcends the immediate needs of life and imparts meaning to the action. All play means something.'[15]

Equally, play has been defined in terms of what it is not. Hence, it can be seen in terms of oppositional dualities: as extraordinary rather than ordinary, abstract rather than tangible, fun rather than serious, a sign of freedom rather than restriction, mobile rather than static, voluntary rather than involuntary, temporary rather than permanent. As Huizinga notes, play is

> a free activity standing quite consciously outside 'ordinary' life as being 'not serious,' but at the same time absorbing the player intensely and utterly. It is an activity connected with no material interest, and no profit can be gained by it. It proceeds within its own proper boundaries of time and space according to fixed rules and in an orderly manner. It promotes the formation of social groupings which tend to surround themselves with secrecy and to stress their difference from the common world by disguise or other means.[16]

These negatives or binaries may enable play to be defined with regard to what it is not, but at the same time they highlight the inherent complexities and ambiguities of the term and its associated activities.[17]

The phrase 'to stress their difference from the common world by disguise or other means' is as an apposite description of cosplayers' social activity, but it does not provide a psychological rationale for their specific motivations, the how and the why of play. For this, we can initially turn to Huizinga's functional distinction between play 'as a contest *for* something and as a representative *of* something.'[18] Applied to cosplay, it appears that play functions in two senses: by competing for, and existing in place of, something. These elements can, of course, occur in tandem. For example, as discussed in the next chapter, some cosplay events are organized around competitions—for the best individual costume, scene enactment or best performing Japanese girl pop music band, and so on—with cosers vying for the gaze of competition judges. Yet most cosplayers derive their primary satisfaction from representing a chosen character, and pose more casually for photographs in the hallways of conventions or in private studio settings, which carry less obvious forms of reward, such as fan capital.[19] This competing for, on the one hand, and existing in the place of something being represented through costume, on the other, can be linked to the idea of extrinsic versus intrinsic reward.

In cosplay performance, play also involves the representation of something through display, evoking Plato's idea of life lived as a play. In this conception, the playing of games, song and dance achieves the ends of mollifying the gods, defending against enemies, and surviving in the process of winning in the game of life. This ritual depiction of play in the form of ceremonial enactments in ancient or archaic cultures is based on the re-presentation of real events to simulate the change of seasons, or to occasion a good harvest. This kind

Figure 1: A female cosplayer duo at a Hong Kong university cosplay event, 2013. © Anne Peirson-Smith.

of 'sympathetic magic' operates in methetic forms rather than in mimetic terms, with the participant actively involved in, but not imitating or becoming, the part that they are performing. Here, ritual play and other forms of human play, including cosplay, appear to diverge. While each is transcendent and knowingly transports the participant to another world or imagined state, the sacred ritual is more representative of symbolic actualization at the cognitive level operating within prescribed, rule-based structures. As Joel Gn observes of the mimetic process of cosplay: 'Unlike stage performers who re-enact and adhere to the narrative of the text, cosplayers place a greater focus on the "likeness" and aesthetics of the imitation.'[20]

The animated and materially divested body, enrobed in spectacular costume, complete with cosmetic mask and supported by props creating magical allusions in the process of mimicking the character, transports the player mentally and bodily to inhabit another persona. By inhabiting the fictional world of, say, Hogwarts in *Harry Potter* (2001–11) or Volantis in *Game of Thrones* (2011–),[21] cosers also figuratively transport themselves to an imagined place. The illusory world and its inhabitants provide a frozen, fleeting, momentary, fantastical existence: psychologically and physically, in real-time and as photographic record. This role play experience affords players the heightened pleasures of traversing normative, sensory boundaries as a form of intensified reality in the transfer of 'linear visual images into amazingly tangible three-dimensional figures, conveying texts and feelings in visual forms.'[22] Scott Duchesne observes the contradictions in these transformations as a polysemic form of play based on

> the awareness that many of us are mere chattels coupled with the dream, nurtured and encouraged within the liminal frame of the convention, that one can briefly pretend to be a chattel in a science fiction epic. These profitable breaches in normative roles allow cosplayers to be reintegrated into a 'mundane' world.[23]

Play in cosplay, then, is premised on the duality of existing in this world yet being able to transform and traverse boundaries into other worlds, as in Michael Taussig's notion of mimesis and alterity.[24] This is to suggest that the cosplayer makes an embodied play of selected character (as mimesis), yet is always aware of the non-reality of their performance (as alterity).

The same would hold true for childhood fantasy costume play. In the gap between reality and fiction, cosplayers do not intend to faithfully re-create their characters; instead they 'can never do more than approximate their intended form.'[25] However, assumptions to the contrary still prevail in some scholarly quarters suggesting that

> even the most splendid of these getups is at best a disappointment. Every seam, every cobweb strand of duct-tap gum, every laddered fish-net stocking or visible ridge of underpants elastic—every stray mark, pulled thread, speck of dust—acts to spoil what is instantly revealed to have been, all along, an illusion.[26]

Ramifying this anxiety are those spectators at events or in online communities who criticize or make fun of cosplayers who display less than perfect bodies. This stands at odds with the cosplayer's intent to present their own interpretation of a chosen character playfully, given that, as Kane Anderson proposes, instead of reproducing 'impossible bodies that exist only [in] fiction, costumed players consciously remake themselves in homage to corporealities that cannot operate in our material plane.'[27] Equally, this observation also suggests that the notions of free play in the cosphere are often challenged by competing value systems intent on applying their own rules to make sense of this form of play.

Rules of the game

Usefully, Caillois makes the distinction between rule-based 'ludic' play and free-form 'paida' play. Ludic play is based on a set of rules and often works within institutional frameworks, as exemplified by ritual activity. Caillois argues this might not best be understood as play, as it operates within a sacramental function, where such 'play' assumes an obligatory essence. In other words, players are duty-bound to play out the ritual practice. In contrast, paida play is open to wider interpretation, as typified by childhood imaginative play. Our understanding of the nature of the cosplay experience may benefit from similarly differentiating between the ways in which play manifests itself on a sliding scale from the open-ended, unstructured, improvised 'paida' style of play, to the more rule-based and conventional 'ludic' approach.[28]

Cosplay appears to represent both of these types of play activity. Paida-type play manifests itself in the range of characters that a coser is free to choose to inhabit. The prescribed components of the 'look' of a chosen character, the regular attendance at cosplay conventions and the organized costume, song and dance competitions entered into by cosplayers seem to accord with the more ludic dimensions of play. There is a sense in Asian cosplay circles that novice cosplayers often begin by being part of a more structured Japanese girl gang or similar 'team,' and later progress to playing individual characters as they became more confident, thus graduating from ludic to paida play as they evolve and become more experienced. One cosplayer respondent noted that:

We have options at events about how to cos. You can be on your own or with a group and there are competitions for bands or skits sometimes too. Many young cosplayers start at about the age of 14 or 15 start as part of a group. That's often how it develops. Like the choice of characters the choice of how to cos is very open and is up to us.

(Jin, 20, male student, Hong Kong)

However, it is the notion of mimicry where the subject, as Caillois notes, 'makes believe or makes others believe that he is someone other than himself.'[29] Regarding cosplay as traversing the line between child and adult provides further insight into the nature of cosplay. Indeed, the type of fictitious, popular media characters being emulated in cosplay dress-up routines suggest a reversion to childhood paida-style mimicry, via the process of dressing up and assuming the identity of the characters that cosers admire enough to expend their time playing. It is also part of the rhetoric of play as a form of identity whereby such mimicry operates to confirm, maintain or develop the player's sense of self—or self-in-character.[30]

At this point, we should also make a distinction that applies within the dressing-up activities of both children and adults. The costume itself may visually transform the outward appearance of the dresser, and enable them to create the illusionary identity of their chosen superhero or manga character, without one symbolically *becoming* them. Conversely, it can enable the coser to fully embrace the imagined persona, thereby projecting him or herself into a material change of identity. Tracey Fullerton et al. make a useful distinction between these two basic modes of dress-up play in their study of online game culture.[31] They distinguish between 'doll-play,' where the player controls and dresses up a character in analogue/digital form and 'identity/avatar costume play,' in which the player actually or virtually appears *as* the character. Cosplayers who regularly role play their characters assume the second mode of dress-up, thereby establishing their difference from the norm by transforming their identities, and thus appearing to be cognitively involved, affectively committed to as well as behaviourally aligned with these assumed costumed identities. Hence, cosplay dress-up can be seen as a ubiquitous pattern of play, across a range of cultural contexts, facilitating a state of transformation through themed play routines, enabling cosplayers to assume many roles in the process of discovering both their self-identity and social connectedness. Cosplayers are thus simultaneously operating across these two dimensions, by performing and presenting both individual and collective identities, with the cosplayer's physical presence in costume, assisted with props and make-up, operating as a type of 'visual metaphor for identity'[32] via transforming into another persona that is read accordingly by the onlooker.

Of course, the cosplay community also has its own ludic rules, in terms of the expectations of how to behave at events. Therefore, this is not a free-floating universe in a behavioural sense. It is generally expected that cosers should respect their character while in costume and act appropriately by taking the event seriously, at the risk of being isolated from the group. Although the rules may be tighter in Asia, this also operates in the west. As one Canadian respondent explained:

> Once the costume goes on you have to be in character and not do the things that you would do in your normal life—no smoking as an example—that's just not right and is disrespectful and looks so bad. Players like that are not dedicated and will not last, and other cosplayers will not support them.
>
> (Kate, 22, female student, Canada)

Yet play of all types—ritual and childhood, paida and ludic—shares common characteristics, including the separation of play activity from everyday life, operating within its own boundaries of time and space, its sociocultural function and the capacity to be mobile. These aspects of play are worth nuancing further in order to better understand how the critical play element in cosplay works. They include why cosplay manifests itself in terms of the deeper motivations of cosers in social, cultural, psychological and corporeal forms, and how it is fundamentally dependent on transformation and mobility.

The magic circle of play

The ubiquity of play in everyday life suggests that it fulfils a need for both the individual and the collective of 'being apart together'.[33] The co-creation of a temporary world of play inhabited by players with a shared interest in meeting up, dressing up and playing in a specific zone that is spatially separated from everyday life can be explored by applying the metaphor of the playground or magic circle. For Huizinga, this manifestation of play was evidence of the parity between ancient and modern designations of space, in that 'there is no distinction whatever between marking out a space for sacred purpose and marking it out for purposes of sheer play. The turf, the tennis-court, the chess-board and pavement-hopscotch cannot formally be distinguished from the temple or the magic circle.'[34]

In this context, play is often conducted in a temporary, physically or mentally bounded space set apart from ordinary existence in terms of place, space and temporality. It is further distinguished by rules specific to the play community, which enable play to take place. As Huizinga further observes:

> All play moves and has its being within a play-ground marked off beforehand either materially or ideally, deliberately or as a matter of course. Just as there is no formal difference between play and ritual, so the 'consecrated spot' cannot be formally distinguished from the playground. The arena, the card-table, the magic circle, the temple, the stage, the screen, the tennis court, the court of justice [...] are all in form and function play-grounds, i.e. forbidden spots, isolated, hedged round, hallowed, within which special rules obtain.[35]

Play in this sense is set up in opposition to ordinary being and behaving. It is extraordinary, in that the player steps out of real life into a transitory sphere of existence constituting 'an interlude in our daily life' with its own atmosphere. Such spaces 'are temporary worlds within the ordinary world, dedicated to the performance of an act apart.'[36] The form of play circle discussed in the next chapter, the cosplay convention, is both a space apart and is one composed of an ever-shifting diaspora of actors.

The wearing of an extraordinary costume connected to a theme symbolically transforms the identity of the player, enabling them to re-present their ordinary self in a new guise through role play, made possible only 'by doffing their ordinary dress and donning extraordinary dress so that play may proceed. Playing the role of the other requires that the player *dress out* of the role or roles that are acknowledged to be his [sic] own. Costume therefore is a kind of magical instrument.'[37] Gregory Stone's analysis of the transformative quality of fantasy costumes adopted by children at play during their early phases of socialization is pertinent here. It can be applied to the general process of costume dress-up and to the activities among people of all ages appearing in a range of contexts from theatre, festivals and masquerade events to fan-based subcultures. However, social interaction and collusion with a knowing audience are also required to validate the deliberate misrepresentation of self through costume play. The wearing of a costume visually denotes the boundaries between the costumed player and the non-costumed other, as 'the "differentness" and secrecy of play are most vividly expressed in "dressing up." Here the "extraordinary" nature of play reaches perfection. The disguised or masked individual "plays" another part, another being. He is another being.'[38]

Within the temporary boundaries of this magic circle of play, 'absolute and peculiar order' prevails. As Katie Salen and Eric Zimmerman suggest, the 'magic circle of a game is the boundary of the game space and within this boundary the rules of the game play out and have authority.'[39] Here, play is based on its own rules and the norms that define it as a certain

Figure 2: Group of cosplayers at Hong Kong university cosplay event, cosplaying characters from *Code Geass: Lelouch of the Rebellion* (2006–07). First row (*left* to *right*): Anya Alstreim; C.C; Nunnally Lamperouge; Shirley Fenette; Kallen Stadtfeld. 2 Second row: Lelouch Lamperouge; Suzaku Kururugi; Zero/Lelouch Lamperouge (Emperor); Suzaku Kururugi (Knight of Zero); Anya Alstreim (Knight of the Round); Lelouch Lamperouge, 2013. © Anne Peirson-Smith.

type of play. In the case of cosplay, this requires the coser to dress-up and make-up in a way that transforms his or her outward appearance into a re-presentation of fictional characters. This is something quite distinct from a subcultural or fashion style like Lolita, Gothic or punk. These style tribes exist and transact within the bounds of daily life, as opposed to something existing metonymically outside of it, such as at a cosplay convention.

More recent work has applied this idea of the magic circle to online and virtual games,[40] thereby downplaying the sacred and cultural aspects of play in the bounds of the magic circle. These games, after all, derive from and form part of the pervasive technoscapes[41] of late capital. However, this approach still acknowledges that gameplay operates in what Salen and Zimmerman call a 'special place in time and space created by a game.'[42] It is a finite and infinite realm where 'magic'—that is, the transformation of meaning—occurs in a temporary, rule-bound world within a circle with permeable borders:

The fact that the magic circle is just that—a circle—is an important feature of this concept. As a closed circle, the space it circumscribes is enclosed and separate from the real world. As a marker of time, the magic circle is like a clock: it simultaneously represents a path with a beginning and end, but one without beginning and end. The magic circle inscribes a space that is repeatable, a space both limited and limitless. In short, a finite space with infinite possibility.[43]

Interestingly, magic is a term that was often used by cosplayer informants when describing their empowering cosplay experience:

I feel that the atmosphere is often magical at 'cos' events. It's as if there is something in the air and I do feel that I have magical powers too—as if I could fly or do magic like Harry Potter or Hermione, and all of us in this group believe that too. It is a powerful thing and maybe that's why we do it as it gives us great positive energy!

(Jax, 21, female student, Hong Kong)

Cosplayers' conscious awareness of having a transformative experience when entering the magic circle of an event contrasts with findings in other studies about online gamers, given that the latters' engagement with the game is far less defined by place and space since they can play online at home, at work or while waiting for a bus. Unlike cosplay, the separation of public and private gaming spaces is more fluid and can take place in the margins of the play zone. Further differences exist between cosplayers and gamers in terms of their preparation before they enter the magic circle of play as the former are prosumers[44] engaging in the active production of their outfits and physical personas, whereas the latter largely tend to be consumers, albeit (inter)active in their play pursuit, with the exception of those creating and playing as their own avatars.

The concept of creating order in play is important, because through the rules of the game the player creates a temporary, unadulterated zone. This stands in marked contrast to the complications of the real world, tainted as it is by norms meted out through various sources of authority that are imposed on the player, often outside of their control and impervious to their desires. In this sense, cosplayers can be seen to be taking control by creating their own worlds in contradistinction to more controlled zones administered by hegemonic forces. In doing so, they are representing an alternative way of playing life out that is in opposition to the status quo and ideological apparatuses of the state (governmental or corporate)—of the governing mediascapes, technoscapes, financescapes and ideoscapes of late capitalism.[45] Granted, this resistance is not overtly political but manifests itself in ways of being and becoming, expressed in terms of cosplayers' spectacular assumed appearance and spent leisure time. Interviews with cosers suggest that they are aware of the separation between working life and their cosplay activity, and that this empowered and enabled them to escape from the pressures of 'real life.' As one coser noted:

When I do cosplay it's like going into another world and it's so good to be able to switch off from work deadlines and difficult clients and bad bosses or people I work with. This is very important for me and it keeps me on balance and lets me deal with my life in a better way as cosplayers create no pressures for me and I am feeling so very happy in that place.

(Edi, 24, female office worker, Hong Kong)

As neo-Marxist thinkers suggest, tensions between work and play that emerged in the industrialized era were based on the division of labour principle that regarded the leisure time enjoyed in pre-industrial societies as undesirable and set it against the interests of productivity and capitalistic success.[46] This viewpoint still prevails in some cultural locations—especially in Asia—despite the liberating forces of technological development and the once promised leisure society, so that downtime is often treated with suspicion in the workplace and relegated as worthless outside it. Therefore, tension is very much evident in the cosplay community. Younger respondents often admitted, for instance, that they were only allowed by their parents to engage in the activity if they attained good school grades. As one respondent observed:

When I first started 'cosing' two years ago my parents strongly discouraged me from it, thinking that I was dressing up like this to be in an adult porn video. That really concerned them and they gave me a hard time, to be honest. They also told me that it was a big waste of time and money and that it would make me become a failed student.

(Kat, 19, female student, Hong Kong)

This perspective further underlines the insider/outsider dynamic of cosplay. As Stanley Cohen suggests, a contentious situation occurs when a 'condition, episode, person or group of persons emerges to become defined as a threat to societal values and interests.'[47] Some journalists and editors in Asia have denounced and labelled such deviant and delinquent youths as 'folk devils'[48] who are a threat to the social structure—often based on a concern for existing values and beliefs. Youth are often 'soft targets' of criticism for their reduced agency in the 'battlefields of cultural politics.'[49] These negative reactions to cosplay and the regulation of the content of youth-oriented trends, such as the content of *yaoi* or BL (Boys Love) manga, are also a reflection of the innate conservatism of older generations and social institutions that prevails in some Asian nations.[50]

Other cosplayers explained that they would never disclose the true nature of their secret 'hobby' to co-workers at risk of being ridiculed or of it having a negative impact on their career development. As one younger coser recounted:

I've been a regular cosplayer for six years now and spend most of my time outside of work either planning my costumes on 'cos' social media sites or at events. My work mates ask me what is my hobby and what do I spend time doing and I tell them I like anime and that's it. I would never tell them what I do really as they would not understand, and if my boss found out he would have negative thoughts about me which would maybe affect my job in future, which I worry about.

(Ting, 23, male accountant, Hong Kong)

Conditional parental and societal responses to cosplay highlight the deep-rooted suspicion that some in authority hold towards play more generally in late capitalism. Of course, these very same social expectations may encourage transgressive behaviours among some cosplayers, despite the fear of negative responses or punishment from parents or colleagues if their activity were to be disclosed. In the words of one respondent, 'I tend to sneak out of home with a small suitcase when I go off to events and I store my costumes with my friend or deep under my mattress as my parents would ban me from going out if they found out that I was cosplaying' (Cate, 16, female student, Hong Kong).

Policing by outsiders, such as parents and employers, is in contrast to the regulations imposed by cosplay event organizers across the globe, who exhibit their own types of boundary control. This occurs on two levels: in managing the 'real' world space outside of the convention, while also managing behavioural expectations within its magic circle. The biannual Comiket (Comic Market) in Tokyo issues a set of rules to ensure that cosplayers are not *meiwaku* or a 'nuisance' to other non-cosplayers, and that they comply with Japanese laws and the edicts of Tokyo Metropolitan government.[51] These typically order participants not to enter the event space dressed in cosplay outfits. Equally, certain outfits, including real uniforms, are expressly forbidden, in addition to the use of potentially dangerous materials or hazardous costume construction with spikes or wired parts, signalling a real demarcation line between narrative fantasy and structural reality. This is exemplified in the following excerpt from the Comiket rules issued to cosplay participants:

It's against the rules to arrive at Comiket or return home from Comiket while in costume. When arriving by car it is also forbidden to change in your vehicle. Please make use of the changing rooms [...]. Before preparing your costume, please note that some costumes and props are forbidden or limited. Those in violation will not be allowed to enter the cosplay area until the offending items have been removed [...]. Police uniforms appearing in anime and manga, real officer uniforms, original police uniforms, firefighting uniforms, the uniforms of rescue workers, or government officials are strictly forbidden.[52]

In light of these kinds of real world controls, the notion of the magic circle representing bordered activities has been much critiqued for being too artificial in its representation of play.[53] As a result, alternative metaphors have been proposed to more accurately represent the bounded experience of play, including the membrane, net, screen or bubble. In essence, this effectively replaces one metaphor with another, rather than offering a different approach to understanding play, and seems like a circular argument. Yet most commentators agree that play operates within demarcated boundaries separated from everyday existence, despite the fact that the mobility between the worlds of play and non-play are often fluid and

Figure 3: Cosplayers enter the magic circle of play at Extra/ordinary Dress Conference event, Cattle Depot Art Space, Hong Kong, 2009. First row: Kikuri from *Hell Girl* (2005–); Ciel Phantomhive from *Black Butler* (2006–). Second row: Roxas from *Kingdom Hearts* (2002–). © Anne Peirson-Smith.

dynamic. Moreover, play can be explained as a cognitive, emotional, and socio-cultural phenomenon, and these three dimensions are now considered to be equally important ways of further understanding cosplay.

Cognitive boundaries

When considered in terms of the player's mindset, play accounts for the phenomenological experience and emphasizes the cognitive function of play activity. The interviewees for this chapter appeared to acknowledge that individual cosers shared a predisposition specifically based on their deep interest in anime and manga, superhero characters or Japanese culture per se. This was a like-minded community defined by possessing a pre-requisite to entry based on a mutual knowledge base and shared cultural capital. As one respondent explained:

We all think alike—we love the characters, which makes us want to cosplay. We are very understanding of the anime and manga sources or the online games. In many cases, we have grown up with this and it is our life so we know all about it and wearing a costume, as [being] a cosplayer is an expression of our Japanese knowledge.

(Danni, 20, male student, Macau)

They also noted that the motivation to cosplay emerged initially from the experience of being immersed in these media texts from an early age and having grown up with them as a form of entertainment and escapism. These preconditions form a shared mediascape, or 'image-centred, narrative accounts of strips of reality' that 'offer to those who experience and transform them [...] a series of elements (such as characters, plots and textual forms) out of which scripts can be formed of imagined lives.'[54] Nevertheless, many acknowledged that while their peer group could enjoy and consume these texts in the same way, not all had the same predispositions to re-present and re-mediate them. Rather, the underlying motivations are often based on deep affective connections with the specific characters, directing the choice of costume.

Many of the informants reported that in choosing and planning their next character, they would daydream about the costume and imagine themselves projected into it before actually crafting it, or commissioning it to be made. This response accords with Sutton-Smith's notion of 'mind or subjective play, dreams, daydreams, fantasy, imagination, ruminations, reveries.'[55] The choice of character may be based on the nature or form of the character or cultural proximity. Asian cosplayers, for example, mainly tend to prefer to cosplay Japanese manga and anime protagonists. Of course, the reverse is also true: that negative associations also dictate cosplay choice, as characters are rejected on the basis of their lack of aesthetic or cultural appeal.

The rhetorics of cosplay

In attempting to rationalize and provide a semblance of order for the inherent ambiguity of such play, Sutton-Smith presents seven rhetorics of play framed as 'a persuasive discourse, or an implicit narrative, wittingly or unwittingly adopted by members of a particular affiliation to persuade others of the veracity and worthwhileness of their beliefs.'[56] Each of these—from the 'ancient rhetorics' of fate, power, identity and frivolity to the more contemporary play orientations of progress, self and imaginary—are applicable to the practice and process of cosplaying to varying degrees. These rhetorics share common features such as 'a historical source, a particular function, a distinctive ludic form, and specialized players and advocates.'[57] While they have their historical foundation in ancient belief systems tending to be more extrinsic, emotive and collective in nature, the modern versions are rooted in the intellectual and philosophical movements of the past 200 years, notably dominant ideoscapes[58] of 'the Enlightenment, romanticism and individualism.'[59] In particular, The rhetorics of progress, self, imaginary, power and identity are useful conceptual tools for unpacking the complex dynamics of what is at play in cosplay.

While plots based on fate may constitute some of the anime or game narratives underpinning cosplay activity, such as *Fate/Stay Night (Feito/Sutei Naito)* (2006),[60] the role of destiny in relation to the actual cosplay process is ambiguous and may be loosely connected to the chance of winning a cosplay competition or the possibility of meeting friends at an event. Equally, while a shared frivolity and sense of fun are an important part of the social aspects of cosplay, the ancient carnivalesque challenge to the ordered world posed by tricksters and fools perhaps finds its parallel in the extraordinary act of the cosplayer as a disruption to the regular ways of being, appearing and behaving. Transgression also lies at the heart of both the rhetoric of identity and of self. While the former is concerned with communal roles, the latter is individually focused. Cosplay operates on both levels. On the one hand, cosplay culture constitutes a recognized collective, social activity and a unique form of embodied and performative fandom related to, yet different from, other fan cultures featuring shared narratives and characters—such as the adoption of avatars in online gaming.

Differentiation based on cultural identity can also be seen across different geographic locations in which cosplay is practiced. Cosplayers in interview often commented, for example, on the distinction between cosplay in Hong Kong and Asia in general, with higher expectations of authenticity compared to America or the United Kingdom, which seemed more relaxed, inclusive and less rule based. Equally, there is a strong universal etiquette associated with cosplay where the boundaries are clearly defined, such as no touching or requesting permission for phototaking.[61] On the other hand, cosplay is a distinctively individual pursuit driven by intrinsic motivations and self-discovery in the cognitive and physical blending of fantasy with reality. It is invested with fun, relaxation and the aesthetic satisfaction of having replicated and performed a selected character. This also provides a parallel with the identity play traditionally practiced in masked play at balls, festivals and masquerades.[62] The cosplayer performs as another persona and in doing so can traverse established bodily boundaries and assume a different gender (from female to male or male to female, as in the 'fake girls' of crossplay)[63] or can temporarily adopt a non-humanoid form.[64] As Shih-chen Chao explains about the presentation of crossplay, a 'female cosplayer can choose to assume Naruto, the leading male from the Japanese manga *Naruto*, likewise a male cosplayer is welcome to assume Usagi Tsukino, the leading female character from the Japanese manga *Sailor Moon*.'[65]

The rhetoric of progress, based on the belief that mimetic and imitative childhood role play is useful as a form of preparation for adult life, also has credence for cosplay. Cosplayers in interview often comment on the benefits of role play participation in terms of gradually gaining self-confidence and self-empowerment. The fantasy performance crosses boundaries by bolstering the cosplayer's everyday existence and normal persona. As Jenn observed:

The more I cosplayed the more I learned that you could change your persona and the way you looked by using costumes, wigs and make up and then feel really special about it. Also, it gave me the confidence to pursue a career in the beauty industry as I could experiment with myself, and how I looked and then become confident in transforming appearance.

(Jenn, 23, female hairstylist, Hong Kong)

Empowerment is also at the core of the rhetoric of power in cosplay, given the rewards that cosplayers claim to gain from it as a form of wish fulfilment, by satisfying a desire to create and perform a version of the selected character. Yet power is also founded on conflict and is based on order and logical expression, in contrast to open play, chance or frivolity. Cosplay perhaps can be considered to fluctuate between order and chaos, between open and closed forms of play. While cosers are observed to be having fun in a relaxed social setting with like-minded people, conflict may arise in terms of personal commentary on the authenticity of costumes, both in real time and online, which can cause issues. As Rachel Leng writes, the

rhetoric of play as the imaginary, usually applied to playful improvisation of all kinds in literature and elsewhere, idealizes the imagination, flexibility and creativity of the animal and human play worlds [...] sustained by modern positive attitudes towards creativity and innovation.[66]

Clearly, the role of the imagination is critical to the cosplay engagement alongside self and identity, as a part of the creative process from the ideation stage of choosing the character through its material re-creation. Here the coser's imagination gives rise to creative displays of a costume- and character-based performance art form. This accords with Mihaly Csikszentmihalyi's notion of the 'playful mindset' or playfulness as a form of imaginative flow state experienced by those who focus their 'attention on limited stimulus field.'[67] Those located in this stimulus field adopt a mindset based on intense focus that operates as a screen to isolate them from the realities of everyday normative operations. Paradoxically, the cosplayer is both in the world and without it;[68] both creating another world yet doing so with ideas, narratives and materials from this one.

Hence, while cosplay is a fun-based activity, the preliminary planning and creative processes that enable the chosen character from the fantasy realm to be actualized and performed in costume requires serious preparatory work in the real world. This comprises a form of 'research' and also involves creative ability and aptitudes for project management to source the materials and craft them into costume, or to direct the design project and have it made by a third party. As one respondent explained:

Usually, I start deciding on my character about two-to-three months before an event. I will find as many images as I can of it online and maybe I will sketch this out too to get the feel of the costume. Then, I will go to Sham Shui Po to source the materials and trims and to Jordan or Mong Kok for the accessories and wigs. For shoes or boots I may go to

China. Then I will take around a month to make the outfit at home. It's a long process but it's all part of the fun of actually cosplaying—it is part of it all.

(Dina, 20, female design student, Hong Kong)

The act of prosumption involved in choosing and making costumes is clearly a source of agency. Innovation and craft based talents find an outlet in material and physical form. This can be seen as evidence of play operating as an expressive form of affirmation for the cosplayer when re-creating their fictional personas.

Mind games, membranes and social play

Michael Apter's notion of telic and paratelic states, albeit located in a psychological paradigm based on scientific psychometric assessment testing, also echo the serious-fun duality of cosplay activity. The former involves a considered, thoughtful state of mind while the latter represents a freer, playful approach, akin to Caillois' binary model of ludic and paida play. For the player, this protective frame constitutes a psychological bubble, in parallel with Goffman's interaction membrane, between the game's reality and the realities of the everyday world, providing a sense of security and familiarity. As Apter explains, this protective boundary

> stands between you and the 'real' world and its problems, creating an enchanted zone in which […] you are confident that no harm can come. Although this frame is psychological, interestingly it often has a perceptible physical representation: the proscenium arch of the theatre, the railings around the park, the boundary line on the cricket pitch, and so on. But such a frame may also be abstract, such as the rules governing the game being played. In the end, whether one is experiencing what one is doing as being within a protective frame or not, is a matter of one's own phenomenology.[69]

Cosplayers regularly talk about their positive feelings when at events and how identifying the space to play both mentally and physically is so important to them. While they are signalling their deviation from normal ways of dressing and being in their extraordinary presentation of self, they are doing so within the safe confines of the cosplay collective. The personal commitment to cosplay underpins how within this secure haven the individual player becomes predisposed to partake in the activity before, during and after events.

This ludic attitude[70] is a necessary precondition for active cosplay and for entry to the magic circle of events, as opposed to attending events and not wearing costume. Yet the mental state of play only goes so far to explain the cosplay phenomenon and the full motivations of the cosers: social and cultural aspects of play provide further clues to the drivers behind this play phenomenon.

Play can be seen as essentially a social construct. For Bateson the meta-communicative signal that 'this is play'[71] sets the tone and the play boundaries, framing play in opposition to non-play activities, which are always present in play. This dualism extends to the presence of the players themselves whereby the player is an individual, yet, in terms of the rhetoric of self at play, plays within a group setting where the intrinsic and aesthetic experience of performing the character is paramount.[72] Even if they enter the magic circle of play alone, say at a cosplay convention, the cosplayer accesses a social realm, real or imagined, whereby they seek out and encounter other players. Hence, cosplayers are ever aware that even if they plan to attend an event as an individual attendee they will inevitably meet others and take photographs or be photographed, both individually and in groups. For most cosplayers, attending an event (or entering the magic circle) is a social occasion, presenting the opportunity to meet existing friends and to find new ones in a self-affirming setting. As one respondent explained:

> I love going to events because I can express my individual love for the character among players who understand what I am doing and why. I first went to a university event two years ago on my own and met so many people, many of whom are now my true friends who would do anything for me. And we go to events together and cos together as a team sometimes. This has opened many friendship doors for me and I always have such fun.
>
> (Della, 19, female student, Hong Kong)

This observation underlines the expressive qualities of play as constituting a social function, offering a distraction or some downtime from everyday life by complementing and adorning it.[73]

The social aspects of cosplay are clearly important, as in any collective activity, where players reinforce common ground through the development of a shared community and friendships. These small group cultures are identified through an adherence to an individual character or small cast of characters from an identifiable franchise, such as *Star Wars, Gundam, Final Fantasy* or *Game of Thrones*,[74] which is signalled visually through the creation and wearing of the physical artefacts of costume as embodied performance.

Habermas' concept of communicative action suggests that humans engaging in social activity make sense of our lived existence through language and self-reflexive discussion.[75] This is done in the process of constructing one's own rational worldview based on an individual's idea of truthfulness, often in opposition to, and critical of, existing institutions of power, whose goals and actions frequently conspire to obliterate the viewpoint of the individual. These ideas can be applied in the broadest sense to the social aspects and agendas of play that are geared up to the need to understand regular, everyday life. Moreover, play in this sense can enhance this knowledge by creating and occupying alterative life-worlds for the subject based on an individual's own normative systems and discursive relations.

The Habermassian communicative action system suggests that communication is 'oriented to achieving, sustaining and reviewing consensus—and indeed a consensus that rests on the intersubjective recognition of criticizable validity claims.'[76] In this way, both verbal and

Figure 4: Two cosplayers enact *Star Wars* scenes from
Episode 1: The Phantom Menace (1999) as a stormtrooper
and Obi Wan Kenobi with Death the Kid from *Soul Eater*
(2004) at Ani-Con and Games event, Convention Centre,
Hong Kong (2015). © Anne Peirson-Smith.

non-verbal discourse is important in creating a communicative rationality that operates not just through linguistic but also aesthetic means, whereby a performance demonstrates and communicates value. In the case of cosplay, cosers communicate consensus through shared interest in a specified cultural form, and at the same time present an alternative way of being. Further, they re-create and project themselves into a world founded on narrative content in popular media texts that paradoxically challenge the hegemonic and unconscionable regimes of institutional power—including dominant mediascapes—that control the individual, and champion their overthrow by a seemingly weak minority. As one informant explained while describing the character behind their costume at an event, 'My character is from the *Gintama* story—we are the good guys who save other people from the evil people, [which] makes us feel good' (Bik, 20, male student, Hong Kong).

Cosplayers are consciously playing and using physical and material cues to signify their character. In this way, characterization is signalled from cosplay's foundational nomenclature to the extraordinary costumes and props worn by the cosers, and by their formalized behaviours, including repeated, stylized posing in character for spectators (onlookers and photographers). This comprises a critical meta-communicative aspect of the performance, and also signifies the accrual of cultural capital talked about in Chapter 2. As noted by one respondent:

> At events you have to act out your character in a real way so we study them in detail and maybe watch the anime many times over to get that really right—it's like our research. And you have to let others and the photographers know that you are acting the character. So, if the character like Haurei Reimu from the *Touhou Project* frowns then you have to do it just like they do or it doesn't work for anyone.
>
> (Win, 21, female student, Hong Kong)

By extension, Goffman sees play as framing social and shared scenarios via an interaction 'membrane' which facilitates a meaningful social encounter between cosplayers, such as occurs at cosplay events, that often would have little relevance outside of the specific frame.[77] Play as fundamentally a social activity is framed by a shared event or scenario such as an organized convention or event.

For Goffman, we make sense of the ordinary and institutional existences that we all lead by complex keying, re-keying, bracketing and laminating activities, thus negotiating meaning inside and outside of the primary and social frames.[78] As he further elaborates: 'It has also been argued that a strip of activity will be perceived by its participants in terms of the rules or premises of a primary framework, whether social or natural, and that activity so perceived provides the model for two basic kinds of transformation—keying and fabrication.' Goffman goes on to suggest that

> these frameworks are not merely a matter of mind but correspond in some sense to the way in which an aspect of the activity itself is organized—especially activity directly involving social agents. Organizational premises are involved, and these are something cognition somehow arrives at, not something cognition creates or generates. Given their understanding of what it is that is going on, individuals fit their actions to this understanding and ordinarily find that the ongoing world supports this fitting. These organizational premises—sustained both in the mind and in activity—I call the frame of the activity.[79]

Goffman also touches on the fluidity of the boundary between play and everyday life. This may pertain to other play-based communities such as online gamers, where the boundary crossings are more fluid and can be undertaken in the margins of life, such as traveling to work. But for cosplayers, as noted above, there is a distinct physical separation between daily existence and dressing up.[80]

The organizational premises vary in terms of the location for play both globally and within regions, especially Asia, but all emphasize the importance of the physical domain of cosplay: its physical locus. Certainly, cosplayers dress up within the frame of events in pre-allocated spaces such as convention centres, university clubs or other specifically organized forums. Often transporting their outfits and props in packs or suitcases, they are rarely seen wearing costumes in everyday life. As one respondent said:

Although many people are much more aware of cosplay as it's been around here for over a decade now I still feel that there are misunderstandings about it and negative feelings in society here. So, we would not go out on the bus or street dressed up as our character in case we had bad comments. Also, it's better to get ready at the event and that's a fun thing to do with others—even though it may take time to get ready—others help you out and chat—its all part of the fun.

(Tin, 21, male student, Hong Kong)

A rare exception to this might be when professional cosplayers are hired to open new shops in shopping malls, for example, but even then they operate within another frame where a performer dressed in extraordinary costume indexically signifies the novelty of the opening event. At the same time, for many cosplayers, this may represent cosplay as 'our' play being appropriated to a commercial zone—something quite removed from its original intent. Cosplayers clearly make a distinction between commercial play and hobby play as a defined boundary and often can be negative about or dismissive of its commercialized appropriation or parody,[81] essentially believing it to be 'fake' play.

On the one hand, this form of commercial application may be seen as evidence of 'fake' cosplayers selling their souls and disrupting the magic boundary between the play world and the real world by tainting their play with market-driven practices,[82] thereby negating the power of the players and disrupting the open and improvisational ethos of play. As one respondent observed:

You get some commercial cosplayers who are paid to open shops or appear at culture events organized by the government but they are not respected by us as they are not real cosers and are doing it for the money. They are fake cosers. It's the same with some regular cosers who think that they will become famous models by cosplaying but that's not right and it's not what it's all about, and even worse it gives it a really bad reputation and people think that we're all about that and it's not true.

(Val, 22, female student, Hong Kong)

Therefore, a distinction can perhaps be made between those cosplay participants who are hired from other communities of practice to supplement the cosplay event or experience. On the other hand, there appears to be a growing community of entrepreneurial cosplayers globally who have crossed the boundaries between amateur and professional play to monetize their craft skills or performative involvement either by happenstance or by design. Given the significant financial outlay involved in doing cosplay, in terms of crafting costumes and accessories, in addition to the time expended backstage to prepare for the front stage performance, the practice may also be driven by pragmatic commercial concerns for covering the costs of made to order costumes. Being commissioned to source and craft a costume or to perform artfully in costume, may equally be recognized as a mark of social capital whether exhibiting craft or performance skills. For other cosplayers, turning their hobby and passion into a viable commercial concern may be regarded as a way of living their dream[83] and the freedom to opt for a chosen way of life.[84]

Generally, cosplayers are very much in the moment of play, operating within their own different versions of a single frame, as 'for every utterance and action only one frame is relevant'[85] and is 'keyed' in opposition to their everyday personas. In the moment of cosplay, the coser symbolically 'becomes' the character, in a meta-communicative sense, by changing their demeanour and physical stance to align with the character role being performed.[86] However, as we have seen, they obviously do not actually become their chosen character in reality, and cosplayers seem always to be intuitively aware of the distinction explored above between mimesis and alterity. Cosplayers consistently explain that, although they chose their characters based on their affection and admiration for them, and perhaps due to some passing physical resemblance, they did not literally become the character. They changed back to reality outside of the frame and the magic circle after the event. Once the costume, make-up, wigs and accessories were removed and they had exited the boundaries of the convention space, it was back to life as normal.

In this sense, cosplay also accords with Goffman's notion of the 'rules of irrelevance' in the context of frame theory, whereby the player leaves behind their trials, tribulations and the minutiae of everyday life by moving into and inhabiting a liminoid state aided by the transformative, magical power of costuming.[87] The player voluntarily enters the social construct of the 'playworld'[88] or 'finite provinces of meaning'[89] shared among a community of practice.[90] Those who inhabit this cosplay cosmos recognize the assumed characters, but these personas may have little (or at least limited) meaning in a different life frame. Yet, despite the relatively porous nature of the so-called magic circle, interaction membrane or frames of play, cosers can project their identities both in real time at the event and capture and share this online afterwards via social media platforms.

Play cultures

The cultural significance of cosplay is also bounded by rules that define ways of being and behaving. Whether cosplayers create their play culture as they begin playing[91] or whether it exists prior to the play act,[92] being based on the mediated worlds of anime, manga and digital game narratives, it is a distinctive culture recognized by its members. It also operates in set locations relevant to purpose. In Hong Kong, for example, cosers congregate at the weekends in public spaces such as the parks in Tai Po or Mei Foo, or in themed cafes in the central city areas such as Causeway Bay and Mong Kok to take photos, role play and socialize. They may alternatively gather at commercial and non-commercial anime conventions and comic book festivals, competing at the same time for best song and dance routine or most accomplished costume. The informal, non-commercial events are mainly organized on university campuses by student-based comic and animation societies, while the annual, commercial conventions are masterminded by the comic book publishers, game and animation producers. These commercialized events are the most visible public showcase for cosplay, and attract significant media coverage.

Cosplay as a play culture can be seen as an embodiment and articulation of belonging to a spectacular subcultural collective. We might then suggest that the player's affective individuality and personal predispositions towards mediated narratives and characters in popular media texts are key factors in the co-creation of self-identity, group identity and their cultural belief systems. This takes place within the wider struggle to create a subjective space, enabling them 'to move between specific identities and nominal groups.'[93] In this sense, cosplay is connected, and refers, to other fictional worlds and assumes cultural forms within a semiotic domain that includes costumes and artefacts, in addition to recorded and shared images of the coser on social media platforms.[94] The replication of the chosen anime and manga character in material form as an online image shared across various digital platforms also ensures that this is a representational cultural practice.

Figure 5: Cosplayer as Red Riding Annie in *League of Legends* (2009–) being photographed by a group of hobby photographers at a Hong Kong Baptist University cosplay event (2014). © Anne Peirson-Smith.

When engaging in the fictional worlds of cosplay through the knowledge of their assumed personae and social interaction, the participants are thus both individually and collectively constructing their own meaning systems based on a shared fantasy experience. As Gary Alan Fine suggests: 'Fantasy role-playing games are cultural systems. They are finely woven worlds of magic and belief. They have social structure, norms, values, and a range of cultural artifacts, which if not physically real, are real to those who participate in them.'[95] The larger universe of cosplay thus comprises many sub-worlds or 'idiocultures.' These have been defined as a

system of knowledge, beliefs, behaviors and customs peculiar to an interacting group to which members refer and employ as the basis of further interaction. Members recognize that they share experiences and that these experiences can be referred to with the expectation that they will be understood by other members, and can be employed to construct a shared universe of discourse.[96]

From a social interactionist perspective, meaning is socially constructed in the world of cosplay, where cosplayers choose their costumes more or less individually, and then come together collectively to enact their private fantasies publicly among peers, who are simultaneously actors and audience. Thus, they create an alternative, fantastical world of meaning—the cosphere—in contrast to the other aspects of their everyday lives. Fantasy enables the cosers to transcend the normative constraints of the other worlds and cultures that they inhabit, and further empowers them to believe that they have control in a world where anything goes, where anything is possible in that moment of assuming the guise of a fantastical other.

Cosplay culture's rationale is, therefore, arguably rooted not in the terms of subcultural rebellion and resistance to the dominant ideology as espoused by the neo-Marxist, new subcultural scholarship from the Centre for Contemporary Cultural Studies (CCCS) school, whose theoretical approach has often been criticized for overextending itself. More usefully, answers may be found in the notions of a fragmented self-identity, stylistic ambiguity, cultural fluidity and the dilution of a dominant culture, which lie at the heart of post- or neo-subcultural approaches. Here, an understanding of subcultural existence is espoused where 'there are no rules, there is no authenticity, no ideological commitment, merely a stylistic game to be played.'[97] Yet caution should perhaps be exercised in according subcultural status of any kind to cosplay activity on the basis that it might more usefully be categorized as a non-mainstream leisure activity. Another way to describe this is as a leisure-based culture representing an aggregate of individuals bonded by common interests, voluntarily joining in cosplay activities and escaping outside of their traditional social networks and everyday activities. As one cosplayer said: 'We are not doing cosplay as a style thing like the Lolitas or hipsters. It is not about fashion at all, but is all about cosplaying. You may call it a hobby but even that doesn't get it right really' (Jasper, 21, male office worker, Macau).

As we have already noted, cosplay is a rule-based culture governing its play practices in terms of both paida and the ludic. Such rubrics reinforce cultural practices and the practice of play. Hence, an understanding of aesthetic prescriptive rules of what to wear and how to wear it carries significant weight among the cosplay community. On the one hand, everyone appears to be invited to the party within the magic circle if they are wearing a costume and have made an effort to dress-up. But cosplayers regularly criticize each other and label others as outsiders for the lack of care in devising their costumes, or in failing to assume a pose authentically suggestive of the character, or for other rule-breaking behaviour. As one respondent recounted:

The biggest problem about some cosers—often new, younger ones—is that they don't follow the rules very much. They sometimes ignore the rules and may cause inconvenience and cause problems for others. So they may climb onto buildings to take photos or leave lots of litter and the estates management get angry and refuse the permit for the next event—this is happening a lot now.

(Lin, 20, female president of University anime and manga society, Hong Kong)

There is an understanding that those who have made the effort to make their own costume are keeping the cosplay faith and acquiring greater cultural capital within the given community of practice, especially among the hobby photographers in attendance at the events. By the same token, those cosplayers who have bought cheap costumes online from Chinese or North American websites are often considered to be undesirable and are often not befriended by others at events.

Transgressive or permeable play boundaries

The notion of a bounded play community[98] is challenged by some as being too fixed or rigid, or for failing to acknowledge the permeability of the sites of play, set against the dynamic activity of playing itself.[99] The boundaries delineating play are admittedly more fluid than traditional play theorists often give it credit for. Richard Schechner terms the fluidity of play as a 'netting,' that is, 'a porous, flexible, gatherer: a three-dimensional, dynamic flow-through container,'[100] while others concur that players tend to negotiate the boundaries of play.[101] Clearly, play involves a complex performance on behalf of the various parties involved, which would suggest that there is the potential for conflict, as in all communities of practice involving people with varying agendas. Hence, play is potentially transgressive. In this way, the rhetoric of play as frivolous[102] can be inverted to explain play not just as a pure, hedonistic—and by implication shallow—pursuit typified by the negative or dismissive media coverage that cosplay has received. Nor is it simply a matter of cosplayers consciously or subconsciously railing against authority along with its traditional and normative values when they don cosplay costumes. Rather, it can be seen as a disruptive play practice that is 'artifactual'[103] in the sense that it provides a socially constructed alternative world experience, if not a deliberate escape from everyday life, in opposition to regular ways of dressing and being. It is in this overt display of otherness that cosplay has often created moral panics among the media and other hegemonic apparatuses.

Within the cosplay community itself, transgression is also stigmatized when cosers criticize the lack of authenticity of others' costumes, both face-to-face and online, which accords with Schechner's notion of 'dark play' occurring 'when contradictory realities coexist' and which 'subverts order, dissolves frames, breaks its own rules.'[104] It also evokes ideas about the rhetoric of play as a power game where human conflicts and contestations that are masked deep within the play experience surface.[105] Other dark practices can emerge, for example, from non-players attending the events as 'hentai-lech'[106] hobby photographers intent on pursuing their own private fetishes. As one respondent explained:

> I'm not always happy to let any photographer at the event take my photo because you just don't know what they do with them. One friend found her image on a porn website and she was heartbroken. That's very bad and is an increasing risk. Equally, you have no control over any of the images and where they can be shared—that is troubling to me these days.
>
> (Fiona, 23, female designer, Hong Kong)

Trust among the cosers is essential in the process of playing together. When broken, it can make some players less relaxed and more wary of the intention of photographers at events.

As we have seen, in the context of play theory, cosplay comprises and is bounded by three play zones, the psychological, the social and the cultural. Individual cosplayers share both a cognitive and an emotional connection with other players, in that they inhabit a mutual world based on their interest in re-animating media characters in material form. Cosers also enter into a social contract in the magic circle of cosplay through the act of playing meta-communicatively. While the borders of this play zone may be porous, enabling the multiplicity of characters chosen, and a range of players and non-players to attend the events, the very act of playing the role of the character in costume is prescribed and set apart from everyday life. Finally, the cultural zone of cosplay operates according to prescribed rules and often comprises the physical space that the cosers inhabit to activate play and the material artefacts—costumes and accessories—that enable play. As such, they need the social act of play to occur and to activate them. The social and cultural aspects of cosplay operate across various frames and signifying practices, given that at any one event there are a wide range of characters or activities and competitions taking place.

Cosplay epitomizes the ambiguities and complexities of play and the separation of play activity from everyday life. It operates within its own boundaries of time and space. The cognitive and physical realms of the magic circle offer recognition and relative security for the cosers to play out their fantasies in extraordinary costume. Yet the challenges to this safe playworld are all too apparent in the form of negative feedback at the convention and in online discussions, which may well represent a more generic spectatorial unease with the

Figure 6: Cosplayers enact a Japanese Noh inspired skit on stage at Macau Animation and Comic Culture Industrial Association event (2014). © Anne Peirson-Smith.

transformed, transgressive, abject body. As the next chapter will explore, the magic circle of cosplay is not just bounded within a specific community between cosplayers and non-cosplayers, but also operates from region to region and country to country. These bounded differences manifest themselves in terms of the rules and behavioural expectations, the mindset and seriousness with which the practice is undertaken by cosplay practitioners and aesthetically in terms of source and character choice or the emphasis on crafted authenticity based on DIY (do-it-yourself) skills.

The mobility of the cosplayer to play across a range of spaces and places, constituting the fluidity of cosplay, in both real and digital modes, evokes Christopher Moore's notion of the online gamer or 'gameur' who

adorns him or herself with different characters and digital artifacts, seeking out and moving between play experiences in games, forums, blogs, machinima and mods. Gameurs are the modifiers of the software and hardware of their game experiences, and by 'conceptualizing contemporary notions of play and mobility' they reinforce, shape, resist and change the commodification of the experiences of play.[107]

While the fluid agility of the gameur obviates the necessity for a magic circle of play, for the cosplayer or 'cosplayeur,' it signals an unequivocal invitation to play in a performance that is always a work in progress.

Notes

1   Jean Lave and Etienne Wenger, *Situated Learning: Legitimate Peripheral Participation* (Cambridge: Cambridge University Press, 1991), 29–36.
2   Brian Sutton-Smith, 'Play Theory: A Personal Journey and New Thoughts,' *The American Journal of Play* (Summer 2008), 114.
3   Brian Sutton-Smith, *The Ambiguity of Play* (Cambridge: Harvard University Press, 1997), 9–14.
4   Johan Huizinga, *Homo Ludens: A Study of Play Elements in Culture* (Boston: Beacon Press, 1955), 28–30.
5   Gregory Bateson, 'A Theory of Play and Fantasy,' *Psychiatric Research Reports* 2 (1955), in *The Game Design Reader: A Rules of Play Anthology*, eds Katie Salen and Eric Zimmerman (Cambridge: MIT Press, 2006), 319–20.
6   Penny Holland, *We Don't Play with Guns Here* (Maidenhead: Oxford University Press, 2003), 70–71.
7   Jean Piaget, *Play, Dreams and Imitation in Childhood* (Abingdon, Oxon: Routledge, 1951), 5–10.
8   Gary Alan Fine, *Shared Fantasy: Role Playing Games as Social Worlds* (Chicago: University of Chicago Press, 1983), 3–5.
9   Sutton-Smith, *The Ambiguity of Play*, 40–41.
10 Gary Kelly, *English Fiction of the Romantic Period, 1789–1830* (London: Routledge, 1989), 99–100.
11 Michael Chabon, 'Secret Skin: An Essay in Unitard Theory,' in *Superheroes: Fashion and Fantasy*, ed. Andrew Bolton (New York: The Metropolitan Museum of Art, 2008), 13, original emphasis.
12 Erving Goffman, 'Fun in Games,' in *Encounters: Two Studies in the Sociology of Interaction*, ed. Erving Goffman (Harmondsworth: Penguin, 1961), 15–72.
13 Sutton-Smith, 'Play Theory,' 114.
14 Catherine Garvey, *Play* (Cambridge: Harvard University Press, 1990), 4–5.
15 Huizinga, *Homo Ludens*, 1, original emphasis.
16 Ibid., 13.
17 Sutton-Smith, 'Play Theory,' 2–3.
18 Huizinga, *Homo Ludens*, 13, emphasis added.
19 Wang Ying, *Secrets of Cosplay* (Harrow, Middlesex: Cypri Press, 2014), 40–41.

20 Joel Gn, 'Queer Simulation: The Practice, Performance and Pleasure of Cosplay,' *Continuum*, 25, no.4 (2011), 589.

21 *Harry Potter and the Philosopher's Stone*, directed by Chris Columbus (New York: Warner Brothers, 2001), Film; *Harry Potter and the Chamber of Secrets*, directed by Chris Columbus (New York: Warner Brothers, 2002), Film; *Harry Potter and the Prisoner of Azkaban*, directed by Alfonso Cuarón (New York: Warner Brothers, 2004), Film; *Harry Potter and the Goblet of Fire*, directed by Mike Newell (New York: Warner Brothers, 2005), Film; *Harry Potter and the Order of the Phoenix*, directed by David Yates (New York: Warner Brothers, 2007), Film; *Harry Potter and the Half-Blood Prince*, directed by David Yates (New York: Warner Brothers, 2009), Film; *Harry Potter and the Deathly Hallows—Part 1*, directed by Mike Newell (New York: Warner Brothers, 2010), Film; *Harry Potter and the Deathly Hallows—Part 2*, directed by Mike Newell (New York: Warner Brothers, 2011), Film; *Games of Thrones*, directed by David Benioff and D. B. Weiss (New York: HBO, 2011–), TV series.

22 Ying, *Secrets of Cosplay*, 48.

23 Scott Duchesne, 'Little Reckonings in Great Rooms,' *Canadian Theatre Review* 121 (Winter, 2005), 24.

24 Michael Taussig, *Mimesis and Alterity: A Particular History of the Senses* (Hove, UK: Psychology Press, 1993), xv–xvi.

25 Kane Anderson, 'Becoming Batman: Cosplay Performance, and Ludic Transformation at Comic-Con,' in *Play Performance and Identity: How Institutions Structure Ludic Spaces*, eds. Matt Omasta and Drew Chappell, *Routledge Advances in Theatre Studies* (New York: Routledge, 2015), 114.

26 Chabon, 'Secret Skin,' 17.

27 Anderson, 'Becoming Batman,' 114.

28 Roger Caillois, *Man, Play and Games*, trans. Mayer Barash (Chicago: University of Illinois Press, 1958), x, 13.

29 Caillois, *Man, Play and Games*, 6–7.

30 Sutton-Smith, 'Play Theory,' 2–15.

31 Tracey Fullerton, Janine Fron, Celia Pearce, and Jackie Morie, 'Getting Girls into the Game: Towards a "Virtuous Cycle,"' in *Beyond Barbie and Mortal Kombat: New Perspectives on Computer Games*, eds. Yasmin B. Kefer, Carrie Heeter, Jill Denner, and J. Y. Suns (Cambridge: MIT Press, 2007).

32 Fred Davis, *Fashion, Culture and Identity* (Chicago: University of Chicago Press, 1992), 25.

33 Huizinga, *Homo Ludens*, 12.

34 Ibid., 20.

35 Ibid., 10.

36 Ibid., 10.

37 Gregory P. Stone, 'Appearance and the Self,' in *Dress and Identity*, eds. Mary Ellen Roach-Higgins, Joanne B. Eicher, and Kim P. Johnson (New York: Fairchild Publications, 1962), 19–39.

38 Huizinga, *Homo Ludens*, 13, emphasis added.

39 Katie Salen and Eric Zimmerman, *Rules of Play Game Design Fundamentals* (London: MIT Press), 2004.

40 Christopher Moore, 'The Magic Circle and the Mobility of Play,' *Convergence: The International Journal of Research in New Media Technologies* 17, no. 4 (2011), 373-87.

41 Arjun Appadurai, 'Disjuncture and Difference in the Global Cultural Economy,' *Theory Culture Society* 7 (1990), 297.

42 Salen and Zimmerman, *Rules of Game Design*, 95.

43 Ibid.

44 George Ritzer and Nathan Jurgenson, 'Production, Consumption, Prosumption: The Nature of Capitalism in the Age of the Digital "Prosumer,"' *Journal of Consumer Culture* 10, no. 1 (2010), 13–36.

45 Appadurai, 'Disjuncture and Difference,' 296–300.

46 Chris Rojek, *Capitalism and Leisure Theory* (New York: Routledge, 1985), 46.

47 Stanley Cohen, *Folk Devils and Moral Panics: The Creation of the Mods and Rockers*, 3rd ed. (London: Routledge, 2002).

48 Ibid., 1.

49 Ibid., xii.

50 Fran Martin, 'Girls Who Love Boy's Love: BL as Goods to Think with in Taiwan,' in *Boy's Love, Cosplay and Androgenous Idols: Queer Fan Cultures in Mainland China*, eds. Maud Lavin, Ling Yang, and Jing Jamie Zhao (Hong Kong: Hong Kong University Press, 2017), 195–220.

51 Anon., *Welcome to the Comic Market*, accessed 1 January 2018, http://www.comiket.co.jp/info-a/TAFO/C88TAFO/C88eng.pdf

52 Anon., 'Comiket Cosplay Rules,' accessed 1 January 2018, http://www.cosplay.com/showthread.php?t=228152

53 Daniel Pargman and Peter Jakobsson, 'Do You Believe in Magic? Computer Games in Everyday Life,' *European Journal of Cultural Studies* 11 (2008), 225–43.

54 Appadurai, 'Disjuncture and Difference,' 299.

55 Sutton-Smith, *The Ambiguity of Play*, 4.

56 Ibid., 303.

57 Ibid., 214.

58 Appadurai, 'Disjuncture and Difference,' 299.

59 Sutton-Smith, *The Ambiguity of Play*, 52.

60 *Fate/Stay Night (Feito/Sutei Naito)*, directed by Yuji Yamaguchi (Tokyo: Studio Deen, 2006), Anime TV series.

61 Alyssa Rosenberg, 'Convention Etiquette 101: How to Avoid Crossing the Line at Comic-Con,' 15 July 2013, accessed 1 January 2018, https://www.wired.com/2013/07/convention-etiquette-comic-con/

62 Terry Castle, *Masquerade and Civilization: The Carnivalesque in the Eighteenth-Century English Culture and Fiction* (Stanford: Stanford University Press, 1996).

63 Rachel Leng, 'Gender, Sexuality, and Cosplay: A Case Study of Male-to-Female Crossplay,' *The Phoenix Papers: First Edition* (April 2013), 106–7.

64 Lauren Orsini, *Cosplay: The Fantasy World of Role Play* (London: Carlton Books, 2015), 228.

65 Shih-chen Chao, 'The Queered Ke'ai of Male Cosplayers as "Fake Girls,"' in *Boys' Love, Cosplay and Androgenous Idols: Queer Fan Cultures in Mainland China*, eds. Maud Lavin, Ling Yang, and Jing Jamie Zhao (Hong Kong: Hong Kong University Press, 2017), 20.

66 Ibid., 11, original emphasis.

67 Mihaly Csikszentmihalyi, *Beyond Boredom and Anxiety* (New York: Jossey Bass, 1975), 81, 182.

68 Gregory Bateson, 'A Theory of Play and Fantasy,' in *Steps to an Ecology of Mind: Collected Essays in Anthropology, Psychiatry, Evolution, and Epistemology*, ed. Gregory Bateson (Northvale: Jason Aronson, 1987), 138–48.

69 Michael J. Apter, 'A Structural-phenomenology of Play,' in *Adult Play: A Reversal Theory Approach*, eds. John H. Kerr and Michael J. Apter (Amsterdam, The Netherlands: Swets & Zeitlinger, 1991), 15.

70 Caillois, *Man, Play and Games*, 13.

71 Gregory Bateson, *A Theory of Play and Fantasy* (Chicago and London: The University of Chicago Press, 1972), 180, 182, 184, 190.

72 Sutton-Smith, 'Play Theory,' 11, 75, 175.

73 Huizinga, *Homo Ludens*, 43.

74 *Star Wars I: The Phantom Menace*, directed by George Lucas (Century City: 20ᵗʰ Century Fox, 1999), Film; *Star Wars II: Attack of the Clones*, directed by George Lucas (Century City: 20ᵗʰ Century Fox, 2002), Film; *Star Wars III: Revenge of the Sith*, directed by George Lucas (Century City: 20ᵗʰ Century Fox, 2005), Film; *Star Wars IV: A New Hope*, directed by George Lucas (Century City: 20ᵗʰ Century Fox, 1977), Film; *Star Wars V: The Empire Strikes Back*, directed by Irvin Kershner (Century City: 20ᵗʰ Century Fox, 1980), Film; *Star Wars VI: Return of the Jedi*, directed by Richard Marquand (Century City: 20ᵗʰ Century Fox, 1983), Film; *Star Wars: The Clone Wars*, produced by Dave Filoni (US: Disney/ABC, 2015), Film; *Star Wars VII: The Force Awakens*, directed by J. J. Abrams (Century City: 20ᵗʰ Century Fox, 2015), Film; *Gundam*, created by Yoshiyuki Tomino (Tokyo: Sunrise, 1979–), Media franchise; *Final Fantasy (Fainaru Fantajī)*, Hironobu Sakaguchi (Tokyo: Nintendo Entertainment System, 1987) Game.

75 Jürgen Habermas, *The Theory of Communicative Action: Lifeworld and System—A Critique of Functionalist Reason*, trans. Thomas McCartney (1981; Boston: Beacon Press, 1987), 155, 195.

76 Ibid., 17.

77 Erving Goffman, *Frame Analysis: An Essay on the Organization of Experience* (Boston: Northeastern University Press, 1986), 42–43, 135–36.

78 Ibid., 1.

79 Ibid., 247.

80 Mackenzie Wark, *Gamer Theory* (Cambridge: Harvard University Press, 2007), 24, 222.

81 Dan Harries, *Film Parody* (London: BFI, 2000), 4–7.

82 Anastasia Seregina and Henri A. Weijo, 'Play at Any Cost: How Cosplayers Produce and Sustain Their Ludic Communal Consumption Experiences,' *Journal of Consumer Research* 44, no. 1 (2016), 153.

83   Zara Stone, *Meet the Girls Making a Living from Cosplay* (6 October 2015), accessed 1 January 2018, https://thehustle.co/meet-the-girls-making-a-living-from-cosplay.

84   Alison DeBlasio, Joey Marsocci, and Yaya Han, *1000 Incredible Costume & Cosplay Ideas* (Singapore: Page One Publications, 2013), 7.

85   Goffman, *Frame Analysis*, 8.

86   Bateson, 'A Theory of Play', 188, 261.

87   Victor Witter Turner, *Dramas, Fields and Metaphors: Symbolic Action in Human Society* (Ithaca and London: Cornell University Press, 1974), 14–16.

88   Kurt Riezler, 'Play and Seriousness', *The Journal of Philosophy*, 38, no. 19 (1941), 511.

89   Peter L. Berger and Thomas Luckmann, *The Social Construction of Reality: A Treatise in the Sociology of Knowledge* (New York: Anchor Books, 1966), 25.

90   Lave and Wenger, *Situated Learning*, 29–30.

91   Salen and Zimmerman, *Rules of Play*, 94–95.

92   Huizinga, *Homo Ludens*, 51.

93   Lawrence Grossberg, *We Gotta Get Out of This Place: Popular Conservatism and Postmodern Culture* (New York: Routledge, 1992), 127.

94   James Paul Gee, 'Learning and Games', in *The Ecology of Games: Connecting Youth Games and Learning*, ed. Katie Salen (Cambridge: MIT Press, 2008), 21–22.

95   Fine, *Shared Fantasy*, 123.

95   Ibid., 136.

97   David Muggleton, *Inside Subculture: The Postmodern Meaning of Style* (Oxford: Berg, 1999), 14.

98   Salen and Zimmerman, *Rules of Play*, 488.

99   Richard Schechner, *Performance Studies: An Introduction*, 3rd ed. (London: Routledge, 1982), 24.

100   Richard Schechner, 'Play', in *The Improvisation Studies Reader: Spontaneous Acts*, eds. Ajay Heble and Rebecca Caines (London and New York: Routledge, 2015), 394.

101   Jesper Juul, 'A Casual Revolution: Reinventing Video Games and Their Players', (Cambridge: MIT Press, 2009), 18, 85, 184.

102   Sutton-Smith, 'Play Theory', 100–102, 203, 212.

103   Thomas Malaby, *Beyond Play: A New Approach to Games, Games and Culture* 2, no. 2 (2007), 95.

104   Richard Schechner, *The Future of Ritual: Writings on Culture and Performance* (London and New York: Routledge, 1993), 36.

105   Sutton-Smith, 'Play Theory', 82, 90.

106   Eron Rauch and Christopher Bolton, 'A Cosplay Photography Sampler', *Mechademia* 5, Fanthropologies (2010), 179.

107   Moore, *The Magic Circle*, 384.

Chapter 5

Cosplay Sites

O ver the past twenty years, global commodity culture flows have received attention from scholars in various disciplines aiming to understand the complex movement of goods and ideas as 'cultural interconnections increasingly reach across the world.'[1] Such research has entailed an interest in the mobility of both communities and things— people, capital and ideas. On one level, this approach has 'liquefied geographies,'[2] valorizing a boundary-less, transcultural world[3] based on an identification process that is mixed or multinational. In connecting up the dots of these global flows, however, the local is often back-grounded or bypassed entirely. Conversely, other scholars have highlighted the complexities of globalized cultural trends that resist homogenization, grounding their approach in localized cases and demonstrating the dynamic hybridity of cultural forms taking root in specific places. By focusing on both people and things, as exemplified in a commodity cultures approach, it is possible to study, as Arjun Appadurai puts it, 'the things-in-motion that illuminate their human and social context,'[4] thus acknowledging the highly complex, multi-directional flow of goods and influences operating across seemingly boundless territories. It is within these increasingly fluid ethnoscapes[5] that cosplay's fantastic presentation of self[6] and costumed identity 'based on emotion'[7] takes place.

The chapter examines the global cosplay trend via the intrinsic motivations of individuals situated in cosplay activity at sites across a number of countries where it has taken root. It is supported by interviewee, observational and interactional data running from 2009 to the present and comprising over 100 cosplay participants from a range of countries, including the United Kingdom (5 respondents), North America (10), Canada (3), Australia (3), Hong Kong (60), Macau (20), Beijing (30) and Tokyo (20). The majority were aged between 17 and 25 and some 70 per cent of them were female, reflecting the age and gender dynamics of cosplay in Asia, in particular. In terms of occupation, most of the respondents were full-time students in higher education or were young professionals often, but not exclusively, working in the creative industries. Data was collected using qualitative research methods based on individual interviews, focus groups and observational methodologies.[8] This was recorded as transcripts and then themed and coded for analytical purposes to enable the mapping of trends that emerged from the cosplayers' insights, and the personal and geographical similarities and differences that emerged. In this way, a reputational approach was taken to data gathering to ensure that the subjective, lived experiences of the cosplayers were recorded from their own perspectives.[9]

Figure 1: Three cosplayers as (*left* to *right*) Byakuya Togami, Junko Enoshima and Makoto Naegi from *Danganronpa* (2010–) at Hong Kong University cosplay event. Macau Animation and Comic Culture Industrial Association event (2014). © Anne Peirson-Smith.

Transnational culture flows

The transnational flow of things and commodities is centuries old and allied to the origins of capitalist societies, predicated as it is on trade routes between 'East' and 'West'—across the Silk Road over centuries, for example—facilitating the exchange of precious goods, ideas, languages and cultures.[10] However, just as the global flow of mediated commodities has hugely intensified in the late twentieth to early twenty-first centuries, so has that of cultural products, as media organizations have widely disseminated their offerings. This distribution of popular culture-based ideas and goods has involved ever more efficient production systems and promotional machines, assisted by a proliferation of media channels. While the process has been regarded by some as driven by a western, neo-imperialistic colonization of indigenous or, at least, local cultures, others highlight the shortcomings of this singular viewpoint, based as it is on a unidirectional model of economic and cultural influence. Critics posit an alternative, decentred and dispersed model. Koichi Iwabuchi observes that it is 'too simplistic to straightforwardly equate globalization with Americanization,' and furthermore that

> It is no longer possible to understand the structure of global cultural power as bipartite, with one-way transfers of culture from the center to the periphery [...]. The decentralization of power can be seen in the emergence of multinational corporations from Japan and other non-Western countries as global players, but this does not mean that a new center is emerging to take the place of the United States. Rather, cross-border partnerships and co-operation among media and cultural industries and capital involving Japan and other non-Western developed countries are being driven forward, with the US as a pivotal presence.[11]

Adding credence to this notion of a multi-way circulation of ideas, people and products is the evidence of an intra-regional flow of Asian popular culture products, such as fashion from Japanese street wear[12] or the significant spread of Hallyu (so-called Korean Wave)[13] culture, which is challenging the dominant cultural flow from western centres that characterized much of the twentieth century. In the Asian context, the youth demographic has proved to be active consumers of global popular culture in the form of music, fashion, television shows and films since at least the 1960s. This has been notably the case in ex-colonial territories such as Hong Kong, Macau and Singapore, given that local artistic and cultural expression was often not fostered or sanctioned by the dominant culture.[14] By way of contrast, Japan has generally preserved its political, economic and cultural autonomy into the modern era, despite patches of military and domestic upheaval, inculcating a deep feeling of nationhood. Consequently, national identity has been expressed latterly through cultural output, which from the 1990s took off across the region, generating an intra-circulation of cultural products. As Beng Huat Chua notes: 'Pop culture from different centers flows and crosses porous national and cultural boundaries and is routinely distributed throughout the entire region.'[15]

Part of the allure for young Asian fans of manga, anime, films and television shows has been a sense of connection, temporality or 'cultural proximity' with Japanese culture based on a sense of 'coevalness' with familiar characters appearing regularly in widespread media products.[16] This emerged in the absence of recognition for home-grown versions of popular culture, given the historic over-reliance on western media. Yet, as Iwabuchi explains, the reception of this cultural nostalgic construct of Japanese culture through adherence to mediated representations was not reciprocated by the Japanese themselves as they largely failed to recognize a sense of connection with other nations in the locality.[17] For western audiences, this 'Japanophilia,' as Roland Kelts calls it,[18] is derived from an Orientalist connection with a fascinating 'other' based on the 'libertarian fearlessness of Japan's creators of popular culture [of which] manga and anime are at the cutting edge.'[19]

Across Asia, Japanese comics or graphic print narratives (manga) and animated media (anime) have acquired global popularity, moving outwards from their Japanese sources from the 1960s and 1970s onwards.[20] This transfer was founded largely on a significant global marketing push by Japanese animation and publishing houses.[21] It was also encouraged by the Japanese government's investment in promoting soft power, which, in turn, exercised a significant influence on other Asian countries' comics and animation industries in terms of narrative content, artwork design and format. Indeed, these soft power outputs have taken root globally in the local popular cultural landscapes. The manga and anime subculture has also affected the lives of young fans who devotedly follow mediated cultural products, thereby suggesting a close alliance of interests and predispositions based on shared experiences across demographic groups of young people in Asia and beyond.[22] This has occurred despite criticism from older segments of the population and talking heads fearful of Japanese cultural hegemony, often based on accusations of insensitivities to past historical events.[23]

The sheer scale of narrative content produced across the past 40 years of Japanese anime and manga output has provided a huge pool of characters to choose from, from science fiction and fantasy to high school and romance genres. This 'flying geese trend'[24] of the appropriation of cultural processes is notably evident among the dressing-up activities of Asian cosplayers who take inspiration largely from imported Japanese characters. In effect, the local comic and animation industries and their consumers have appropriated and adapted these texts both linguistically and artistically. In doing so, they have added new meanings, thereby creating unique, hybrid cultural products—as in the appropriation of elements of what was once known as 'Japanimation' into Hong Kong martial arts comics, exemplified by *Supergod Z* (1993), which also took inspiration from Japanese video games such as *Street Fighters* (*Sutorito Faitā*) (1987–).[25] Another example of localization is the practice of cosplay in Mainland China modelled on Chinese mythology. Equally, though Hollywood- or MTV-sourced superheroes and protagonists are more typically performed at events outside of Asian cons, they remain a common subject of cosplay in Asia due to the global reach of US media products.[26] This cultural borrowing and appropriation of cosplay ideas from both Japanese anime and manga and western superhero comics and films highlights the normative aspect of cultural hybridity in the practice of cosplay. Thus, superheroes such as Iron Man can be seen rubbing shoulders with anime heroes such as female protagonist Hatuki Fujioka from *Ouran High School Host Club* (*Ōran Kōko Hostu Kurabu*) (2002–10),[27] in both Asia and the west.

However, in Asia this cultural mixing more often tends to be a one-way flow based on a unidirectional trajectory of cultural influence out of Japan. Hence, for example, the majority of cosplay characters in Hong Kong and Taiwanese conventions are commonly based on familiar Japanese manga and anime sources, given that these narratives and characters were often part of the socialization process of the mediascapes[28] of young people who grew up reading and watching them. As one respondent explained:

We love Japanese culture and it has always been there for us as we grew up reading Japanese comic books and watching anime. It is usual that we would identify with a heroic character such as Naruto or Gohan in *Dragon Ball X* and sort of grow up with them. And then as a cosplayer we want to pay homage to them by recreating them which is based on memory and knowing them well. Our favourite characters really do seem like friends to us as they have been through it all with us—all our school, family and friendship problems. They were there for us all of the time in their own world that we could visit anytime. And they had big problems too but they showed us how to survive them. Of course, some cosplayers also 'cos' American superheroes or *Star Wars* characters as we grew up with them too and admire some of them. But they are from another language and culture and not as many do 'cos' them here.

(Ginti, 23, male student, Macau)

Taken as a whole, cosplay is comprised of situated, intertextual acts based on cultural borrowings or 'textual poaching'[29] by a fan base from a familiar and popular narrative corpus involving a re-creation of authorship and ownership, as discussed in Chapter 1. As Matthew Hale observes, a cosplayer typically signifies

a nongeneric dramatis personae that has enough circulation amongst con attendees that it can act as an intertextual medium of exchange [...]. They have distinctive costumes, personalities, backstories, and histories of circulation that make them cohesive, recognizable, and thus iterable forms that can be differentially shared between individuals with varying familiarity with the source text(s).[30]

At the same time, this viewpoint illustrates how these derivations influence the creation of imagined communities based on adaptation and interpretation. Hale goes on to make the distinction between two types of character representation at large in the North American conventions that he staked out for his ethnographic research, namely discrete representation and generic representation. The former involves the embodied replication as a citational act of a familiar subject from a popular textual source, including 'the representation of nonfictional personalities like historical figures, reality television show stars, politicians, religious figures, internet memes, and popular advertising imagery,' thus 'the majority of cosplayers represent fictional characters from comics, video games, television programs.'[31] Generic character representation, on the other hand, involves

a practice that does not focus on reproducing a specific character from a given text like Optimus Prime, Wonder Woman, or Mystique, rather it engages a general character typology like a robot, superhero, or supervillain. These general forms are conventionalized conceptual categories.[32]

It is interesting to note that while discrete character representation at Asian cons is the norm, generic representation is rare if not non-existent, unlike North American experiences and other global sites of cosplay conventions. In the same way, there is always a significant presence of Japanese manga- and anime-sourced characters at cons both within and outside of Asia.

Figure 2: Two cosplayers as characters Shaytan (Demon of Flame) and Layla (Beautiful Maiden of the Night) from *Sound Horizon* (2001–) at Macau Animation and Comic Culture Industrial Association event. Macau Animation and Comic Culture Industrial Association event (2014). © Anne Peirson-Smith.

This gives further credence to Edward Said's notions of the mythical constructions of the 'East' and the 'West' whereby such 'locales, regions, geographic sectors as "Orient" and "Occident" are man-made. Therefore as much as the West itself, the Orient is an idea that has history and a tradition of thought, imagery and vocabulary that have given it reality and presence.'[33]

Orientalizing tendencies have a track record. As Mark Holborn suggests, 'Oriental views have provided the West with spectacle'[34] from the mid-nineteenth century onwards in the aesthetic integration of Japanese motifs into western art and design. Certainly, the appeal of manga, anime and online game characters lies, in part, in the exoticization of Japanese particularism and difference.[35] This is evidenced from Roland Barthes' fascination with Bunraku puppetry and Japanese signifiers in *The Empire of Signs* (1970)[36] to the popular fascination with cosplay superhero characters or heroic archetypes with magical or cyborg powers, suggesting a postmodern and popular culture interpretation of Orientalism. The appeal of imagined settings and the option to inhabit them mentally, physically and affectively may also reside in self-Orientalism, whereby a culture seemingly adopts and absorbs western hegemony in the process of mining Orientalist views based on the intention of transforming the self into a cultural 'Other.'

This is typified by the longstanding tradition of the use of exoticized *shōjo* (girl's) manga narrative settings across a range of genres from historical romance to sci-fi aimed at the teenage female market. An example is Julietta Suzuki's shōjo manga series, *Beginning Life as a God (Kamisama Hajimemashita)* (2008–16).[37] The plot is founded on the Orientalist notion that the east is a spiritual reflection of the west, based on a longing of the latter to escape from mindless capitalistic pursuits as embedded in the female teenage protagonist, Nanami, who morphs into a local deity assisted by male fox *yokai* (demon) Tomoe. She, thus, acquires spiritual powers, based on a tense romantic attraction that, according to a divine decree, can never be fulfilled. In the process of mythically presenting the east as a place of mystery and eroticism, Japanese self-identity is actually strengthened,[38] while playing on the sense of pleasure that western readers and viewers experience when encountering and immersing themselves in the aesthetics of Japanese mythology.

While this may be mirrored in cosplay practice, by using both eastern and western sources as inspiration for their embodied practice, cosplayers are creating and inhabiting their own hybridized space between the real and the imaginary. As Frenchy Lunning observes: 'Characters from such sources as the *Harry Potter* stories, the film *Sweeney Todd*, fanfiction, video and online games, Renaissance festivals, re-enactors and the various Japanese Lolitas and fetish zoku or "tribes" can appear at an anime convention.'[39] One cosplayer reflected in conversation on this universality of costumed representation:

> In the 'cos' universe there are a never ending range of personas to choose from, so it's about big decisions every time! But that is also part of the fun of cosplay—it's like a kid in a sweet shop really as the choices can be too much but we can do more than one character per season, and also we can save our favourites to 'cos' again. We do love Japanese culture so those are often the characters that we 'cos,' but some groups also specialize in their passion for a movie like *Star Wars* or *Twilight*.
>
> (Jen, 20, female student, Canada)

The complementary cosplaying of western sources in Asia, when it does occur, could be seen not so much as cultural imperialism but as a form of Occidentalism, whereby an imaginary west is constructed and exploited for fantasy purposes by cosplayers in a region that is on the rise.

Transmutable cosplay origins

Significantly, the origins of cosplay, as with its manga and anime roots, are founded in its transmutability. Chapters 1 and 2 discussed how the term 'cosplay' emerged in 1983 and gained currency in the wake of Japanese reporter and manga publisher Nobuyuki

Takahashi's attendance at the Los Angles WorldCon where he was 'overwhelmed' by fans' arrestingly embellished outfits as well as the wearers' frequent refusal to break character while in costume. To him, the play-acting element made the hobby a practice to be differentiated from regular old costume wearing. In order to explain this novel dress-up practice to his Japanese readers, he coined the term 'cosplay,' a decidedly Japanese contraction for the two English words 'costume' and 'play.'[40] Other scholars have located the immediate origins of cosplay in the more anonymous trend for costume parties in 1980s Tokyo. However, their acknowledged source of inspiration is still linked to American costuming activity at Worldcons and comic conventions, which developed out of the prior practice of costuming,[41] suggesting an—albeit self-assured—form of cultural appropriation.

For centuries, global cultural hegemony meant a predominantly one-way flow of influence, and an embodied form of cultural control, that was highly Eurocentric. Hence, the colonial powers dominating the Asian political landscape during the period of European cultural ascendency largely failed to recognize the validity of other, non-western cultural forms. They tended to engage in conventional one-dimensional Orientalizing, as when appropriating Japanese kimonos, qipaos and other parodied oriental signifiers, for instance, into their own art forms and consumer worlds, as discussed in Chapter 7.

However, this cultural neglect may have unwittingly provided an inviting cultural space for local cultures to create their own forms, albeit sometimes manifested as a facsimile, parody or pastiche of western outputs. This transmutability and cultural exchange found expression, for example, in Japanese manga texts that have their roots in late nineteenth-century magazines published in Japan. Graphic storytelling elements carried across from the west include the use of temporal and spatial framing for content and speech bubbles to convey character-based conversations. Japanese artists also found inspiration in US comics of the early twentieth century published in Japan, creating their own Japanese versions.[42] The outcomes of this cultural hybridity were on full display in the work of Disney-inspired manga and anime master Osamu Tezuka from the 1950s, through iconic texts such as *Mighty Atom (Tetsuwan Atomu)* (in Japan from 1952), also known as *Astro Boy* (in North America from 1964). As Kelts notes:

Aside from the American influences [...] (visible in the wide eyes and rounder shapes of Tezuka' work versus that of others in the anime tradition) [...] Tezuka created the blueprint for Japanese manga and anime artists—and it was vast. All subject matter was fair game, and expressions could be bleak, violent and apocalyptic, in addition to being humourless and hopeful [...]. He focused on story and he was a voracious reader of both eastern and western sources.[43]

The transcultural roots of these texts are integral as the source of inspiration for the characters that cosplayers draw on in this dynamic, creative practice. Regionally within Asia, the popular uptake of cultural forms, such as Japanese anime and manga, and their creative expression and appropriation in youth practices, such as cosplay, evoke forms of modernity for participants. In doing so, they highlight the similarities and differences within Asian cultures, given their essential heterogeneity. This has obvious appeal in terms of enabling young people to make sense of their often pressurized lives by immersing themselves within mediated narratives that are largely familiar through cultural and geographic proximity, yet also have important points of divergence and difference. At the same time, both the intra-regional and wider global cultural flows of such textual content arguably represents a decentring trend in relation to western cultural outputs—or at the very least, a broadening out or re-calibration of the actors involved in popular culture outputs.[44]

The centre–periphery model of cultural flows, directed from west to non-west, has been extensively examined within the globalization debate,[45] and clearly no longer necessarily prevails as the dominant influencer when examining aspects of transregional and transnational cultural borrowings that often direct cosplay practice. Even notions of western cultural imperialism are fraught with stereotypical assumptions about the tyranny of cultural colonization by North American media corporations such as Disney[46] or digital colonialism by multimedia behemoths such as Viacom or Google. While there is strong evidence for western products dominating other cultures, values and behaviours,[47] this cultural dominance thesis may no longer hold complete sway, given that these products are not necessarily passively consumed or used by fans. Added to this are the specificities of localized uptake,[48] in the transformation of characters and their original narratives across geographies and cultures, reflecting different positions in relation to modernity or postmodernity. A reworked perspective is required if we are to more accurately represent the range of globalized and 'glocalized' cultural outputs that have recently emerged, given the considerable complexity and fracturing of transglobal flows of both goods and ideas across multiple-scapes in late modernity.[49] This glocalization process suggests that there are complex and dynamic global flows of cultural goods, such as manga and anime texts, narratives and characters, in terms of their fan bases and markets outside of Japan. While, at the more micro-glocalized level, various versions of Japanese-influenced *kawaii* (cute) or *moe* (character-based affective behaviour) will be on display at a cosplay event in Hong Kong, for example, there will also likely be a team performing song and dance routines imitating Korean band Girls' Generation, alongside a group of singing synthesizer applications of *Vocaloid* characters such as Hatsune Miku[50] in long turquoise blue wigs with portable mics, in addition to stormtroopers and Jedi knights.

In many ways, therefore, cosplay typifies the re-centring trend from western cultural dominance to other centres of cultural interest. This has followed in the wake of western culture's relative displacement by the rise of Japanese soft power, reflecting its economic strength in the 1990s and concomitant newly dispersed transnational cultural circulation from other rapidly emerging engines of pop culture, such as South Korea. This apparent cultural displacement also reflects the evolving South-East Asian urban entertainment landscape, where players and fans are expressing themselves as active pro-consumers or 'prosumers'[51] of manga and anime in the entertainment economies of China, Hong Kong,

Figure 3: Cosplayer as Asuka Langley Sohryn from *Evangelion* (1995–2012) at Macau Animation and Comic Culture Industrial Association event. Macau Animation and Comic Culture Industrial Association event (2014). © Anne Peirson-Smith.

Indonesia, Singapore, Thailand, Malaysia and beyond. This regional and global emergence, however, is not solely user driven, having been accelerated by the activities of Japanese media producers who have aggressively made their cultural products, especially manga and anime, available at every level.[52] Nevertheless, this product push by an efficient and aggressive production system cannot alone explain the significant pull of consumer popularity that these cultural products have enjoyed, nor can it totally account for their transnational impact and varied manifestations across the Asian region, in particular.

The conditions underpinning cosplay as a creative, transcultural practice across Asia and the globe need to be examined further to establish how cosplayers as active consumption and re-production agents create new imaginaries that are re-worked across a range of localized and globalized cultural zones.

Lunning notes that the two-way flow underpinning the cosplay craze dating from 1970s Comic-Cons highlight the complexities of locating its true origins, while foregrounding the fluidity and non-homogeneity of the phenomenon:

In July 1979, the San Diego Comic-Con, visited by a touring group of Japanese mangaka (comic artists), became the first convention in the United States to include several anime characters in its masquerade. During the 1980s as anime and manga began to circulate in the West anime increasingly became a prominent portion of convention activities, and anime characters were included in the masquerades.[53]

The contention here is that cosplayers are not essentializing Japanese cultural characteristics because of mere alignment with 'cultural proximity'[54] or the representation of familiar Asian values, or even in the lure of the 'other.' Rather, they are attracted to cosplay on the basis of its capacity to create alternative identities based on axiomatic, or at least familiar, reference points. Further, this cosplay activity offers active participation in a cultural practice that is fluidly interpretative rather than rigidly fixed. As a result, it is highly appealing to a youth demographic in search of agency and identity, given the multi-levelled pressures of contemporary life from parental, peer and social sources.

Tracking cosplay communalities and sites of difference

Tracking similarities and differences in the appropriation of cosplay culture is a useful way of understanding its appeal and the cosers' motivations. Also relevant is the question as to whether the global—versus distinctively local—interpretations of the practice are based on unifying or dis-unifying principles. As Appadurai observes: 'The most valuable feature of the concept of culture is the concept of difference [...] that can highlight points of similarity and contrast between all sorts of categories: classes, genders, roles, groups, nations.'[55] In this sense, cosplay is a practice with cultural dimensions founded on a mix of histories, influences and irregular mobilities wherever it locates itself. This takes the form of 'situated difference [...] in relation to something local, embodied and significant.'[56] On one side of the coin, communalities are evident whereby cosplayers globally and locally share a love of costuming, creative skills and the display of affective participatory fandom often based on a deep and nuanced knowledge of the text. On the other, there are observable divergences in terms of the characters chosen, motivations, costume creation, protocols and spatial settings for cosplay.

Effectively, the practice is located in the representation of relative agency and power among cosers that is based on the political, economic and cultural characteristics of their given geographic location. These characteristics include having the economic ability to produce and distribute cultural goods; the cultural ability to produce and circulate form and meaning; and the latitude for shaping desire, fantasy and imagination against the backdrop of prevailing social and political ideologies. Despite cosplay's culturally diverse origins, there is a global unity in cosplay practice in its embodied presentation of the spectacular self based on a specific costumed character, and the affective transformation of mind and body that this involves. As Xin, a 22-year-old female office worker from China commented:

I become the character when I cos and put on my costume like San from *Princess Mononoke* and not only do I look like them and not myself I feel different. I am truly changed and can do anything—that makes me feel so good and really powerful to be honest.

(Xin, 22, female office worker, China)

Cosplayers are constantly traversing boundaries: physically when they put on the costume and transform their appearance, cognitively as they think like the character and feel consequently empowered, affectively as they experience a changed emotional state, behaviourally when they pose and act 'in character' and virtually when they share their captured cosplay images across multiple digital platforms.

The interplay between and correlation of these factors, however, can vary both among and within different nations. Moreover, the level of engagement and the boundaries that are crossed, from real to imaginary, may also differ depending on individual cosers and their level of experience across different generations of cosplayers. As veteran cosplayer Tanya explained:

Figure 4: Cosplayers pose as manga artist Matsuri Hino-inspired characters at a University of Science and Technology cosplay event (2013). © Anne Peirson-Smith.

152

I consider that newer and younger 'cosers' today often are not as involved in it. I mean they might dress up as their character, but it is a surface connection with it. I mean they might look really good, but they don't really think or feel deeply inside that they are really Aerith from *Final Fantasy VII* or Knight King from *Game of Thrones* [...] and this is really true of what I see at Asian Cons and also in North America too. I guess it's a thin line between having fun and being serious about it. As an old timer doing cosplay for 10 years it's all about serious fun for me, in that order, with full engagement, from looks to thoughts and feelings.

(Tanya, 29, female cosplayer, Canada)

Cosplay also involves many complex crossings of self to other based on reforming images and texts from other cultures, nations and enterprises. As Rachel Leng observes, cosplayers inhabit a transitory world of border crossings that provides the space for social transgression and gender performance, in that

crossplay practices epitomize how cosplay conventions and fandom provide a transitional space where boundaries between self and world are encountered, crossed, and reconstructed [...] not only to challenge hegemonic norms about masculinity and femininity, but also to facilitate the construction of new modes of fan identity and creative expression.[57]

The subject of gender, crossplay and queer is explored in Chapter 8, but in terms of ethnicity, based on personal observation there can be a tendency for Asian players to lean towards Japanese characters. Cosers outside of Asia may lean more towards Hollywood and superhero characters, though as previously noted Japanese sources have a huge following. Globally, many of the characters chosen often reflect the latest popular film or release from a popular franchise—*Harry Potter, Iron Man, Game of Thrones, Star Wars* or *Pokémon*, along with many others—highlighting the significant influence of the media conglomerates on choice for cosplayer fans.

One site of significant difference is that character is central to anime and manga narratives rather than the storyline itself.[58] As Ian Condry has shown, Japanese anime creators are largely character-driven and create characters that they become emotionally connected with, like friends:

In the case of anime, it is seldom narrative coherence—the story—that provides the link across media. Rather, it is the characters. In this respect, anime can deepen our understanding of media anthropology in part because of the blurred boundaries between media on the screen, whether packaged, broadcast, theatrically released or streamed on the Internet, and the emergent potential of character-related businesses and activities later, from lucrative licensing deals with pachinko manufacturers to such non-commercial fan uses as cosplay (dressing in costume as one's favourite character).[59]

Figure 5: Two male cosplayers photographed crossplaying at
Hong Kong university event (2012). © Anne Peirson-Smith.

The fascination with fictional characters flows from producer to consumer turned
prosumer.[60] It is also possible to see the popular cultural circulation of fictional characters
in anime, manga, comics and cartoons as part of inexorable media convergences and
communal modes of reception of characters and narratives.[61] Across platforms, fans engage
with media content for their particular use and gratification,[62] to bring it to life and reach
beyond its textual existence. As with many popular cultural forms, the reification of the
image is arguably more important than the commodified object and becomes the source of
affect that flows across a socially mediated universe that spans cultures.

This may help to account for why character persona rather than the storyline is a central
focus of cosplay dress-up activity. Creators and players often activate their practice starting
with a character. Practitioners and hobbyist-fans across the globe, when asked about their
cosplay choices, often elaborate with enthusiasm on the finer details of their character and
the profound admiration they espouse for them, as opposed to contextualizing this purely
within a compelling storyline. This characterological affinity, for example, was found in
field research to be a motivator for fans of the *Harry Potter* (1997–2007) books in Hong
Kong and China, who compared their own characteristics and personalities with the literary
characters and associated them aspirationally with their magical, empowered world.[63]

However, even within Asia there are visible differences in character choice, often guided by societal pressures embedded in anti-Japanese sentiments. In China, for instance, cosers are encouraged by con organizers at the local and national levels to cosplay legendary Chinese figures such as *The Monkey King* or more 'odourless'[64] texts such as *Final Fantasy* (1987–)[65] (odourless in this case meaning that they are not overly contaminated by Japanese cultural traits, from plot elements to the portrayal of characters with large eyes and neutral skin tones). Nevertheless, informants in this region again professed their preference for, and devotion to, Japanese texts and personas. This suggests that even if the characters are made to appear more neutral or culturally proximate by their creators, the country of origin and its positive connotations still remain as a powerful signifier for fans, affecting cosplay preferences.

Interestingly, many anime, manga and game narratives are set in a western or non-Japanese frame such as *Spice and Wolf (Ōkami to Kōshinryō)* (2008)[66] and *Pandora Hearts (Kuroshitsuj)* (2006–15),[67] but the characters always have a distinct aesthetic in terms of their hair or clothes signifying their origin, which for many cosers would seem to be a critical attraction. The costumes can often stereotype nationalities, ethnicities and histories as a pastiche,[68] a form of mimicry highlighting the hedonic pleasures gained from this imaginary experience based on the creation and inhabiting of multifarious imagined communities. At a recent, privately organized Hong Kong event of web-comic-turned manga and anime, *Hetalia: Axis Powers (Hetaria Akushisu Pawāzu)* (2010),[69] the 200 attendees all dressed as characters representing different regions around the world, based on their chosen character's personality profile. As cosplayer Toby with a group of respondents explained:

Figure 6: A team of cosplayers perform *Final Fantasy V* (1992) on stage at the China Joy Competition in Beijing (2009). © Anne Peirson-Smith.

We are all APH characters and come from different regions around the world—and there are some others keep being added. It's set during the Second World War when these nations are struggling for power and it's quite historic and military in a way with the axis power countries of Germany, Japan and Italy against the allied countries of Britain, America and Russia. Each character represents a nation so I represent Germany because the character is attractive to me as he is serious and sort of handsome with blond hair and blue eyes and is the one trying to make the countries work together. This one represents New Zealand and she is Hong Kong. We all carry flags of those countries to show our nationality off and we study the personality of the character very much and then chose one type that we find attractive.

(Toby, 20, male student, Hong Kong)

Nevertheless, the ethnicity of the characters was not always discernible, other than perhaps in the variations in the colour of wigs, with blond hair representing the mythic Anglo-Saxon heritage and a punk hairstyle signifying the British persona. At the same APH event, a

Figure 7: An individual cosplayer as the character France in the *Hetalia: Axis Powers (2009)* European Cosplay event in Hong Kong poses in front of a poster of the same anime featuring the character (2010). © Anne Peirson-Smith.

17-year-old boy wearing a Uniqlo *Star Wars* t-shirt and jeans was bemused to be invited on stage in front of the 200 assembled cosplayers after winning the lucky draw for a box of customized anime illustrated cola bottles, with the crowd responding wildly. 'Ahh it's so amazing!' exclaimed a female dressed as France with stylish blue and gold frogged cape, red pantaloons, brown buckled boots and nut brown flowing locks. 'It's as if Britain has come alive here today—this is magic and a lucky day for us all and it adds to our pleasure!' Afterwards, cosplayers representing all nationalities queued up to have a photograph taken with him as if to heighten the intensity of the mimicked cosplay experience or pastiche moment.

Glocalized production centres

The creative skills necessary to plan and compile outfits and their component parts, including accessories such as wigs and coloured contact lenses, is an intrinsic part of the cosplay process—from designing, sourcing, drawing, cutting and sewing to prop making. This craft-based, creative endeavour appears consistently to be undertaken in the interests of creating an authentic re-presentation of the character where attention to detail is essential:

> My cosplay characters [...] have a deep meaning for me and I spend hours getting this right from planning to the end point of the event. I breathe life into my characters so the outfit has to be perfect—down to the sword and the wig and the eye colour achieved though coloured lenses. It's disrespectful to the character of say Gundam or Boba Fett and the creator of the original game or anime if you don't do this.
>
> (Jett, 20, male cosplayer, Macau)

Creativity in cosplay is the subject of the next chapter, but the role of craft consumption is in evidence here. In some cases the product concerned is essentially both made and designed by the same person, and is thus a process to which the prosumer typically brings skill, knowledge, judgement and passion,[70] while being 'motivated by a desire for self-expression.'[71] In this sense, a coser could be regarded as 'a self-conscious manipulator of the symbolic meanings that are attached to products, someone who selects goods with the specific intention of using them to create or maintain a given impression, identity or lifestyle.'[72]

Arguably, wherever and whenever cosplay occurs it involves the transubstantiation of knowledge and a passion for turning a mediated object with symbolic meaning into a form of material representation as a display of creative skill. The cosplayer represents an active prosumer engaged in an activity in which

> individuals not merely exercise control over the consumption process, but also bring skill, knowledge, judgment, love and passion to their consuming in much the same way that it has always been assumed that traditional craftsmen and craftswomen approach their work.[73]

Here the cosplayer does not just take possession of their chosen character, but also invests it with their own personal interpretation, re-contextualizing the commodity and transmuting it into a 'potentially inalienable culture'[74] shared by the cosplay community itself:

> For me it's all is about improving your craft and it's a development process. When I started out six years ago I just did simple stuff like *Sailor Moon* and now I'm doing *Amano Girl* which is a much more complex costume with a dramatic blond wig unlike my black hair and I just keep improving my craft by just doing it.
>
> (Mini, 22, female student, Hong Kong)

However, differences emerge in terms of the ability to access materials to create a costume. There is a universal recognition that the resources of time and money critical to the endeavour are not always evenly accessible. Cosplayers in Hong Kong, Macau and China are located close to the sources of raw materials and global centres of production, enabling them to create their costumes in shorter time frames and at lower cost. This results in Asian cosplayers having more outfits and placing a high value on replicating a perfect outfit. By contrast, cosers interviewed in North America or the United Kingdom often lamented the reverse situation, explaining how they often had to improvise when they were unable to access certain materials. Some, however, are starting to use 3D printing services to make costumes and props, while others order costumes from online sites with a view to further DIY customization. As a consequence, they tended to regard their costumes as a work in progress, unlike their Asian counterparts who aim for a flawless ensemble each time. As one respondent said:

Figure 8: Cosplayers as *Final Fantasy V* (1995) characters assist each other in getting ready for ChinaJoy cosplay competition in Beijing (2009). © Anne Peirson-Smith.

I can't always get the materials to make my characters as I would like to do but it is amazing what can be done by customizing and recycling household materials and anything that I can get my hands on—charity shops can be useful in that way too. And there is always someone online with advice to offer a useful demo of how to make that material work into a costume. You just have to be very resourceful and get it as close as you can knowing that you can improve on it next time.

(Tammi, 20, female student, United Kingdom)

Here, the process and practice of playing became the focal point for those located outside of Asia, with a considerable amount of improvisation in the DIY process of making or customizing costumes bought online. Nevertheless, on cosplay forums such as Cosplay.com, CosplayLab and dedicated YouTube channels, there is a sense of a supportive global community offering all manner of advice, from costume construction to obtaining materials and accessories off and online. This feedback and advice provides the sense of a globally networked cosplay tutorial system representing the flow of shared knowledge capital across the cos-scape.

Fan geographies and cosplay kinships

Globally, cosplay can be considered as a form of 'participatory' fandom. This is supported by Henry Jenkin's point that a growing number of 'active' or 'participatory' fans[75] are exhibiting a sense of ownership, involving an investment in the creative activity and development of a fan-fuelled universe.[76] As consecrating agents[77] fans often possess detailed insider knowledge and contribute to the symbolic value of their fan practice, while also evaluating the symbolic capital of creative producers. Fans as active cultural agents share three main features in their engagement with a chosen fan universe: a predisposition for close textual reading; the creation of 'folk culture' based on the selection and appropriation of texts, discourses and images; and in addition the utilization of technology as a basis for consumer activism.[78] These variations largely pertain to the global manifestation of cosplay practice, yet there are local variants subject to cultural and background influences.

While each of these characteristics is consistently evident in cosplay, there are differences in how they manifest themselves. Though some specialized knowledge of the character source—manga and anime, film, music band or online game—is a given, this operates on a sliding scale often dictated by cultural circumstance. Cosplayers in Asia have grown up immersed in manga and anime from an early age. While this is now true for many non-Asian cosers, others may have had to actively seek it out, sometimes literally translating content into their own language through the fan practice of 'subbing' (subtitling video content).[79] While this situation does not impact substantially on knowledge capital or connoisseurship among cosers, it does suggest that they are informed in different ways, which may further heighten the desire for fandom[80] and the need to turn knowledge into an experiential moment.

159

Along with such mediascapes, late capitalism's technoscapes are also hugely important.[81] Clearly, technological engagement has also transformed the cosplay experience, in line with many fan communities contributing to its global spread. Yet again, the engagement on social media sites and online generally—in terms of sharing images and advice—varies across place and space. This ranges from the limited scope in countries such as China, where communication is tightly controlled, to the relatively limitless opportunities for connecting with fans online across a range of multi-platforms in other parts of Asia and around the world.

The motivations for cosplay across the globe conform to the universals of having fun through creating costumes and dressing up in character among a collective of like-minded players. Most informants from Hong Kong, Beijing, Singapore, New York, Dallas, Melbourne and London agree that the activity has both a personal and a group dimension. The sharing aspect seems important, in that it reflects the value of teamwork and group-play involved, particularly for those who need to enact scripted scenes together from, for example, the *Star Wars* franchise, to ensure that the character costumes align with each other:

We meet every week in the run up to the events to plan our outfits and accessories like our light sabers and helmets which are critical for the Clone Troopers and Darth Vader. We have all been working on the light sabers for two years now and they are getting better which is satisfying. We also practice our moves too because although we don't act out scenes at events we do need to act like the troopers or Luke Skywalker has to use his light saber properly like a real Jedi knight or there's no point to doing it.

(Grant, 27, male electronic engineer, Hong Kong and United States)

In conversation with respondents, again, the concept of love for the character (*moe*) that they are 'cosing' and, often, the original manga and anime source appeared to be paramount, with deep affective display as a key motivator in parallel with other fandom phenomena.[82]

I love this character Hermione from *Harry Potter* deeply—she makes me feel strong as a girl and you can see how much effort I've placed into making the costume and it goes deep. I also love being at these events and feel so good being with people who really understand why we need to do this and what the benefits are in our lives.

(Tina, 20, female student, United Kingdom)

The notion of the existence and importance of the 'cosplay family' also emerged strongly among the Asian cosers as a metaphor for validating their practice and as a way of legitimizing their actions. This may be because family values are strong in Asia, yet it could also be a manifestation of latent social issues. Young people in Asia are often collectively enfolded in the safety of their peer group friendships, the social norm in a region where children spend more time with friends than family, as traditional Asian values are shifting in post-industrialized centres such as Hong Kong. In other respects, this may be seen as an escapist trend for young adults to turn to popular culture's sci-fi manga and anime fantasy worlds as a refuge from the pressure cooker of urban life. In this fantasy world, a sense of belonging and the self become invested in re-mediated characters. Such a connection to a potentially outsider culture, however, is often at odds with traditional values, as embodied in the *kawaii* ('cute') demeanour, for example. Certainly, some of the informants confided that they had to persuade their parents of the social benefits of cosplay, and demonstrate that it did not interfere with their schoolwork or career plans.

It may also be possible to see cosplay involvement as a rite of passage, or even as a way of maturing and forging an individual identity. Growing up amid the constraints of Hong Kong's crowded housing estates, cramped urban places and residential spaces, and being all the while subjected to the highly pressurized expectations of school and workplace, it may be no surprise that these young cosplayers look outwards and escape to fantastic universes. Cosplay also provides a way of connecting with the fictional friends that they have made through the many hours of reading manga and watching anime TV shows over the years, and with whom they have possibly spent more active time than their 'real' family. Clearly, wherever it takes root cosplay is not a solitary but an overtly social activity, with the support of peers acting as a validating audience. Hence, there is a common duality observed in cosplay. On one side, the individual coser is presenting his or her secret or private self through a re-presentation of chosen character, yielding an intrinsic experience through a change of identity. On the other, the channelling of the character is only validated in the presence of the collective of others—players, helpers, friends, fans, spectators, hobby photographers—and is further extended into the digital domain via selective image sharing.

Locational protocols and spatial settings

Variation in how cosplay is performed is further determined both regionally across Asia and globally by the specific locales where it occurs. There is a sense of more serious, formal cosplay activity taking place across Asia, while players in non-Asian centres appeared to be more relaxed in their approach. As a measure of this, one female cosplayer reflected that, having left Hong Kong to pursue a university degree in America, she had found an alternative world to replace the cosplay universe that she had inhabited in Hong Kong, based on her own cross-cultural exposure and her acquired ability for cultural accommodation:

I cosplay both in California and Hong Kong when I come back in the summer after my university studies to see my family. I'm not really into the scene here as I used to be when I was younger and starting out—I was an early adopter then. Now many of my friends have left or moved on with their hobbies and interests. Me too as I have changed. And cosplay is different now—it's much more competitive in Hong Kong to present a totally perfect self—the make-up, costumes, the total look all have to be completely perfect or you feel that you are not really doing it properly [...]. But in the U.S. things are much more relaxed and there is less pressure because when you cosplay there it's just accepted if everything is just ok and you've made some effort. That's more how I feel these days. I can see that it's about the fun of getting together with friends, sharing interests and enjoying that moment without stressing out.

(Clara, 24, female student, Hong Kong and North America)

Evidence of comparative approaches to cosplaying also emerged in conversation with a Dutch cosplayer visiting the Jingu Bashi (Harajuku Bridge) area in Tokyo once synonymous with cosplay, though in actuality the scene has since moved on:

I'm here dressed as Reimi today, an archer from the game *Star Ocean*, and it's a great feeling to be in Tokyo like it's ground zero for all of this special culture that we admire from Europe. But what I've noticed is that things are taken much more seriously here in Japan, not just in getting that perfect outfit and your presence must appear totally right, but also how you play the character as the posing has to be good too. There's also not much laughter going on here either unlike my experiences of the Comic-Cons in America where people make lot of noise and fool around. It's just a different way of doing things but with everything really I see big time differences of culture and that also applies to cosplaying.

(Jayna, 23, female designer, Netherlands)

These comments also suggest that the rules, norms and values of cosplay will vary according to the cultural location in which it is being practiced. Moreover, there is an accepted notion of cultural difference in how it is played out in various locations. Such differences also can be found in inter-Asian settings, where cosplay as a fun activity shows variances in the type and form of play, becoming a measure of the varied value systems in place across the region, and the different manifestations of power relations on display between cosplayers and institutional actors.

Both the unstructured style of play (paida) and the more structured (ludic) type discussed in the previous chapter can be differentiating factors in the form cosplay takes in the Greater China region. Given the relatively liberal economics, quasi-democratic leanings and postcolonial heritage of Hong Kong and Macau, there is a concomitantly open type of play based on the free choice and wide range of source material that cosers present at public conventions, university anime and manga society events, cosplay cafés or in private get-togethers. Meanwhile, cosers in Tokyo traditionally converged at Harajuku Bridge to 'play' in a different manner. Here they arranged themselves in a free-form way, clustering territorially in small groups in the corners of the open public area, redolent of cliques forming in the school playground having little active connection with each other. The boundaries here operate as a meeting zone, a tourist attraction and a cultural showcase of soft power. These factors do not, however, always elide harmoniously. Recently, the Harajuku Bridge scene has suffered precipitous decline as cosplayers have been put off by the intensity of tourist and media focus on their activities.

Figure 9: A team of three cosplayers gather at Harajuku Bridge, Tokyo (2009). © Anne Peirson-Smith.

In mainland China, cosplay space must contend with different challenges. Content and structure are more ritualized and controlled by ludic rules. Events are organized by the authorities or private operators centring on competitive, regionally based, local government-run or large commercialized events, such as the China Joy national and regional competitions. The prohibitions against Japanese source media have already been mentioned. In addition, the nature of play is also more structured, taking the form of a well-rehearsed skit honed over months of planning, with the group composing soundtrack and script to be played out as a competitive staged performance before a panel of judges. Agency is negotiated between the cosers and the authorities, who recently banned 'overly revealing' costumes in the puritanical interest of preserving moral values at the 2015 China Joy competition.[83] By contrast, in Hong Kong and Macau, forms of social regulation are limited to negative media coverage of cosplay, discouraging some youth from getting involved on the basis that it allegedly wastes time and money, or where parents only grant permission to cosplay if their children secure good school grades, due to the focus on academic attainment as a form of individual and familial progress in many Asian cultures.

With these caveats in mind, the relatively open culture of cosplay in most geographic locales is apparent in the social settings chosen for this activity. As Ellen Kirkpatrick observes: 'Cosplay can happen automatically, anywhere and at any time—it is not limited to convention halls or cosplay parties and gatherings.'[84] Yet there are fine-grained local differences in terms of where it occurs, as noted above, and in the ways that the activity is played out. Cityscapes become the site of leisure or activity systems where individuals and groups can engage in expressive, cultural scenes[85] for photo taking and posing in character, which also maps in various ways onto a city, as suggested in Chapter 2 in relation to the Seattle Sakura-con. Indeed, conventions globally are often considered safe havens for cosplayers to perform with a level of confidence engendered by relatively supportive and responsive audiences.

Again, there are levels of usage of these prescribed spaces in which to perform cosplay, as Nicole Lamerichs notes,[86] from lobby photo-shoots to fashion shows, cosplay competitions and skits. There is also an observable difference within Asia and beyond, in terms of where cosplay takes place and what cosers are comfortable with in their choice of play locations. This highlights the various mobilities of the players themselves as they traverse the cityscape or even the globe to attend events and cons in different locations. Cosers adopt urban spatial settings by manipulating and aligning place as an extension of costuming, and as a space for creative expression and performed identity. The draw for a city-based youth demographic in appropriating urban spaces for their personal leisure time may also be compounded by the need to find a refuge that affords a physical and psychological outlet from the stresses of life in the cramped living and working spaces of densely populated urban settings.

While cosplayers interviewed in Hong Kong and Macau, for example, did admit to dressing up and practicing character poses at home, in the secret spaces of their bedroom or at small, private events, most tended to appropriate the public spaces of the city in private meetings, in a group or as part of a larger event. Backdrops that mimic the manga and anime/comic book or cartoon settings themselves can be particularly important in framing the play experience, in terms of the look, feel and *mise-en-scène* of the storyworld that the character inhabits.[87] Hence, for photo shoots and private meets, Hong Kong cosers often seek out older buildings, such as disused Second-World-War troop barracks, or choose fantastical locations, such as Hong Kong Disneyland. As one informant explained:

We sometimes book a hotel room at Disneyland and it is the perfect location for us as we wear our costumes and can be photographed in the amazing locations and settings like a film set—the maze, the raging river, the castle—and so we feel transported to another world just like our characters in the game or series—this makes them really come to life. If we wear costumes from *Rozen Maiden* for example, we look like Disney Princesses and visitors there think that we are employed there so we do let people have photos with us there.

(Kitty, 22, female office worker, Hong Kong)

Cosplay may not be permissible in other theme parks globally and cosplayers in Hong Kong are discreet about where they display their costumes, many preferring the more secluded location of the Disney hotel and its private gardens and maze. The notion of a 'symbolic pilgrimage'[88] within cultural geographies is useful here, whereby people can symbolically visit places and spaces through print, broadcast or digital technology, or in the realms of their imagination. But cosplay represents an extension of this in appropriating physical spaces that often approximate the imaginary or hyper-real settings represented in the original texts on account of their aesthetic, sociocultural or historical value.

Significantly, manga and anime creators are on record as having been drawn to particular cultural settings for their stories, with the anime series creator of *Emma: A Victorian Romance* (*Eikoku Koi Monogatari Emma*) (2006–08),[89] Kaori Mori, for example, claiming direct inspiration from English Victorian architecture and design. These transnational borrowings, as Rayna Denison suggests, create an attractive make-believe scenario that anime and manga fans—and cosplayers by extension—wish to inhabit through active engagement with the text:

> Playing into the first category of branded Englishness, this borrowed iconography lifts details from English history and re-imagines them in this anime as part of an overtly consumerist discursive repertoire. For example, in *Emma* differences in households are represented through numbers of servants and the types of beverages served to visitors. Moreover, shopping, as pastime for the rich, and job for servants, is frequently depicted in *Emma*, which includes lingering sequences in antiques stores, department stores, markets and other sites of consumption.[90]

Such hyper-real settings offer a re-imagined world for its users or fans: an imaginary sphere that cosers also try to re-create and inhabit when seeking out historic backdrops for their activity and photo shoots.

As a further extension of imagined tourism, the cultural landmarks used in manga and anime narrative settings potentially increase the desire to replicate the character in situ, enhancing the authenticity of the play, as with any performance. For example, a popular Asian cosplay character, demonic butler Sebastian Michelis from the manga *Black Butler* (*Kuroshitsuji*) (2008–09),[91] usually serves his aristocratic master, detective Ciel Phantomhive, high tea and cakes from high-end English grocer, Fortnum and Mason. Meanwhile, the mythic Crystal Palace site is also used in *Emma*, as according to Rayna Denison it 'provides an easily nostalgized, romanticized and "othered" space in which the central romance can unfold. The Crystal Palace is, therefore, simultaneously familiar and unfamiliar as an inaccessible, past world space.'[92] It is also pertinent that this was the historic site of London's Great Exhibition in 1851 and the showcasing of Japanese culture in the western domain, pre-figuring the resumption of international trade with Japan in 1868.[93]

This underlines how the shared practice of cosplay often, and even preferably, takes place in a community of visitors immersed in fantastical places to extend the experience beyond the confines of the bland, corporatized convention hall that will be captured

Figure 10: Two cosplayers as Hanabusa Aido from *Vampire Knight* (2000) and Sebastian Michaelis from *Black Butler* (2008–09) at Hong Kong University Cosplay event (2011). © Anne Peirson-Smith.

photographically. Consequently, cosplaying communities can be understood in terms of Appadurai's ethnoscapes, defined as 'the landscape of persons who constitute the shifting world in which we live.'[94] Cosplayers are, in this sense, one of those 'other moving groups' of late capitalism, alongside tourists, immigrants, refugees, exiles and guest workers in the globalized world.[95] Yet at the same time, these shifting communities of cosplayers appropriate sites of cosplay performance, even if the ultimate control of the spaces in which cosplay occurs is in the hands of hegemonic powers. Cosers often evaluate events in online chat forums or in conversation in situ based on the aesthetics or atmosphere of the cosplay performance setting, which also points to the ways in which this cosplay practice is constructed and negotiated through and against recognized connoisseurial standards.

Public display of this type is often discouraged and uncommon in China, however, further highlighting geographic differences in practice, and thus the varied opportunities for negotiated hegemonic responses and performative interpretations. Nevertheless, research fieldwork in Beijing conducted in 2009 revealed that one group of local cosplayers regularly chose historic locations in the city for their photo-shoots, such as the 798 Art District, complete with its derelict 1950s East German-designed electronics factory warehouses and rusting old steam train. The transgressive aspects of their activity enhanced the 'liminal/ liminoid' experience,[96] as this ad hoc way of playing is not sanctioned on the Mainland. Yet the players relished recording the visually incongruous juxtaposition of the formalist architectural setting with their spectacular cartoon costumes—ironically, alongside couples taking wedding photos. As a Beijing based photographer/cosplayer elaborated:

> What we are doing is not really allowed but it is worth the risk because the setting is so perfect for our purposes because the light is good the mood of the old factory is dark and dramatic and it turns our work into real art which is also another reason for doing it, and that makes us happy and gain respect for us from others who are not part of it.
>
> (Fran, 22, female student, China)

Overall, the global recognition of cosplay as a performance art form dependent on a space in which to display it is also a unifying theme, given the accomplishments of cosers in

Figure 11: An individual cosplayer as vocaloid character Hatsune Miku from the song '1925' (2009) in a private photo shoot at 798 Art District, Beijing, for an atmospheric photographic backdrop (2010). © Anne Peirson-Smith.

creating their spectacular outfits and capturing them in photos or on videos shared across social media platforms. As Craig Norris and Jason Bainbridge note: 'In its purest form cosplay is akin to performance art, taking on the habitus of a particular character through costume, accessories, gesture and attitude; it is therefore not simply "dressing up" but rather inhabiting the role of a character both physically and mentally.'[97] This framing of cosplay as performance art may also contribute to recognized standards of practice that can enable validation, yet at the same time might exclude those who transgress the rules or fail to match up to set standards or expectations. A global response appears to emerge from dialogue with other fan communities who noted the downside of becoming obsessed with the perfect image. Over-critical comments about misaligned body image or sub-standard costuming were a troubling trend, heightened by the ease of posting such commentary on social media.

In summary, the multiple transnational and transcultural journeys that cosplay involves cover those of individual self-discovery and identity formation, across cultures, geographic localities and online sites. It also traverses personal cognitive and affective spaces in exploring and reforming identities based on derivative work. Technology may accelerate these globalized cultural flows, creating a sense of placelessness with fluid identities as a precursor for textual play that is founded on reworked material styles and visual forms

Figure 12: A group of three female cosplayers perform at Melbourne Comic-Con as the White Queen, Red Queen and Alice from *Alice in Wonderland* (anime version, 2010) (2012). © Anne Peirson-Smith.

that are expressions of consumer culture and commodity fetishism. These are imagined communities beyond Benedict Anderson's notion of the national, operating at a supranational level. Overall, there appear to be more commonalities than otherwise among cosplayers globally in their core motivations, dressing-up activities and performance—rooted as these are in a common visual language of character play where the individual 're-forms' identity within a public, collective setting based on affective connections.

As cosplay finds expression in various regions and localities across transitional, transcultural and transmediated global circuits, there are also commonalities seen in the motivations underlying the dress-up practice based on shared interests driven by desire. Although the focus here has been largely on Asian cosplayers, it would seem that the differences are rooted in local cultural tendencies, levels of engagement with consumerism and choice of play locations. They may also, however, be administered ideologically by external structures such as media, government and parents. Technology, and the social media platforms it supports, can itself be hegemonic, but its availability has also assisted this heterogeneity and enabled greater access to knowledge sharing, as well as access to the cultural commodities that bring cosplay to life.[98] This has established a transcultural, borderless community—or globally distributed ethnoscape—which is able to communicate in the common lingua franca of a cosplay discourse based on recognizable images, characters, costumes, settings and narratives. At the same time, the formation of digital cosplay networks has given rise to the universal pressures of attaining high standards by which cosplayers are judged in their re-creation of mediated sources, especially online, whatever their geographical setting. In re-mediating popular culture sources and images by bringing fictional characters to life in costume, cosers are constantly crossing the borders of self to other, and as such are always in a state of transition.

Notes

1   Ulf Hanertz, *Cultural Complexity: Studies in the Social Organization of Meaning* (New York: Columbia University Press, 1992), 218.
2   Philip Crang, Claire Dwyer and Peter Jackson, 'Transnationalism and the Spaces of Commodity Culture', *Progress in Human Geography* 27, no. 4 (2003), 438–39.
3   Thomas Friedman, *The World Is Flat: A Brief History of the 21st Century* (New York: Farrar, Strauss and Giroux, 2005), 78.
4   Arjun Appadurai, 'Introduction: Commodities and the Politics of Value,' in *The Social Life of Things: Commodities in Cultural Perspective*, ed. Arjun Appadurai (Cambridge: Cambridge University Press, 1986), 5.
5   Arjun Appadurai, 'Disjuncture and Difference in the Global Cultural Economy,' *Theory Culture Society* 7 (1990), 297.
6   Anne Peirson-Smith, 'Fashioning the Fantastical Self: An Examination of the Cosplay Dress-up Phenomenon in Southeast Asia,' *Fashion Theory* 17, no. 1 (2012), 77–78.

7 Michel Mafessoli, *The Time of the Tribes: The Decline of Individualism in Mass Society* (London: Sage, 1996), 10–11.

8 A. Michael Hubermann, Matthew B. Miles, and Johnny Saldana, *Qualitative Data Analysis*, 3rd ed. (Thousand Oaks: Sage Publications, 2014), 69–75.

9 Paul Willis, 'Notes on Method,' in *Culture, Media, Language*, eds. Stuart Hall, Dorothy Hobson, Andrew Lowe, and Paul Willis (London: Hutchinson, 1980), 88–95, 91.

10 Valerie Hansen, *The Silk Road: A New History* (Oxford: Oxford University Press, *The Silk Road*, 2012), 5.

11 Koichi Iwabuchi, 'Introduction: Cultural Globalization and Asian Media Connection,' in *Feeling Asian Modernities: Transnational Consumption of Japanese TV Dramas*, ed. Koichi Iwabuchi (Hong Kong: University of Hong Kong Press, 2004), 27.

12 Junita Kawamura, 'Japanese Teens as Producers of Street Fashion,' *Current Sociology* 54 (2006), 785–86.

13 Seiko Yasumoto, 'Korean Wave: Towards Regional Cultural Diffusion,' *Journal of Literature and Art Studies* 3, no. 2 (February 2012), 102.

14 Ackbar Abbas, *Hong Kong: Culture and the Politics of Disappearance* (Minneapolis: University of Minnesota Press, 1997), 4–5.

15 Beng Huat Chua, *Structure, Audience and Soft Power in East Asian Pop Culture* (Hong Kong: Hong Kong University Press, HKU, 2004), 9.

16 Koichi Iwabuchi, *Recentering Globalization: Popular Culture and Japanese Transnationalism* (Durham, NC: Duke U.P., 2002), 122.

17 Koichi Iwabuchi, 'Uses of Japanese Popular Culture: Trans/nationalism and Postcolonial Desire for "Asia,"' *Emergences: Journal for the Study of Media & Composite Cultures* 11, no. 2 (2001), 199–200.

18 Roland Kelts, *Japanamerica: How Japanese Pop Culture Has Invaded the U.S.* (New York: Palgrave Macmillan, 2006), 5.

19 Ibid., 6.

20 Anne Allison, 'Sailor Moon: Japanese Superheroes for Girls,' in *Japan Pop! Inside the World of Japanese Popular Culture*, ed. Timothy J. Craig (New York: M.E. Sharpe, 2000), 259–78.

21 Sharon Kinsella, *Adult Manga: Culture and Power in Contemporary Japanese Culture* (Honolulu: University of Hawaii Press, 2000).

22 Frederic L. Schodt, *Dreamland Japan: Writings on Modern Manga* (Berkeley, CA: Stone Bridge Press, 2011), 190.

23 Tze-yu G. Hu, 'Animating for Whom in the Aftermath of a World War,' in *Japanese Animation: East Asian Perspectives*, eds. Masao Yokota and Tze-yu G. Hu (Jackson: University Press of Mississippi, 2013), 128–129.

24 Peirson-Smith, 'Fashioning the Fantastical Self,' 82.

25 Benjamin Wai-ming Ng, 'Street Fighter and the King of Fighters in Hong Kong: A Study of Cultural Consumption and Localization of Japanese Games in an Asian Context,' *Game Studies* 6, no.1 (2006), 1–20, accessed 1 January 2018, http://gamestudies.org/articles.

26 Laura Orsini, *Cosplay: The Fantasy World of Role Play* (New York: Carlton Books, 2015), 8–9.

27 Bisco Hatori, *Ouran High School Host Club (Ōran Kōko Hostu Kurabu)* (Tokyo: Hakusensha, 2002–10).

28 Appadurai, 'Disjuncture and Difference,' 299.

29 Henry Jenkins, *Textual Poachers: Television Fans and Participatory Culture* (New York: Routledge, 1992), 1–5.

30 Matthew Hale, 'Cosplay: Intertextuality, Public Texts, and the Body Fantastic,' *Western Folklore* 73, no.1 (2014), 10.

31 Ibid., 10.

32 Ibid., 12.

33 Edward Said, *Orientalism* (London: Vintage Books, 1978), 4–5.

34 Mark Holborn *Beyond Japan* (London: Barbican Art Gallery Publications, 1991), 18.

35 Anne Allison, 'The Attraction of the J-Wave for American Youth,' in eds. Wantanabe Yakushi and David L McConnell, *Soft Power Superpowers: Cultural and National Assets of Japan and the United States* (London/New York: Routledge, 2015), 99–110.

36 Roland Barthes, *The Empire of Signs,* trans. Richard Howard (1970; New York: The Noonday Press, 1982), 48–55.

37 *Beginning Life as a God (Kamisama Hajimemashita)*, Julietta Suzuki (Tokyo: Hakusensha, 2008–2016), Anime TV series.

38 Koichi Iwabuchi, 'Complicit exoticism: Japan and its other,' *The Australian Journal of Media & Culture* 8, no.2 (1994), 49–82.

39 Frenchy Lunning, 'Cosplay,' in *Berg Encyclopedia of Dress and Fashion, Vol. 10—Global Perspectives,* ed. Joanna B. Eicher (2011), accessed 1 January 2018, http://www.bergfashionlibrary.com/view/bewdf/BEWDF-v10/EDch10024.xml .

40 Orsini, *Cosplay,* 11.

41 Brian Ashcraft and Luke Plunkett, *Cosplay World* (Munich: Prestel, 2014), 9.

42 Frederik L. Schodt, *Dreamland Japan: Writings on Modern Manga* (Berkeley: Stonebridge Press, 1996), 24–26.

43 Kelts, *Japanamerica*, 43.

44 Joseph S. Nye, 'Foreword,' in *Soft Power Superpowers: Cultural and National Assets of Japan and the United States,* eds. Wantanabe Yakushi and David L. McConnell (London and New York: Routledge, 2015), 4–10.

45 Lane Crothers, 'Cultural Imperialism,' in *The SAGE Handbook of Globalization,* vol. 1, eds. Manfred Steger, Paul Battersby, and John Siracusa (London: Sage, 2014), 166–67, 166–78.

46 Armand Mattelart, Ariel Dorfman, and David Kunzle, *How to Read Donald Duck: Imperialist Ideology in the Disney Comic* (New York: International General Publications, 1975), 20–28.

47 James L. Watson, *Golden Arches East: McDonald's in East Asia* (Stanford: Stanford University Press, 1997), 5–6.

48 Micky Lee and Anthony Y. H. Fung, 'One Region, Two Modernities: Disneyland in Hong Kong and Tokyo,' in *Asian Popular Culture: The Global (Dis)continuity,* ed. Anthony Y. H. Fung (New York: Routledge, 2004), 42–58.

49 Appadurai, *The Social Life of Things*, 3–63.

50 *Hatsune Miku V4X Bundle* (Chūōku, SPK, Japan: Crypton Future Media, 2007–), Computer game.

51 Alvin Toffler, *The Third Wave: The Classic Study of Tomorrow* (New York: Bantam Press, 1980); George Ritzer and Nathan Jurgenson, 'Production, Consumption, Prosumption,' *Journal of Consumer Culture* 10, no. 1 (2010), 13–36.

52 Koichi Iwabuchi, '"Soft" Nationalism and Narcissism: Japanese Popular Culture Goes Global,' *Asian Studies Review* 26, no. 4 (2002), 447–69; Koichi Iwabuchi, 'Cultural Globalization.'

53 Lunning, 'Cosplay,' n.pag.

54 Iwabuchi, 'Uses of Japanese Popular Culture,' 199–200.

55 Arjun Appadurai, *Modernity at large: Cultural Dimensions of Globalization* (Minneapolis: University of Minnesota Press, 1996), 12.

56 Ibid., 12.

57 Rachel Leng, 'Gender, Sexuality, and Cosplay: A Case Study of Male-to-Female Crossplay,' *The Phoenix Papers: First Edition* (April, 2013), 92.

58 Ian Condry, 'Anime Creativity,' *Theory, Culture & Society* 26, no. 2–3 (2009), 63–139.

59 Ibid., 11.

60 See Ritzer and Jurgenson, 'Production, Consumption, Prosumption,' 13–14; Katherine K. Chen, 'Artistic Prosumption: Cocreative Destruction at Burning Man,' *American Behavioral Scientist* 56, no. 4 (April, 2012), 571.

61 Henry Jenkins, *Convergence Cultures: Where Old and New Media Collide* (New York: New York University Press, 2008), 26.

62 Jay G. Blumler and Michael Gurevitch, 'Utilization of Mass Communication by the Individual,' in *The Uses of Mass Communications: Current Perspectives on Gratifications Research*, eds. Jay G. Blumler and Elihu Katz (Beverly Hills: Sage, 1974), 22–25.

63 John Ngyet Erni, 'When Chinese Youth Meet Harry Potter: Translating Consumption and Middle-class Identity,' in *Asian Popular Culture: The Global (Dis)continuity*, ed. Anthony Y. H. Fung (New York: Routledge, 2014), 21–41.

64 Koichi, 'Cultural Globalization,' 1–22.

65 *Final Fantasy*, created by Hironobu Sakaguchi (Tokyo: Square Enix, 1987–).

66 *Spice and Wolf* (*Ōkami to Kōshinryō*), directed by Takeo Takahashi (Tokyo: Imagin Studio, Madman Entertainment, Chiba TV, Funimation Channel, 2008), Anime TV series.

67 Jun Mochizuki, *Pandora Hearts (Kuroshitsuj)*, in *Monthly GFantasy* (Tokyo: Square Enix/ Yen Press, 2006–15), Manga.

68 Richard Dyer, *Pastiche* (London: Routledge, 2007), 415–20.

69 *Hetalia: Axis Powers (Hetalia Akushizu Pawāzu)*, directed by Bob Shirohata (Tokyo: Studio Deen, Madmen Entertainment, 2010), Film.

70 Will Brooker, *Using the Force: Creativity, Community and Star Wars Fans* (New York: Continuum International Publishing Group, 2002), 4–6.

71 Colin Campbell, 'I Shop therefore I Know that I Am: The Metaphysical Basis of Modern Consumerism,' in *Elusive Consumption: Tracking New Research Perspectives*, eds. Karen M. Ekström and Helene Brembeck (Oxford: Berg, 2004), 23.

72 Ibid., 24.

73 Daniel Miller, *Material Culture and Mass Consumption* (Oxford: Blackwell, 1987), 214.

74 Ibid., 215.

75 Henry Jenkins, *Textual Poachers*, 46.

76 Henry Jenkins, *Fans, Bloggers and Gamers: Exploring Participatory* Culture (New York: New York University Press, 2006), 148.

77 Pierre Bourdieu, 'The Market of Symbolic Goods', in *The Field of Cultural Production: Essays on Art and Literature*, ed. R. Johnson (1971; New York: Columbia University Press, 1993), 112–41).

78 Jenkins, *Textual Poachers*, 278.

79 Patrick W. Galbraith, *The Otaku Encyclopaedia: An Insider's Guide to the Subculture of Cool Japan* (New York: Kodansha Press, 2014), 20–25.

80 Patrick Drazen, *Anime Explosion: The What, Why, & Wow of Japanese Animation* (Berkeley: Stonebridge Press, 2003), vii–xiv.

81 Appadurai, 'Disjuncture and Difference', 297, 299.

82 Matt Hills, *Fan Cultures* (London: Routledge, 2002), 41–43.

83 Eric Liu, 'China Joy Cleavage Crackdown', *CNN.Com* 2015, accessed 1 January 2018, http://edition.cnn.com/2015/05/22/asia/chinajoy-cleavage-crackdown/

84 Ellen Kirkpatrick, 'Toward New Horizons: Cosplay (Re)imagined through the Superhero Genre, Authenticity, and Transformation', *Transformative Works and Cultures* 18, Performance and Performativity in Fandom (2015), para 6.3.

85 Will Straw, 'Cultural Scenes', *Society and Leisure* 21, no. 2 (2014), 411–12.

86 Nicolle Lamerichs, 'Stranger than Fiction: Fan Identity in Cosplay', *Transformative Works and Cultures* 7 (2011), para 2.3.

87 Condry, 'Anime Creativity', 20.

88 Roger C. Aden, *Popular Stories and Promised Lands: Fan Cultures and Symbolic Pilgrimages* (Tuscaloosa: Alabama University Press, 1999), 10.

89 Kaoru Mori, *Emma: A Victorian Romance (Eikoku Koi Monogatari Emma)* (2006–08), in *Monthly Comic Beam* (Tokyo: Enterbrain, 2006–8), Manga.

90 Rayna Denison, 'Transcultural Creativity in Anime: Hybrid Identities in the Production, Distribution, Texts and Fandom of Japanese Anime', *Creative Industries Journal* 3, no. 3 (2011), 227.

91 *Black Butler (Kuroshitsuji)*, directed by Toshiya Shinohara (Tokyo: Madmen Entertainment, Animax, 2008–9), Anime TV series.

92 Denison, 'Transcultural Creativity', 228.

93 Joy Hendry, *The Orient Strikes Back: A Global View of Cultural Display* (Oxford: Berg, 2000), 50–53.

94 Appadurai, 'Disjuncture and Difference', 297.

95 Ibid.

96 Victor Witter Turner, *From Ritual to Theatre: The Human Seriousness of Play* (New York: PFA Publications, 1982), 33–36.

97 Craig Norris and Jason Bainbridge, 'Selling *Otaku*? Mapping the Relationship between Industry and Fandom in the Australian Cosplay Scene', *Intersections: Gender and Sexuality in Asia and the Pacific* 20 (2009), para. 9.

98 Susan J. Napier, *From Impressionism to Anime: Japan as Fantasy and Fan Cult in the Mind of the West* (Houndmills: Palgrave Macmillan, 2007), 149–67.

Chapter 6

Cos/creation

C reativity has many and competing definitions. But from a cultural perspective it can be defined as the ability to articulate a message visually or verbally, in abstract or material form, through the bringing together of previously unconnected ideas and combining them in a unique but relevant way. The creative individual is thus somebody who

> actively seeks new knowledge, who is motivated by curiosity and who wants to achieve something [...]. [L]ifestyle and being in the right place at the right time play a major role in creativity. To know when and where the right time and place indicates that factors outside the creative individual are at play.[1]

Creativity can be used to challenge the status quo and find artistic or personal expression in hybrid, adapted and fantastical cultural forms. Hence, cosplay can be considered as an intrinsically creative practice, bringing together the elements of play and situatedness discussed in the previous two chapters. In this chapter, concepts of and processes underpinning creativity will be addressed, before turning to examine how members of the cosplay community exercise it in devising and presenting their costumed identities. Accounts by cosplayers suggest that through cosplay they transform their everyday selves by drawing on the combined resources of interpretation, co-operation and interaction in the material creation of a spectacular self. The central argument presented here is that cosplay is an illustration of creativity-in-action expressed as a range of activities by individuals and groups operating within a creative and cultural domain. In this sphere, creativity is a collaborative effort that operates as an expression of individual agency and resistance based on cultural appropriation and re-creation.

Creativity defined

Before labelling cosplay as both a site and an expression of creativity, we need to be clear about what we mean by the latter term. Yet defining creativity is not unlike the proverbial game with three blindfolded people describing the elephant. One feeling its trunk declares that it is a snake, the other running their hand along the thick skinned girth of the leg proclaims it to be a large tree, while the third, touching the large, mobile ears assures the others that it is indeed a type of bird. Similarly, creativity has been framed by discipline-specific discourses, from psychology and biology, sociology and anthropology, to critical discourse analysis. Each perspective either subscribes to or dismantles a set of creativity myths that have evolved over time and across cultures. However, they all share an understanding of creativity as a process for generating something unique, original and appropriate to the task in hand; namely, the ability to produce relevant but unexpected connections from different sources of inspiration and modes of thought.

For psychologists, creativity is an individually generated and applied phenomenon, resulting from routine cognitive processes based on sustained effort, aligned with combined conscious and subconscious insights, and is consistently domain specific.[2] The biological take on the subject represents creativity within an evolutionary, Darwinian framework. While not necessarily genetically coded, nor emanating from a particular region of the brain, it is adaptive and is thus neither attributable to mental instability nor necessarily differentiated from the species norm.[3] Anthropologists, by contrast, frame creativity's processes and products firmly in the context of a given culture, and its individualist or collectivist tendencies.[4] The creative artist is thus defined in terms of their contribution to continuing tribal traditions, on the one hand, or to innovative, progressive work on the other. Finally, discourse analytical approaches tend to locate creativity in the realm of language and ideology,[5] suggesting the term is a modern one that has been progressively elaborated by association with governing metaphors such as 'exploration' and 'work.'[6]

Historically, notions of creativity have largely been framed by western-centric, Renaissance, Romantic and modernist takes on artistic expression being seen as the unique preserve of the artist as mythic solitary genius.[7] As Elizabeth Wilson observes of the romantic bohemian myth around which such ideas crystallized:

the idea of the artist as a different *sort of person* from his fellow human beings—is founded on the idea of Artist as Genius developed by the Romantic movement in the wake of the industrial and French revolutions. The romantic genius is the artist against society. He or she embodies dissidence, opposition, criticism of the status quo; these may be expressed politically, aesthetically or in the artist's behaviour and lifestyle. Components of the myth are transgression, excess, sexual outrage, eccentric behavior, outrageous appearance, nostalgia and poverty.[8]

This viewpoint, redolent of Giorgio Vasari's notions of the artist as supreme creator, was largely superseded from the mid-twentieth century on two fronts. First, a more scientific assessment of creativity espoused the cognitive ability to problem-solve based on personality types and traits associated with creativity in the production of creative products.[9] Second, there was a shift from regarding it within an individualist to a collectivist framework, whereby creativity became a collaborative work effort, though neo-liberal discourse continues to ally it with innovative output as a form of cultural production often framed in the context of post-industrial cities in late capitalism.[10] The instrumentalist view of creativity that comes out of this approach regards self-expression as effected within collaborative effort that is geared to maximize original, innovative output in socioeconomic terms.

Other sociocultural approaches to creativity acknowledge the less universal and more grounded interpretations of creative expression by artistic workers seen through the lens of local cultural practices and ways of being and becoming.[11] Acknowledging that creativity is often based on the efforts of an individual within a collective setting, Mikhail Csikszentmihalyi suggests that 'creativity is as much a cultural and social as it is a psychological event. Therefore, what we call creativity is not purely the product of single individuals, but of social systems making judgments about individual's products.'[12] He notes further that the sociocultural preconditions for creativity are based on three components—the individual perspective, the domain and the field. Here the creative environment comprises

a cultural, or symbolic, aspect [...] called the domain; and a social aspect called the field. Creativity is a process that can be observed only at the intersection where individuals, domains, and fields interact [...]. For creativity to occur, a set of rules and practices must be transmitted from the domain to the individual. The individual must then produce a novel variation in the content of the domain. The variation then must be selected by the field for inclusion in the domain.[13]

From a sociocultural perspective, creativity is a socially based process, constructed and regulated by a contextualized, complex social system. This 'field' is populated by cultural intermediaries and powerbrokers located in the circuit of cultural production and consumption.[14] These experts define, judge, support and disseminate creativity and creative works as cultural capital residing in 'knowledge skills, and other cultural acquisitions exemplified by educational or technological qualifications,' in alliance with 'symbolic capital [...] accumulated prestige or honour.'[15] This occurs in addition to, and in connection with, the 'domain' embodying all of the shared conventions, codes, discourses and creative products systemically defining the creative field itself. The creative processes of cosplay can be seen as operating within such a domain, which individual cosplayers can gain access to and become involved with. This also occurs within the process of acquiring rule-based knowledge about cosplay as participants become experts in the mediated cultures that the practice emanates from. Once this information is acquired, the cosplayer processes it, resulting in its application to, and their symbolic and material interpretations of, a freely chosen fictional character from a finite universe of options, subject to the recognition and approval of other members in the field.

The following discussion deploys the latter, sociocultural approach to evaluate the phenomenon of cosplay as a creative activity by recognizing creativity as a collaborative and social phenomenon.[16] This stance assumes that creativity as a process is responsible for producing a range of visually based genres that are expressed multimodally in a given cultural context. They are also dispersed across city spaces by a range of neo-style tribal players.[17] Cosplay challenges the elitist myth of creativity as the sole preserve of the individual artist whose artworks are elevated by the establishment into the benchmarks of a national, aesthetic achievement. It is a case study of how expressions of symbolic creativity are located

Figure 1: Cosplayers at 2013 Hong Kong University cosplay event as characters from *Inu X Boku SS* (2012). First row: Banri Watanuki; Ririchiyo Shirakiin; Banri Watanuki; Ririchiyo Shirakiin (half oni version); Karuta Roromiya (maid version); Karuta Roromiya. Second row: Zange Natsume; Soshi Miketsukami; Soshi Miketsukami; Kagero Shoklin; Nobara Yukinokoji; Rensho Sorinozuka. © Anne Peirson-Smith.

in everyday life, and are collectively driven by 'ordinary' people and their interface with the mediated commodities of popular culture.[18] Given the youth-oriented demographic profile of most cosplayers, this can be usefully framed within the study of youth culture overall, whereby

> young people use, humanize, decorate and invest with meanings their common and immediate life spaces and social practices—personal styles and choice of clothes, selective and active use of music, TV, magazines, decorations of bedrooms; the rituals of romance and subcultural styles; the style, banter and drama of friendship groups, music-making and dance.[19]

Here, meaning is created by youth using popular culture commodities in their own expressive way. By extension, the wider spectrum of contemporary youth cultures—where cosplayers reside alongside, and in distinction to, other neo-style tribes such as Goths or Lolitas—is evidence of appropriated symbolic creativity within the domain of commodity culture.[20]

Cosplayers, unlike street-style tribe members, are not limited to a particular idiom but have the flexibility to dress as one or many of their personal fictional heroes from the narrative reveries of manga, anime, fictional and filmic texts. They can also opt to symbolically 'take their place' in the cast's line-up in the process of making intertextual sense of their own lives. While cosplayers are required by the collective to follow certain rules and guidelines during the creation process (e.g. authentic hair style, costume colour, specific poses, venue policies and common courtesy), there is also latitude for individual interpretation that can be respected by the group. Whether or not predominantly youth-based activities such as cosplay consciously challenge the prevailing ideology of commodity aesthetics through the manipulation of images,[21] which could be interpreted as a creative act of undermining the status quo and challenging the dominant discourse from within, they are evidence of creative participation and performance, performance art or work at play.[22] This runs in stark contrast to what Paul Willis calls 'the myth of the special, creative, individual artist holding out against passive mass consumerism.'[23] Taking this approach, cosplay can be considered

Figure 2: A group of six female cosplayers pose after performing a Japanese song and dance routine at a Hong Kong university cosplay competition (2009). © Anne Peirson-Smith.

as a creative practice in a number of ways: in the adaptation of material and virtual means to create costumes; when organizing and rehearsing; the real-time cosplay performance itself; and both in the actual or virtual creative collaboration of the cosplay community with its individual and team-based performances. As Nicolle Lamerichs suggests, these articulations include 'fandom itself: a discourse that emphasizes fiction, camaraderie, and the art of costume design.'[24] Finally, and crucially, cosers and their associates often record their cosplay persona and share their performances via social media channels.

Cosplay as creative discourse in action

Cosplay exemplifies creative discourse in action. Here, discourse can be defined in its broadest paralinguistic and extralinguistic senses as a form of social action that communicates visually and, in the case of cosplay, in a spectacular, extraordinary way. This is actualized through symbolic borrowings from popular narrative texts and is represented in the crafting of physical artefacts of clothing, accessories and body modification.

The discursive form that cosplay as a visually 'performed genre'[25] takes is multimodal and polysemic.[26] Observations on communicating through mediated forms provide useful insight into the ways in which these social actors are created using material tools. [27] Cosplayers communicate their identity by dressing into their community as an expression of symbolic consumption, using a complex visual vocabulary to express their connection with an assumed identity and create an alignment with a particular cultural perspective—be it the local settings where the cosplay takes place, the consumer culture that underpins the practice or in virtual worlds. In this transformative process, they resist and differentiate themselves from other mainstream ways of dressing and being. On the surface, commonalities exist between cosplay and other forms of dressing up in socially differentiated ways. However, intention is the key differentiator between these and other costumed practices. Isaac Gagné, in his study of Gothic/Lolitas as a linguistic community,[28] shows how hyper-feminine verbal and kinetic language is employed to communicate a 'true self.'[29] Yet the cosplayer's representation of a costumed self appears to go beyond a latent connection with the characters that they are presenting. As Erving Goffman notes, the belief in the part that one is playing is essential to the performance as 'the performer can be fully taken in by his [sic] own act; he can be sincerely convinced that the impression of reality which he stages is the real reality.'[30] These strategies are in contrast to critical views of cosplay as a purely mimetic representation staged in the interests of gaining attention and fame, and thus lacking authenticity.[31]

As seen in previous chapters, since the 1970s, Japanese manga and anime have gained in popularity beyond their point of origin.[32] This is a form of cultural transfer, founded largely on a significant global marketing push by the Japanese animation and publishing houses.[33] It has been offered as a prime example of the soft power emanating from the creative outputs

182

of 'Cool Japan.' Such products have exerted a significant influence on regional comic and animation industries, taking root in the local popular cultural landscape in terms of the narrative content, artwork design and format of these imported cultural products. Tze-yeu Hu explains:

> In Japan, the idea of 'Cool Japan' has also captured the idea of government officials searching for new avenues to reinvigorate a recession-stricken economy. The promotion of Japanese media arts as 'soft power' has become an exciting enterprise in realizing Japan's leadership abroad. Surrounding countries also desire to produce and adapt forms of Japanese animation for domestic use, consumption and even for export motives.[34]

While the Cool Japan brand has faced strong headwinds recently,[35] the soft power located in such cultural exports is not only about creating brand nationalism to boost the cultural economy at a national or structural level.[36] The cosplay phenomenon and its textual sources of inspiration are also located in creative interactions at a micro level whereby fans tap into the character role within the context of a storyline.

Hence, the manga and anime subculture has affected the lives of young consumers who avidly follow these mediated cultural products in places such as Hong Kong, an active importer of Japanese subcultural trends and commercial Japanese products since the 1970s.[37] This suggests a close alliance of predispositions based on shared experiences across demographic groups of young people in Asia and beyond. In effect, the local comic and animation industries' appropriation of these texts, by creating their own versions inspired by the originals, parallels fan based practices such as dubbing and fan-subbing. These borrowings have lent new creative meanings to the original texts, thereby creating derivative yet novel, hybrid cultural products. An example is the incorporation of elements of 'Japanimation' into Hong Kong martial arts, kung fu or *wuxia* (martial arts and chivalry) style comics. As Wai-ming Ng observes: 'Most Asian comic and animation artists are under very strong Japanese influence in terms of drawing, format, atmosphere, perspective, story and plot, and the production system.'[38]

Specifically, the manga and anime industry's expression of hybridized modernity has given rise to various popular cultural forms radiating out from its cultural centres. One example is *dōjinshi*, Japanese amateur comics created by avid manga fans who publish their own artwork globally.[39] Further, the influence of American comics and cartoons on Japanese and Hong Kong cultural output from at least the 1960s is significant, and illustrates the multi-way flow of cultural influence that is typified by cosplay.[40] Cosplay is a creative practice based on the interpretative borrowing and melding of ideas with physical materials to create a persona in material form, which is then reproduced digitally in virtual formats across social media platforms. Nevertheless, despite its inherent globalism, there are culturally specific features germane to the cosplayer operating across different cultural settings. This is not to suggest that cosplay is limited to any one geographical frame—quite the reverse, as the trend is rapidly globalizing and regular events are now taking place from Shanghai to Seattle, and from Helsinki to Auckland. Nevertheless, each cultural frame must be acknowledged and factored in when trying to understand the motivations behind cosplay behaviour.

Hong Kong youth provide a textbook example of how cosplayers' affective attachment to their characters, and emotional needs that the activity fulfils, may be located in such a cognitive space. It takes place in a territory characterized by the absence of any national religion or moral book for young people to guide their lives by, with significant pressures to succeed financially and professionally, and a cultural tendency to focus on contextual behaviour above moral considerations.[41] In this context, the worlds of anime, manga and comic book superheroes, fantasy film characters and online game characters provide an essential, affective support. Enacted by a cast of thousands, cosplay can be performed across multiple genres, which effectively comprise a field of endless narrative possibility.[42] As one of the respondents observed:

Figure 3: Female cosplayer in *Alice in Wonderland*–styled outfit at Hong Kong University cosplay event, 2013. © Anne Peirson-Smith.

I have cosplayed about 15 characters over five years and they are all of my favourite ones—some old from my childhood—and some new online game or anime characters. There's a lot of choice—in fact it can be a hard choice to make but in the end after all of the work it is the right one and it's funny there is always someone else in the same character!

(Tin, 23, male waiter, Hong Kong)

The theme of escape from, and control over, self and everyday reality is often cited as a key motivator for cosplay practice. This operates as an aid to the creative process that is visibly expressed through the making and wearing of a spectacular costume.

Creative cosplay domains

As in any creative domain, cosplay practice is guided by protocols designed to regulate the activity, to delineate and distinguish it from other creative practices. Creativity, as Csikszentmihalyi states, 'presupposes a community of people who share ways of thinking and acting, who learn from each other and imitate each other's actions.'[43] Likewise, the evolutionary biologist and ethnologist Richard Dawkins has suggested that these units of imitation or 'memes' constitute the foundations of any culture. In cosplay, this operates not so much in a biological context but rather in an educational and cultural one where members of the domain can learn how, in this case, to cosplay. The domain-based rules governing cosplay can be typified as both formalized and free, ludic and paidic,[44] as discussed in Chapter 4. Such rules and information sets are ways in which domain cultures validate themselves to preserve and demarcate their presence. Formal and informal rules and norms are accessed by cosers online in cosplay forums, on social media sites and at events themselves. Online and offline, they tend to share information and offer support. In ludic terms, there are also a number of published guides instructing players how to cosplay. Tips include how to source costumes and accessories, craft costumes and apply make-up and contact lens, devise cosplay skits and film videos spanning a range of skill sets, from craft and design to technology.[45]

This begs the deeper question of whether creativity can be learned and how far the rules governing a community of practice actually compromise creativity. The notion of imitative cosplaying based on an originating text, as Matthew Hale observes, again highlights the tensions involved in cosplay based on

the capacity to both engender and delimit a cosplayer's aesthetic and performative choices, particularly if one's goal is to maintain fidelity within their adaptation of a given text. With that said, all communicative acts are, in some sense, reconfigurations or modulations of existing repeatable forms built from dynamic semiotic structures.[46]

In this sense, through the 'replication, revision and modulation'[47] in the embodied form and concrete practice of cosplay, cosplayers exercise a contained creativity that can be seen to enhance the creative process. As cosplayer Nina observed:

I do think that cosplay is a very creative thing as we are able to create and craft our own version of the character that we choose. Sure there are rules about how to do that in terms of wanting to make the character as accurate as possible and also rules about how cosplayers are meant to behave at cons and in public. But we are given freedom to create our own version of say Rei Ayanami or Shinji Ikara in *Evengelion* and to bring them to life in our own way. And that is a real chance to be creative.

(Nina, 23, female office worker, Singapore)

The cosplay domain and its contingent rule system distinguishes it from other zones of real life and other forms of creative play, finding ultimate expression in the costuming of a spectacular self that visibly signals one's cognitive, affective and corporeal difference from others who are not cosplaying at that moment in time.[48] The free-form paidic rules are played out in the broad choice of characters to cosplay. Moreover, the sheer scope of anime and manga products, constituting a continuous flow of media products consumed on a weekly basis, means that the cosplaying fans have a rich resource to draw from, but one that also necessitates a total immersion in their fantasy world of choice.

Given that many manga and anime narratives are also available as computer games consumed online, the relationship established between coser and narrative is interactive and all-inclusive. Assuming the form of a virtual character on screen is just one step away from physically replicating the character through costume play as private selves enter the public domain. Yet the ludic constraints are always present as costume control is located in cosers' expectations that the costumed self that is presented should be as authentic as possible, thereby necessitating careful planning and preparation, which is considered to be part of the cosplay 'discipline' by many respondents. As one informant explained:

My *Gintama* outfit today took about two months and 100 hours of my time to plan and make it, with some help from a friend who is much better at sewing than me. But that is also part of what we do and it's a good feeling to think that I have done this and when people ask me where did I get the costume they are impressed that I did this.

(Kat, 22, female student, Hong Kong)

By the same token, when creative practices occur in other cultural domains there will be space for a broader paidic interpretation because geographic location or economic activities are subject to other normative influences. Hence, as cosplay is practiced in different locations in the world, it tends to take on different forms in terms of the type of characters, the source and quality of the costumes and the nature and location of the cosplay events.

As observed in Chapter 4, this cultural difference is generally accepted and accommodated among the globalized cosplay community. As one respondent who had actively cosplayed in both Hong Kong and North America noted:

The differences in cosplaying in Asia, America and Canada are very big. Here it is more formal and people are really caught up on the authenticity of the costume and how you look—it has to be perfect! There it is more about the playing and that you have made an effort to put on a costume even if it's not great but that you are there at the event and have made an effort to dress up and make up like your character. We all accept that, as cosplayers outside of Asia have a different understanding on Japanese culture, maybe, and also do not have the resources that we have here.

(Jan, 23, female student and entrepreneur,
Hong Kong and Canada)

The majority of interviewees here have practiced their craft in Hong Kong and the China region, yet are often aware and accepting of the nuances in location-based practice. Some informants noted that, as a general observation, cosplay in North America was more relaxed and inclusive to a point, while in New Zealand the focus was on the cultural capital of demonstrating craftsmanship, in Australia photo shoots and skits were often the main focus, in Europe it is moving from real-time to digital engagement,[49] whereas in Singapore and Hong Kong, character fidelity was crucial. Such variations suggest that cosplay is an evolving, dynamic, creative phenomenon—not only because of the constantly emerging mediated characters, but also the increased use of social media and the technological competencies of a digital generation who are now playing and sharing their lived experiences online.[50] In this sense, cosplayers constitute an affinity group or a universe of affinity groups.[51] Collectively, they represent a knowledge system founded on sharing ideas and knowledge in different communicative modes, verbal and visual, about texts, characters, costume sourcing and construction.[52]

The creative cosplay field

The cosplay field conceals an inherent tension between free expression and regulation, acceptance and potential exclusion. Cosplay is an urban, festive instance of the carnivalesque, 'a second life' occurring according to specified dates and spatial frames. Like historical carnivals, cosplay events temporarily disrupt and invert everyday life with 'the suspension of hierarchical precedence'[53] through sanctioned, playful activity that is a creative display and outlet for emotions. By radically changing one's appearance and behaviour through masquerading in the public domain in embodied material forms based on Japanese and North American superhero cultures, cosers exercise control over their reworked and multiple identities. In this way, they are representing themselves creatively through a variety of personas based on affective connections. But as suggested above by the cosplay informants themselves, there are rules, and even within disruptive play communities breaching those rules can carry penalties depending on the geographic location of the practice, from online criticism of disrespectful behaviour while in costume to the types of costumes that are allowed or disallowed. Outsiders may also view the practice unsympathetically, marking cosplayers socially as fantastical 'others' in all the wrong ways, and may seek to restrict the practice. Again, this highlights the inherent tensions within creative expression in the public domain where individual effort is often regulated by the collective.

Through cosplay, players seek a sense of belonging to a recognizable youth or neo-tribe style[54] as a form of playful and entertaining 'disindividuation' premised on collaborative creative practices that actively involve both themselves and spectators. This participatory loop emphasizes 'the role that each person (persona) is called upon to play within the tribe.'[55] Cosplay can, of course, be all about having fun and finding self-gratification. Certainly, from close observations of various events, there is frequently a party atmosphere, with laughter in the air and high excitement when players appear to be enjoying the celebratory experience to the full. As one informant said, 'it is really good fun to dress up with your friends and share the love for this culture. We feel so happy here at these places being in our costumes. It's really about having a great time doing what we really love for ourselves' (Luna, 20, female student, Hong Kong). The opportunity to creatively transform and control the remediated self may explain why cosplay is increasingly becoming popular in transglobal youth cultures, with the proviso that it usually manifests itself in localized and individualized interpretations.

As with many creative activities, cosplay is also a cooperative pastime based on playful group work, requiring the existence of, and engagement with, onlookers who add a broader communicative dimension by critiquing costumes in the real-time physical spaces of events or distributing photographic images across social networking platforms. It also involves a cast of players 'backstage,' some of whom actively support the cosplayer's 'front-stage' presentation of self.[56] Characteristically, at a private or commercial event, the scene is reminiscent of that encountered in a dramatic performance, with a group of helpers often assisting the cosplayer inhabit and fine-tune costumes, attach accoutrements such as swords, helmets and wings, tweak wigs with hair gel or scissors and apply make-up. Some informants claimed that close family members, and even teachers, were supportive of their 'cosplay hobby,' considering it to be a healthy pastime, offering advice and support in the form of costume modifications and photographic assistance. Although some failed to disclose the actual amount of money they spent on costumes, cosers often received financial support from their parents to help construct their costumes, suggestive of family approval and collaborative support in material and financial terms.

However, as much as the costumed self can be legitimized by other social players—parents, friends, the media or strangers—it can also be challenged. While many of the female cosplayers said that they enjoyed being looked at and photographed at the various events, for instance, and male cosplayers welcomed being observed and admired in their 'cool outfits,' most appeared to be very self-conscious about venturing outside of the field alone in their costumes. They professed to feel safer when together as a group, based on the mutual respect it engendered. Especially in Asia, this insecurity on behalf of the players might suggest an awareness of the social stigma attached to wearing a spectacular, individualistic costume in collectivistic, traditional cultural settings. Such concerns also undermine the branding of cosplay as a subcultural articulation since players do not wear their costumes in everyday life as a signal of individuality or rebellion, unlike fashion subcultures such as Lolita and Goths. This suggests the cosplay field is a place to meet like-minded others and share creative practices that stand outside the norms of everyday life and yet to also challenge it. As respondent Jenna explained:

In my costume, I'm not always ready to take on the real world on my own. If I dare to wear a costume in the street people would stare and point at me, I may feel safer if I was with a friend but it's best to dress up at the event only. Sometimes, they are nice and genuinely interested in the outfit, but other times people are rude and critical, implying that I'm crazy and I don't always feel in the mood to deal with that.

(Jenna, 18, female student, Hong Kong)

Female cosplayers, in particular, express the ambivalences of dressing up in costume that visually sets them apart from others. Many cosers appear to find the emulation of their idealized other to be empowering in the search for the potential self.[57] Yet the multi-coloured wigs, tight silver lamé space suits and vertiginous black sequined platform boots may engender a crisis of confidence if the presentation of the singular self jars with their collective selves. Young women appear more prone to a heightened awareness of the gaze of others, with a consequent avoidance or denial of their sexualized selves. More practical concerns tended to weigh on male cosplayers, as their costumes were often so complex and bulky in their construction that they needed help to assemble them and don their persona. Traversing a busy city street as an imperial guard, for example, might prove impractical.

Collaborative creativity can be understood to triangulate the cosplayer, text and others. Rob Pope usefully adds intertextuality to its definition in order to explain the social dimension of creative process, wherein it 'basically means "operating together" and can be more precisely defined as *working and playing with and with respect to others* [...]. It is a shared, ongoing process of change through exchange.'[58] The point here is that, in their collaborative efforts, cosers interact creatively with materials, which becomes a textual stimulus to create or modify subsequent performances enacted by themselves and others. This is exemplified by the experience of one informant who explained that at a recent commercial Asian Games Show (AGS) event at the Hong Kong Convention and Exhibition Centre, he encountered another coser dressed as the same character, Gin Ichimaru from the anime *Bleach (Burīchi)* (2004–12),[59] with blood red contact lenses, silver hair and long V-necked serge grey, black-lined kimono robe and matching trouser suit:

I had made a great effort to make my outfit and character look as good as the old anime version 300 or something and felt good about how I looked [...] he's one of my big heroes. Then I saw another guy across the room and he was the same character. Then he came over to me and said my hair was very wrong and that he looked better. The hair is the most important thing about him. That is where his name comes from [...] Gin is silver hair. I felt bad then and this character doesn't smile and I looked at him like I could kill him [...]. But later a girl dressed as another *Bleach* character came up to me and asked if I could have a photo taken with her and others cosing *Bleach* hung out around me and we all had photos taken and it was good then.

(CK, 19, male trainee accountant, Hong Kong)

Collaboration based on change through exchange and creative interaction is largely in evidence in cosplay activity, from the attempt at authentic replication through critical exchange with the replicated character, to the validated collective exchange with the other *Bleach* or *Game of Thrones* cosplayers. As this account suggests, the social environment changes both the behavioural and affective states of the individual cosers, their relationship with each other and the wider social relationships that they experience in their everyday lives.

Creativity, in this context, resides in the interaction between cosers and their facilitators, which appears to have fluidity in terms of the roles played. One informant explained how it had changed her whole approach to life, connecting her up with a community of like-minded people.

I was part of a group doing the same story. When we got to the place we all started to help each other get ready—putting on make-up and combing out wigs. It was friendly

Figure 4: Cosplayers work collaboratively in getting ready backstage at China Joy event Beijing (2009). © Anne Peirson-Smith.

and caring for each other. A girl in the group I didn't know before helped me put on the wig and combed it over my eyes like the character I was 'cosing.' She is now my best friend. She didn't have a costume that day but now we always 'cos' together. It was the most fun I had and we started to take photos of each other and it felt really good and strange at first. Then a photographer asked us to take a photo all together and then more came and we had lots of photos taken. It was a special day for me and these are still all my friends […] this was a good experience for me. I am more confident now I am studying to become a hairdresser or beautician which is also very good for 'cosing' and then I help out sometimes at events instead of being a character.

(Belle, 25, female cosplayer, Hong Kong)

The appraisals of others seemed to matter greatly to all of the informants, and all noted both negative and positive feedback from external sources. Generally, there was a sense that Hong Kong society was now more accepting of the cosplay trend because of its recent track record or increasing familiarity with the practice, to the extent that observers did not tend to ridicule, stare or comment adversely. This, the respondents believed, was also reflected in a change in local media reportage. Whereas five years ago, cosers were branded as psychologically unbalanced and pornographic, currently the Hong Kong media coverage— in the mass circulation newspaper *The Apple Daily*, for instance—was largely positive. This shift in media interpretations may reflect the fact that the style has impacted mainstream local fashion, and has also been embraced and endorsed by cultural powerbrokers in the creative and entertainment industries, including local celebrities. Cosplay-themed events have also been taken up commercially, and are sometimes being used to open new Hong Kong shopping malls, for example.

Outside of this relatively supportive kinship circle or cosplay 'family,' some female informants received more sinister appraisals from outsiders, again reinforcing the validity of the collective as a safe haven to practice creative play. Online communication channels were acknowledged as legitimate sites of appraisal. One player explained that on her online message board she is often told to change her character by some male commentators: 'Others have told me anonymously that I am the wrong shape for some characters but I tend to ignore this and my friends in my team always support me on this, which is actually a big comfort for me' (Kim, 18, female student, Hong Kong). Her feisty response and those of others to (largely male) critical feedback about their cosplay images is significant, as such young women appear to be demonstrating a form of female empowerment invested by their idealized costumed selves within a shared cosplayer ideology.

The judgemental nature of the feedback received, particularly from the online communication channels and chat rooms, was perhaps an indication of a younger generation obsessed with idealized body images and celebrity culture, according to one female cosplayer:

I often get comments online saying that I'm too fat to wear my Chi robot outfit, or that my skirt is too short for the shape of my legs. Yes, it bothers me because these young people are missing the point and don't understand the true nature of cosplay. Instead they are looking beyond the costumes and being critical of the real body and the normal person and matching them up to some celebrity or supermodel's perfect image, when they should really be appraising the authenticity of the costume, the construction of the accessories, and most of all, how it all comes together in the aura of the player's character.

(Cam, 22, female stylist, Hong Kong)

The critique of the cosplayer's corporeal form was also evident in the increasing trend for subtle forms of censorship operating among some of the photographers at cosplay events, who often would be highly selective in choosing their subjects on the basis of their physical appearance, as one female player observed:

Some of the photographers are there just to focus on pretty faces and beautiful bodies or the most flesh revealing outfits and this just cheapens the whole cosplay scene in my view. And sometimes you have a meeting of minds or bodies as some cosplayers are not

Figure 5: Cosplayer as vocaloid Hatsune Miku in *Snow Miku Fluffy Coat* (2012) being photographed at Ani-Con event Hong Kong (2012). © Anne Peirson-Smith.

genuine—they are wannabe models or actresses wanting to get exposure, particularly at the big commercial cosplay exhibitions.

(Tabi, 21, female student, Hong Kong)

The visual nature of the cosplay experience and the need to record it photographically either as individual shot or as a group *mise-en-scène* appeared to be a given among the participants, yet there was also a feeling that the boundaries of control between the player and the photographer as voyeur could sometimes be violated, which was of real concern to some of the female cosplayers, in particular. In many ways, the social world of cosplay is a contested site, subject to the playing out of different personal agendas and gender differences, both among the cosers themselves and with the intermediaries involved. They may sometimes be at odds with the original collective cosplay norms and values, which could occasion an individual cosplayer to eventually opt out of the scene if their self-image was sufficiently threatened.

The individual domain

As seen above, creativity was traditionally and historically attributed to individual genius, but this is clearly not how the creative process operates in the contemporary social domain. The individual needs to appreciate the rules of the domain before admission to the field, which is based on collective acceptance and action, given that in order 'to function well within the creative system, one must internalize the rules of the domain and the opinions of the field, so that one can choose the most promising ideas to work on, and do so in a way that will be acceptable to one's peers.'[60] Nevertheless, the role of the individual is pertinent to understanding how creativity operates within the cosplay collective, as this duality is a necessary part of the creative process. Cosplayers have been labelled as *otaku* or as geeky outsiders in the past,[61] as with similar communities of practice, such as online gamers. However, this negative connotation largely appears to be dissipating as these fans and their fandom become more mainstream, widespread, legitimized and on trend.[62] Sometimes cosplay informants appeared to desire more societal acceptance of what they were doing, a form of producing and creating that begs recognition as performance art.[63] Yet, paradoxically, validation and appropriation by mainstream commercial institutions stand to render cosplay less meaningful by diminishing the value of the field and its domain of insider knowledge capital. This situation can be observed in the reaction of cosplayers to its over-commercialization, and in the token use of the activity as soft power, by media celebrities, corporations and even national governments. Conversely, a marginal or neo-tribal status can help legitimize the creative domain and field.[64]

The demographic profiles of the cosplay informants involved here were not homogeneous, as their occupations ranged from school and university students to service-based professionals, with a wide variation in income. Many of the players in full-time occupations tended to work in the creative industries as designers, stylists and beauticians. Many are female and from a youth demographic typically ranging from 14-25. Although this did not seem to create a social imbalance ('cosplayers are all a supportive bunch,' noted Carmen, 20, female retail assistant, Macau) and there appeared to be no discrimination on the basis of socioeconomic status, there was no evidence of the sharing or direct handing on of costumes. This would appear to reveal the limits of a wider collectivism. According to cosplayer Rinka, her circle would often 'borrow and share each other's ideas, strengths and talents, while also providing honest feedback for improvement of each other's costumes,' but the actual exchange of artefacts or outfits was not commonplace. This denoted a personal, possessive aspect of the devotion to a chosen character—possibly because each cosplayer appeared to make their choices based on an alignment that had in most cases evolved over time, often from childhood. It also suggests a desire for authenticity not just in the faithful representation of character, but also in the individual evocation of that embodied self.

In the same way, unlike other geographic locations it is rare in Hong Kong to source second-hand costumes, where an individual's choice of a particular cosplay costume aligns

Figure 6: Cosplayer as vocaloid character Hatsune Miku in *Project DIVA-2nd – Mikuzukin* (2010) at Macau Animation and Comic Culture Industrial Association cosplay event (2014). © Anne Peirson-Smith.

squarely with their engagement as fans with the source manga and anime. These are followed loyally—often over years—for the duration of the mediated narrative, with significant affective responses often erupting among the fan base when an anime series is axed. This may spring from a profound and sustained identification with the character being played that extends through and beyond the cosplay context. As one player explained of her deep connection to the main protagonist in the anime film *Spirited Away (Sen to Chihiro no Kamikakushi)* (2001):[65]

I'm a lifelong fan of *Spirited Away*—I've always related to the main female hero Chihiro and her predicament when the witch magically turns her parents into pigs and she becomes trapped in the spirit world beyond the great river. She was there when I grew up and her personality is a bit like mine—she can be quite moody. The costume is a classic one too—everyone knows it with the robe and belt and it's easy to do and to wear and I feel very special and different like wearing it.

(Isa, 18, female student, Macau)

Here, the individual coser appears to be re-creating her identity by projecting her secret self into the public domain, adapting Joanne Eicher's typology of the three selves manifested through dress via the public, private and secret selves.[66] According to this model, in communicating an identity the public persona is revealed to everyone, signalling the demographic features and professional garb of the wearer, whereas the private self, familiar to friends and family, is based on the clothing of relaxation and leisure, and the secret self is a restricted zone reserved for the individual and intimates based on the wearing of fantasy dress.[67] This model also has gender implications according to Eicher, who proposed that women tended to pursue their fantasies by dressing up as their secret selves, while men were more confined, as a rule, to expressing themselves only in public and private dress.[68] While there tend to be more female participants than males in global cosplay communities, this gender bias seems to be eroding and certainly both male and female cosplayers engage in the practice with the same motivations to publicly represent secret identities.

Applying this typology to cosplay suggests that cosers reconstitute their identities, notwithstanding gender differences. In dressing up, they place the hidden, secret self on public display in the quest to express their devotion to the character with like-minded others in the field. Cosplay as creative role play offers scope for playing with socially constructed and performed roles not only of gender but also of social propriety. As Victor Turner puts it, 'outside the restricting frames of masculine domination and everyday appearance using accessories and costumes.' Masquerade of this kind becomes 'a sort of visual performance through artefacts: a vehicle for constructing and deconstructing identities.'[69] This represents challenges to socially prescribed ways of being, often evoking hostility from institutions in the form of moral panics in the media where it is often framed as deviant behaviour. The Asian cosplay community often appears particularly uncomfortable with open expressions of the gendered other, for example. Consequently, some players are at pains to stress that crossplay is largely removed from expressions of alternative sexualities, given that individual character choice is based on affective connections with their persona irrespective of their gender. As one respondent explained:

> I'm a male yes, and you know this is a female character, Reisen Udongen Inan from the *Touhou Project* that I really admire a lot. When I dress up as a girl like this with purple hair many people look at me bizarrely. They say 'how come he dresses as a girl—crazy-la!' But most of the characters in this anime that we all like in this group are female—and don't forget many girls here today are doing male characters as well.
>
> (Jet, 21, male student, Hong Kong)

Choices of character may also revolve around the sense of empowerment provided by playing a figure with magical powers or attributes. As another respondent said:

> My character from *xxxHolic*, Kitsune, is able to morph into a fox and their enemies and I feel the power when he is with me especially when I attend cosplay events when I might dress up like him and then I feel like I also have those magical powers. I feel like today I can control the rain and the wind—I have real power!
>
> (Cyn, 22, female teaching assistant, Hong Kong)

This response suggests that the player is projecting their identity onto the character costume and animating their character by dressing up both 'as' and 'with' them. The acquisition of agency through creative efforts helps relieve the stresses of life for young people, given that they are often subjected to huge parental and institutional expectations to succeed academically and professionally above all else. As a respondent noted, 'I do this as a release from the trouble in my life. When I watch the animation, I can think what my future is. Some elements of the anime represent myself, and who I am and really want to be in this character Diva that I chose today' (Carmen, 16, female student, Hong Kong). Much of the narrative content of the original sources are based on plotlines tracking the triumph of good over evil or the small and powerless over the big and powerful, thereby enabling cosers to mimetically deal with their personal anxieties and daily situations. Other stories concern the ability of characters to escape from danger or retreat into a nostalgic past, as one respondent explained: 'My character is Princess White Rose from a game. She is the princess of a country kidnapped by an evil person but she and the main male character manage to escape together—it's very exciting and a good ending' (Dana, 22, female student, Hong Kong).

Identification with the selected character may, therefore, go beyond the surface level of merely 'dressing up.' Cosplayers are not only emotionally transformed by the costume, but in wearing it both cognitively and affectively 'become' the imagined persona at events, and carry this through into other social worlds. Teri Silvio suggests that the cosplayer does not project their individual personality through the character as the 'whole idea of animation is to give characters "lives of their own."'[70] In this sense, cosers are channelling their characters as opposed to controlling them, as the puppet is controlled by the puppet-master. Yet the player is puppet master over his or her own assumed persona by taking the character out of the narrative and situating them in the specific contexts of cosplay events. This occurs not just in terms of the choice of character that is brought to life, but compiling each part of their anatomy—eyes, wigs and skin tone, for example—as the ultimate form of *moe*, the deep intense love for an avatar. As one respondent typically noted:

> We deeply love the characters that we choose to do—that is the main point. I am Anlayami from *07-Ghosts*—he's the main part—a boy who has lost his memory back in the past— we have to find it. The character is good and it's a good story too.
>
> (Mint, 24, male computer programmer, Hong Kong)

Ironically, some cosers may present their character in public, yet keep the practice private: that is, hidden from their parents or co-workers. Equally, others may conceal the form and intention of their cosplaying, as when they are crossplaying, from others, which highlights the fluidity of the boundaries that are often traversed from the expression of secret to private to pubic selves.

Processes of cosplay creativity

The material creation of outfits and a made-up appearance, along with their subsequent photographic capture and circulation, enables cosplayers to reaffirm their identity and find solace in social connectedness with like-minded coser. These tools also enable the player to visibly signal their creative competencies[71] in compiling their outfits, and visibly communicate the fact that they are a legitimate member of a particular group or 'nexus of practice.'[72]

Significantly, interviewees claimed that the main benefits of their creative hobby comprise not only the creative skills required in assuming the 'mask,' or in role playing their characters and creating a 'front' before observers, but also in the project management skills and teamwork abilities needed to plan and execute group performances. In addition, acquiring the technical know-how to construct outfits and deliver an authentic public performance of a recognizable character is substantial.[73] The self-sufficiency of players, and their divergence from over-reliance on commercial sourcing or passive consumption, is also on show. The continual challenge is to locate, adapt and make one's own costumes and accessories, which is fundamental to the participatory, hands-on DIY (do-it-yourself) nature of the cosplay process globally. Frenchy Lunning acknowledges the role of the 'cosplay designer' and their wider influence on the domain of fashion in representing 'a global response to anime and manga that moved it from an obscure and marginal practice to a well-known source of popular-culture style that has had a profound influence on fashion.'[74] As she observes:

Designers revel in the specific freedom of expression that cosplay affords them, which is not limited by the constraints of everyday ready-to-wear clothes. Cosplay costumes demand creative and highly imaginative solutions as the images on a screen are adapted to create a three-dimensional wearable costume. Cosplay calls on the designer to use unconventional materials and processes to replicate objects and clothing that do not actually exist. Most poignantly, cosplay allows for an extended performance of a fantasy of identity through costume and makeup: a potential for creating fantasy.[75]

The significant investment of time and money in the creative process, design and customizations of an entire and invariably complex cosplay ensemble is a measure of its importance as an increasingly popular pastime. Criteria for success are based on the application of innovative aesthetic and technical competencies, whether as designer, customizer, stylist, make-up artist, photographer or videographer. Once the character is chosen and the requisite materials are sourced in the correct fabric texture and colour, a skilled processes takes place of

draping, adapting commercial patterns, and purchasing pieces. Extensive yardage can be required to form capes and flowing skirts, generally from inexpensive fabrics […]. The particular fall of a cape, opening gracefully to reveal the golden interior, which may add so much to the romantic flair of an anime character, is a highly manipulated aspect of the costume design: The folds are carefully stitched, glued, or even pinned into shape. Detailing on the gauntlets and chest ornament is carefully reproduced.

Lunning goes on to note that '[a]ll parts of the costume must not only look as exactly like the anime as possible but must also allow the cosplayer to perform in the manner of the character. The costume must be durable and yet flexible, visually accurate yet innovative in terms of materials and processes.'[76]

As an expression of creative and innovative practice, the desire, inclination and ability to re-create and re-present fictional characters in meticulously embodied material form principally emerges from domain-based knowledge. Cosplayers clearly must possess a deep knowledge, and a wealth of cultural and knowledge capital about the sources of their costumed inspirations as a precursor for entry to both creative domain and field. As one respondent noted:

From the age of two or three, I was watching Japanese anime—Pokémon, Digimon, Sailor Moon—on TV and they were my original memories, and very strong ones. They coloured my world then, as a young child growing up—I saw the work through the eyes of these characters and the challenges that faced them became my challenges. I still cannot separate the character from my life in many ways.

(Tam, 19, male student, Macau)

There is a logical connection with having been immersed in, and socialized via, these fictional worlds at impressionable stages of life and acquiring the motivation to represent the character and re-create its existence in real time, according to the norms and creative practices of the cosplay domain.

Certainly, the interviewees for this chapter recognized the importance of this innovative process as the basis for creating their outfits. Most cosers explained that they would typically start to plan their character choices some months before an event, spending considerable time privately researching online, scanning and monitoring forums and social media sites. In the following stage of mulling over different character ideas leading to the execution of their costume, players often admitted that they would 'carry this around with them' while traversing other areas of their life such as work. The ideational stage allowed them to park the idea for their character and costume at the back of their mind to let it crystallize or incubate into a firmer notion of what was needed in terms of the raw materials and component parts needed, which one coser termed waiting for the arrival of his 'light bulb moment.'

> When I realize what I want to do as a character and what can be achieved in bringing it all together it's a good feeling but that can take weeks or months so you have to give yourself enough thinking and prep time. You have to be realistic but at the same time you have to take a few risks in making it happen. I knew that the robot costume that I was making for the AniCom event could be sculpted out of polystyrene, spray-painted and embellished with chrome paint that looks just like metal parts. It really worked and I won the competition on the day.
>
> (Jasper, 30, male technician, Hong Kong)

The final stage of the creative process tended to be shared with others to verify and validate the choice by drawing on the collaborative expertise of the field and in some cases soliciting help in sourcing costumes, wigs and accessories, and in making and customizing outfits.

Subcultures of spectacular consumption

Cosplayer activity can also be understood from a creative consumption-related perspective.[77] This is based on the notion that cosplayers are tapping into and re-creating cultures of consumption,[78] characterized by Robert Kozinets as 'a particular interconnected system of commercially produced images, texts, and objects that particular groups use—through the construction of overlapping and even conflicting practices, identities, and meanings—to make collective sense of their environments and to orient their members' experiences and lives.'[79] The subculture thus defines its unique boundaries and determines both individual and collective meaning when taking contrasting positions to its traditional cultural framework and related indigenous norms.

Given that cosplay is a form of extraordinary presentation of self, the practice could also be viewed as a form of spectacular consumption through which the relations among cultural forms, the culture industry and individual lived experiences are shaped by public consumption.[80] The character costumes of cosplayers become the material forms or artefacts that re-articulate the original media texts and inhabit a mythical, conceptual space offering an escape from a known and lived reality. Consumption experiences have been compared to sacred practices and the process of 'sacralization,'[81] as they appear to fill an existing affective gap for the consumer as a creative space, satisfied by accessing the large corpus of mythic narratives from which the cosplayers derive their characters. As Kozinets suggests, this sacred consumption practice affords 'a conceptual space that is set apart and extraordinary—an alternate, timeless, mythic, and mysterious reality, an ecstatic place where one can sometimes stand outside of oneself—entertainment consumption may offer, for some, the very quintessence of sacralization.'[82] However, this is active consumption—an act of creation, even—and not a passive form of character admiration or casual citation from the cosplay congregation.

Figure 7: Cosplayer as Chikage Kazama from *Hakuoki Shinsengumi Kitan* (2010) at a Hong Kong University cosplay event (2013). © Anne Peirson-Smith.

The global commodity chain in which goods and services are conceived, produced and introduced into the market[83] is the material context that surrounds and drives cosplay practice. While a fraught and increasingly contested one, it does offer various opportunities for creative, inventive engagement. As Anne Allison argues: 'Technologically advanced capitalism produced a loss of place and community and feelings of alienation from parents and the past and created longings for identity via the friendly chaos of comic books, toys, and cartoons and merchandise emblazoned with images of these characters.'[84] The material aspect necessitates that players turn their affective devotion to the chosen character into physical reality by acquiring the costume. The DIY component of the costumed ensemble is still considered to be the preferred way of re-creating the character, as one respondent observed:

I make my own costumes—it takes time but it is enjoyable and it makes me more patient and skillful. I buy the material in Hong Kong and then the wigs and accessories in Mong Kok markets. Even if my friends buy their outfits online from China or get them made in Shenzhen they will still customize them further so this DIY part is important as it means that you make the character as your own.

(Yu, 23, female designer, Hong Kong)

Notions of authenticity are embedded into the cosplay practice, in terms of creating a faithful representation of a character in 'the origin story,'[85] and in the act of dressing up and publically performing it also operates on multiple levels of 'show and tell.'

This manifests itself as an individual display of affective connect, as a visual proof of craft and of individual willingness to inhabit an imaginary community. Yet authenticity in relation to cosplay is a complex and problematic construct subject to negotiation. As Ellen Kirkpatrick observes:

Authenticity is an intricate concept, shot through with indeterminacy and subjectivity. It evokes many troublesome ideas, not least truth and realness but also power—how does the power to define the authentic circulate? It also concerns identity and ideas of acceptance and belonging, and in terms of cosplay, an authentic reading can secure acceptance as both cosplayer and source character.[86]

As such, the quest for character fidelity is a quintessential creative pursuit, taking unrelated ideas and materials and combining them to produce an associative effect through costume and material culture. Many of the cosplayers interviewed in Asia were fashion, textile or design students who applied their craft-making knowledge and skills to conscientiously creating their costumes, or took commissions for making costumes for others. Despite the earlier female orientation of costume creation, cosplay today does not appear overly determined by gender 'borderwork,'[87] unlike online games. One male cosplayer who worked as an electronic engineer willingly crafted *Star Wars* outfits and light sabers for himself and his troop, liaising with George Lucas' former technician on Facebook to perfect the design

Figure 8: Cosplayers enact scenes from *Star Wars V: The Empire Strikes Back* (1980) as Boba Fett, Obi-Wan Kenobi (stormtrooper) and an Imperial stormtrooper at Ani-Con and Games event Hong Kong (2015). © Anne Peirson-Smith.

process. However, authenticity in cosplay cannot reside purely in the faithful mechanical reproduction of character, given that each costume and spectacular presentation of self is always a re-mediated interpretation of the original source.

The reliance on friends and family to assist in the creation of costumes is another common theme highlighting the collaborative networks that underpin cosplay. Support also assumed the form of assistance at events including dressing-up, make-up and photography. It is not uncommon to see a support team accompanying the player operating as personal assistants and adding to the notion that the creative field of cosplay operates as a 'family' or close-knit kinship group acting in line with the normative aspects of the domain. Although most cosplayers do not make significant money from their activity, cosplay has acquired a commercial dimension when staged in opening shopping malls, or as part of the business-oriented anime and manga fairs and Comic-Cons. Images of cosplayers are also sometimes sold to media outlets by cosplay photographers, often without permission, as one female cosplayer complained:

I was so unhappy when my friends told me that my image was on a big website. This is very wrong and I felt very abused by the photographer, which is like a thief. This makes us wary of having photos taken by those that we do not know or have not seen before at events.

(Jan, 21, female student, Hong Kong)

Generally, however, the entertainment sources of anime and manga and their re-articulation into costume play appear to enable players to guide and empower their self and collective identities as participatory fans. In so doing they establish a *raison d'être* where fantasy becomes a form of reality within a set domain, which also accords with findings from other fan-based subcultural studies based on strong, associative affective connections with the sources and objects of fandom.

Culture creators

This process of transubstantiation in the reshaping and reapplication of material resources across mediated modes from comic books and video games to human performance and photographic record is central to the creative process of cosplay. By engaging in this transformational activity, cosplayers are essentially culture creators[88] communicating through consumption practices, as an emblem of contemporary youth cultures. They are also fans and spectators who indulge in 'textual poaching'[89] that enables them to realize creative acts by consuming, appropriating, modifying, reworking and re-performing the visual, verbal, narrative and pictorial aspects of popular culture. They do this with commodities such as cartoons and comic books, re-presenting these commoditized forms when spectacularly dressing up in the public spaces and places of global cityscapes. In sharing this common ideology or passion, they are actively shaping the evolution of the popular culture landscape.[90] Cosplay events provide an opportunity both for the creation of spectacular forms of self-expression and collective identity formation. This duality is a consistent theme, as a player is integrated into an imaginary world that is visually and physically separate from everyday realities and quotidian modalities.

Cosplay is a quintessentially creative pursuit that draws on the resources of the fantastical imagination. Cosers re-create and re-articulate the original media forms in real time. The individual player's affective individuality and personal predispositions towards characters from these media texts is a key factor in the co-creation of self-identity, group identity and their subcultural belief systems. Cosplay activity is not an end in itself, but an important social and cultural process. It concerns the creation of a social world, the cosphere, whose passport for entry is the sourcing, crafting and wearing of fantastic costume, forming the basis of shared relationships that are dynamic and that shift over time within the structured setting of cosplay conventions, competitions and meetings. At the same time, it affords the

Figure 9: Cosplayers as Super Sonico from *Nitroplus* (*Blue Tiger Parka* version) (2014), Ranka Lee from *Macross Frontier: The False Songtress* (2009) and Super Sonico from *Nitroplus* (*Pink Tiger Parka* version) (2014) at Oz Comic-Con Melbourne, Australia (2012). © Anne Peirson-Smith.

individual player a way of re-creating and celebrating individuality, while expressing and performing the secret self publicly among a group of like minded others.

Notes

1 Tore Kristensen, 'The Physical Context of Creativity,' *Creativity and Innovation Management* 13, no. 2 (2004), 89.

2 Jonathan A. Plucker and Joseph S. Renzulli, 'Psychometric Approaches to the Study of Human Creativity,' in *Handbook of Creativity*, ed. Robert J. Sternberg (Cambridge: Cambridge University Press, 1999), 3–4.

3　Liane Gabora, 'Why the Creative Process is Not Darwinian: Commentary on "The Creative Process in Picasso's Guernica Sketches: Monotonic Improvements versus Nonmonotonic Variants" by D. K. Simonton,' *Creativity Research Journal* 19, no. 4 (2007), 361–65.

4　Elizabeth Hallam and Tim Ingold, *Creativity and Cultural Improvisation: An Introduction,* in *Creativity and Cultural Improvisation,* eds Elizabeth Hallam and Tim Ingold (Oxford: Berg, 2007), 1–24.

5　Rodney Jones, 'Introduction: Discourse and Creativity,' in *Discourse and Creativity,* ed. Rodney Jones (Oxon, Abington: Routledge, 2012), 1–4.

6　Darryl Hocking, *Communicating Creativity: The Discursive Facilitation of Creativity in the Arts* (London: Palgrave Macmillan, 2017), 33–35.

7　Elizabeth Wilson, *The Bohemians: Glamorous Outcasts* (London: Tauris Parke, 2002), 2.

8　Ibid., 3.

9　George Wallas, *The Art of Thought* (1926; Tunbridge Wells, Kent: Solis Press; New York: Harcourt Brace Jovanovich, 2014), 24–35; Plucker and Renzulli, *Handbook of Creativity,* 35–61; Robert J. Sternberg and Todd I. Lubart, 'Investing in Creativity,' *Psychological Enquiry* 4, no. 3 (1993), 229–32.

10　Keith Sawyer, *Group Genius: The Creative Power of Collaboration* (New York: Perseus Books, 2007), xiii; Richard Florida, *Cities and the Creative Class* (New York: Routledge, 2005).

11　Sawyer, *Group Genius,* 70.

12　Mikhail Csikszentmihalyi, 'A Systems Perspective on Creativity,' in *Handbook of Creativity,* ed. Robert J. Sternberg (Cambridge: Cambridge University Press, 1999), 313–35.

13　Csikszentmihalyi, 'A Systems Perspective,' 314.

14　Paul Du Gay, Stuart Hall, Linda Janes, Anders Koed Madsen, Hugh Mackay, and Keith Negus, *Doing Cultural Studies: The Story of the Sony Walkman* (Manchester, UK: Manchester University Press, 1997), 3–6.

15　Pierre Bourdieu, *Language and Symbolic Power* (Cambridge: Polity Press, 1991), 14.

16　Henry Bial, 'What Is Performance?' in *The Performance Studies Reader,* ed. Henry Bial (New York: Routledge, 2004), 57–59.

17　Gunter Kress, *Multimodality: A Social Semiotic Approach to Contemporary Communication* (London: Routledge, 2010), 1–3.

18　Michel de Certeau, *The Practice of Everyday Life,* trans. Steven Rendall (1980; Berkeley: University of California Press, 1984), 1–15.

19　Paul Willis, Simon Jones, Joyce Canaan, and Geoff Hurd, *Common Culture: Symbolic Work at Play in Everyday Cultures of the Young* (Milton Keynes, UK: Open University Press, 1990), 2.

20　Paul Hodkinson, *Goth: Identity, Style and Subculture* (London: Bloomsbury, 2002), 40–42.

21　Stuart Ewen and Elizabeth Ewen, *Channels of Desire: Mass Images and the Shaping of the American Consciousness* (New York: McGraw Hill, 1982), 244.

22　See Joel Gn, 'Queer Simulation: The Practice, Performance and Pleasure of Cosplay,' *Continuum* 25, no. 4 (2011), 583–93; Hans Joas, *The Creativity of Action,* trans. Jeremy Gaines and Paul Keast (Cambridge: Polity Press, 1996), 92–93.

23　Willis et al., *Common Culture,* 1.

24 Nichol Lamerichs, 'The Remediation of the Fan Convention: Understanding the Emerging Genre of Cosplay Music Videos,' *Transformative Works and Cultures* 18, Performance and Performativity in Fandom (2015), para. 1.3.

25 Theo Van Leeuwen, 'Ten Reasons Why Linguists Should Pay Attention to Visual Communication,' in *Discourse & Technology: Multimodal Discourse Analysis*, eds. Philip Levine and Ron Scollon (Washington, DC: Georgetown University Press, 2004), 10.

26 Gunter Kress and Theo Van Leeuwen, *Reading Images: The Grammar of Visual Design* (Hove, UK: Psychology Press, 1992), 159–62.

27 James V. Wertsch, 'The Primacy of Mediated Action in Sociocultural Studies,' *Mind, Culture, and Activity* 1, no. 4 (1994), 202–8.

28 Isaac Gagné, 'Urban Princesses: Performance and "Women's Language" in Japan's Gothic/ Lolita Subculture,' *Journal of Linguistic Anthropology* 18, no. 1 (2007), 131.

29 Edward Hall, *Beyond Culture* (New York: Anchor Books, 1977), 71–84.

30 Erving Goffman, *The Presentation of Self in Everyday Life* (New York: Anchor Books, 1959), 17.

31 Richard Segers, 'The Negativity Behind Cosplaying and How it is Affecting the Culture,' (30 April 2016), accessed 1 January 2018, https://medium.com/@RichardSeghers/the-negativity-behind-cosplaying-and-how-it-is-affecting-the-culture-3076c97973eb

32 Frederik L. Schodt, *Dreamland Japan: Writings on Modern Manga* (Berkeley: Stone Bridge Press, 1996), 19–20.

33 Sharon Kinsella, *Adult Manga: Culture and Power in Contemporary Japanese Society*, (Richmond, UK: Curzon Press, 2000), 19–49

34 Tze-yue G. Hu, 'Frameworks of Teaching and Researching Japanese Animation,' in *Japanese Animation: East Asian Perspectives,* ed. Yokota Masao (Jackson: University of Mississippi, 2015), 5.

35 See Mark McLelland, ed., *The End of Cool Japan: Ethical, Legal and Cultural Challenges to Japanese Popular Culture* (London: Routledge, 2017).

36 Koichi Iwabuchi, 'Reconsidering East Asian Connectivity and the Usefulness of Media and Cultural Studies,' in *Cultural Studies, Culture Industries in Northeast Asia: What a Difference Region Makes*, eds. Chris Berry, Nicole Liscutin, and Jonathan D. Macintosh (Hong Kong: Hong Kong University Press, 2009), 32–36.

37 Y. H. A. Fung, 'Hong Kong as the Asian and Chinese Distributor of Pokémon,' *International Journal of Comic Art* 7, no. 1 (2005), 432–48.

38 Wai-ming Ng, 'The Impact of Japanese Comics and Animation in Asia,' *Journal of Japanese Trade and Industry* (July/August, 2002), 1.

39 R. E. Brenner, *Understanding Manga and Anime* (Westport: Libraries Unlimited/Greenwood, 2007).

40 Wendy Siuyi Wong, 'Globalizing Manga: From Japan to Hong Kong and Beyond,' *Mechademia* 1, Emerging Worlds of Anime and Manga (2006), 23–45.

41 Hellmut Schütte and Ciarlante Deanna, *Consumer Behaviour in Asia*, 1st ed. (London: Macmillan Business, 1998), 60–65.

42 Brenner, *Understanding Manga and Anime*.

43 Csikszentmihalyi, 'A Systems Perspective,' 313–35.

44 Roger Caillois, *Man, Play and Games* (Chicago: University of Illinois Press, 1985), 11–35.

45 Some print or online publications include Yaya Han, Allison Deblaso, and Joey Marsocci, *1000 Incredible Costume & Cosplay Ideas* (Singapore: Quarry Books, 2013), 6–7; Kristie Good, *Epic Cosplay Costumes* (Winterset: Fons and Porter, 2016), Svetlana Quindt, *The Costume Making Guide: Creating Armor and Props for Cosplay* (Oakland: Impact Books, 2016); Miyuu Takahara, *Cosplay: The Beginner's Masterclass* (Scoots Valley: CreateSpace Publishing, 2015); Shawn Thorsson, *Make: Props and Costume Armor* (Sebastopol: Maker Media, 2016).

46 Matthew Hale, 'Cosplay: Intertextuality, Public Texts, and the Body Fantastic,' *Western Folklore* 73, no. 1 (2014), 19.

47 Ibid., 5.

48 Anne Peirson-Smith, 'Fashioning the Fantastical Self: An Examination of the Cosplay Dress-up Phenomenon in Southeast Asia,' *Fashion Theory* 17, no. 1 (2012), 77–111.

49 See Lamerichs, 'Remediation of the Fan Convention.'

50 James Paul Gee, *Situated Language and Learning: A Critique of Traditional Schooling* (London: Routledge, 2004), 70–80.

51 James Paul Gee, *What Video Games Have to Teach Us about Leaning and Literacy* (New York: Palgrave Macmillan, 2003), 27–28.

52 Etienne Wenger, *Communities of Practice: Learning Meaning and Identity* (Cambridge; Cambridge University Press, 1999), 14–15.

53 Mikhail M. Bakhtin, *Rabelais and His World (Tvorčestvo Fransua Rable i narodnaja kul'tura srednevekov'ja i Renessansa)*, 2nd ed. (Bloomington: Indiana University Press, 1968), 10–11.

54 Michel Maffesoli, *The Time of the Tribes: The Decline of Individualism in Mass Society* (London: Sage, 1996), 5–6.

55 Maffesoli, *The Time of the Tribes*, 6.

56 Goffman, *The Presentation of Self*, 106–40.

57 Jackie Stacey, *Star Gazing: Hollywood Cinema and Female Spectatorship* (London: Routledge, 1994), 126–75.

58 Rob Pope, *Creativity: Theory, History, Practice* (London and New York: Routledge, 2005), 65–66, original emphasis.

59 *Bleach (Burīchi)*, directed by Noriyuki Abe (Tokyo: TV Tokyo, 2004–12), Anime TV series.

60 Csikszentmihalyi, 'A Systems Perspective,' 313–35.

61 Patrick W. Galbraith, *The Otaku Encyclopedia: An Insider's Guide to the Subculture of Cool Japan* (Tokyo: Kodansha International, 2009), 1–3.

62 Wai-hung Yiu and Alex Ching-shing Chan, '"Kawaii" and "Moe"—Gazes, Geeks (*otaku*) and Glocalization of Beautiful Girls (Bi Shojo) in Hong Kong Youth Culture,' *Positions: East Asia Cultures Critique* 21, no. 4, (2013), 853–84.

63 Craig Norris and Jason Bainbridge, 'Selling Otaku? Mapping the Relationship between Industry and Fandom in the Australian Cosplay Scene,' *Intersections* 20, no. 1, Gender and Sexuality in Asia and the Pacific (April 2009), para. 1.

64 Zygmunt Bauman, *Liquid Modernity* (Cambridge: Polity Press, 2000), 139–40.

65 *Spirited Away (Sen to Chihiro no Kamikakushi)*, directed by Hayao Miyazaki (Tokyo: Studio Ghibli, 2001), Anime film.

66   Gregory P. Stone, 'Appearance and the Self,' in *Human Behavior and the Social Processes: An Interactionist Approach*, ed. Arnold Marshall Rose (New York: Houghton Mifflin, 1962), 86–118.

67   Joanne B. Eicher and K. A. Miller, 'Dress and the Public, Private and Secret Self: Revisiting the Model,' *Proceedings of the International Textiles and Apparel Association* (Minneapolis: ITAA, 1994), 116.

68   Mary Ellen Roach and Joanne B. Eicher, *Dress, Adornment and the Social Order* (New York: John Wiley, 1965), 230.

69   Victor Witter Turner, *From Ritual to Theatre: The Human Seriousness of Play* (New York: PFA Publications, 1982), 103.

70   Teri Silvio, 'Informationalized Affect: The Body in Taiwanese Digital Video Puppetry and COSplay,' in *Embodied Modernities: Corporeality, Representation and Chinese Cultures*, eds. Fran Martin and Larrissa Heinrich (Honolulu: University of Hawaii Press, 2008), 197–217.

71   Ron Scollon, *Mediated Discourse: The Nexus of Practice* (London: Routledge, 2001), 1–4.

72   Rodney Jones, 'The Problem of Context in Computer-Mediated Communication,' in *Discourse & Technology: Multimodal Discourse Analysis*, eds. P. Levine and Ron Scollon (Washington, DC: Georgetown University Press, 2004), 9, 20–33.

73   Goffman, *The Presentation of Self*, 22–30.

74   Frenchy Lunning, 'Cosplay,' in *Berg Encyclopedia of Dress and Fashion, Vol. 10—Global Perspectives*, ed. Joanna B. Eicher (2011): 3–5, accessed 1 January 2018, http://www.bergfashionlibrary.com/view/bewdf/BEWDF-v10/EDch10024.xml.

75   Ibid., 3.

76   Ibid., 4.

77   Craig J. Thompson and Diana L. Haytko, 'Speaking of Fashion: Consumers' Uses of Fashion Discourses and the Appropriation of Countervailing Cultural Meanings,' *Journal of Consumer Research* 24 (1997), 15–42.

78   John W. Schouten and James H. McAlexander, 'Subcultures of Consumption: An Ethnography of the New Bikers,' *Journal of Consumer Research* 22 (1995), 43–61.

79   Robert V. Kozinets, 'Utopian Enterprise: Articulating the Meanings of *Star Trek's* Culture of Consumption,' *Journal of Consumer Research* 28 (2001), 68, 67–88.

80   Eric King Watts and Mark Orbe, 'The Spectacular Consumption of "True" African American Culture: "Whassup" with the Budweiser Guys?,' *Orbe Critical Studies in Media Communication* 19, no. 1 (2002), 1–20.

81   Russel Belk, Melanie Wallendorf, and John F. Sherry, Jr., 'The Sacred and the Profane: Theodicy on the Odyssey,' *Journal of Consumer Research*, 16 (June 1989), 1–38.

82   Robert V. Kozinets, 'Reviewed Work(s),' *Journal of Consumer Research* 28, no. 1 (June 2001), 85.

83   Terence K. Hopkins and Immanuel Wallerstein, 'Commodity Chains in the World Economy Prior to 1800,' *Review* 10, no. 1 (1986), 157–58.

84   Anne Allison, *Millennial Monsters: Japanese Toys and the Global Imaginary* (Oakland: University of California Press, 2006), viii.

85   Theresa Winge, 'Costuming the Imagination: Origins of Manga and Anime,' *Mechademia* 1, Emerging Worlds of Anime and Manga (2006), 75.

86 Ellen Kirkpatrick, 'Toward New Horizons: Cosplay (Re)imagined through the Superhero Genre, Authenticity, and Transformation,' *Transformative Works and Cultures* 18, Performance and Performativity in Fandom (2015), para 5.1.

87 Barrie Thorne, *Gender Play: Girls and Boys in School* (New Brunswick: Rutgers University Press, 1993), 64–67.

88 Henry Jenkins, *Convergence Culture: Where Old and New Media Collide* (New York: New York University Press, 2006), 2–3.

89 Henry Jenkins, *Textual Poachers: Television Fans and Participatory Culture* (New York: Routledge, 1992), 2–3.

90 Matt Hills, *Fan Cultures* (London and New York: Routledge, 2002), 41–43.

Part III

Provocations

Chapter 7

Proto-Cosplay

Dressing up is central, in more than a few respects, to human society and to civilization. Civilization is predicated on the assignation of ever-more specialized roles, whether of gender or class, to which people are required to conform, and also involves the playing out of roles and the acting out of proxies and aliases. However, dressing up for festivals and dramatic performances has also long allowed disruptive acts and expressions that were circumscribed in everyday life. In the rituals of traditional societies, shamanistic invocation and energetic spillage (abreaction) involved the assumption of identifiable archetypes, in part through accoutrements, such as masks and costumes, that symbolically mediated between the living and the dead, past and present, the seen and unseen. In this way, ritual provided a framework enabling individual and collective renewal. Masking oneself and becoming other in later, secular festive and dramatic performances, such as carnival, burlesque, masques and *commedia dell'arte*, remained a means of resituating the self to deliver a message often beyond the quotidian. That dressing up in both sacral and secular contexts lent itself to transgressive actions made it potentially threatening, and certainly provocative. In so doing, one could become more oneself, so to speak, by overstepping common mores and boundaries.

In assessing the historical development of masquerade in western civilization, it is essential to look at it from two main perspectives. The first is the way in which ad hoc forms of secular ritual coalesced in the carnivals of the late Middle Ages and the Renaissance. The second is the birth of the commedia dell'arte in the later sixteenth century, which occurred at the same time as the development of early modern drama and the operatic genre. These were all-important forms of spectacle in which everyday people often could actively participate. In reflecting on the emergence of the modern subject, role play is central to the expressions of personal possibility and limits, including Orientalist costuming vogues that allowed one to play fantastical others. Such forms provided a means through which people inserted themselves within myth, as active players rather than passive observers. Not only are these issues important for considering the broad cultural historical background to cosplay, highlighting the human need to dress up in costume for a range of purposes, but they also present a set of qualities that cosplay is not, and distinguish it as a cultural practice linked to, yet distinct from, its predecessors.

Carnival and the grotesque

Carnival and masquerade have to be understood against the broader backdrop of satire, comedy and laughter, particularly in terms of the relationship of people to dominant institutions such as king and state. In certain ancient rites, it was commonplace to laugh at a deity, known as 'ritual laughter,' a measure that allowed the one who laughs some purchase in the face of awe and incomprehension.[1] Such laughter also took place, for example, during funeral rituals, in which the deceased was both mourned and satirized. Satire performed the function of making death more palatable by grounding it in what could be experienced and known; it gave the satirist some place within the unknown. The practices of play and humour in the face of authority, observable in numerous cultures, was the subject of a famous anthropological study by Pierre Clastres, *Society against the State (La Société contre l'État)* (1974), which describes the Guayaki Indians of South America, for instance, as engaging in subversive humour against authority as a means of coming to grips with that authority. Here playing out and outrageousness become the expressive surplus value that makes arbitrary power palatable.[2]

Archaic western folk cultural practices evincing similar features appear to have survived into classical calendrical rituals such as the Greek Lupercalia and Roman Saturnalia, which, in turn, survived into the Middle Ages in masked 'squads' (similar to Halloween trick-or-treaters) known as *charivari* who operated during popular festivities. Italian historian Carlo Ginzburg has argued that there is a direct lineage between figures such as Harlequin that are found in Renaissance commedia dell'arte and ancient Eurasian shamanistic practices, via the 'ghostly cavalcade' of the Wild Hunt and similar popular festivities in the Middle Ages that underpinned medieval carnivals.[3] What was distinctive about these gatherings was that they were essentially participatory. As Mikhail Bakhtin observes: 'Carnival is not a spectacle seen by the people; they live in it, and everyone participates because its very idea embraces all the people. While carnival lasts there is no other life outside it.'[4] The key to carnival was escape from the mundane routines of everyday life. People could enter the stories told to them and temporarily become the characters to which they aspired, performing actions symbolically possible in that transitory moment. 'As opposed to the official feast,' Bakhtin continues,

> one might say that carnival celebrated temporary liberation from the prevailing truth and from the established order; it marked the suspension of all hierarchical rank, privileges, norms, and prohibitions. Carnival was the true feast of time, the feast of becoming, change and renewal. It was hostile to all that was immortalized and completed.[5]

The hostility embedded in carnival is based on the idea that people within it had, or had the illusion of having, everything in hand, within reach, but also the possibility of freedoms not permitted in everyday life. During Saturnalia, for example, women of the nobility would throw themselves on paupers, and soldiers would dress as women and prostitute themselves on the streets of Rome. Echoes of this kind of abandon survived into Christian Europe in popular, carnivalesque festivities.

In the perversion of the natural, in stretching the possible, the aesthetic and ethos that is often invoked is that of the grotesque. While already incipient in exaggerated rituals of ancient times, the grotesque comes into its own in the Middle Ages across a variety of media. It was present not just in the performing arts such as theatre, but the visual and plastic arts. Gothic architecture provides a concrete example in the various sculptural elements on the surface of the cathedrals, which are typically referred to as 'grotesques'. The grotesque signified an out of the ordinary state carrying with it elements of the supernatural, the dangerous and the wanton. Medieval grotesquerie, with its earthly, even crude folk humour, was very much something of the common people, and would be successively refined, but never entirely banished, from European cultural life. Bakhtin identified residues of the carnivalesque spirit of the Middle Ages in literary works such as François Rabelais' *The Life of Gargantua and Pantagruel* (*La vie de Gargantua et de Pantagruel*) (1532–52), comprising a genre that he termed 'grotesque realism'.

This sensibility was later reprised in the late eighteenth and early-nineteenth centuries, the early decades of Romanticism, which was also the beginning of the Gothic revival. Romanticism reserved for itself a special place in which fear and foreboding lay in menacing wait as a form of social control, but what the Romantic grotesque revealed was something in abeyance in earlier forms, namely an expression of personal alienation. The grotesque, and to act out in grotesque ways, was ultimately to embrace the contradictions of existence. Arguably, cosplay embodies both the medieval and Romantic grotesque, in its affective continuum between the collective body and personal alienation. It also represents a process by which the carnivalesque returns, like a revenant, to the stage of cultural history.

Masks and the commedia dell'arte

One of the recurring features of carnival was the mask. Masks were used in ancient Greek and Roman theatre, as they were in the most popular comic theatre of antiquity, the improvisatory Atellan farce, otherwise known as the *ludi Osci* or Oscan plays, originally performed in the native Oscan of the Campania. Becoming popular in 400 BCE, it remained for around five hundred years into the first century CE. The Oscan farces were characterized not only by their bawdiness and risqué topics, but for their recurring stock set of characters: Bucco, Manducus, Pappus, Samnio and Dossenus (or Dorsinus), all with distinctive traits tailored for explosive, exaggerated encounters. Bucco was a stout glutton, Manducus the avaricious, big-jawed ogre with an insatiable appetite. As it evolved, these characters became the instruments for popular social satire. It was so effective that in 23 CE the emperor Tiberius sought to banish scurrilous theatrical forms, including Atellan farce, from Rome. There were subsequent cases of Caligula, Nero and Galba all issuing proscriptions in the effort to restore the status quo and to prevent the social critique that emanated from popular satirical theatre. This aside, inasmuch as the Atellan farce relied on a technique where actors inhabited particular character types, it is generally viewed as the main precursor to the commedia. There was also plenty of grotesquerie with rampant priapism, buggery and transvestism, enacted with exaggerated ribaldry.

As with cosplay, a key feature and enabler of such shenanigans was the object of the mask. Unlike dissimulation and pretending, a metaphoric masking linked to lying and presumption, the physical mask, because concrete and unambiguous, opened up limitless possibilities for the one masked. One could literally become a god without reprisal because the act of alteration was writ large. But, paradoxically, it was the very acceptance precipitated by the lack of pretence, the directness of the visual lie that allowed for a more striking illusion. The mask literally acts as both a symbolic and physical portal into another consciousness and a higher, and hence more dangerous, reality. According to Bakhtin, the mask is

the most complex theme of folk culture. The mask is connected with the joy of change and reincarnation, with gay relativity and with the merry negation of uniformity and similarity; it rejects oneself. The mask is related to transition, metamorphosis, the violation of natural boundaries, to mockery and familiar nicknames. It contains the playful element of life; it is based on a peculiar interrelation of reality and image, characteristic of the most ancient rituals and spectacles. Of course it would be impossible to exhaust the intricate multiform symbolism of the mask.[6]

Bakhtin goes on to point out that 'such manifestations as parodies, caricatures, grimaces, eccentric postures, and comic gestures per se derived from the mask. It reveals the essence of the grotesque.'[7]

In light of this, it is both curious and understandable that the commedia dell'arte should come into being in the mid-sixteenth century—like today, a period of uncertainty and unrest—and therefore one to which the aesthetic of the grotesque is singularly at home. As Paul Castagno forcefully argues, the commedia dell'arte, while sharing traits from other dramatic forms such as Oscan drama, is very much a product of its time, namely the period that has since been identified as Mannerism. Mannerism begins roughly in the 1520s, with the death of Raphael, followed by the Sack of Rome in 1527. The latter occasioned the exile of Pope Clement VII himself from marauding troops brought on by the sudden death of Charles V, which was read as a sign of the opprobrium of God, and caused a new era of mass uncertainty. Given also that in 1521 Luther had refused to retract his *Ninety-Five Theses* (*Disputatio pro declaratione virtutis indulgentiarum*), the sack was read as a providential sign, and the discrediting of the Pope caused a breach in spiritual confidence and faith.

It is widely agreed that the art following these events reflected a spiritual unease, an unease that would expand exponentially into that associated with the de-centredness of the modern subject. Some of the music of this period is tempered by dramatic discord, epitomized by the enigmatic composer Carlo Gesualdo. In art, the harmonies and unities of the Renaissance were abjured in favour of gross distortions for the sake of exaggerated elegance (Parimigianino) or the insertion of human forms in settings that presaged Surrealism (Pontormo). The empathetic humanism that had begun with an artist such as Giotto was jettisoned, and in its place were cold, hard, inscrutable faces, their bodies sculpturally rigid rather than made of labile flesh (Bronzino). According to one of the key authorities on Mannerism, Arnold Hauser: 'To mannerism [...] all things presented themselves in distorted forms, under a cloak of concealment that made their true nature impossible to ascertain. The mask was never laid aside, the cloak never thrown off.'[8] Previous chapters of this book will have made the significance of this clearer, in discussing the way in which certain cosplayers only become 'themselves' when in their costume/role—'the mask is never laid aside'—in the attenuated moments of cosplay performance.

The Mannerist universe is one in which the grotesque is never absent, always waiting in the wings, since it would always embrace a non-reality, a life in permanent distortion, if not unrest. Primacy is given to types as opposed to individuals; genera are valued over particularities. As Castagno observes, Mannerism included 'typification of form (lack of individuality, conventionality), focus on surface treatment (costume, excessive ornamentation), lack of dimensionality or depth, exaggeration and distortion, and emphasis on parts versus the unity of the entire design.'[9] The singular body was abstracted, and unmoored from any natural realm or context. This notion of 'typing' is also explored by Constant Mic in his examination of the relationship between the commedia and comedy. He writes:

> Comedy is dominated by types; in tragedy, on the contrary, the living personality of the hero contains and absorbs the complex unity of vices, faults, the various traits that the type schematizes. Bergson makes a striking example for this point: comedies often take a vice or human weakness as their title (*The Miser*, *The Gambler*, *The Distracted One*), whereas the title of dramas is generally the name of the person.[10]

In this regard, commedia provides parallels with the theatrical forms from East Asia, where cosplay also has deep cultural roots. Since the fourteenth century, Japanese Noh theatre employed wooden masks and ornate, shimmering silk costumes to represent set characters conveying emotions in a stylized manner.[11] The more popularly orientated and participatory Kabuki theatre relied on a similar level of contrivance with white rice powder-based mask of make-up overlaid with colours to convey the essence of the character, with red (*aka*) representing passion or heroism and blue (*ao*) the supernatural, and so on.[12]

By the beginning of the eighteenth century—also the era of the growth and entrenchment of masquerade balls, discussed in the next section—the commedia dell'arte had become something of a ubiquitous theatrical and festive feature across Europe. The characters were fairly clearly defined and identified with particular roles and dispositions. In addition to the most famous, Arlecchino (or Harlequin) and Polchinelle/Pulcinella (Punch), other figures included Pierrette, Pantalone, Il Dottore, Colombina and Scaramuccia (Scaramouche). Although they were a convention that posed as a rival to the scripted forms of drama, when not sexually convulsive, the commedia's recurring themes were nonetheless about fidelity, jealousy, miscommunication, class and age. Catherine Velay-Vallantin also remarks that by the end of the seventeenth century, the commedia dell'arte not only had its standardized costumes aligned to characters, but that physical movements had come to be more discernibly mechanized, with an acrobatic element that had a strong visual effect.[13]

It therefore comes as no surprise that marionette theatre, specifically dolls controlled with strings, appeared in central Europe at around the same time.[14] The first appearance of Polichinelle in France is reported as being 1649 and was soon after transformed into the marionette and puppet still loved by children today. Similarly, Japanese Bunraku puppet theatre, originally called *ningyo joruri*, literally meaning 'narrative art with dolls,' dates from seventeenth-century Osaka. Bunraku uses sophisticated, mechanically controlled three-foot high puppets with expressive carved heads, real hair and elaborate traditional costume to represent key characters in the narrative, such as monks, adventurers and warriors.[15] A link to cosplay is found in the way in which the puppet masters breathe life into the puppets, which become human, while that which is human becomes puppetry—that is, an embodied, stylized, structured and sensory performance. As Roland Barthes notes, 'It is not the simulation of the body which Bunraku seeks, it is—if this can be said—the body's tangible abstraction.'[16] Unlike the marionette, which stands in for the live actor, the Bunraku puppetry is a unified, embodied mediation of three parts that become the whole—the wooden puppet, the puppeteer and the chanter.

Another irony of the early modern period is that the mechanical body is also the beginning of the modern body, a concept associated with one of the founders of modern philosophy, René Descartes, who devised the mind-body division, but also conceived of the body as machine. Cartesian conflict between advancing mechanization and humanity as 'antagonistic dualisms'[17] embedded itself in western discourse, serving to rationalize and control otherness. Arguably, by addressing these mythic constructs in popular narratives and embodying them, often by dressing up as a cyborg, mecha (giant robot) or other non- or extra-human character, cosplayers attempt to make sense of and contain the man versus machine dilemma while overcoming their conscious or unconscious fears of a flawed humanity.

Another factor that aligns the commedia to early modernity is the greater sophistication of social strata. European societies had been conveniently divided into king, church and people, as in the *ancien régime* of the French Three Estates. These feudal structures would not, however, survive the mercantilism and technologization that followed in the wake of the Renaissance. This process was also reflected in the evolution of cultural forms. By the end of the sixteenth century not only is the commedia dell'arte in its infancy, but there is also the burgeoning of opera—Jacopo Peri's *Dafne* was written in c.1597 and Claudio Moneverdi's *Orfeo* in 1609—and also what would come to be known as the museum, as in for instance Samuel Quiccheberg's *Inscriptiones*, published in Latin in 1565, arguably the first major, ambitious treatise on museology.[18] Such developments point to a widening and a re-ordering of society as mirrored in art and related cultural practices. In this vein, the commedia dell'arte can be understood as belonging to the taxonomic practice of making sense of society along lines that are no longer solely of class, but according to traits associated with inherent qualities such as ambition, mobility of action and character. According to Michael Quinn, the figures of the commedia

were developed into discrete artistic units, which, in the context of an improvised dramaturgy, dominated the conventional structures of dramatic events. They are also sufficiently static and visually interesting that they were translated into a repertory of figures for painting and carnival disguise. Though conventional figures can be based on particular historic individuals, the commedia types tended to derive their characteristics from several different mimetic relations.[19]

Such relations were historically derived or circumscribed.[20] The costumes and their associated actions and reactions were an amalgam that revolved around customs and values that were, in turn, obeyed or violated. As the characters became recognized, they were known according to visual and other structural signatures (movements, sounds and so on). Clearly, this is the realm of caricature that has always been the province of class and identity—namely the upper classes deriding the lower, or the lower satirizing those above them through comic relief.

Given the itinerant nature of the commedia dell'arte troupes, they were associated right until the early twentieth century with the lower 'gypsy' and itinerant classes (think Picasso's Rose period paintings of the travelling clowns and misfits). Hence the association of comedy—which reaches a climax in the twentieth century in Chaplin—with the tramp, the vagrant, and the down-and-out. The application of this notion to contemporary cosplay is a simple one: it is not to suggest that cosplay is to do with poverty, although there is a level of travel and itinerancy, with many cosplayers being less than pecunious students and other young people; the main point is otherness. Domenico Scagoglio notices that comedy is conceived along the lines of others. Our empathy is always a degree or two removed:

> the comic figure is always the same albeit in different ways, being foreign to the culture he lives in: in Rome one said the Atellan dramatists came from Atella; the comedians of Roman theatre were slaves, and so again foreigners; the buffoons from urban European societies came from the country or were thought to be; the masques of the Commedia dell'Arte of the sixteenth to the eighteenth century were generally ethnic masques that represented, under typologized forms, neighbouring cultures.[21]

This is also partially to ensure that the comedic mishap does not appear to impinge directly on our own lives. Ferdinando Taviani and Mirella Schino divide the various professionals of the commedia spectacle not only into actors, but also as 'charlatans, buffoons and beggars.'[22]

To return to the Cartesian mind-body division, it is feasible to assume that the commedia were a kind of dramatic solution to subjective alienation and the split between mind and body, hence humans and nature. Moreover, it is tenable to argue that the character types of the commedia, with their insistent and associated movements, moods and traits, were tantamount to living dolls; they were characterological machines. For actors to inhabit pre-existing forms with their associated rules of voice and action was, in effect, to insert themselves into a carapace that was pre-formed, known and recognized, and thereby to inhabit a known character, to engage in a degree of ontological certainly unfamiliar to individual subjects. The whole body essentially becomes a mask, and the theatrical stylization of movements becomes similar to the controlled and stilted movements of western puppetry and eastern forms such as Bunraku theatre.

The issue of certainty is central to the problem here. For after all, Descartes asserted that the body was far easier to know than the mind. Bodies, machine-like, the characters pre-ordained—all this allowed the audience anchorage and comprehensibility within the comedic chaos. Ultimately, to play the doll was to renounce the transparency of self, to displace the notion of nuclear self, the Cartesian *cogito*. Similarly, with cosplay the characters are extracted from a closed and known universe. It is known in the sense that even where there are ambiguities and indeterminacies, these are all components within a diegetic framework that operates for the sake of the action of the hero. In computer games, for instance, the certainty consists in the barriers that one's avatar runs up against when straying too far from the game's path or parameters, despite the graphics depicting a beyond (outer space, a forest or whatever). And one's powers are those that can have an effect on one's adversaries. Qualities are fitted to a smooth calibration of cause and effect. The minutiae of variations are infinite, but the trajectory is always the same.

While the commedia would continue until modern times, this dimension of communal life had waned in its influence, and its popularity became sporadic. It would have a powerful presence in the art of the eighteenth century onward, and would fascinate major artists like Watteau, Cézanne and Picasso, sometimes as a way of conveying a particular expression of character, or the condition of the isolated, muted modern artist. The presence of the commedia still persists in modern festivals, such as those of Venice, Siena and Ravenna, and has been productively re-adapted to children's puppet theatre. It is no surprise, however, that the emergence of the commedia dell'arte in the mid-to-late sixteenth century occurred at the same time and pace as that of the masque, the carnival gatherings in which people wore masks and special clothing for the event.

Masque and masquerade

By the early eighteenth century, masquerade in all its various forms was treated with considerable anxiety across several strata of society. The opprobrium was not limited to the upper classes, many of whom liked to indulge. On the contrary, it was a sentiment shared by the clergy (i.e. among those who were averse to indulging themselves), the middle classes and the aristocracy. It was seen as a social practice that allowed for crass and inappropriate behaviour, and for a kind of class mixing that was seen as highly questionable, not to say risky, for the respectable social fabric.

One of the more vocal members of what became known as the 'anti-masquerade movement' was Henry Fielding who, together with Samuel Richardson and Eliza Haywood, aligned masquerade to a form of public debauchery. In his 1728 poem 'The Masquerade' he writes of the mixing of classes and the way they share in lubricious behaviour:

Known prudes there, livertibes we find,
Who masque the face, t'unmasque the mind.
Here, running footmen guzzle tea;
There, milk-maids flasks of Burgundy.
I saw two shepherdesses drunk
And heard a friar called a punk.[23]

Fielding maintains that Christianity's old bête noire, Satan, was the 'first minister of masquerade'.[24] For masquerade was a sure sign of the biblical Fall coming to full fruition, a loss of innocence played out on a mass scale. Alexander Pope would echo this in the 'Rape of the Lock':

What guards the purity of melting maids,
In courtly balls, and midnight masquerades,
Safe from the treach'rous friend, the daring spark,
The glance by day, the whisper in the dark,
When kind occasion prompts their warm desires,
When music softens, and when dancing fires?[25]

Masquerade inevitably led to female defilement and shame. Likewise Fielding mourns:

When love alone could charm the fair:
Such Arcadian nymphs, when love
Beauty alone in men could move.
How happy did they sport away,
In fragrant bow'rs, the scorching day;
Or, to the Nightingale's soft tune,
Danc'd by the lustre of the moon!
Beauteous nymphs, the swains sincere,
They knew no jealousy, no fear:
Together they flock'd, like turtle-doves,
All constant to their plighted loves.
How different is now their fate!
Both equally conspire to cheat.
Florus, with lying billet-doux
The charming Rosalind pursues;
Follows her to the play—to court,
Where-ever the beau monde resort.[26]

The message is simple enough, and it presages in many ways Rousseau's narratives of urban society and corrupted morals that were soon to follow.

While Fielding's satire draws on classical references, it comes directly out of the social conditions of eighteenth-century London, then rivalled only by Tokyo as the world's largest urban metropolis. Masquerade was often viewed by its detractors as a mediator whereby the vices of urban life could have some kind of organizing principle. But there was far more to masquerade than an orgiastic practice of early modernity. For Terry Castle, the appetite for costume and masque that flourished so rapidly in the eighteenth century 'demonstrated a kinship with the traditional rite of reversal, and indeed with all those outbreaks of topsy-turvy-dom manifested in virtually every documented human culture.'[27] In a society where class divisions were increasingly tested, and where the rank and arbitrary rule were becoming dangerously contested, the masquerade and the power of deliberate disguise explored a space in which the artificiality of rank and roles could be seen for what they were, as essentially constructed. In other words, it was precisely through enactment that the artifice of the world could come to light. As Castle continues: 'Besides highlighting structure, rituals of inversion can demonstrate the fictionality of classification systems, exposing them as man-made rather than natural or divine.'[28] In a time also when fashions were very much indicators of class and station, it exposed 'the artificiality of the sartorial code.'[29]

Thus, if the spokespeople against masquerade railed against its moral turpitude, it was also because they were extracting the most graphic and provocative side of its activity, since it can easily be seen as a form of social rebellion. It was easy for a duke to impersonate a servant—which is also represented repeatedly in farces and operas of the time—but it was far more provocative if a servant impersonated a duke. But the former was the more common case, simply because the latter activity was constrained by economics—it was hard for a member of the working class to justify, let alone afford, the finery of the upper classes. The most popular members of the lower classes included shepherds and shepherdesses, millers, slower-sellers and sailors and soldiers bedecked in motley fashion. The repertoire of such types is much in line with what after the 1970s came to be known as 'clones,' particularly as they belonged to that culture (the builder, the sailor, the cowboy and so on).

As well as challenging or undermining class, masquerade also tested the limits of gender, sexuality and ethnicity. As Castle explains:

Transvestite garb began, necessarily, with violation of the basic trouser/skirt opposition: as on the eighteenth-century comic stage, male masqueraders preened and glided in voluminous skirts, while their female counterparts strutted in breeches and jackboots. Simple cross-gender impersonation usually merged with occupational fancy dress: masquerade transvestites as a rule wore costumes suggesting professions or roles associated solely with the opposite sex. Women disguised themselves, thus, as hussars, pirates, bishops, and the like, while their male counterparts metamorphosed into milkmaids, spinsters, and wayward bacchantes. Given the particular metonymic connection between sexuality and masquerade, the costume of a procuress or bawd remained one of the more ironic choices opened to male cross-dressers.[30]

Such extravagancies and indiscretions clearly had a cathartic effect, in which people could entertain indiscretions rather than officially act on them. They could transact them but, as a proxy, it was always a truth spoken in jest.

The pervasiveness of masquerade had inserted itself so powerfully within the fabric of eighteenth-century culture that the anti-masquerade movement in England had spread throughout Europe and by the end of the century called for proscriptions to be effected. The energies surrounding dressing up also penetrated the moralities discussed between various writers, wherein certain characters were deemed ciphers for all manner of iniquity. This brings us back to the commedia dell'arte and the particular controversy that circulated around the character of Harlequin. Some eminent classicists called for, and briefly succeeded in his expulsion from the stage.[31] Harlequin, perhaps the most recognizable and popular member of the commedia dell-arte, was seen as being the archetype of a form of theatre and conduct inimical to theatre and theatricalization. Like the anti-masqueraders, purists of theatre and literature deemed the grotesque not only a poorer form, but far worse, as a kind of aesthetic disease.

Orientalism and costuming

One way of preventing, or at least of sidestepping, this predicament was through the ruses and displacements of Orientalism. The history of Orientalism in dress has a long and intricate history in which masquerade forms a crucial, as well as fluid, part.[32] Another word for fluid is permeable, since wearing one item of Orientalist dress was already to partake in a series of values that pointed to a reorientation of inhibitions or one's scholarly and ideological scope. From the seventeenth century until well into the nineteenth, many 'men of letters,' for example, wore and had themselves depicted as wearing a banyan, the Indian-ified version of the Japanese yukata, the original version of what today is prosaically called the dressing gown (the portrait of Samuel Pepys by John Hayls from 1666 is one notable example of this). Rousseau famously wore Armenian style robes and kaftans to signal his aversion to the worldly wiles of fashion, and that he was the mandarin of his own intellectual domain. There are many more colourful cases, but what all the instances share is the perception that the Orient somehow existed outside of time as the exoticized 'other,' being a place of eternal mysteries and passions.

But the incidence of Orientalism in masquerade per se was so popular that it occasioned the publication of several discrete tomes that served as source books for possible dress ensembles and combinations. These were John Tinney's *Collection of Eastern and Foreign Dresses* (1750) and Thomas Jefferys' *Collection of the Dresses of Different Nations, Ancient and Modern* (1757). These books were a grab-bag of Orientalist dress, as such compilations inevitably were, with references to historical personages and reproductions of copies of artworks. Not only were there material guidelines for dress, but there were instructions on appearance and deportment as well, often bordering on the intriguing and the bizarre. Castle argues that such instructions and what they eventuated in amounted to a 'primitive ethnography.'[33] And while such fascinations could be read in tandem with imperial expansion—the imperial victor having the confidence and shamelessness to mimic the colonized, much in the vein of the upper classes dressing up as the lower orders—she argues that there is a broader instinct at work here that has to do with the engagement with 'otherness itself.'[34] As she states: 'Stereotypical and inaccurate though they often were, exotic costumes marked out a kind of symbolic interpenetration with difference—an almost erotic commingling with the alien. Mimicry became a form of psychological recognition, a way of embracing, quite literally, the unfamiliar.'[35]

Thus, the historic details of Orientalism and masquerade are essential to the genealogy of cosplay, given its joint American-Japanese roots, as discussed in previous chapters. Contemporary criticism in the wake of the key postcolonial critique, Edward Said's now highly contested *Orientalism* (1978), has concentrated on words such as 'exchange' over stealing, as well as inquiring into the various ways in which cultures engage in their own self- or re-Orientalizing. As with India and the re-adoption of the *buta* after it was rebranded 'paisley' from the Scottish town of the same name, or the renewed emphasis on the cheongsam in China, Orientalizing within cultures once amorphously deemed Oriental is a way of remarketing nationhood, as well as revelling in artefacts understood as inextricable from it. Cosplay, as it is staged in Asian countries, is careful to distinguish the Asian from the non-Asian stereotypes, including 'Asian-ifying' western types with signifiers that are close to universal in popular culture, such as large manga-style eyes. What is common to both contemporary and historical Orientalism is the way in which the malleable and changeable dances together with the permanent and the pure. Like all signs of indigeneity and nationhood, as with myth itself, it is constantly being manipulated with the faith in some unalterable fundament, which is nonetheless intangible and unreachable.

One of the more memorable and instructive historic instances of early Orientalist masquerade occurred in 1686 when the court of Louis XIV received a delegation of ambassadors from Siam (now Thailand). This was a period when France was being subjected to a great deal of isolation from the rest of Europe and as a result was looking further afield for allegiances and affiliations. The influence of Siam itself was reflected in what came to be known as *la siamoise*, a light striped cotton or linen garment, which became a short-lived fashion, and was not subject to much imaginative embroidery. Rather, the Siamese visit served to entrench chinoiserie into the French cultural consciousness. Of importance is the way in which, in this case, France, took an 'other,' here Siam, as an excuse and catalyst for stylistic variation and play in a form of active othering that was then performed on clothing, *objets d'art*, furniture, interior decoration and more besides.

King Louis' performance in this historic event is also central. To celebrate the occasion of the visit, he had himself dressed in a costume that was 'half-Persian, half-Chinese' (*moitié à la persienne, moitié à la chinoise*). It is to be remembered that this was an age when cultural sensitivity or cultural faithfulness were little respected. On the contrary, cultures and references attached to them could be mixed and matched and, in this case, more was more. Louis provided a mere opening to what followed: a series of colourful and sumptuous balls *à la chinoise* involving numerous players, including the king and his princes.[36] Undoubtedly chinoiserie was a chimerical platform that allowed for all kinds of play departing from the lineaments of the home culture. And it is again worth emphasizing, against all prurient accusations of inauthenticity, that dressing up in this way furnished a means for expression that allowed one to do things that would have been difficult to justify in everyday life—through such voluntary deceits one could become more of oneself. The close association with play, creation, adaptation, performance and just plain old fun made chinoiserie a highly popular and lasting style. And the fact that it was exotic, unmoored to local mores and beliefs, made it the perfect portal for all kinds of variations and conceits.

Nor can the invention of costumes in the seventeenth and early eighteenth centuries in any way be divorced from smaller accoutrements that could be worn as souvenirs, talismans or trophies, in such magnitude that it became harder and harder to tell which originated in China or in Europe. This stylistic appetite for chinoiserie, the cult of Cathay in France, was given the new name of *lachinage*—literally 'Chinese-ing' or 'Chinese-ifying' (*la chine-age*). It was to become a tendency in fashion and the decorative arts whose equivalent had already come into place in music and theatre. While not part of everyday garb, there are obvious parallels with the many scimitars, *kanzashi* (hairpins) and other Asian objects and devices worn by many western cosplayers at conventions today, in addition to the vast profusion of garments that comprise the primary elements of their costuming.

By the eighteenth century, chinoiserie had melded with the Turkish style, *turquerie*, but variations by degree across the range of Orientalist styles still pertained. One of the more celebrated dramatists that combined fairy tales, exotic styling and the commedia dell'arte was Carlo Gozzi, active in Venice until the end of the century. One of his best-known plays was *Turandot* (1762), a commedia-style adaptation of stories from the *Thousand and One Nights (Alf layla wa-layla)*, which had been translated around fifty years earlier. Given that the *Thousand and One Nights* had become well-trodden territory by this time, in an effort to revive interest while taking advantage of familiarity, Gozzi shifts the action to Peking (Beijing). One of the characters, Truffaldino, initially a servant from Bergamo, becomes the chief eunuch in the seraglio of the king and dressed in 'Chinese style.'[37] Pantalone has travelled from Venice to become the king's advisor. In one of his speeches, he confesses, 'I didn't know a thing about China. I thought it was one of those powders you take for tertian fever. I still can't believe all those vows and beheadings.'[38] He perpetuates a much-cherished belief of China as a place of supreme despotism, as well as of earthly delights. In this way, he also helps to maintain the close relationship between dressing up, the exotic, the dangerous and, by extension, the erotic.

Dressing up, again, is also used as a strategy not only for airing delicate or unwelcome opinions, but also for simplifying certain beliefs. As Quinn explains,

> By setting the scene of his play in a foreign land, Gozzi was able to refer back to a Venice that was not conceived realistically but rather symbolically, as a city that embodied a

particular ideology through the process of figuration. The commedia images, as familiar and historically revered as the lion [the symbol of Venice] itself, became crucial icons in this symbolic expression, which hovered beyond the reach of mundane concerns.[39]

These words can be extrapolated well beyond the reach of the issue at hand, especially phrases such as 'the process of figuration' and 'hovered beyond the reach of mundane concerns.' For Orientalist masquerade was a completely understandable and logical modality in the illogical taxonomy of identities at play, as it engaged with the other par excellence. Unlike the proverbial shepherdesses, mariners or other popular types, to indulge in Orientalist masquerade was not to be accountable to any tangible point of reference. One literally cast oneself far afield, and in doing so sublimated to the highest level. Mundanities were of the least concern.

Continuities and discontinuities

It would be precisely this flight into fantasy and the license that could be taken in masquerade that would continue to be counted as a threat by conservatives and government authorities. When the libretto by Antonio Somma (based on an earlier version by the French playwright Eugène Scribe) was presented to the Neopolitan censors in 1857, it was met with consternation due to the representation of a regicide on stage. It was because of the ensuing legal complications that the action shifted to Boston during the period of British colonization. Complicating things further, the main character, the Earl of Warwick, the governor of Boston, was a direct transposition of the original character, Gustav III of Sweden, who was known as a flamboyant homosexual or bisexual. Masquerade was a way of mobilizing socially unappetizing and risqué behaviour, which the public as viewer and participant, nonetheless, were enthusiastic to consume. Cosplay can be considered in part its modern, if distant, successor, though with some key provisos.

The historical co-ordinates that predate cosplay are many and rooted in adult play, othering, fantasy, masquerade and character typecasting. In view of this genealogy, it might be useful to conclude on a few speculative points on the inherent continuities and discontinuities with modern cosplay. Clearly, like the various models of the past presented above, cosplay allows one to step into character, while occupying a set of rules and qualities oriented around culture and narrative. It allows one to escape the flow of everyday events, to elide reason and to eschew the natural order. There need not be any justification in what one is doing except when one does become the new other, when it is incumbent upon the player to achieve some degree of verisimilitude with the source character. Yet cosplayers also dress up and inhabit their fictional characters as a way of signalling otherness beyond the mundaneness of their everyday existence in the search for, and in support of, an exotic, mythic dimension of existence. This chimes with historical festive practices such as carnival and other exhibitions of the grotesque body that cosplay reclaims from the textual level and reanimates in costumed bodies. Like historical masques and masquerades, cosplay has provoked censure in some quarters for encouraging deviancy.

When surveying the masquerade and the commedia dell'arte since the sixteenth century, however, three differences appear to loom out: one is that commedia dell'arte can be considered as a popular theatrical form of its day being enjoyed by many,[40] while cosplay is a fan-based practice reliant on specific popular culture texts as an inspirational resource.[41] The cosplayer, in effect, apprentices him or herself to whomever he or she plays, and is judged by a community of peers who are, reciprocally, judged in turn. The second issue is that the erotic and the openly transgressive have become sublimated once again. In comparison to the masquerades of the eighteenth century, derided by Fielding and his contemporaries as debauched encounters, from a sexual point of view, cosplay conventions are decorous affairs, despite the moral panics about their value and their deviant nature. Any eroticism is situated in an external realm, such as built into narratives whence the characters are derived, though female cosplayers have been cast by some media commentators as constituting overt displays of hypersexuality (quite separate from the notion of 'cosporn,' which will be discussed in Chapter 9).

Finally, not only Orientalism but Occidentalism (whereby Asian cosplayers, and sometimes the source texts they mine, evoke imaginative constructions of the west) is built into the very caste of cosplay where a duality of otherness is at stake. Representations of an idealized west in Japanese media, for example, include many of the European settings in Hayao Miyazaki's anime and many a *shōjo* BL (Boys Love) manga or anime, suggesting a reciprocal process.[42] While Occidentalism occurs in the idealization and superiorization of western-style characters signified by costume-based superpowers or accessories—magic wands, futuristic armour and mystic cloaks—Orientalism exists as a series of signifiers that have become transhistorical and transnational—such as scimitar swords, samurai swords, beading, harem pants—internal to the stylistic order, and existing across a range of other references.[43] As such, cosplay resides at the intersection of eastern and western culture flows rather than as a site of appropriation of one by the other.

Notes

1   Mikhail Bakhtin, *Rabelais and His World* (*Tvorčestvo Fransua Rable i narodnaja kul'tura srednevekov'ja i Renessansa*), trans. Helene Iswolsky (1965; Cambridge: MIT Press, 1968), 6.

2   Pierre Clastres, *Society against the State: Essays in Political Anthropology* (*La Société contre l'État*) (1974), trans. Robert Hurley and Abe Stein (Cambridge: Zone Books, 1989).

3   See Carlo Ginzberg, *Ecstasies: Deciphering the Witches' Sabbath* (*Storia notturna: Una decifrazione del Sabba*), trans. Raymond Rosenthal (Chicago: Chicago University Press, 1991), Carlo Ginzburg, *The Night Battles: Witchcraft and Agrarian Cults in the Sixteen and Seventeenth Centuries* (*I Benandanti: Stregoneria e culti agrari tra Cinquecento e Seicento*), trans. Anne C. Tedeschi and John Tedeschi (Baltimore: Johns Hopkins University Press, 2013).

4 Bakhtin, *Rabelais*, 7.

5 Ibid., 10.

6 Ibid., 39–40.

7 Ibid.

8 Arnold Hauser, *Mannerism* (Cambridge: Bellkamp Press of Harvard University Press, 1965), 329.

9 Paul Castagno, *The Early Commedia Dell'Arte, 1550–1621: The Mannerist Context* (New York: Peter Lang, 1994), 85.

10 Constant Mic, *La Commedia dell'Arte Oe Le Theatre Des Comediens Italiens Des XVIe, XVIIe & XVIIIe Siecles* (1927; Paris: Librairie Theatrale, 1980), 162–63.

11 Faubion Bowers, *Japanese Theatre* (Rutland: Charles E. Tuttle Co, 1974).

12 Zoe Kincaid, *Kabuki: The Popular Stage of Japan* (London: MacMillan and Co., 1925), 21–22.

13 Catherine Velay-Vallantin, 'Polichinelle dans le colportage au XIXème siècle,' in ed. Brunela Ernuli, *Policinelle* (Charelleville-Mézières: Cahiers Robinson, 1999), 92.

14 Hans R. Purschke, *Die Entwicklung des* (Frankfurt: H. R. Purschke, 1984).

15 Karen Brazell, *Traditional Japanese Theater* (New York: Columbia University Press, 1997), 115–16.

16 Roland Barthes, 'On Bunraku,' *The Drama Review: TDR* 15, no. 2, *Theatre in Asia* (1971), 79.

17 Donna Jeanne Haraway, 'A Cyborg Manifesto: Science, Technology, and Socialist-Feminism in the Late Twentieth Century,' in *Simians, Cyborgs and Women: The Reinvention of Nature* (London: Routledge, 1991).

18 Samuel Quicchebereg, *The First Treatise on Museums: Samuel Quiccheberg's Inscriptiones, 1565*, trans. Mark Meadow and Bruce Robertson (Los Angeles: Getty, 2013).

19 Michael Quinn, 'The Comedy of Reference: The Semiotics of the Commedia Figures in Eighteenth-Century Venice,' *Theatre Journal* 43, no. 1 (March 1991), 73.

20 Ibid.

21 Domenico Scafoglio, 'Pulcinella/Policinelle: *Méethodologique et perspectives de recherche*,' in *Policinelle*, ed. B. Ernuli, 14. See also Gerald Sandy 'Habinnas' where a slave takes up some of the slack, giving samples of his virtuoso abilities as a 'Vergilianist' and as a performer of Atellan farces (68.4–5), with his master reporting additional details of his talent as a mimus (68.6–7; cf. 69.4–5). It is of some interest that the slave's mingling of different verse forms is reminiscent of Livy's famous description of the introduction of drama, i.e. Atellan farce, to Rome (7.2.II). 'Scaenica Petronia,' *Transactions of the American Philological Association (1974–)* 104 (1974), 336.

22 Ferdinando Taviani and Mirella Schino, *Le Secret de la Commedia dell'Arte*, trans. Fr. Yves Liebert (1982; Florence: La Casa Usher, 1984), 129–62.

23 Samuel Fielding, 'The Masquerade, A Poem' (Warwick Lane, London: J. Roberts, 1728), 3.

24 Ibid., 5.

25 Alexander Pope, 'Rape of the Lock,' Canto I, *The Works of Alexander Pope* (1712; Hertfordshire: Wordsworth Poetry Library, 1995), 89.

26 Ibid., 7.

27 Terry Castle, *Masquerade and Civilization: The Carnivalesque in Eighteenth-Century English Culture and Fiction* (Stanford: Stanford University Press, 1986), 87.

28 Ibid., 88.

29 Ibid.

30 Ibid., 64.

31 Bakhtin, *Rabelais*, 35.

32 Adam Geczy, *Fashion and Orientalism: Dress, Textiles and Culture from the 17th to the 21st Century* (London and New York: Bloomsbury), 2013.

33 Castle, *Masquerade and Civilization*, 60–61.

34 Ibid., 61.

35 Ibid.

36 See Hugh Honour, *Chinoiserie: The Vision of Cathay* (London: John Murray, 1961), 62–3; Dawn Jacobson, *Chinoiserie* (London: Phaidon, 1993), 31.

37 See also Quinn, 'The Comedy of Reference,' 85.

38 Carlo Gozzi, 'Turandot,' in *Carlo Gozzi: Five Tales for the Theatre*, eds. A. Bermel and T. Emery (Chicago: Chicago University Press, 1989), 139.

39 Quinn, 'The Comedy of Reference,' 86.

40 Raymond Williams, *Keywords: A Vocabulary of Culture and Society* (London: Fontana, 1976).

41 John Fiske, 'Cultural Economy of Fandom,' in *The Adoring Audience: Fan Culture and Popular Media*, ed. Lisa A. Lewis (London: Routledge, 2003), 31.

42 Examples include *Lupin the III: The Castle of Cagliostro (Rupan Sansei: Kariosutoro no Shiro)*, directed by Hayao Miyazaki (Tokyo: Tokyo Movie Shinsha, 1979), Anime film; *Laputa: Castle in the Sky (Tenkū no Shiro Rapyuta)*, directed by Hayao Miyazaki (Tokyo: Studio Ghibli, 1986), Anime film; *Porco Rosso*, directed by Hayao Miyazaki (Tokyo: Studio Ghibli, 1992), Anime film; *Howl's Moving Castle (Hauru no Ugoku Shiro)*, directed by Hayao Miyazaki (Tokyo: Studio Ghibli, 2004), Anime film. See Tomoko Aoyama and Barbara Hartley, *Girl Reading Girl* (London: Routledge, 2010) or Laura Miller and Jan Bardesly, *Bad Girls of Japan* (London: Palgrave Macmillan, 2005).

43 See discussion of the 'transoriental' in Geczy, *Fashion and Orientalism*.

Chapter 8

Cosgender/Cosqueer

While gender is widely featured in discussions of cosplay, the term 'cosqueer' and its fellow traveller 'cosgay' are largely limited to online forums and have not yet made their way into the critical lexicon. The coinage of the term 'crossplay' is used to refer to the practice of female players dressing as male characters, and vice versa, but while this may be a form of drag there is no automatic presumption of queer sexuality attached to such gender-bending costume play. Yet it seems only a matter of time before the terms cosplay and queer, each relatively new, would be soldered together and deployed to describe a dimension of cosplay distinct, though overlapping in some respects, from the crossplay genre. This is not only because of the rising prevalence of queer studies, as the term originated from the 1990s, and more recently what is cumbrously known as LGBTQIA (lesbian, gay, bisexual, transgender, queer, intersex and asexual) studies interrogating sexuality from multiple positions in the gender continuum, but also that cosplay itself fits into a general definition of queer. For queer—which like all such terms relating to class, race and identity are porous, hotly debated and contested—is not limited to signify being gay or lesbian, but embraces all the variants of identity types that do not comply with, or are indifferent to, what queer studies calls 'heteronormativity.'

True enough, a good many of the characters that cosplayers seek to emulate are highly compliant with sexual norms and stereotypes, but cosqueer can be said to boil down to two basic concepts. The first is grounded in those characters that do not fit these norms, or of players who choose to undermine such norms in their presentation of characters. The second is grounded in difference itself: difference not only as sexual difference but also as bodily and character difference. The latter thematic can be traced back to the tragic story of Victor Frankenstein's monster, an amalgam of human parts forced to inhabit a terrifying skin, a shell he could not shake, and who was thereby condemned to be treated as eternally repugnant and an object of disdain.[1] Today, with the notion of the cyborg alongside the popularity and growing normalcy of body modification, the line between the terrifying and desirable appears to be an enormously fluid concept. Like all queer communities, cosplayers celebrate their difference, in the desire to escape what is regularly deemed natural and normal.

Queer

It may be that readers involved in cosplay find themselves divided at this point: some revelling in being called queer, others resentfully uncomfortable with a term that portrays a group as errant and odd. This is a divide that may never be filled, but it is a conflict that is built into queer theory from the very outset, particularly in a refusal to be normalized, which is conceived as an absorption into an inhibiting set of rules.[2] '"Queer"' writes Judith Butler, 'derives its force precisely through the repeated invocation by which it has become linked to accusation, pathologization, insult.'[3] Queer theory, and its successors in LGBTQIA studies, developed out of second-wave feminism and postcolonial theory in the 1980s, a period that witnessed the outbreak of the AIDS virus across the world. The key founders of queer theory include Eve Kosofsky Sedgwick and Guy Hocquenghem, theorists who defended the need for a greater homosexual presence in art, literature and life. Sedgwick, predominately a literary theorist, drew attention to homosexual undercurrents in the works of writers such as Charles Dickens and Henry James, arguing that it is not philosophically responsible to overlook such readings of canonical texts, as they underscore certain inner meanings and interpretations of their work.

Another important notion to derive from the 1980s was that of 'technologies of gender,' a provocative phrase coined by Teresa de Lauretis in order to describe the way in which gender is constructed from a variety of elements according to systems and rules. Drawing from Louis Althusser's theories of ideology and Michel Foucault's notions of the (female) body as object of knowledge, Lauretis discerns four main considerations for a better grasp of gender: first, gender is 'representation—which is not to say that it does not have concrete or real implications, both social and subjective, for the material life of individuals.'[4] Second, the 'representation of gender *is* its construction—and in the simplest sense it can be said that all western art and high culture is the engraving of the history of that construction.'[5] Third, the construction of gender 'goes on busily' in various areas of social activity, from schools to courts, to the family, to what Althusser calls 'ideological state apparati.'[6] Fourth, and most complicatedly, gender, since not fixed, is defined by a series of other factors that both support and undermine it, given that 'gender, like the real, is not only the effect of representation but also its excess.'[7] Lauretis concludes that gender, which is always a mobile and febrile construct, takes place in an oscillation between male representations and all that such representations omit. Hence, gender can only be thought of according to spaces that are unthought, unseen and unknown.[8] Lauretis effectively lays the ground for much queer theory to follow, especially in emphasizing the manner in which things are unfixed, displaced and non-unified. Queer theory is subversive for such reasons, and not least in that it sets up the grounds for asserting that all gender is in fact queer, in parallel with the rather challenging but curiously tenable argument that S/M (sadomasochism) is the purest form of sexual congress for enjoyment since it occurs in the mind and in language, while the body is but a support.

Roughly contemporaneous with Lauretis is the work for which Donna Haraway is best known, namely the connection between women and cyborgs. Like Lauretis and her many contemporaries, Haraway supports gender as a construction, and therewith, 'nature' as a construction as well. In her 'Cyborg Manifesto,' cyborgs are introduced into the gender mix in order to 'suggest a way out of the maze of dualisms in which we have explained our bodies and our tools to ourselves.'[9] Haraway deploys the concept in an effort to move away from the fantasy, cherished by many feminists of the 1980s (and a concept that Lauretis also deplores) of an exclusive and pure feminine space, generally referred to metonymically as 'the goddess.' Rather, for Haraway the cyborg is a way of foregrounding the mobilizations by which gender is implemented, introduced and moulded. As she writes: 'The machine is us, our processes, an aspect of our embodiment.'[10] In another essay ('"Gender" for a Marxist Dictionary') Haraway draws attention to the way biology, in this case as related to human sex and gender, is used in such a way as to designate some unalterable and essential limit, a myth that involves both obfuscation and a manipulation. '"Biology"' she writes, 'has tended to denote the body itself, rather than a social discourse open to intervention.'[11] As a result feminists, she argues, have been caught on 'biological determinism,' which has hindered the critical analysis of 'how bodies, including sexualized and racialized bodies, appear as objects of knowledge and sites of intervention in "biology".'[12] Words such as these will prove enormously useful in looking at the way in which gender is expressed, organized and played out in cosplay. With cosplay everything is openly a construct, and as the sizeable resources for cosplay globally derive from popular media such as manga, anime, comics, cartoons, television shows, music bands and video games, they already may in some cases have a cybernetic edge implicit in their storyworlds and characters.

As a name for an object of study, as well as a personal reference, queer came to circulate more freely in the 1990s, with the arrival of a new generation of lesbian, gay, bisexual and transgendered individuals. This heightened awareness of difference was indicative of a number of factors, including the development of anti-retro-virals for AIDS victims and the fading of the age of accusation that called AIDS a scourge of retribution for the 'illness' of homosexuality. It was in the coming-out of greater discussion, at least in western countries, around gender, creating a climate of more robust self-examination and discursivity. It also coincided with the beginning of a digital age, which witnessed the circulation of new virtual identities. Through these more public debates, many who identified as gay and lesbian saw the need to define themselves according to a greater breadth of scope. Writing in 1993, Judith Butler observed that 'the term "queer" itself has been precisely the discursive rallying point for younger lesbian and gay men and, in other contexts, for lesbian interventions and, in yet other contexts, for bisexuals and straights for whom the term expresses an affiliation with anti-homophobic politics.'[13] The last members of this category are a moot, but highly significant, point: moot because some lesbians and gays, needing to stake a claim for the otherness they inhabit and which is imposed on them on a daily basis, are unwilling to admit straight people into their communities, and therefore choose not to adopt 'queer' as a preferred term. But at the same time, the inclusion of 'straights' thereby opens up a new space that highlights the importance of politics in the negotiation of gender. It also opens 'queer' up to being an umbrella term for all deviations, all perturbations of the norm, where the norm is defined according to strict presumptions of nature, culture and economy (primarily that heterosexual sex is normal because it is the natural and therefore correct way to produce offspring, all other sexual congress being lustful and wrong).

Gender performance

In her now classic book, *Gender Trouble* (1990), Butler, in an effort again to escape some of the gridlocks of the social, psychoanalytic, scientific and feminist conceptions of sex and gender, defines the latter as performance. Here the emphasis is laid on the event of the performance in its present moment, and how different features are constellated according to linguistic, cultural exchanges. In the lead up to this, Butler systematically establishes that sex is something that is culturally fabricated for the sake of maintaining a particular status quo. Working from the ideas of Foucault, Butler notes that the sexual binary of man-woman is a simplification that enables one to quell thoughts about any potential variations between the two, where in fact all there are, arguably, is variations—an observation that lies at the core of queer theory:

> For Foucault, the substantive grammar of sex imposes an artificial binary relation between the sexes, as well as an artificial internal coherence within each term of that binary. The binary regulation of sexuality suppresses the subversive multiplicity of a sexuality that disrupts heterosexual, reproductive, and medicojuridical hegemonies.[14]

Such a way of reading sex as an artificial binary, and by extension the way in which humans are defined and situated within society according to a system of unfixed laws and unmoored from stereotypes, is highly subversive and, to some, dangerous, because pre-assumed laws no longer blindly apply. For sex and gender are, under this understanding, considered as manifestations of the distributions of power, language and knowledge. And the way they are identified is always subject to these conditions.

Another important factor in the determinations, and blurrings, of sex and gender is that of the guises that the sexes—and primarily women—are placed under: in other words, masquerade. An important theoretical touchstone in the genealogy of this idea is Joan Riviere's essay from 1929, 'Womanliness as Masquerade.' Riviere conceives of femininity as working according to particular roles and tropes, which are required or imposed by the (aggressive) conduct of men. She argues that women are often forced into positions of entering into a particular modality of womanhood that is not theirs in order to make their audience more comfortable. For what Riviere discerns is that there are a multitude of what she calls 'intermediate types,' that is, people with characteristics that are more like those typical of the opposite sex. As Butler unpacks this theory:

> Riviere calls into question these naturalized typologies through an appeal to a psychoanalytic account that locates the meaning of mixed gender attributes in the 'interplay of conflicts.' Significantly, she contrasts this kind of psychoanalytic theory with one that would reduce the presence of ostensibly 'masculine' attributes in a woman to a 'radical or fundamental tendency.' In other words, the acquisition of such attributes and the accomplishment of heterosexual or homosexual orientation are

produced through the resolution of conflicts that have as their aim the suppression of anxiety.[15]

This highlights the traumatic core of sexual orientation. Heterosexual men, for example, exaggerate their heterosexuality to combat homosexuality—both from outside and within themselves. Masquerade's fortunes are therefore a mixed blessing. On the one hand, it enframes the imposition of forms of behaviour, and of dress, deportment and disposition. On the other, it allows one to resolve certain conflicts, indecisions and anxieties through compliance, through entering into or inhabiting one or another social modality of sex and gender. Men who opt for the masquerade of femininity or women for masculinity do so because they wish to enter into a particular form of social exchange. Men acting out 'as men' know to expect certain strategies, certain reactions.[16] This will again be important to bear in mind when thinking of cosplay. For becoming one character or another can be done for the sake of wish-fulfilment (such as becoming more a man/woman than you think you are capable in everyday life) or cathartic release (the expression of certain covert desires that the subject is less comfortable doing as their 'real' selves).

Read in retrospect, the itinerary towards the metaphor, or model, of gender as performance seems fairly clear. Butler argues how the body is typically and habitually viewed under the aegis of nature 'that appears to be a passive medium that is signified with an inscription from a cultural source figured as "external" to that body.'[17] This is also endemic of the Cartesian mind/body dualism, where the body is a machine and a device for the mind's choosing. However, this way of considering the body as somehow prior, and exempt from cultural inscription, is inadequate, given that the body only really becomes body once it is inscribed, once it is designated, named and thereby ordered according to its component parts. A body with breasts, for example, immediately leads to the supposition that the body is female.

But this is where the issue gets unstuck. Breasts were an example used advisedly. Paradoxically, the evidence for gender performance is best demonstrated in the practice of drag. In the west, at least, a drag queen will often display large breasts, big lips, long hair, long legs. At least, it does not serve the drag performer's avowed shift to have small breasts and to wear make-up. For a transsexual to announce him/herself as such is to have large breasts and a large penis—at least for him/her to be 'marketable.' Not to have both of these is, so to speak, to ruin the balance and to become more one than another as opposed to radically in-between. As Butler writes, '[t]he performance of drag plays upon the distinction between the anatomy of the performer and the gender that is being performed.'[18] What is effected is the combination of three contingent factors: 'anatomical sex, gender identity, and gender performance.' Thus:

As much as drag creates a unified picture of 'woman' (what its critics often oppose), it also reveals the distinctness of those aspects of gendered experience which are falsely naturalized as a unity through the regulatory fiction of heterosexual coherence. *In imitating gender, drag implicitly reveals the imitative structure of gender itself—as well as its contingency*. Indeed, part of the pleasure, the giddiness of the performance is in the recognition of a radical contingency in the relation between sex and gender in the face of cultural configurations of causal unities that are regularly assumed to be natural and necessary.[19]

This is where the agonistic but never separable relationship between homage and parody comes in. In drag, it is through the amplification, the hypostatization of gender that gender meets its parody. But what is unmistakable is that neither of these poles is on the spectrum of what is generally considered normal. They may be desirable to some, but it is also because of their exceptional status that they are coveted and admired by both performers and spectators.

The 'limits,' as Butler calls them, of gender performance lie in what is covered or modified. The performing subject employs a form of extraction that is tantamount in classic Freudian terms to a castration, which can lead to mourning. The process of playing out the part of the other is at the expense of what one was before the dressed-up state. And further, particularly in reference to 'straight' men dragging, 'drag exposes or allegorizes the mundane psychic and performative practices by which heterosexualized genders form themselves through the renunciation of the *possibility* of homosexuality.'[20] This notion of mourning is necessary to keep in mind when we turn to cosplay. Although cosplay is a celebratory, carnivalesque form, it must at the same time operate according to a decisive renunciation of the self for the sake of self-transformation. In its performance it lays claim to something that the other self was not and in reality can never be.

The question of cosplay as queer

This chapter opened with the provocation that all cosplay is in some way playing into the queer paradigm, for greater or lesser. Perhaps surprisingly, scrutiny of the conjunction of cosplay and queer to date has been limited, for the most part, to a scattering of journal articles. Among these commentators, Craig Norris and Jason Bainbridge have applied Butler's notion of gender as a performance to cosplay in a 2009 article, arguing that if, 'as Judith Butler suggests, gender is performative—something we unconsciously do, inscribed by societal norms and repetition—then cosplay is a performance, through costume and the assumption of another identity, that reveals the performativity of gender.'[21] They go on to associate this with costume, both literal and metaphoric, in the cosplaying context:

Ironically it is through the wearing of another layer that the true nature of gender is revealed; the cosplay character creates a critical distance, a point of disruption, a vantage point from which the gender of the wearer can be critiqued, negotiated and explored. In this way, cosplay becomes a way for anime and manga fans not only to identify, align and belong but also to question their own socially- and culturally-constructed notions of what it means to be masculine and/or feminine.[22]

Crucially, therefore, cosplay 'is not simply the fannish act of dressing up, but rather the act of "queering" gender roles and stepping outside hetero-normative behaviours through the assumption of fictional identities.'[23]

Noting that Norris and Bainbridge 'build upon [Butler's] framework in their study,' Joel Gn's evocatively titled article 'Queer Simulation: The Practice, Performance and Pleasure of Cosplay' is nonetheless critical of their claim 'that the "queering" of cosplay, as a means of deviating from heteronormative behaviours, parallels Butler's construction of drag as a parody of the gender binary.'[24] As Gn writes:

> I would argue that their dialectic for subversion not only leaves the character of affective individuation unresolved, but also presumes a reductionist strategy that overlooks critical aesthetic positions, or stylistic devices within the object of the animated body. If the latter is indeed an exemplification of gender as performance, does it re-enact an ideal of the gender dichotomy or is it 'gendered' by a series of visible markers which, as iterated by Butler (1990, 10), constitute a discursive effect brought about through a 'convergence among culturally and historically specific sets of relations?'[25]

Daisuke Okabe's tangential treatment of the matter in a chapter from *Fandom Unbound: Otaku Culture in a Connected World* (2012), which includes case study and interview material, provided grist for Patrick W. Galbraith to tease out a distinction between the apparent 'naturalization of sex in crossplay as practiced by Okabe's informants' which 'seems to diverge from drag as described by Judith Butler, who saw in it the potential for destabilizing norms.'[26] Galbraith complains that 'Okabe tells his readers that no matter how queer cosplay performances and desires get, his informants "lead conventional adult lives,"'[27] suggesting that the queer in cosplay is all performance and in fact serves as an instrument to reinscribe the dominance of heteronormativity back in the ordinary world.

This disavowal is reiterated by a male cosplayer, quoted in an article by Rachel Leng, who exclaims: 'Let's get one thing straight. I am not gay. I like girls a lot. That's why most of my favorite anime characters are girls. I like them so much that I sometimes dress up like them.'[28] This foregrounds love of character over drag—as another subject exclaims: 'Good crossplay reveals the pure love for an anime character [...] that is at the heart of all cosplay, regardless of the gender of [the] cosplayer or the character being cosplayed. In my perspective, it takes a real man to dress like a 10-year-old girl.'[29] Yet another comment located cosplay more in the realm of the ludic than of queer, in that 'traditional societal perceptions of gender are no fun anyway. I can't fire, earth, water, or air bend so I Gender Bend [*sic*].'[30] While Leng discusses crossplay in terms of drag, revealingly, the term 'queer' is never used.

One window into the crossovers between drag and cosplay is provided by its parallels with the fashion subculture of Lolita. The proviso here is that Lolita culture represents a style statement and taste community affiliation on behalf of the wearer, which is not synonymous with cosplay costuming, or performing a fictional character. The two phenomena are strictly distinguished by both popular culture scholars and practitioners. As Isaac Gagne notes, this style subculture is 'characterised by dressing in Victorian and Rococo-inspired fashions and affecting a "princess-like" demeanour.'[31] Most Lolitas are unaware of, or ambivalent about, the eponymous character from Vladimir Nabokov's novel,[32] so are in no way role playing a literary prototype. While Lolitas are sometimes seen at cosplay events, especially in Asia, they are usually either availing themselves of a dress-up opportunity, or, in some cases cosplaying a character associated with Lolita-esque costume from popular manga and anime, such as the eponymous heroine from *Rozen Maiden (Rōzen Meiden)* (2002–2007).[33]

Nonetheless, Lolita provides one important parallel, in that the performance of gender is achieved through dressing up in non-normative outfits. The intersection of the two lies in the fact that, as with cosplay, Lolitas do not simply wear a costume but rather symbolically *become* Lolita—in the sense that they embody what Lolita represents within the wider taste community. Contrary to the western associations of the term 'Lolita,' this involves performing a 'girly' form of hyper-feminized but innocent and (apart from in the subgenre of ero-lolita) decidedly non-sexualized character persona. Boy Lolitas, although rarer, don equivalently ornate male garments. This tends to mitigate the notion of gender performance insofar as performance is always a *playing at* while (pure) being is not. What is true of both Lolitas and cosplayers, then, is that to undertake a new alias, either in a temporary or permanent capacity, is to modify the conditions of the assumption of gender that occurred in the processes of socialization since birth. The 'normal' assumption of gender is expected to be understood as precisely not something shaped, assumed, imposed, represented, mimicked or modelled, while the adoption of Lolita and cosplay identities is self-consciously all of these things. The subject willingly enters into a myriad of symbolic codes and quite distinctive visual or narrative references.

In effect, cosplayers are choosing a variety of signifiers that express parts of their desires, personalities, aspirations, inhibitions or inclinations. 'For the cosplayer,' remarks Gn, 'it is not only the modification of the text that is liberating (or, in other instances, subversive), but also the consumption of the image that becomes a pleasurable, embodied experience.'[34] This can mean in certain instances that 'cosplay can take the form of "crossplay," in which the socially accepted gender of the subject is at odds with that of the character.'[35] The net effect is one of artificiality for the purpose of participating and generating spectacle that all but rules out conventional applications of gender norms.[36]

One quality that is particularly significant to cosplay identity is that of *kawaii*, an adjective that has become so metonymic of the 'cute' or 'loveable' endemic to Japanese aesthetics that it is often used in English as an abstract noun. Kawaii can be invoked in the context of queer in respect of the justifications made above, namely that it distorts the gender relationships, and places them into a neighbouring terrain: in some cases, girls assume typically male characteristics of power and agency, while boys may appear pretty and effete. Girls and women in Japan, in particular, may modify their appearance through make-up and even surgery to achieve a kawaii effect, most typically unnaturally large, doe-eyes. Being queer in this regard resides in being constructed, mediated and paraded with the artificial qualities foregrounded. Among the many reference points for kawaii are popular media franchises such as *Hello Kitty* and *Pokémon*, and goods produced by companies like San-X and Sanrio. Kawaii is distinctively child-like, conveys a sense of innocence, vulnerability and even embarrassment, and with that a vulnerability that is deemed lovable and worthy of attention. In the kawaii equation, cuteness is mixed with self-consciousness and disingenuousness. The endearment related to the distant and untarnished joys of childhood that kawaii is expected to elicit is not the same as a western Rousseaueanism, however. Rousseau's childhood innocence is intimately caught up with quite strict and ardent presumptions about a state of nature in which there is some deep connection between natural forces and human drives. By stark contrast, kawaii is highly contrived, and therefore its claims to nature are seen through a lens of distortions and tropes. In this regard, it is far closer to camp and its mannered theatricality.

The simpler way of approaching this is that the 'nature' from which kawaii derives is one that it is entirely represented, from its eleventh-century literary origins to its current forms in the artificial fictions of animation, cartoons and games.[37] As Gn observes: 'Reading animated bodies along the same lines as a "living subject" would thus negate the ways in which they will always "fall inside quotations marks"; they are, essentially, virtual objects capable of shifting between different systems of representation.'[38] While it may be true that the cosplayer is embarking on some return to childhood roots of pleasure and blamelessness, the fact that this imaginative journey is conducted through a very distorting 'comic-book' lens means that the return to childhood is not to their actual childhood but a metaphor, and something that needs to be considered according to different categories and values. The appeal to 'accuracy' is no longer there. For with animation the need to distinguish between the biological body and that of the artificial body dissolves. Further, animation is also predisposed to camp because of the way in which it need not adhere to any strict, normative rules about the body and by extension gender identity. By definition the comic body is a caricatural body, distorted and, by extension, on the queer scale. As Sam Abel argues, the 'animated cartoon is the ideal camp medium' for the way that its figures employ a double-movement of 'simultaneously an embodiment of the target and a parody of it.'[39]

This dynamic germane to camp also helps to explain the complex, and multivalent, relationship to childhood within anime and cosplay. The aesthetics of cute is closely allied to the *youjika*, the 'infanticization of culture,' which, as distinct from 'infantilizing,' is a process of altering things and people so that they appear to come from the framework of childhood, and one largely manufactured through the framework of animation. But along with this is a return to types who have next to no sexual orientation, an androgyny that derives from an undeveloped (or underdeveloped) sexuality. However, such a transitional or liminal space provides the possibility of characters crossing, or perhaps going back and forth to either side, of the proverbial fence: the androgynous can be, vicariously, male or female.

Imaginative recourses to the state of childhood of this kind are a prime mobilizer in cosplay performance akin to the pleasures of the carnivalesque.

More problematically, Japanese 'lolicon' culture since the early 1980s has traded in manga and anime images that blur the lines between pre-pubescence and adult sexuality. Unlike the Lolita fashion subculture that postdates it, lolicon (from 'Lolita-complex') is explicitly named after Nabokov's motif of the underage girl and generally refers to a taste culture comprising (relatively) older male spectators. Although lolicon depictions occur in purely drawn form, unlike photographic images, it has led to accusations in western media of Japan being the 'Empire of Child Pornography,'[40] and subsequent United Stated-led legal bans on such images. Galbraith has framed this in terms of largely western-inspired moral panics, while Gn argues that 'the corporeal effects of these images are more compatible with an embodied materiality based on affects, as opposed to dominant meanings of deviance.'[41]

At this juncture it is important to emphasize, however, that we are in no way contending that childhood sexuality (or the projection of such by adults) is necessarily queer, but rather the way that childishness is troped and manipulated in order to enter into different terrains of gender conduct. The space of simulated childhood gives the cosplayer the opportunity not just to 'be' but to 'become.' It allows for the continuous prospect of evolution into something else, into virtual and possible spaces of identity and gender. And since the child is noticeably evolving in an ecstatic state, as opposed to the devolution and depredation of old age, it is *ipso facto* the site of impermanence and change. For outside of the tabulation of numerical years, the defining boundary of biological childhood is when one ceases to grow. The shoe size stays the same, and with it, sexual orientation (or so it is expected).

It is also this imaginative recourse to the state of childhood that is prime mobilizer in cosplay performance to the pleasures of the carnivalesque. Within Japanese culture especially, in which expectations of appearance and behaviour are more encoded and monitored than in 'permissive' western cultures, youjika serves an analogous function to the eroticism and transgression that occurred in more traditional, western eighteenth-century masquerade. Its gender spaces are malleable and fluid, but activated in a largely more decorous manner.

Drag and dolls

To return to the Lolita fashion subculture—which, again, is not to be confused with lolicon, the former being built in large part on the rejection of the sexualizing male gaze through the accumulation of multiple layers of clothing—one common thread emerges from testimonials to analyses. That is the extent to which Lolitas take themselves very seriously (even as an object of play) and that they have very strong, if nevertheless never homogeneous, opinions about who they are and how they are to be received. The Lolita is in part a reaction to the extremes of teenage dress that came from the protest era of the late 1960s and the 1970s, which led to a sartorial lingua franca in the western world that verged in the direction of androgyny: T-shirts, jeans, sneakers. By dramatic contrast, Lolitas are a staging of a very studied and highly performed femininity. 'Broadly speaking,' writes Isaac Gagné, 'Lolita is a predominantly female subcultural aesthetic whose participants strive to embody a "princess" theme through fashion and mannerisms. Whereas the ethos of casual was content over form, for the Lolita, form is all.'[42] Lolitas in many ways represent a kind of unspoken group revolt against what Frenchy Lunning condemns as

> The banal sartorial culture of the dumpy middle-aged adolescent [...] the baggy T-shirt, frumpy jeans, the dirty flip-flops of the American public, who wear this dreadful uniform all over the world: to the theatre, museums, restaurants, and even the church. It is a style no one looks good in, yet it afflicts all classes, all ages, and all genders. One porcelain-skinned Lolita, Crystal, lovely in a vintage white linen dress, poignantly told me that she adopted the Lolita style to regain a never-experienced girlhood of innocence.[43]

One point of origin is that of social media, where people perform the self and where self-images are meticulously shaped and continually perfected. Lunning goes on to describe how Crystal 'had found a group of like-minded people in the Lolita community, a global band drawn to the ultrafeminine styles of the Victorian era, whose complex aesthetics have become sundered into many different genres.'[44] She cites the influences of well-known Lolita designers, like Samantha Rei, who contributes to what she calls the 'Fancy Movement,' which is used to describe not just Lolitas but Goths and other fashion tribes, all of whom wish to share in the escape from codes of dress that are makeshift, standard and unremarkable. Again, while distinct from cosplay, these performances arguably are all forms of dragging since they involve some form of exaggeration and they are the result of a series of conscious decisions as to how they are being seen and understood.

Lolita also helps us to locate the doll in relation to cosplay and how it is performed across different, assumed personas. The doll and its relationship to costume and dressing up were already mentioned in relation to the *commedia dell'arte* in the previous chapter. But another, eastern progenitor to cosplay is *shōjo*, which predates both anime and manga in Japan. Mizuki Takahashi discusses shōjo as a highly stylized illustration that was popular since the early twentieth century, which may have drawn inspiration from nineteenth-century mythic representations of girlhood as seen in Lewis Carroll's protagonist, Alice.[45] The main publication was *Shōjo kai* (*Girls' World*) (1903–12), which was an early version of the kind of fandom that today is associated with the Barbie universe, in which the fashionable girl is depicted together with settings and accessories that complement her look, from stationery to homeware. It was also a significant milestone in how popular media related to young females, encouraging them to participate in their own identity, but an identity whose emphasis lay in regulated forms of appearance and behaviour that was uncannily tied to the prettiness and contrivance of the doll.

Mari Kotani and Thomas LaMarre contextualize the wider emergence of shōjo culture across literary and cultural referents in the Shōwa period (1926–89):

the shojo fantasy begins with the culture of the bourgeois daughters of downtown Tokyo who took the imported culture of Europe and America and made it their own; it then entered into the postwar world where it was popularized and thoroughly saturated with capitalist development; it was finally reconstructed as a culture that demanded a certain degree of literacy. It was then that the ability to appreciate its aesthetic qualities gained high esteem.[46]

Today shōjo continues to function as a subgenre of manga and anime, referring not just literally to 'girls' but to what Kotani and LaMarre refer to as 'a juvenile existence prior to the adult female, that is, prior to the adoption of adult femininity. Within the system circumscribed by patriarchy, insofar as it secures future femininity, shōjo is a period when girls are protected and indulged, handled like dolls.'[47] Via manga and anime sources, the shōjo figure is a major influence on cosplay, given that the majority of players, especially but not exclusively in Asia, are younger women. Thus, the meaning of shōjo in all these various social theatres is a constructed identity to which 'girliness' and its performance are a critical part of the enactment of the fantasy. Yet the gap between performer and their performed girliness in cosplay is a way of bringing agency over shōjo, given that, as Kotani and LaMarre point out, its iteration 'must be inscribed somewhere. Otherwise we will be drawn into a hegemonic structure that simply makes girls into girls.'[48]

It is worth commenting here on the Barbie figure, since she is central to the intimate but still fluctuating relationships between stylized (and unrealistic) body types, dress and the social aspiration to become the doll. Barbie is the modern counterpart to the traditional doll but as a symptom and as an instrument of late capitalism, insofar as she conjoins childhood longing with commercial interests that in turn are linked to highly specific aspirations concerned with body type, gender, class and even race. Although more recent iterations of Barbie have diversified her in terms of both ethnicity and, to some degree, body type, classic (mid-twentieth century) Barbie would long reign as unrivalled benchmark for women's bodies, with drag-like long legs, small waist and pronounced, improbably (before plastic surgery) horizontal breasts. In contrast to cultural icons such as Marilyn Monroe, or Elvis, or fashion icons from Twiggy to Naomi Campbell, Barbie is a fictional and fanciful icon who stands somewhere between superheroes and celebrities. She shares with the celebrity the promise of what one could be, but also stands as a paragon of female physical desirability. Barbie evolved from her German cousin Lilli who was an object of male delectation, a 'comical gift,'[49] to become a paragon of cultural styling and female identity. At the end of the twentieth century, Ruth Handler, her 'mother,' is reported to have stated that 'Barbie is an institution, and has been copyrighted as a work of art.'[50]

In Barbie we find encoded a series of highly pronounced and recognizable traits of femininity that are anchored in a signature prettiness and daintiness. If she is dressed as something more butch, such as a cowgirl, her suit is in white satin and has silver trimmings,[51] and any other ensembles with trousers are offset with one or more visual cues associated with decorative and delightful womanliness, whose underpinnings are in leisure and luxury (though Barbie has had many careers, from police officer to astronaut). Barbie's ubiquitous, multilayered and intimate attachment to the fashion industry also serves to exemplify another point, which has to do with the complementarity if not the inextricability between body and dress. Furthermore, it is haute couture's taste for outrageousness at its most experimental and indulgent that also necessitates equally outrageous body types. As Mary Rogers declares, 'Barbie's style might be called *emphatic femininity*. It takes feminine appearances and demeanor to unsustainable extremes.'[52] The use of the word 'unsustainable' has many trajectories, in particular the way in which some commentators have inverted the ubiquitous critiques over her feminine stereotyping. Erica Rand, for example, argues that these traits and trappings are so unsustainable, so emphatic that they stretch the limits of plausibility such that she retreats from being a full-blown woman to becoming a drag queen.

Rand argues that in Barbie we witness a regular playing out of this configuration through the re-instatement, overstatement and parody that is found in male drag queens. Meanwhile, Ken may be ostensibly Barbie's boyfriend, but seems inscribed with a gay identity (a fact not lost on the gay men who fetishized him, resulting in the release by Mattel of an explicitly gay Ken doll).[53] While interviewing gay and lesbian adults, Rand shows how Barbie was significant to their own identity building.[54] One factor in all of this is that gay and lesbian identity is not buttressed by the fiction of heteronormativity, of all that is deemed safely rational and right. Queer identity has claims and recourse to artificiality,[55] so it would follow that Barbie or Ken, also heavily constructed and artificial, could play central roles. Rand tells of how Barbie, for instance, has participated in the identity of femme lesbians, who are not necessarily complicit in imposed norms, but rather are conscious of their construction.[56] She describes the way in which Barbie was treated or refitted by girls who became lesbians, such as being 'rolled in dirt or dressed like the hot baby-sitter next door.'[57] It is precisely Barbie's pronounced femininity that makes her so liable for subversion and desecration, a perfect sexual object ready to be spoiled and messed-up.[58] It is her perfection that makes her prone to be the site of children's, and adult's frustrations and left-of-field desires.

Barbie, as an idea, provides an unexpected historical precursor of cosplay, and is sometimes literally requisitioned as a cosplay character, since she epitomizes (as object and as idea) the successful conflation of the doll and the female body. The otherworldly allure of the doll[59] lies in its embodiment of the 'departure from the mundane or real' and how transformation 'needs to be performed, and performed outrageously, in an alien manner, rather than appear as a facsimile of something in existence.'[60] As Kotani observes, in this respect 'Barbie is not so much the image of an adult woman as a gynoid alien, the very essence of a cosplay body.'[61] Hence Barbie is also an archetype for gender that undermines gender determinacy as much as she instates it, helping to formulate the assertion that cosplay is a form of drag for the new millennium.

Dragplay

The close connection between dolls, drag and cosplay returns us to the relationship, almost so basic as to be in danger of being overlooked, that dragging and cosplay both share the common quality of play discussed earlier in this book. True enough, all masquerade involves play to some degree, since disguise and therefore deceit can give license to the individual that affords him or her a temporary release into states of being that may not all be necessarily controllable. And while contested among some groups, the term 'gay' carries connotations of festivity, closely linked to the celebrations of Mardi Gras, that fly in the face of opprobrium and which instead emphasize shamelessness and pride (hence 'gay pride'). Thus, in their 2013 article 'Posthuman Drag,' Bainbridge and Norris cite 'three reasons why cosplayers *cosplay*: to play with gender, to play with race and to play with reality.' Presciently they consider cosplay according to 'a pre-digital form of social networking, posthuman drag that sutures the real to the unreal.'[62]

But first, what is posthuman, and what is its relation to gender and drag? Posthumanism is a concept first advanced by Judith ('Jack') Halberstam, Ira Livingston and Katherine Hayles in the mid- to late 1990s.[63] Partly as a response to Haraway's introduction of the cyborg into the debate about gender, posthumanism was, and is, invoked, in order to shift the debate away from the proverbial 'man-woman problem' (in which is also, by extension, contained the man-man and woman-woman problem), to recreate the approach to gender relations through drawing notice to the way in which gender, self and humanity are mutually exclusive co-ordinates. Posthumanism is an attempt to sidestep conceptions of homogenized, essentialized humanity that was raised to the status of cultural ideology in the eighteenth-century Enlightenment. In their early study of the concept, Halberstam and Livingston argue that the gendered body must be understood phenomenologically, that is, seamless with stimuli and movement. Gender is also a coming-to-visualization of forces of ideology, technology and biology. The body is a site of mediation, mutation and representation. To think gender can be easily and coherently grasped is to be deceived, as it is an increasingly mobile and fabricated element with changing forces in which the borderline between passive and active is progressively challenged.[64] Not only are neat definitions of gender exploded in favour of concepts that abjure the static and the stable, but posthumanity also relocates the presumption of a clean difference between what is human and what is inhuman.[65]

It is indeed both instructive and ironic that the theorization of posthumanism since the mid-1990s has occurred contemporaneously with the rise of cosplay, which also occurs at the same time as the rise of digital prosthetics and the decreasing stigmatization of body modification, including tattoos, piercing and cosmetic surgery, as a means of self-enhancement. As Stefan Herbrechter remarks:

> On the one hand, one needs to reject the metaphysical idea of the 'natural body' and human 'nature,' which is still more or less compatible with transhumanist techno-prophecies even though or rather because they embrace the idea of augmentation in general to improve

human (and nonhuman) life. On the other hand, one needs to critique posthumanism in cultural, materialist fashion, as part of an ideology of a technoscientific capitalist society. Economic neoliberalism, free market ideology and late capitalist individualism can no longer be separated from the various technological posthumanization processes.[66]

But as for the latter, negative aspect, cosplay can be read as a symptom of the 'technological posthumanization,' in not only the destabilization of gender norms but also the need for recourse to 'deep' subjectivity. Here Marx's alienation of the proletariat takes a radical turn, in which alienation of subjectivity changes to renunciation. Cosplayers renounce subjectivity and opt for a play of surfaces and signifiers.[67]

To call cosplay a manifestation of 'posthumanist drag' is necessarily to invoke Lunning's definition that 'cosplay accepts and recognizes all body forms, genders and sexualities of the fan community in practice.'[68] While referencing the virtual, cosplaying is pre-eminently embodied and material; from the point of view of gender, the encounters are physical, lived and constantly negotiated. Cosplayers act within their character, but at the same time enact acceptable variations to distinguish themselves from other cosplayers who adopt the same character. These enactments are never free of gender and, like the drag performance, seek to distinguish the theatricalized identity from the quotidian one. As Bainbridge and Norris suggest, cosplay is in some ways closer to drag than 'fannish dressing-up' because 'it is not merely an act of becoming a particular character, or marking out a particular alignment, but of disruption.' For them, the play boils down to 'a play with gender identity.'[69] This play is not necessarily one of celebration, but one that deals with particular anxieties and uncertainties of what gender should constitute. And the more it is negotiated, the more the lines of demarcation remain uncertain. Nicolle Lamerichs underscores that cosplay always participates in identity construction.[70] It is a construction in which 'core' identity is not preserved as some essential originary component, but rather something that exists as the instigator of a construction—the construction and the constructedness is what counts.

There appear to be two positions with regard to the relationship between cosplay and dragging. One is that of sexual subversion (supported by Gn), another is 'that the drag act is as much about playful engagement with the simulation itself' (Bainbridge and Norris).[71] Put another way, cosplay actively initiates an identity that is different from the one shaped by 'natural' cultural forces through the playing up to a persona—which can only be achieved through ensuring that that persona is read as such, which is no different from the drag queen (or drag king) bearing the obvious imprimatur of what consensually constitutes gender. The latter position does not use drag metaphorically, however; it is always concerned with gender to a greater or lesser extent. As the next chapter, on cosplay and pornography, explores in greater detail, cosplay is a multivalent form of desire worn on the body, and the obsession with a character cannot be divorced with various forms of fetishism. Fetishism is about lack, just as dragging is, since the drag queen (to continue to use the dominant example) announces his lack of 'the Thing' through its surfeited and ample demonstration, much as the disavowal is a registration of a hidden wish.

Something that has been established already in this book is that cosplay is much more than just dressing up, it is an act of becoming, and it is the ritualization of transformation. Victor Witter Turner's comments about theatre can be conscripted to refer to other orders of performance, including that of cosplay: 'Theatre is, indeed, a hypertrophy, an exaggeration, of jural and ritual processes; it is not a simple replication of the "natural" total procession pattern of the social drama.'[72] But within this process cosplay is also a form of mimesis, of character and of gendered behaviour with a group that is expected to read these variations and inventions with pleasure and approval. Moreover, the cosplayer is not simply one who has 'come out' in the traditional sense of the phrase, but rather relocates to a space that is also 'impossible' according to everyday reasoning and values. While more traditional dragging takes place with some cosplayers, dragging also occurs in cosplay itself, a practice and a zone of visualization that is replete with variables, and whose terms of reference in signifiers and performances, are seldom stable for long. With traditional drag certain gender norms are reinstated through parodic hypostatiation. By contrast, cosplay is far more the play of gender shifters, where the certainty expressed in one character is challenged by the rhetorical certainty of another. It is through the constant social and material collisions and juxtapositions that gender's mobile and protean nature is confirmed.

Notes

1   Mary Shelley, *Frankenstein; or, The Modern Prometheus* (London: Lackington, Hughes, Harding, Mavor and Jones, 1818).
2   See Adam Geczy and Vicki Karaminas, *Queer Style* (London and New York: Bloomsbury, 2013).
3   Judith Butler, *Bodies that Matter: On the Discursive Limits of Sex* (New York: Routledge, 1993), 226.
4   Theresa de Lauretis, *Technologies of Gender* (Bloomington and Indianapolis: Indiana University Press, 1987), 3.
5   Ibid., original emphasis.
6   Ibid.
7   Ibid.
8   Ibid., 26.
9   Donna Haraway, *Simians, Cyborgs, and Women: The Reinvention of Nature* (New York: Routledge, 1991), 181.
10 Ibid., 180.
11 Ibid., 134.
12 Ibid.
13 Butler, *Bodies that Matter*, 230.
14 Judith Butler, *Gender Trouble* (New York: Routledge, 1990), 19.
15 Ibid., 50–51.
16 Ibid., 52.

17 Ibid., 129.

18 Ibid., 137.

19 Ibid., original emphasis.

20 Butler, *Bodies that Matter*, 235, original emphasis.

21 Craig Norris and Jason Bainbridge, 'Selling Otaku? Mapping the Relationship between Industry and Fandom in the Australian Cosplay Scene', *Intersections: Gender and Sexuality in Asia and the Pacific* 20 (2009), para. 11.

22 Ibid.

23 Ibid.

24 Joel Gn, 'Queer Simulation: The Practice, Performance and Pleasure of Cosplay', *Continuum: Journal of Media and Cultural Studies* 25, no. 4 (2011), 586.

25 Gn, 'Queer Simulation', 586.

26 Daisuke Okabe, 'Cosplay, Learning, and Cultural Practice', in *Fandom Unbound: Otaku Culture in a Connected World*, eds. Mizuko Ito, Daisuke Okabe, and Izumi Tsuji (New Haven: Yale University Press, 2012), 225–48, 229, quoted in Patrick W. Galbraith, *Intersections: Gender and Sexuality in Asia and the Pacific* 32 (July 2013), para. 11.

27 Ibid.

28 Quoted in Rachel Leng, 'Gender, Sexuality, and Cosplay: A Case Study of Male-to-Female Crossplay', in *The Phoenix Papers: First Edition* (April 2013), para. 1.1 (2014), 89–110.

29 Ibid., 89.

30 Ibid.

31 Isaac Gagne, 'Bracketed Adolescence: Unpacking Gender and Youth Subjectivity through Subcultural Fashion in Late-Capitalist Japan', *Intersections: Gender and Sexuality in Asia Pacific* 32, no. (July 2013), para. 1.

32 Vladimir Nabokov, *Lolita* (Paris: Olympia Press, 1955).

33 Peach Pit, *Rozen Maiden* (*Rōzen Meiden*) (Tokyo: Monthly Comic Birz, 2002–07), Manga; *Rozen Maiden* (*Rōzen Meiden*), directed by Kou Matsuo (Tokyo: Nomad, 2004), Anime TV series. *Rozen Maiden: Träumend*, directed by Kou Matsuo (Tokyo: Nomad, 2005–06), Anime TV series.

34 Gn, 'Queer Simulation', 584.

35 Ibid.

36 Ibid. See also Kim Toffoletti, *Cyborgs to Barbie Dolls: Feminism, Popular Culture and the Post-Human Body* (London: I.B. Tauris, 2007), 103.

37 See Kanako Shiokawa, 'Cute But Deadly: Women and Violence in Japanese Comics', in *Themes and Issues in Asian Cartooning: Cute, Cheap, Mad and Sexy*, ed. John A. Lent (Bowling Green: Bowling Green State University Popular Press, 1999), 93–12.

38 Gn, 'Queer Simulation', 585.

39 Sam Abel, 'The Rabbit in Drag: Camp and Gender Construction in the American Animated Cartoon', *Journal of Popular Culture* 29, no. 3 (1995), 184.

40 Jake Adelstein and Angela Erika Kubo, cit. in Patrick W. Galbraith, '"The Lolicon Guy": Some Observations on Researching Unpopular Topics in Japan', in *The End of Cool Japan: Ethical, Legal and Cultural Challenges to Japanese Popular Culture*, ed. Mark McLelland (London:

Routledge, 2017), n.pag., accessed 1 January 2017, https://books.google.com/books/about/ The_End_of_Cool_Japan.html?id=23e3DAAAQBAJ&redir_esc=y

41   Gn, 'Queer Simulation,' 586.

42   Isaac Gagné, 'Bracketed Adolescence: Unpacking Gender and Youth Subjectivity through Subcultural Fashion in Late-Capitalist Japan,' *Intersections: Gender and Sexuality in Asia and the Pacific* 32 (July 2013), 1.

43   Rio Saito and Frenchy Lunning, 'Out of the Closet: The Fancy Phenomenon,' *Mechademia* 6 (2011), 140.

44   Ibid.

45   Mizuki Takahashi, 'Opening the Closed Word of Shojo Manga,' in *Japanese Visual Culture: Explorations in the World of Manga and Anime*, ed. Mark MacWilliams (Armonk: M. E. Sharpe, 2008), 117. See also Jason Bainbridge and Craig Norris, 'Posthuman Drag: Understanding Cosplay as Social Networking in a Material Culture,' *Intersections: Gender and Sexuality in Asia and the Pacific* 32 (2013), 2.

46   Mari Kotani and Thomas LaMarre, 'Doll Beauties and Cosplay,' *Mechademia* 2 (2007), 60.

47   Ibid., 56.

48   Kotani and LaMarre, 'Doll Beauties,' 60.

49   David Groves, 'A Doll's Life,' in *The Los Angeles Times* (15 December 1994), cit. in Kristin Weissman, *Barbie: The Icon, the Image, the Ideal* (Boca Raton: Universal Publishers, 1999), 11.

50   Ibid., 12.

51   Laura Jacobs, *BarbieTM: What a Doll!* (New York and London: Artabras of Abbeville, 1994), 42.

52   Mary Rogers, *Barbie Culture* (London: Sage, 1999), 4, Original emphasis.

53   See Mel Melendez, 'Show Me Your Billy,' *Prism* 1 (Fall, 1997), n.pag., accessed 1 January 2018, https://web.archive.org/web/19980220181319/http://www.journalism.sfsu.edu/www/ pubs/prism/oct97/P1.Billy.html.

54   Erica Rand, *Barbie's Queer Accessories* (Durham: Duke University Press, 1995), 93–148.

55   Geczy and Karaminas, *Queer Style*, 'Introduction' and passim.

56   Rand, *Barbie's Queer Accessories*, 109–11.

57   Ibid., 115.

58   Ibid., 150.

59   Kotani and LaMarre, 'Doll Beauties,' 56.

60   Carrington et al., *Generation Z*, 78.

61   Kotani and LaMarre, 'Doll Beauties,' 54.

62   Bainbridge and Norris, 'Posthuman Drag,' 1, Original emphasis.

63   Judith Halberstam and Ira Livingston (eds.), *Posthuman Bodies* (Bloomington: Indian University Press, 1995); Katherine Hayles, *How We Became Posthuman: Virtual Bodies in Cybernetics, Literature and Infomatics* (Chicago and London: Chicago University Press, 1999).

64   Halberstam and Livingston, *Posthuman Bodies*, 3ff.

65   Stafen Herbrecheter, *Posthumanism: A Critical Analysis* (London and New York: Bloomsbury, 2013), 49.

66   Ibid., 55.

67   See Adam Geczy, 'The Psychology of Cosplay,' *Journal of Asia-Pacific Pop Culture* 1, no. 1 (2016), 18–36.

68   Frenchy Lunning, 'Cosplay, Drag, and the Performance of Abjection,' in *Mangatopia: Essays on Manga and Anime in the Modern World,* eds. Timothy Perper and Martha Cornog (Santa Barbara: ABC-CLIO, 2011), 76.

69   Norris and Bainbridge, 'Selling Otaku?,' para. 9. See also Bainbridge and Norris, 'Posthuman Drag,' 4.

70   Nicolle Lamerichs, 'Stranger than Fiction: Fan Identity and Cosplay,' *Transformative Works and Cultures* 7 (2011), para.3.3.

71   Bainbridge and Norris, 'Posthuman Drag,' 5.

72   Victor Wittter Turner, *From Ritual to Theatre: The Human Seriousness of Play* (London: PAJ Publications, 1982), 11.

Chapter 9

Cosporn

Science is the ultimate pornography, analytic activity whose main aim is to isolate objects or events from their contexts in time and space. This obsession with the specific activity of quantified functions is what science shares with pornography.

J. G. Ballard, *The Atrocity Exhibition*[1]

Finding a satisfying definition of pornography is tantalizing, and disappointing. A common theme is the depiction of sexually explicit material, which in today's permissive and hedonistic age would make most developed countries steeped in pornography. Pornography comes from the Greek, *porne*, meaning harlot, or prostitute, while *graphy* refers to the treatment, or the 'description of manners.'[2] So pornography is the way in which whores conduct their business. This is still too narrow and insufficient, which makes J. G. Ballard's comment all the more satisfying: pornography deals in objectification, isolation and reduction. His invocation of science encapsulates the particular quality of pornography, which is its renunciation of naturalness. A love scene in film is considered unpornographic because of its verisimilitude, equally so in literature: the love scene between the aged protagonists in Gabriel Márquez's *Love in the Age of Cholera* (1985) is not pornographic, while the forensic, and at times, laconic objectivity of the Marquis de Sade is.

To use the term 'pornographic' in a figural sense is to imply the extraction of a quality out of its causal frame of reference and to situate it in an unselfconscious and decontextualized place that gives it an air of fecklessness and obscenity. The conflation of cosplay and pornography in the throwaway term 'cosporn' seems a natural progression, an easy fit, following on from the earlier chapters of Part III dealing with its historical antecedents in masquerade as well as the curious interplay between cosplay and drag. As we have outlined already, cosplay is by degrees the result of processes of sublimation, a form of asserting and expressing desire through identification (and 'actually' becoming) a certain character and the narratives associated with it. Pornography enjoys an important place in cosplay for the following reasons: the body's extraction from the real life-world and the everyday; the objectification of bodies; the obsession with artificial and unnatural bodies and thus either loosely or literally the doll, the identification of the body as a system of parts; and seamless relation between the body and items of clothing with special respect to the fetish; and finally, if the above categories do not already imply this, the premium placed on contrivance. This chapter is not only about the structural and affective qualities that pornography shares with cosplay, but also the more direct examples of cosplaying in the realm of pornography.

The problem of pornography

The convergence of cosplay and pornography, which this chapter will reveal, is far from gratuitous or indulgent. There are not only numerous connections, but also it is noteworthy because cosplay is a historically new phenomenon, while the age-old phenomenon of pornography is chronically under-theorized and, for something so well-known, under-defined. Both, then, retain a certain element of contingency and indeterminacy, which from a philosophical (and philological) perspective can be both an advantage and a disadvantage. In a meditation on the definition of pornography, Michael Rea argues that the lack of insight around what pornography actually is can be seen as 'lamentable' and questionable because the 'stakes are high' since it causes offense, while for others to censor it would be a deprivation of civil freedom:

> But it is precisely because the stakes are high that it is so surprising that relatively little serious philosophical work has been done toward providing an adequate definition of 'pornography.' What is truly lamentable is not the fact that 'pornography' is difficult to define, but that the difficulty has served in many cases as an excuse for frivolous work or for ignoring the project altogether.[3]

This said, Rea also admits that this omission does elide several problems, since pornography is not easy to pin down, as it is not just about the reproduction of sex and/or nudity, but is rather more inclusive of the reaction to its reproduction. He further breaks this definition into six categories:

> (i) those that define 'pornography' as the sale of sex for profit, (ii) those that define it as a form of bad art, (iii) those that define it as portraying men or women as, as only, or only as sexual beings or sexual objects, (iv) those that define it as a form of obscenity, (v) those that define it as a form of (or contributor to) oppression, and (vi) those that define it as material that is intended to produce or has the effect of producing sexual arousal. Definitions in the latter three categories are by far the most prominent. Some definitions fall under more than one of these categories; and some pornography has all of the characteristics picked out by these six categories.[4]

But none of these definitions is adequate, since all of them take 'for granted either that pornography is sexually explicit material of some kind or that pornography is (in some sense) material that is intended to appeal to the audience's sexual interests.'[5] He concludes that 'being pornography' is not an intrinsic property, but is consequent upon the intentions and uses of particular material, codes of display and the extent to which social mores are upheld or violated.[6] He also makes a useful comparison to establish this point. Jane Campion's film *The Piano* (1993)[7] was erotic and involved sexual exploitation of the female protagonist's lover. Being erotic, and involving what may be deemed objectionable behaviour does not, nevertheless, constitute it as pornographic. On the other hand, Paul Verhoeven's *Showgirls* (1995),[8] while intended as erotic, fell far short of the mark and ended as trashy and pornographic. Rea ends on a purposely ambiguous note asking when, and by whom, the work by D. H. Lawrence would be deemed pornographic, a point that exposes the circumstantial and contextual modulators of response and expectation.[9]

While not a criticism of what is a sizeable and thorough analysis, what is not given serious attention in any way is the role of artificiality in defining the difference between the erotic and the pornographic. The success of *The Piano*, to many people's minds, was that it was not contrived, while *Showgirls* was almost unanimously recognized as implausible, highly orchestrated and mannered. This does not mean that the latter did not elicit enjoyment, as it fits into a category that is camp, and it is well known that camp is a category in which contrivance and artifice stand at the fore.[10] Cosplay sits well in this debate since it divorces itself from the natural world. This is not by any means to suggest that cosplay is pornographic per se, or to frame cosplay performance as pornography against the avowed wishes of its practitioners, but rather to suggest a place of affinity, of symmetry.

The unnaturalness that is central to pornography is conveyed and staged on a number of levels. One is that the goings-on anticipate and are conscious of being filmed or represented in some way. Indeed pornography is steeped in contrivance. For it is now an integral part of the genre itself as it has become entrenched and proliferated online, so that the narrative sequences, should they be there, are stilted to the point of self-parody. It would be tenable to assert that what was once criticized as a sign of the debasement of pornography—that it showed the weakest and shallowest kinds of verbal exchanges—is now an expected quality and a given, as if this ceremonialized insincerity is something to be expected and inherent to the form itself. This leads to another key quality, which is that, because the sexual action is there for representation and spectatorship, it is inimical to the 'natural' process of procreation. In this regard, it flies in the face of biologically oriented justifications of sexual coupling and brings the act front and centre into that of gratuitousness and lust. But the lust and the desire are themselves of a very particular sort since they, again, are not spontaneous, but rather are part of an organized system. The pornography actors are doing a job, and that job is to play out a simplistic and droll scenario and to enact desire. Whether or not they themselves as individual subjects are raised to the level of pleasure is immaterial so long as the effect is preserved.

Playing porn

At the risk of making an analogy that might at first sound perverse, another way to consider the pornographic actor is as a professional sportsman or sportswoman. After all, they are valued for their prowess at being able to maintain particular physical states for relatively prescribed periods. Hence again the pertinence of Ballard's ironic statement about pornography's scientific systematicity, its ordering and isolation of parts, its partitioning and division of body parts, sexual positions, and sexual acts. Porn stars are expected to perform a variety of acts, willingly and with the requisite level of responsiveness. In short, they are professional *players* who perform for the sake of the enjoyment, titillation and gratification of a set of spectators.

Let us then return to the concept of play, considered in a sociological frame in Chapter 4 and more historically in Chapter 7. As we have seen, play in the form of masquerade reaches a highly visible and convulsive climax in the eighteenth century. Among other things, the eighteenth century, before the French Revolution at least, is also seen as the final flowering of Baroque excess. The Rococo style, an umbrella term used well after the period for all art of this nature around Europe, is dainty, hedonistic and often with sexual undertones, associated with the pleasure-seeking upper classes. The eighteenth century also witnessed the hitherto greatest proliferation of pornography. Thousands of lurid and lascivious engravings of people, known or nameless, engaged in explicit carnal acts were circulated, together with the rising interest in publications for public consumption, the *affiches* and the *feuilletons*, which were in effect the incipient forms of newsprint. Political and social scores were waged on the pornographic platform: eminences were depicted, caught in outrageous acts of licentiousness in order to expose their hypocrisy and allow the public to vent their distaste. One of the greatest casualties of this new form of covert communication was Marie Antoinette herself, the 'Austrian whore.' While her court painter Vigée-Lebrun had created a small scandal by representing her in free-flowing dress as a kind of high-blown shepherdess, the pornographers exposed her to countless bogus scandals, propagating a stream of groundless rumours, including one that she had had an affair with the Count d'Artois, Louis XVI's youngest brother (later Charles X).

Finally, the eighteenth century, which saw the birth of wholesale (as opposed to isolated) pornography, also introduced art as a form of play. This was far beyond the kinds of play represented on decorative wall-panels of shepherds and nymphs, the elegantly wistful *fêtes galantes* of Antoine Watteau and his epigones. Aesthetics as a mode of philosophical thought was given its first extensive critical treatment by Alexander Baumgarten with his *Aesthetica* from 1750, which was subsequently followed by Kant in his *Critique of Judgment* (1791). The association of art with play unmoors art from life's action and of rationality. As such, it also relieves art from an intrinsic correspondence to nature; rather the relationship would be metaphoric and contingent. Gianni Vattimo writes observantly of the relationship between art, modernism and play, and the disengagement of art from particular forms of thought and of social roles. His comments are worth quoting at length:

While the basic assertion that the European aesthetics of the nineteenth and twentieth centuries is an aesthetics of play may sound paradoxical, it is nevertheless understandable once we specify that the term 'play' is intended to point to any vision that places art outside, above, or beyond any 'serious' (i.e. moral and cognitive) activity with respect to the world or, more generally, to being. The reactions against Hegelian rationalism, on the one hand, and the affirmation of positivism and the parallel attempts of experimental, psychological, and sociological aesthetics, on the other, allied themselves to deprive art and the aesthetic sphere of their 'ontological' value, thus confining art to the secondary, or at least disengaged (i.e. disinterested) activities of the human being. Kierkegaard's category of [sic] aesthetic stage—an existential category characterized by immediacy, disengagement, and lack of historicity—seems to acquire a prophetic meaning with respect to the developments of nineteenth- and twentieth-century poetics.[11]

For Kierkegaard there were three basic modes of life, the aesthetic, the ethical and the religious. The ethical is rationally self-involved, the religious is bound up with faith, while the aesthetic lives according to life's pleasures and makes choices accordingly. The aesthetic mode of life is detached from both far-sighted reasoning and the deep, often tragic contradiction of the religious deliberation, preferring instead a life of spontaneity and immediacy—in a word, play.

At first glance, it would seem implausible to extrapolate philosophical aesthetics into cosplay and pornography, but a close reading of the passage above will suggest that the ingredients are all there. This is especially true with regard to the way in which both cosplay and pornography eschew the natural world, manipulating it to their needs, which are based on personal and group spectatorship. As in the grounding of aesthetics since the eighteenth century, like art, cosplay and pornography are freed of utility, and since divorced from analogical attachments to utility and aetiology, the possibilities of what they can indulge in are potentially endless. But unlike art, what cosplay and pornography both share is a *discernible* internal logic and ritualized systems, so discernible, in fact, that they are what govern their position as separate from 'natural' rules and social organization. For both cosplay and pornography, nature and society are just raw materials for new variations in which the result need not have any true, plausible reference to the origin.

Pornography and the fetish

Both the concepts of fashion and dress, and that of dressing up, operate by the basic understanding that there is an inside and an outside, that of the natural core of the naked body that is then covered by clothing and any other additions such as body piercings, scarification or tattoos. In this regard the concept of clothing and dress is additive, and there is an assumption of a qualitative difference between body and clothing. These notions are built on the habitual binaries of nature and culture, inside and outside, unmediated as against mediated. It is also a relation that resides at the root of the difference between nude and naked, in which nude is an expression of a state of bodily felicity and grace, whereas naked is a state of insecurity and vulnerability due to the lack of covering. The first implies a mentality and a place in which clothing has no consequential value (if it is there it is for the sake of emphasizing nudity per se); the second is where it is always implicated in the body's placement in the world. It is a division that in western cultural history also implies the transition of bodily innocence before the biblical Fall to a state of irrevocable shame.

The notion of the Fall will also have a bearing on the section to follow, but for now it can be used as the buttress of the internal relationship of fetishism to pornography, and the difference between the erotic and the pornographic in western philosophy. While acknowledging the lack of strict demarcation between the two, the erotic is to the nude what the pornographic is to the naked. The former allows for a state of grace and dignity and the universally sanctioned—the comforting ideology within the idea of the natural—while the latter is stigmatized with deprivation and lack. In the well-known, if contested, definition by Sigmund Freud, the fetish is precipitated by the young male child's realization that his mother lacks a penis. For Freud this is a traumatic realization, *trauma* coming from the ancient Greek word for 'wound.' The mother's wound is therefore double: the wound of the vaginal crack and the wound of the imagined castration performed on her. But in order to compensate for this wound, as well as to shield himself from the initial psychic trauma, the male subject invents for himself a series of compensations, a series of interests that come 'to a halt half-way, as it were; it is as though the last impression before the uncanny or traumatic one is retained as a fetish. Thus the foot or shoe [...] fur or velvet [...] crystallizes the moment of undressing.'[12] (Lacan would later take the castration complex, of which fetishism is the most salient symptom, as a symbol of the fundamental lack that the subject feels in relation to the other, the basic alienation that fuels desire). For Freud, isolated body parts and tactile objects are ways of overcoming the lack of wholeness of women. But since this perceived incompleteness is precisely perceived and imagined, its re-imagination and re-assignment with the aid of something else is only fleeting and ultimately inadequate.

In terms of pictorial representations, the signal watershed that brought fetishism and pornography into direct notice and dialogue was Édouard Manet's *Olympia* (1863). In a work that, in effect, conflates academic painting with the erotic/pornographic photography of the day, Manet exposed the academic nude for what was, namely a fetish, a pornographic object hiding behind a mendacious pantomime of the erotic. The original nudes used for artistic studies were, after all, drawn from the lower classes, subjects who were happy to be paid for their artistic posing rather than for hard labour. (This was also one of Degas's important contributions, to represent the women at work, from milliners to washerwomen, rather than displacing them and sanitizing them). *Olympia* is literally awash with signs that disallow it from collapsing into the innocuousness and safeness of myth, despite the allegory-arousing title itself. One could even go so far as to say that in view of the many signifiers to the contrary, the title has an ironic effect and infects other contemporary paintings with similar titles. She is being brought flowers by a black woman, signalling difference and servility—her own difference and servility that is, from respectable middle-class women. A cat on the bed rears up animatedly, suggesting animal desire. And Olympia is not nude, but rather wears a collar and her feet play coquettishly with a pair of house shoes, even though she lies on a bed, posing with her hand near her hip in reference to Titian's *Venus*, commonly associated with ushering in the primacy of the female nude over that of the male in pictorial iconography. The net products of all of these factors in *Olympia* have a destabilizing force that tips it into the lurid, and the pornographic. However, the work is generally seen as being more of a meta-commentary on pornography, using visual devices that would be later taken up by feminist artists as measures of pictorial deconstruction.

Photography of the naked women of this period has an overwhelming commonality, which is to deploy the fetish often to the point of overstatement. In her book on the areas of convergence of pornography and art, Kelly Dennis shows how photographs of nude women were generally divided into two types, ones that sought to emulate paintings, and others that clearly wished to distinguish themselves from painting and be pornographic. Being painterly meant mimicking poses from paintings from the traditional odalisque to the upright 'source' (source of a river or spring) poses. But again, there are no clear lines of demarcation. Further, she observes that

> the formal evolution of the pornographic nude in photography traced photography's technological development. The first photographic nudes, like daguerreotypes themselves, were luxury items: unique, one-of-a-kind images under glass, of necessity encased in a frame and often concealed in a velvet-lined case or 'jewel box.' Like lingerie and fur, velvet is one of those tactile elements Freud would later identify as a 'fetish,' a displaced signifier of female genitals; thus, these shocking, early photographic glimpses of female pubic hair would have been erotically charged by the auxiliary experience of the touch of a proximate thumb or fingertip on the surrounding velvet.[13]

Hence the excitement and the meaning of the image were caught up in the accoutrements, the additional elements surrounding the body, and it was these elements that conferred the greater meaning to the body itself.

To put it another way, the body in pornography is never complete without the other things that 'dress it': an observation that equally pertains to cosplay, excepting the brief fashion for nude masquerades in the 1970s. The porn body is a tissue of partial objects in which natural and fetish have become confounded, or fused. Or to use the words of Berkeley Kaite, 'the pornographic body is a textual body replete with fetish inscriptions.'[14] Underwear, so important to pornography, was also an invention that occurred at the same time as the earliest photographs. Valerie Steele draws attention to the fact that underwear only became used towards the end of the nineteenth century, which predictably gave rise to discussion about it. As she puts it: 'Like the corset correspondents, underwear enthusiasts argued that the modern man resisted marriage, "putting his attentions in quarters where the question of intentions is never raised"; so it was necessary to use erotic lingerie to "pique" his imagination.'[15] Early photographic pornography must thus be viewed as part of a plentiful, narrativized commentary and journalism about the functions of garments in and out of the bedroom.[16]

The second half of the nineteenth century was also a time that witnessed a rise in men's serials. One such was *The Exquisite*, which could be called the *Playboy* of the Victorian era, with 'men's advice' on subjects ranging from venereal diseases to erotic fiction. These periodicals predated the widespread use of photography by a slim margin, but they set the model for patterns that photographic pornography would assiduously take up. As Tracey Davis asks:

If it is true that the clothed female performer was interchangeable with other erotic stimuli, particularly nudes, how did the eroticism of the actress's clothes function? The *Exquisite* relied on costume fetishism—borrowed wholesale from the theatre—to attract men. Theatrical costume flagrantly violated the dress codes of the street and drawing room, flaunting the ankles, calves, legs, thighs, crotch, and upper torso. Cross-dressing as males was sometimes the pretense, but even as animals or inanimate objects female performers were costumed as gendered objects of display. In the Victorian theatre, adult female performers were never sexless: sex was always apparent in gendered costume, whether through tights, breeches, skirts, corseted silhouettes, hairstyles, or headgear. Cross-dressing highlighted sexual difference, it did not disguise it. Femininity was intractable, and the point was to reveal, not disguise it.[17]

This revealing tendency could only be occasioned with two layers: clothing and role play. Davis goes on to describe how tenacious this was well into the early years of the next century. Sadomasochistic themes were prevalent, and catered for a rich variety of fetishistic references.[18]

It is instructive, but by no means surprising, to observe the close relationship that pornography had with dressing up. And this need not be limited to the visible things themselves, for it was also commonplace for pornographic models to invent new names for themselves that fitted the equally fabricated life-stories. Pornography is a web of fictions that generates fraudulent mystery. Similarly, cosplay draws on a web of fictions to represent this in costumed form. As Frenchy Lunning comments, cosplay is 'about sexuality, whether or not it is purposeful. Some characters are innately sexy or crossgendered—it is about flirting and exploration—sexual exploration without consequences.'[19] The fabrication of multiple identities in pornography also lies at the heart of what Lunning, after Félix Guattari, calls a 'transversal' state with cosplayers

slipping and sliding into all manner of identities that have no name but are identifiable through their rapid-fire snippets of gestures, manic vocal peculiarities, and poses, to become popular cultural iconic characterizations and quotations of exotic, erotic and gendered types. This display of multiple identities eruptions begins precisely as the costume is put on and the subject encounters other cosplayers.[20]

Clothing+body+fetish

While it is commonplace to assign pornography to an activity after the Fall in western epistemology, cosplaying is implicated in the same way, for the reason that dress and identity are indissoluble from the body. Moreover, cosplaying suggests a transformation of the inside from the outside, a transmutation that distinguishes it from simple masquerade. An analogy from film serves to make this clearer. In Jon Watt's *Clown* (2014),[21] the titular character played by Eli Roth is a real-estate agent who finds a clown costume in the attic of a house he is selling, and wears it at the birthday party of his son. Exhausted after the party, he falls asleep still wearing the costume. After he wakes, he finds that he cannot remove the suit, the nose or the hair, as they slowly and insidiously become part of his bodily tissue. Together with this metamorphosis, he becomes progressively more derailed and his appetite rises. He sequesters himself from his family and encounters a series of grisly contretemps in the process of trying to free himself from the clothing/persona of the clown, including a failed suicide attempt that leads to the murder of a child. He learns that the suit is the avatar of a demon, which can only be satisfied by preying on children, several of whom he hunts down and devours. He is finally subsumed by the demon before it retires back into the suit.

Clown is a striking example, but far from unique in the horror genre, which only serves to compound the point that once the leap to a change of identity is made irrevocable the results are monstrous, since it signifies a break from the order of nature. Both cosplaying and, by analogy, pornography are monstrous insofar as they seek an escape from the first order of life, gender and identity. Yet cosplay is not a permanent state of being but a cyclical one, in that it only occurs while the player is in costume, and in this sense represents a temporary form of monstrosity. As Jason Bainbridge and Craig Norris note:

> Part of the cosplayer's role is to be in character at all times the costume is worn, to be ready to perform, or pose when requested. This is why some cosplayers change into 'casual' clothes at conventions; the assumption of the costume is the assumption of the role. They cannot step out of that role unless they are out of costume.[22]

In this, cosplay again resembles pornography, in that porn actors play their parts for a fixed period of time for financial rewards, where cosplayers instead accrue fan capital. However, some professional cosplayer figures discussed below such as Yaya Han—who overtly plays to her eroticization—increasingly blur the line.

To make this analogy less far-fetched, what the cosplay body and the pornographic body share, at least at their borderlands, is a fascination with extreme body types, where drag represents gender and identity play writ large. It is for this reason that the classic Barbie continues to be an ongoing stereotype for what a woman should supposedly aspire to, but, more instructively, Jessica Rabbit: one is a doll, the other is cartoon. With over 90 per cent of girls between the ages of 3 and 10 in the United States estimated to own a Barbie,[23] she is still, in the words of Jacqueline Urla and Alan Swedlund, 'an incredibly resilient visual and tactile model of femininity for pre-pubescent girls headed straight for the twenty-first century.'[24] But it is now far from exceptional for women to front up to cosmetic surgeons with a picture of Jessica Rabbit, or something very similar, with the request that this is how she wants to look.[25] Both Barbie and Jessica Rabbit have been widely cosplayed, the latter recently, and notably, by Yaya Han, in a demonstration of the ironies of the requisition by young women, in particular, of hypersexualized representations as sources of self-empowerment (not least economic). The obsession with *kawaii* from anime and manga is also sometimes a decisive factor in making cosplayers want to modify their bodies in order to look like the characters they play. Unsurprisingly, the most popular recourse is breast augmentation.

For the sake of making the analogies with cosplay clearer, let us return at this point to the role of body and dress in pornography. The term 'natrificial' was coined by Adam Geczy for the cross-relation of body, dress and fetish within pornography.[26] (The study was on straight, as opposed to queer and other 'marginal' forms of pornography, for the reason of its dominance by dint of sheer quantity, and for the way that the normativity of 'straight' has created in Internet pornography a roughly normative sequence for which all others are the exception). Natrificiality involves two interlocking factors: first the altered or 'worked' body and second the way in which the bodily mediations are complemented and indeed made continuous with visibly material additions to the body, which can be anything from a metal stud to a body-stocking. The use of the phrase *visibly material* serves temporarily to clarify a distinction, which will then be discredited, between mediations in the body (implants) and mediations on the body (rings, studs, clothing, even make-up).

By the early 2000s, sales of established pornographic periodicals such as *Playboy*, *Hustler* and *Penthouse* had begun to drop off at a sizeable rate, but it was a trend that was predictable by the mid-1990s when the Internet had become a fact of life and had penetrated into the average home in the developed world. The early years of the Web, and its gradual domestication, also saw a revival of the debates that had occurred in the 1970s about the pros and cons of pornography, especially as anxieties rose regarding its mass availability. What is just as striking in the new millennium is the degree to which such debates have subsided. Anxiety appears to have given way to an acceptance of something that cannot be controlled. The explosion of pornography occurred as a result of technological advancements that developed together with other developments such as availability and improvements in cosmetic surgery techniques. What emerged from all of this was a certain convention, or ritual to the pornographic sequence. While of no absolutely fixed standard, there is extraordinary uniformity to the way that the pornographic narrative unfolds, which includes the transition from different poses and actions to denouement. There are, of course, variations, but these only serve to emphasize the normativity of the default sequence. Moreover, together with this stylization, there was also a particular body type that fitted into it, which for a woman was a draggish—that is hypertrophied—version of the Barbie doll. The male body was also sculpted and an echo of the pumped body popularized by Arnold Schwarzenegger and his contemporaries, when gym culture entered the mainstream in the 1980s, at least in western, Euro-centred pornography.

The natrificial as it is applied to the porn body and the associated fetish dress is understood according to two basic principles. The first, which we have covered already, is the renunciation of naturalness in favour of a sham. The second is that the body is as much *worn* as it is possessed. In the case of porn, the masquerade no longer begins once the body is covered; rather it begins with the skin and what lies beneath it. The dress fetish exists together with the 'porn body.' In parallel, many cosplayers express their difference from traditional masqueraders insofar as the costume is a catalyst to an alteration of what is also within; it is not a mere covering up. Both the cosplay outfit and the look—make-up, hair, nails and so on—are the result of serious effort, work involving design and craft. Rachel Leng argues that

> both contribute to a visual transformation of the fan into a specific fictional character's simulacrum. The process takes a lot of effort, money, and emotional investment: once a cosplayer decides to make a particular costume, they have to collect multiple images of that character in the same clothing design from different angles. They then have to purchase fabric, cut, sew, make patterns.[27]

Bainbridge and Norris likewise observe of the dedicated labour involved in the craft process presaging cosplay:

> the 'set of clothing,' functions as a suture not just between the unreal character and the real performer, but also between the real performer, the larger cosplay community, the performer and the spectator. Importantly this set of clothing is created; the authenticity of the costume very much depends on the craft that goes into its making, bringing to the fore skills in needlework and design.[28]

Cosplay is also often gendered to the extent that while many female practitioners design and construct costumes, male cosplayers appear more likely to engage in construction processes akin to engineering projects. Among professional and semi-professional cosplayers, body maintenance is also a major concern.

Similarly, the porn body shows evidence of all kinds of 'work.' The muscular male body is the result of hours of work in the gym. The cosmetic enhancements on women are signs of 'having had work done.' The man 'works on' the woman in having sex with her, and vice versa. She might also have had other kinds of work done on herself, such as fake long nails. What all of these have in common is that it is a form of work that sits well outside of the basic Marxist economics of work and production. This is work of a decisively post-industrial, new millennial kind, in that it produces nothing, and as for instance in the case of the long nails, it is work that perforce prevents many other forms of potential labour. It is also a fundamental characteristic of pornographic sexual congress that it is not aimed at producing babies—procreation is the remotest thing on the agenda and reference to it is to be avoided. If the work in cosplay produces an outcome, it is one that is highly abstract, aesthetic, driven by perception and consensus, and therefore highly unstable.

Another key aspect of natrificiality that shares many traits with cosplay is that it is not just played out on the surface but in the way in which the body moves. The body is, therefore, not only the site of technology (work) but performs technologically. Almost taken for granted are the ungainly poses on Internet porn staged in order to reveal genitals for the camera. The body in this case becomes something of a marionette. An example is where the woman lies down and extends one leg high while the man penetrates her from behind; another is where the woman performs a similar yoga move while leaning against a bench or table. Moreover, the bodies are as often clothed as they are naked. The men might wear sneakers (following the rugged tradesman or sportsman stereotype, also known as 'rough trade') and the woman may wear stilettoes, or might have a body stocking or have a garment that has been lowered and hiked up. One or both will have tattoos. To dress up as the porn actor is to anticipate the state of semi-undress. The intimate is made specular and the body mimics, or becomes, the clown of technology, delimiting coupling and love to a genital act. Thus the natrificiality of straight porn is a condition that represses 'natural,' non-pornographic sexual relations. It brings to the fore the way in which the subject perpetually clothes the other with our needs, desires and expectations.

Similarly, the cosplayer displays natrificial characteristics and is marionette-like in the layering of the natural body with costume, cosmetics and accessories.[29] They contribute to what Judith Butler calls a 'radical theatrical remaking of the body.'[30] The cosplayer's costumed body also moves in a prescribed manner to simulate the character being mimicked, where the signature pose is an integral part of the performance beyond the surface presentation. This serves to express a desire on the part of the player to display an alternative identity, while generating voyeuristic desire and gratification among spectators. Natrificiality is the space of fantasy, desire and lack grafted onto the body with exaggeration and with extended play, where tattoos, body modification, cosmetic surgery, athletic work, make-up, shoes and other fetishes become simultaneous and unified.

Cosporners

For the remainder of this chapter, it is useful to look into several examples of cosplay pornography and their proponents. Calling up 'cosporn' on a casual Google search will retrieve some results, but not overly many. The existence of the neologism cosporn is understandable, given its simple euphoniousness and that it does the work of what it sets out to denote.

For the most part, cosporn leads to predictable sequences of girls in cosplay suits having sex or masturbating. This has little to do with cosplay proper as viewed through the frames of critical and ethnographic practice in previous parts of this book. But the advantage of a serial grouping of these examples is to expose particular aesthetic patterns. For one, the outfits identifiably mimic cosplay's popular media tropes: the hair is typically pink or dyed to some other extreme, the suits will have a manga or anime-like look to them and footwear consists of brightly coloured synthetic boots. What these patterns once again show us is a quality that is especially germane to pornography, which is to match exaggeration with a *reductio ad absurdum*, so that there is no room for ambiguity. Other searches reveal that the term 'cosplay' itself is sometimes used rather loosely to designate pornography that involves dressing up, which, as we have seen, is close to ubiquitous in one way or another. Favourite costumes include the schoolmistress and the nurse, which are also staples in the BDSM (bondage and discipline/dominance and submission/sadism and masochism) repertoire. When the cosplay clothing is more in the manga/anime style, there is an emphasis on shiny, synthetic fabrics. The clothing has a lustrous, almost armour-like quality. It is seldom fully removed, as that would no doubt deprive the image of its cosplay signature.

If cosporn in this less theoretical, more mass cultural frame had to be reduced to a single archetype, it would be the female body that has been altered to look like an erotic anime cartoon; that is, long and thin legs and arms, and voluminous, melon-like breasts. The human body literally assumes a cartoon shape. Perhaps the most celebrated performer to succeed in this regard outside of Japan is currently the French-Canadian cosplayer and model, Marie-Claude Bourbonnais.[31] While the distinctions are perhaps too subtle to follow, her overall look is different from Barbie, precisely because of the dramatic contrast in proportions, and the enormous breasts whose bulbousness is impossible from a natural point of view. Although Bourbonnais does not engage in hard-core sex videos, naked images of her in numerous poses are freely available online. On her website, the section, 'About Me', begins as follows:

> Marie-Claude Bourbonnais is a French Canadian costume maker, model, cosplayer and former fashion designer. People associate her trademark oversized breast augmentation with her modeling career, but MC actually received her first surgery when she was 23, years before she started as a model. As a teenager, she was fascinated by the extreme body shapes of both American comic book and Japanese anime characters. Her interest in costumes and clothing production led her to complete studies in Fashion Design.[32]

Her first major foray into public cosplay came with a personally fabricated costume of the character 'Frost' from *Mortal Kombat* (1982–),[33] 'and was a tribute to the videogame she had been a fan of as a teenager.' The page also states:

> In 2010, MC attended her first comicon [*sic*] and convention, wearing costumes she had made herself. Through her modeling work, she had met people from Polymorphe, a Montreal based latex clothing company who had sponsored her during the previous years. MC had an idea to develop, with Polymorphe, a cosplay costume using latex,

material which was still pretty underground at the time and that was mainly worn and used through the fetishist community. They made a latex version of Sue Storm from the Fantastic 4 that MC wore for NYCC 2010. The costume was a huge hit and pictures of MC as Sue Storm soon could be found all over the Internet, making MC one of the most popular North American cosplayers at the time. That latex costume created a precedent in both the cosplay and the fetish scenes. From that moment, various companies started to produce superhero costumes for cosplayers. Because of MC's influence, some fetish models, who were strangers to the cosplay world until then, started to include various characters' costumes made out of latex in their modeling work.[34]

Apart from being an interesting account from the point of view of recent cosplay history, this narrative brings attention to yet another allegiance between cosplaying and sex work. This is hard to document, but it is now plausible to assume that as cosplay, at least in terms of its western cultural influences, is due also in no small part to the unflagging popularity of films based on Marvel and DC comics, that BDSM mistresses may possess the means in their wardrobes to dress up as superheroes.

An overview of Bourbonnais's 'Gallery' also proves it to be full of surprises. Congress with the highly sexual imagery available is nonetheless retained with links to lingerie commercials and to coy soft porn. ('Flower Fields,' where Bourbonnais is naked except for underwear, covering her nipples with her hand while standing in a sea of yellow flowers in bloom). The now famous Sue Storm outfit with her in it is also featured. What binds all of these images is that they revel in their respective ways in structured and modified identities, maintaining a tight relationship to pastiche and mimesis, with strong focus given to rendering the boundary between what is real and what is cartoon all but redundant. This can also be said to be true for all cosplay. But what is instructive here is that mimetic play is carried out on numerous levels. One line of images entitled 'Japanese Anime Cosplay' is of Bourbonnais imitating contemporary Japanese, girlish kawaii street style, so that she is not so much dressed in cosplay but dressed as someone who has adopted a cosplay-oriented style. 'Vampirella and art by Bruce Colero' is Bourbonnais in a black wig and a sheer, red, latex costume with thigh-length vinyl boots and a red cloak in a dark faux-castle setting, with an overall aesthetic redolent of the 1980s fantasy image painters such as Boris and Frank Frazetta. Bourbonnais also manifests as a '1:6 Scale Collectable Hornet Figure' where the eponymous figure is from the Canadian web series *Heroes of the North* (2010–11).[35] The caption reads that it is a '[h]igh quality articulated body with enhanced breasts and removable clothes.'[36] Finally, there is the thumbnail simply titled 'Art' that contains commissioned and gifted images of her in a variety of fantasy incarnations. The main image is a cartoon of an as yet more disproportioned Bourbonnais, rearing up on all fours on a beach, naked save for a thin one-piece strap-around, often used in porn imagery.

For embedded cosplay commentator Kane Anderson, '[f]etish and fandom seemingly go hand in hand,' serving to perpetuate the 'myth of cosplay as sexual practice,' which he considers to have become 'ingrained.'[37] As he explains, 'the uninitiated associate cosplay with sexual practices like bondage and discipline, masochism and sadomasochism, or other kinky behaviors.'[38] Yet he is keen to avoid the automatic assumption that cosplay represents a transfer of sexual energy. Rather, in signifying cosplay as fetish, Anderson locates it as a form of fetish that rails against sexualization: 'if superhero cosplayers fetishize cosplay they fetishize the impossible. They deny the sexualization of the character as they "boy-ize" them.'[39] A distinction can also be made with 'costumed playing outside these environments (e.g. sexualized acts and within superhero[ine] costumes),' which more accurately equates with 'costumed role playing as a means toward separating cosplay at Comic-Cons from fetishized kink.'[40]

However, as in the case of Bourbonnais, this does not necessarily correspond to cosplay as sexualized imagery or sexualized performance, which often evokes mixed moral responses. Anderson cites the sexualized performances of the deliberately controversial cosplay idol, Yaya Han, and her assertion to have reclaimed and countered the objectification of female cosplayers by explicitly cosplaying superheroines, thereby challenging onlookers and critics to overcome their own tendencies to tokenize, objectify and exoticize. In the artifice and deliberately provocative embodiment of hypersexualized characters, Han claims to find empowerment yet, as with Bourbonnais, in many ways, still objectifies herself in the process of overt character display. Further, both women can be seen as complicit in the commodification of cosplay, Han in her television idol persona, and Bourbonnais in her commercial enterprises. But in a sense Bourbonnais can conversely be seen to be appropriating the latter to another kind of subculture: that of fetish and kink, which have been embraced by many feminists as a revolutionary denaturalizing of both gender and sex. More generally, cosplay pin-ups of cosplay idols such as Han, Jessica Nigiri, Katyuska Moonfox and others abound on sites such as Patreon, where fans pay monthly subscriptions for updated pics on photo galleries that tend towards the titillating. Like Manet's nudes, these women profit by their labour; unlike his models they control the means of production, if not always of circulation.

A discussion of Han, Bourbonnais and the many other female cosplay idols who have made a business out of cosplay—whether one chooses to view this as objectification, professionalization or a mixture of both—is the best place to end an analysis of the relationship between cosplay and pornography. What the foregoing suggests is that the respects in which cosplay and pornography are different is only by degree, not kind—though not in the crudely obvious sense that cosplayers may wear costumes based on hypersexualized source characters, and commodify themselves in varying degrees of cosporn. Like the definition of pornography itself, which was essayed at the beginning of this chapter, in which the necessity of a definition is disproportionate to the number and quality of them, the connection is perhaps too close for many to wish to give the subject too much scrutiny. It begins with the auto-eroticism inherent in role play and fantasy, and it spreads across to fetishism, which is a compensation of what you do not have, as well as the primacy given to play, and the redundancy of work.

Notes

1   J. G. Ballard, *The Atrocity Exhibition* (London: Double Day and Company, 1970), 44.

2   *The Concise Oxford Dictionary* (Oxford: Oxford and the Clarendon Press, 1964), 946.

3   Michael Rea, 'What Is Pornography?', *Noûs* 35, no. 1 (March 2001), 119.

4   Ibid., 123.

5   Ibid.

6   Ibid., 135ff.

7   *The Piano*, directed by Jane Campion (USA: Miramax Films, 1993), Film.

8   *Showgirls*, directed by Paul Verhoeven (USA: United Artists, 1995), Film.

9   Rea, 141.

10 See Susan Sontag, 'Notes on Camp,' in *Against Interpretation,* ed. Susan Sontag (New York: Farrar, Straus and Giroux, 1966).

11 Gianni Vattimo, *Art's Claim to Truth*, ed. Santiago Zabal and trans. Luca D'Isanto (1985; New York: Columbia University Press, 2008), 39.

12 Sigmund Freud, 'Fetishism,' *The Standard Edition of the Complete Psychological Works of Sigmund Freud*, trans. James Strachey (London: Hogarth Press, 1927), 21, 155.

13 Kelly Dennis, *Art/Porn: A History of Seeing and Touching* (London and New York: Berg, 2009), 75–76.

14 Berkeley Kaite, *Pornography and Difference* (Bloomington and Indianapolis: Indiana University Press, 1995), 91.

15 Ibid.

16 Valery Steele, *Fashion and Eroticism: Ideals of Feminine Beauty from the Victorian Era to the Jazz Age* (Oxford and New York: Oxford University Press, 1985), 200

17 Lucy Davis, 'The Actress in Victorian Pornography,' *Theatre Journal* 41, no. 3, Special Issue, 'Performance in Context' (2011), 298.

18 Ibid., 306.

19 Frenchy Lunning, 'Cosplay, Drag, and the Performance of Abjection,' in *Mangatopia: Essays on Manga and Anime in the Modern World*, eds. Timothy Perper and Martha Cornog (Santa Barbara: Libraries Unlimited, 2011), 78.

20 Frenchy Lunning, *Fetish Style* (London: Bloomsbury Books, 2013), 137.

21 *Clown*, directed by Jon Watts (Los Angeles: Cross Creek Pictures, 2014), Film.

22 Jason Bainbridge and Craig Norris, 'Posthuman Drag: Understanding Cosplay as Social Networking in a Material Culture,' *Intersections: Gender and Sexuality in Asia and the Pacific* 32 (2013), 12.

23 Julia Griffin, 'Academics Like to Play with Barbies, Too,' in *Pacific Standard* (9 March 2009), accessed 1 January 2018, https:/psmag.com

24 Jacqueline Urla and Alan Swedlund, 'The Anthropometry of Barbie: Unsettling Ideals of the Feminine Body in Popular Culture,' in *Feminism and the Body*, ed. Londa Schiebinger (Oxford and New York: Oxford University Press, 2000), 389.

25 Conversation with Dr. Darryl Hodgkinson, December 2015.

26 Adam Geczy, 'Straight Internet Porn and the Natrificial: Body and Dress,' *Fashion Theory, The Journal of Dress, Body and Culture* 18, no.2, Special Issue, Fashion and Porn, eds. Pamela Church Gibson and Vicki Karaminas (April 2014), 169–88.

27 Rachel Leng, 'Gender, Sexuality, and Cosplay: A Case Study of Male-to-Female Crossplay,' in *The Phoenix Papers: First Edition* (April 2013), 94.

28 Bainbridge and Norris, 'Posthuman Drag,' para. 9.

29 Teri Silvio, 'Informationalized Affect: The Body in Taiwanese Digital-Video Puppetry and COSplay,' in *Embodied Modernities: Corporeality, Representation, and Chinese Cultures*, eds. Fran Martin and Larissa Heinrich (Honolulu: University of Hawai'i Press, 2006), 195–96.

30 Judith Butler, *Bodies that Matter: On the Discursive Limits of 'Sex'* (London: Routledge, 1993), 66.

31 Anon., 'Marie-Claude Bourbonnais,' accessed 1 January 2018, http://mcbourbonnais.com/en/home/.

32 Anon., 'About Me,' accessed 1 January 2018, http://mcbourbonnais.com/en/pages/about-us/

33 *Mortal Kombat*, created by Ed Boon and John Tobias (Burbank: Warner Bros., 1982–).

34 Ibid.

35. Heroes of the North directed by Christian Viel et al. (Montreal: Movie Seals Productions Inc., 1982–).

36 Ibid.

37 Kane Anderson, 'Becoming Batman: Cosplay Performance, and Ludic Transformation at Comic-Con,' in *Play Performance and Identity: How Institutions Structure Ludic Spaces, Routledge Advances in Theatre Studies*, eds. Matt Omasta and Drew Chappell (New York: Routledge, 2015), 112.

38 Ibid., 111.

39 Ibid., 112.

40 Ibid.

Conclusion

Cosplay Futures

I want… to change things. I want to believe that anything can be changed. The moment I met you, a new world opened up for me. You see, after wandering in the darkness for so long, a light brought me happiness. It's all thanks to you.

Chrono Crusade[1]

You can take away my suits, you can take away my home, but there's one thing you can never take away from me. I am Iron Man.

Iron Man[2]

When cosplayers are asked what the future holds, naturally enough, many respond subjectively, claiming that they will continue to be involved with the practice ad infinitum, being unable to imagine their lives without this major source of pleasure and enjoyment. As one young cosplayer stated: 'Well, I will just keep on going, I guess—it's my life and my friends are all in it together. It makes me happy and helps me deal with life's problems so I can't honestly give it up' (Jil, 22, female student, Hong Kong). This display of deep affect is typical to expressions of fandom, suggesting that this fan community has a future—at least in the minds of its participants—and will be passed on, even if existing cosplayers hang up their *Avengers* or *Evangelion* outfits.[3] The collaborative nature of the practice also means that in addition to performing the character in costume, various roles can be played backstage or post-event, such as sharing advice or images in the digital cosphere.

In response to questions regarding the predicted longevity of cosplay, others reflect on the differing catalysts, desires or personalities of cosplayers that influence character predilections, thereby highlighting the complex motivations attached to the practice. Another cosplayer observed that cosers typically exhibit three outlooks in their community:

Focusing on the past means that a coser thinks a lot about their past actions and the past actions of others. They believe that the past were golden days and imagine that they had more fun than they actually had—this is the nostalgic link to childhood characters that we all loved back then. Those fixed on the present are more relaxed as they live for now and don't dwell on what they have done right or wrongly—they just love to have fun. Future dwellers are always looking ahead to a place where it will be so much better to be. They dream of a better life and more happiness as they see the past as a bad, unhappy place that they need to escape from at all costs. And cosplay really helps them achieve their aims in different ways depending on the character they choose and their connected life story.

(Tom, 24, male cosplayer, United Kingdom)

Many manga, anime and online game narratives are also premised on futuristic storylines, albeit in settings ruled by totalitarian or alien regimes, in the face of resistance from the heroic cast. This means that cosplayers are highly familiar with traversing the liminal spaces of imagined pasts, presents and futures. Source media storylines are often set in a dystopian future, such as *Pale Cocoon* (*Peiru Kokūn*) (2006), while others, such as *In Search of The Lost Future* (*Ushinawareta mirai o motomete*) (2010) and *Erased* (*Boku dake ga inai machi*) (2016), play with time, enabling their heroes to travel back into the past or forward into the future, in order to save loved ones from their fate.[4] Here cosplaying fans can choose from a range of futuristic, time-based narratives in the search for a fitting avatar. This offers a nostalgic connection with a mediated object, which, while impermanent, seems charged with future possibilities. Disillusioned with the prospects of a relatively bleak future and the challenges of finding gainful employment, many young people in post-industrial societies seek to be master of their own destiny through the costumed other.

While the characters that are cosplayed are fixed on the page and screen, their interpretation by cosplayers adds a new dimension based on age, ethnicity and gender. This fluidity of identity is exciting, vicarious and subversive. The choice of character for recreation may enable the coser to turn back time itself and recreate childhood innocence through the visible attachment to a refashioned persona. Western cosplayers can play as Japanese avatars and superheroes, and vice versa. Female cosplayers play *bishōnen* (beautiful young men) and male cosplayers *mahō shōjo* (magical girls). Each cosplayer appears to make their choices based on the alignment of personal qualities between themselves and a selected character, rather than on the basis of age, ethnicity or gender. Subtle variations occur depending on the demographic and geographic placement of the individual coser and the choice of source text. Fidelity displayed in the selection of a particular cosplay costume aligns with the personal engagement of fans and the popular media sources they have been exposed to. These may be followed loyally, often for years, suggesting continuance in some modality—real or virtual—into their future life projection.

As a relatively recent fan practice, the longer-term trajectory of cosplay is still uncertain. In the face of globalization and technologization, as well as the de-institutionalization of life in a corporate age, the traditional social structures of family, government and media are seemingly eroding. Former twentieth-century popular culture role models of how life should be for each age group are now disintegrating, especially due to the individualistic trends driven by social media and the Internet more generally.[5] Consequently, our location in family, educational and working lives is increasingly uncertain, yet open to interpretation. In this fluid and uncertain landscape, the search for a sense-making anchor is increasingly taking root in fandom and fan communities. While they do not provide all of the solutions or ultimate security in the face of such uncertainty, they do offer some opportunities and challenges. In this sense, fandom and the associated worlds of cosplay are emotional and psychological touchstones that fill the gaps that have emerged in the wake of structural changes. For fandom offers what Larry Grossberg calls 'mattering maps' for future survival and well-being.[6] These emotive maps provide the necessary mental compass to guide us through life's ambiguities and uncertainties. This holds true for both adolescents and adults. Significantly, cosplay involves a broader range of ages as it takes root across the planet. There is also a fluidity attached to cosplay performance that is not confined to age or ethnicity—the normal demographic markers of consumption communities.

It has been argued that contemporary fandom finds its dominant form of expression through consumption. Cosplay is correspondingly a consumption-based community or tribe connected by emotional connections to objects located in mediated texts.[7] But cosplay is also creative, and one of a range of prosumer fan practices[8] that appropriate media products to their own ends. Performing a character in costume enables cosers to cope with their lives without sacrificing their identity, given that they can explore it through the acquisition of multiple personas. Further, the individual operates both outside of a routine existence and dresses into the collective settings of the cosphere. This affinity group is based on a passion for the media object as the main requirement for membership. As a participatory fan culture, cosplay offers the opportunity to establish closer support among cosplayers built on the sharing of collective intelligence and skills—both craft-based and digital.[9] The increasing popularity and acceptance of cosplay is a significant move away from the Puritanical and even modernist stigmatization and suspicion of pleasure.[10] Although its emergence in new places and spaces may continue to witness moral panics by opinion leaders who equate it with projected social and cultural ills, they are unlikely to be able to put the genie back in the bottle.

Nor is the future of cosplay in both the west and Asia necessarily dependent for its survival on the production of new anime and manga output—although this shows no signs of slowing down. The fan networks surrounding this cultural practice are as active as ever in related activities such as dubbing or 'fan-subbing.' Yet the Japanese manga and anime industries themselves, as a ground zero source for cosplay, are under financial strain. The average annual sales of 200 billion yen during the decade of the 'animation bubble'—in the heady days of anime and gaming mega franchises stretching from *Doraemon* (1969–) to *Final Fantasy (Fainaru Fantajī)* (1987–)—are now slowing down.[11] Ironically, as the global fan base for anime expands in the seemingly insatiable overseas markets within Asia and beyond, the standard industry business model is disintegrating in the wake of Japan's prolonged economic downturn, with shrinking advertising income having a further knock-on effect on animation budgets. The effect on the volume of animation being produced is significant, with claims that this creative industry is also under siege by free online streaming sites. However, the threat of this to cosplay is debatable, given that characters from existing narrative archives are ever popular and fans are still spoilt for choice. Hence, the seemingly never-ending cast of characters in both Japanese and western narrative media represents a rich resource that looks set to fuel cosplay practice for the foreseeable future.

Looking into the future direction of any popular cultural phenomenon involves reflecting on the macro-social, political and economic transformations that will inform the narrative scripts of cultural life. There is a curious tendency for commentators, when future focused, to dwell on the end of things rather than on their beginning or evolution into something more positive embedded with opportunity.[12] We commonly see pronouncements by futurist gurus about the end of popular culture, the end of childhood, the end of adolescence, the end of the family, the end of work and the end of meaningful communication between humans— all of which have the potential to affect cosplay practice, if these gloomy prognostications are fulfilled. Not that the genuine cultural anomie and ennui associated with existential threats in the age of global warming, far-right politics, corporate cronyism and terrorism should be dismissed, but to prophesy the end of cosplay would seem to be premature as long as there are popular media narratives with a cast of characters for fans to mine.

In the realms of fan studies, however, academic debates have posed questions about the potential end of fandom, even the end of the fan. These positions revolve around the paradoxical notion that we are now all fans, or perhaps that none of us are any longer fans in the original sense of the word.[13] Yet as this book has demonstrated, this is not likely to be an end of the kind of fandom exemplified by cosplay, but perhaps another beginning, in the sense that fandom is an ever-moving target. Renewel can be seen not only in the constantly evolving league of extraordinary fictional characters available to 'cos' from Japanese manga and anime sources, Hollywood superheroes and online games, but also in terms of cosplay's rapid geographic spread across cultural spaces and places, real and virtual. This has resulted in glocalized interpretations of the cosplay practice within the multiple, hybrid forms that it assumes wherever it takes root. At a more grounded level, the future of cosplay will depend on how cosplayers interact, and how they relate to media texts and to the producers of these texts. Less than a decade ago, cosplay was a relatively specialized, unknown and misunderstood practice of marginalized *otakus*, yet it has now gained in recognition and understanding due to technological exposure in popular culture.

As with most fan communities, cosplay initially relied on real-time encounters at commercial conventions and private meets, from North America's Worldcons, Comic-Cons and Anime Expos (AX) to Comiket in Japan and Gamescon in Germany. Now websites are used to circulate the photographic archives of cosplay moments, as discussion forums for establishing a public presence, and to share ideas about costume making and best practice. In recent years, with the general digitization and virtualization of lived experiences through mobile devices and social media, cosplay engagement has become more multi-modal. Cosplay has always had a dominant visual dimension, capturing and sharing the embodied performances of character in photographic format from cosplayer to cosplayer.[14] Now the global coser community has the technology to match its ambitions, and has recently gained wider media attention in relation to photographic and video material distributed over a variety of visual platforms. As Lucy Bennett observes of the extended creativity of fandom communities, in general, via digital channels:

> The Internet and social media has fostered the prospect of these activities within fandom to be circulated more easily and quickly than before, potentially reaching larger audiences, with fan studies scholarship similarly continuing a focus on these activities.

Fans can create videos of themselves performing, compose fanvids, remixes and mashups and upload these to video platforms such as YouTube, circulating the links widely.[15]

This has broadened cosplay's reach and pushed the fan experience into other dimensions, such as music video production on photo hobbyist and social media sites, giving rise to its iteration as 'digital cosplay' by fans of clothing companies.[16] As Paul Booth explains, the social media website Polyvore, for example,

> has become a site for participants to enact digital cosplay. Polyvore is funded by fashion companies and enables users to collect images of clothing from around the web, create new fashions by combining them into outfits, and then display these outfits for others to browse [...] demonstrating the convergence of top-down and bottom-up content creation [...]. By integrating pastiche with parody and nostalgia with novelty, digital cosplay enables a new understanding of digital fandom in our culture and functions as a symbol of media play [...] costuming without physicality, drag without performance.[17]

The evolution of new, immersive forms of communication technologies, such as virtual reality (VR) and augmented reality (AR), will also affect how any future fan community interacts with its sources. They will enable mixed or virtualized presentations of self, which may reshape the material dimensions of cosplay practice and its DIY culture. Yet as an embodied performative practice, digital or virtual dimensions may still prove to be more of a complement to cosplay's core materiality, physicality and social psychology than an existential threat.[18]

Citing Pierre Levy's visionary work, *Collective Intelligence* (1999), Henry Jenkins argues that the emergence of self-organized community with the arrival of digital technologies has de-territorialized knowledge, signalling the demise of traditional organic groups such as the family, or organized groups such as commercial institutions. In its place emerges a 'cosmopedia' representing new forms of community and citizenship. According to this vision of the future, groups based on knowledge production and exchange in the new knowledge communities

> will be voluntary, temporary, and tactical affiliations, defined through common intellectual enterprises and emotional investments. Members may shift from one community to another as their interests and needs change and they may belong to more than one community at the same time. Yet, they are held together through the mutual production and reciprocal exchange of knowledge.[19]

In many ways, this view consolidates existing realities as fan communities are already connecting up across multiple platforms and technoscapes. These expansive, self-organizing groups are focused around the collective production, debate and circulation of meanings, interpretations and fantasies in response to various artefacts of contemporary popular culture. Online fan communities might well be the most fully realized versions of Levy's cosmopedia.

Fan communities have long defined their memberships through affinities rather than in terms of specific localities. Fandoms were 'imagined' and 'imagining' communities, long before the introduction of networked computers.[20] Yet—and perhaps this is the point—the medium for cosplay is first and foremost a message in an embodied form, with digital encounters on Instagram and Snapchat furthering, but not replacing, the original performance and the DIY culture associated with it. Digital cosplay, as Booth points out, is quite different in the sense that it operates at a physical remove from the body and the performance, although it inhabits a parallel universe of fandom. In essence, it is a playful, pastiche-oriented activity based on a consumption-based performance. But arguably 'in person' cosplay is, and will remain, more pleasurable and transgressive, especially where sensuous dimensions of physical embodiment such as cosqueer and cosporn are concerned.

The usefulness of technological advancements for knowledge exchange also suggests that the future of cosplay may come to represent a particular form of agency. This operates both individually and collectively. Indeed, as a measure of this potential cosplayers are already running tutorials both on and offline.[21] Sites such as Kamui Cosplay[22] provide cosplayers with a step-by-step, thirty-stage guide teaching them how to tailor-make their own costumes from raw materials. These include the design and the fabrication of body armour, including the use of 3D printing production techniques and 3D modelling softwares (3D Studio Max, Rhino and Maya), enabling cosplayers to bring their 'own inner superhero to life.'[23] In assisting the DIY aspects of the culture, the technology enables cosplayers to make more realistic armour, for example, saving time and money in the process.[24]

The roots of cosplay are indubitably commodity-based, as with many fandoms, given that characters are located in largely mainstream popular culture texts that are the source of pleasure as pastiche, mimicked re-presentation or textual reproduction for the cosplayer. As Jenkins observes, the 'emergent knowledge cultures never fully escape the influence of the commodity culture, any more than commodity culture can totally function outside the constraints of territoriality [...] within the culture industries, where the commodities that circulate become resources for the production of meaning.'[25] This may further presage the blurring of lines between cultural producer and consumer, industry and interpreter, 'to form a reading-writing continuum, which will extend from the machine and network designers to the ultimate recipient, each helping to sustain the activities of the others.'[26]

The creative aspects of the practice are likely to continue to develop, from costume making and photography to competitive performances at commercial events and cons. Cosplay practitioners buy into the experience, from the text, at one end of the continuum, to the material manifestation of their practice, at the other. Their exchange values vary according to geographic location and their proximity to centres of industrial production. In China, for example, outfits and accessories can be sourced, crafted and customized at relatively low cost. Allied to this need, cosplayers may also increasingly become producers and prosumers. Cosplay entrepreneurship or fantrepreneurship is a controversial but growing trend whereby cosers sell their skills. These are businesses in the niche entrepreneurial economy where play becomes work constituting a form of emotional labour.[27] As Yaya Han, judge and former contestant from Syfy Channel's *Heroes of Cosplay* (2013–14) and *Cosplay Melee* (2017–) reality television show, spins it: 'Beyond the fun and fulfilment of hands on crafting, cosplay also is a confidence builder, a great way to make friends and be social, a fitness motivator, and for some people, inspiration to pursue a creative field.'[28] Complaints against the show and Han's particular role in it for the moment aside, it is possible, however, that putting cosplay in the public eye (and a commercial frame) may begin to erode the relatively relaxed attitude towards intellectual property (IP) that rights holders appear to have had towards cosplay.

Some physically based technologies may also prove disruptive, such as 3D printing, which is already being deployed in the manufacture of some cosplay garments, saving significant labour.[29] Creative technologies may or may not prove to be a major motivator for cosers, as their involvement often emerges from affect and the expert knowledge acquired over time that is applied to and extended across the performative cosplay moment. There can, of course, be such a thing as overexposure, and a cultural phenomenon can become over-appropriated by commercial enterprises, awakening the latent tensions that exist between producer and consumer. *Heroes of Cosplay*, for instance, notoriously featured the exploits of a group of cosplayers as they compete in events across the United States. Rather than enhance understanding of the cosplay phenomenon among a viewing public, for many viewers and cosplayers the show isolated and stigmatized it by trivializing the underlying impetus to cosplay within

> [a] really terrible, manipulative, mean-spirited reality TV series that completely misrepresents the entire hobby and craft of cosplaying, makes cosplayers look like a bunch of backstabbing harpies and generally does a disservice to the already widely-misunderstood world of people who just like making costumes and showing them off at silly nerd conventions.[30]

Among the shows' sins were making the female caste appear overly dependent on the men, undermining a major site of female agency in DIY practice. These stereotypical images of fan production, as Suzanne Scott writes, 'not only persist but also are often used to reentrench the notion that male fans are more adept at professionalizing their labor and discursively discipline female fans who make similar efforts to monetize their mimetic fan works.'[31] In this way, the embodied performance of identity in material form masks existing hierarchical power relations. Interestingly, Syfy's revised approach to cosplay in the updated televised form of *Cosplay Melee* suggests that cosplay creation has proved to be viable entertainment content that was sustainable, at least as reality TV. Concerns about the competitive ethos of the elimination style format aside, viewed generously it affirms that cosplay practice is not a shallow, sensationalist, freaky pursuit, but rather a competitive showcase of accomplished craft, artistic and theatrical competencies in 'an epic showdown of creativity, eye popping costumes and one of a kind characters [...]. Each week four world class cosplayers compete to create not only intricate full-body costumes—but fully-formed characters that they must bring to life through their own realistic performance.'[32]

Nonetheless, negative responses to cosplay are widespread and, as with comics in the 1950s, reflect concerns, if not panics, by liberals (racism, female objectification, tokenism and exoticization) and conservatives (deviancy, hypersexuality and queering). There is also the flaming of cosplayers who are supposedly guilty of inauthentic character representation, being overweight, of the wrong 'race' or so on. Such reactions can be considered as symptomatic of sociocultural anxieties about negotiating diverse identities within the cosphere. Cosplayers largely appear undeterred by such negativity or the framing of it as 'dark-play' in what Richard Schechner calls its 'disruption, deceit, excess and gratification.'[33] Often this notion of cosplay as a transgressive and liminal performance only serves to amplify cosers' resolve to continue with their creative pursuit, while legitimizing it in opposition to a normative world that they are perhaps also keen to escape. Increasingly, there are numerous examples cited in the public domain of cosplay becoming normalized and being integrated into normative spaces such as in advertising or store openings, weddings or libraries.[34] When cosplay occurs in social and commercial settings not normally associated with the practice, the fan performance becomes naturalized and is opened up to a wider community of interest. However, tensions also emerge when the enactment of cosplay is (neo)liberalized and the rules of the game are challenged, or not faithfully adhered to, due to ignorance, non-engagement or in the deliberate affronts to existing ways of being and doing.

Debates about the future of fandom, in general, often centre on the offline versus online duality and importance of fan participation.[35] Received wisdom appears to concede that both sites of engagement are important to the fan experience and to the formation of identity that appears to be residing at the core ethos of fandom. Both online and offline forms of cosplay engagement are here to stay, given the symbiotic nature of the two. As Paul Booth and Peter Kelly suggest:

> Despite the widespread adoption of the Internet into fan practices, it's the *in person* community that seems to matter much more. Like a family meeting for holidays or birthdays, being online helps organize but does not replace the sense of belonging. This is not to say that all fans participate in their fandom offline: for many, circumstance, limited mobility, and/or finances prevent attendance at conventions. For these fans, the computer and social media specifically are ways of deepening the ties between fan communities and have become influential on their fan practices. But for fans that have the financial and social capital, traveling to conventions remains an important fannish event, augmented by online messages but reliant on in-person dialogue.[36]

On the one hand, the dual, dialogic identity of individual cosplayers and the coser as part of a wider group has been seen as a visual metaphor that anchors fans' singular identities in the collective context of a wider fan community.[37] On the other hand, the desire to be connected and to be engaged in between real-time connections also continues to drive online interactions. Thus, one can simultaneously satisfy an affective need to be connected to an imaginary world and its inhabitants while sharing a deep devotion with like-minded others.

It seems likely that future cosplay practice will continue to traverse geographic, cultural, public, private, commercial, social, psychological, affective real-time and digital spaces and places. In doing so, it may transcend new boundaries as emerging hybrid forms of cosplay continue to develop in future. Perhaps in Asia, for example, we will see more of a loosening up of prescribed and imitative ways of cosplaying characters, with more open interpretations and hybrid character forms appearing at cons and photo shoots, with semiotic meaning founded on creating an ironic distance between the original source and the intertextual interpretation. There is an inherent inclusivity to spaces when participants choose to make the effort and dress up as their favourite character, irrespective of age, gender, ethnicity or sexual orientation. This also aligns with the postmodern trend towards more gender, racial and sexual inclusivity.[38] Of course, the global cosplay community has not been protected from wider culture wars, with heated discussion surrounding issues of authenticity—as to whether, for example, a person who does not share the same ethnicity or skin colour as the original character is a viable cosplay choice. Yet, on the whole, the tolerance for character interpretation, as exemplified by crossplaying, for example, is broad, and relatively without judgement or issue.[39]

The affirmative role of cosplay in this respect, as well as its socio-cognitive dimensions, could see a role for it in educational practice concerned with developing critical literacies[40] or as a kind of performative correlate to narrative therapy.[41] In a recent article Shonagh Walsh has discussed how cosplaying in her self-made costumes, along with designing or fixing them for others, provided self-treatment for her depression:

> I have a huge amount of fun at conventions. I dress up and don't have to be me, I can forget my typical world worries for a while […]. People talk to me about common interests, which helps with my anxiety greatly […]. Cosplay has helped me in a lot of ways. When I started, I had huge stage fright and hated public speaking. Now that I'm invited as a guest, and asked to do talks about cosplay, I've got so much better at that. What was at first terrifying I'm now fairly confident with […]. No matter where you go in the world, or no matter what club you join, there are always going to be negative people who will be nasty. But at the end of the day, we're just a bunch of nerds in costumes just trying to have fun.[42]

Rates of disaffection and indeed depression appear to be at all-time highs across the developed world, especially among youth, who are struggling to stake a viable claim on a crowded planet that is itself imperilled by political and environmental ennui.

What, then, will the future of Planet Cosplay look like? Will it resemble a traditional masked ball out of a *Rose of Versailles (Berusaiyu no Bara)* (1979–80)[43] narrative by Riyoko Ikeda, where female protagonist Oscar adopts gender fluid guises at the pre-revolutionary court of Marie Antoinette in order to uncover anti-monarchy plots and intrigue? Or will it resemble a neo-Utopian state—'a dream of a better world'[44]—after Plato's *Republic* or Thomas or Moore's *Utopia* (1516),[45] perhaps via constructed augmented spaces where people exist in virtual harmony. Similar worlds have been conjured in anime with *Aria The Animation's* (2005–15)[46] paradisal, terraformed, home planet, Aqua, where we follow young female protagonist Akari Mizunashi as she trains to be an apprentice gondolier in its peaceful, waterlogged landscape. Equally, in *Time of Eve (Eve no Jikan)* (2008–09),[47] the young male protagonist Rikuo Sakisaka grapples with the most appropriate way of engaging with the storyworld's omnipresent androids, raising vexed questions of whether artificial intelligence (AI) can or should ever be equal in a society that is totally reliant on it. All of which recalls the paradox that utopia cannot perhaps exist without dystopia, or at least makes little sense without the existence of an opposite state of play and conflicting characters with competing moral compasses. Devastated, post-apocalyptic worlds are common subject matter not just for popular Hollywood fare such as the recent film franchise (2012–15) adaptations of Suzanne Collins' young adult novel series, *The Hunger Games*,[48] where teenagers are pitted against each other in combative public games in the deadliest fight for survival. Many anime storyworlds, such as *Wolf's Rain (Urufuzu Rein)* (2003–04) by Keiko Nobumoto,[49] evoke a near future dystopia, though there is always the spectre of hope. Here, the solution to a poverty-stricken world resides in the shape of ancient wolves that assume human form and know the secret location of an earthly paradise.

While many cosers partake in dystopian, politically and environmentally ravaged universes—both fictional and real world—where totalitarian elites regularly mete out savage and inhumane treatments on their citizens, they often choose to represent characters who are fighting to remedy such inequities and preserve some semblance of justice. Post-apocalyptic worlds depicted in popular mediated narratives represent an exaggerated form of reality, yet are extrapolating on real issues faced in everyday existence in late capitalism. Cosplayers are not just escaping their pressured lives and inhabiting a fictional persona and fictitious universe, but also perhaps using cosplay to make sense of, and deal with, their everyday existence. The deep gratification in interpreting, creating and controlling another persona often motivates character choice, empowering the cosplayer and reinforcing their agency. As Dan explains:

When I'm Obi Wan or a Stormtrooper I do feel so much more confident—it's as if I've tapped into a powerful force and I can't be defeated. I feel like I could do anything and be anyone and whatever came my way I could deal with it. My pressurized work life seems like it's in a galaxy far away and I feel much more positive about everything. And it doesn't just work on the surface cosplay presentation as I have made and customized every part of my outfit. I get a lot of praise about that which also makes me feel as if I have really achieved something which I can honestly say doesn't happen at work—where I'm actually a work slave. For most of the day in the office I'm criticized for not getting things right and where I do not feel powerful in any way. But as a cosplayer I don't have to go through that. I feel in charge and in control of my life and that's a powerful way to be.

(Dan, 25, male trainee accountant, Hong Kong)

Despite the fragmented ethnoscapes of the postmodern, and perhaps posthuman, world, cosplay provides spaces of *communitas* that develop their own internal social structure and ways of operating. These are based on the inner resources of its participants who act as 'liminaries' and mobilize 'sensorily perceptible rituals and symbols which frame and consolidate their existence as a community'[50] in opposition to the norm.

In sum, while it faces multiple challenges and the ever-present threat of co-option and récupération, it seems likely that cosplay will continue to function as a therapeutic and empowering site for cosplayers. With the recent regressive turn in western politics, cosplay's fluidity of identity and mixing and matching of global culture seems more vital than ever. It has even been explicitly linked with ludic protest against ethnic prejudice.[51] Perhaps this transgressive dimension comes with the territory. After all, cosplay habitually plays with multiple possibilities and can accommodate many stories and characters. Across the mutable, bounded yet borderless universe of the cosphere, where the social, cultural and affective intersect, cosplayers look set to continue to engage in transformative acts that allow them to discover new forms of agency, inhabit new identities and explore alternate sexualities. In this, Planet Cosplay is a type of heterotopia, an ideal universe based on the extraordinary celebration of diversity and deviance in a world that is increasingly dystopian yet aches with possibility. On Planet Cosplay, every abject body is invited to the party—to have fun, transgress and to demonstrate their innate craft, while practicing creative, artistic and performative skills and knowledge. In the words of one superhero: 'The future is worth it. All the pain. All the tears. The future is worth the fight.'[52]

Notes

1   *Chrono Crusade*, directed by Shoten Kadokawa (Tokyo: Madmen Entertainment, 2003), Anime film.

2   *Iron Man*, directed by Jon Favreau (Hollywood: Paramount Pictures, 2008), Film.

3   See *Marvel's The Avengers*, directed by Joss Whedon (Burbank: Walt Disney Studios Motion Pictures, 2012), Film; *Neon Genesis Evangelion (Shin Seiki Evangerion)*, directed by Hideki Ano (Tokyo: TV Tokyo, 1995–96), Anime TV series.

4   *Pale Cocoon (Peiru Kokūn)*, directed by Yasuhiro Yoshiura (Tokyo: Studio Rikka, 2006), Anime film; *In Search of the Lost Future (Ushinawareta Mirai o Motomete)*, created by Trumple and Atelier High Key (Tokyo: Comp Ace, 2010), Manga; *Erased (Boku dake ga Inai Machi)*, directed by Tomohiko Itō (Tokyo: Fuji TV, 2016), Anime TV series.

5   John Fiske, *Understanding Popular Culture* (London: Unwin Hyman, 1989), 24–25.

6   Larry Grossberg, 'Is There a Fan in the House?: The Affective Sensibility of Fandom,' in *The Adoring Audience: Fan Culture and Popular Media*, ed. Lisa Lewis (New York: Routledge, 1992), 60–65.

7   Michel Maffesoli, *The Time of the Tribes: The Decline of Individualism in Mass Society* (London: Sage, 1996), 5–6.

8   Roberta Pearson, 'Fandom in the Digital Era,' *Popular Communication* 8, no. 1 (2010), 84–95.

9   Henry Jenkins, 'Afterword: The Future of Fandom,' in *Fandom: Identities and Communities in a Mediated World*, eds. Jonathan Gray, C. Lee Harrington, and Cornell Sandvoss (New York: New York University Press, 2007), 357–64.

10 Joli Jenson, 'Fandom as Pathology: The Consequences of Characterization,' in *The Adoring Audience: Fan Culture and Popular Media*, ed. Lisa A. Lewis (Hove, UK: Psychology Press, 1992), 9–29.

11 Fujiko F. Fujio, *Doraemon* (Tokyo: Shogakukan, 1969–), Manga; *Doraemon* (Tokyo: Nippon TV, 1972), Anime TV series; *Doraemon* (Tokyo: TV Asahi, 1979–2005), Anime TV series; *Doraemon* (Tokyo: Asahi TV, 2005), Anime TV series; *Final Fantasy (Fainaru Fantajī)*, Hironobu Sakaguchi (Tokyo: Nintendo Entertainment System, 1987–), Console game.

12 Janet H. Murray, *Hamlet on the Holodeck: The Future of Narrative in Cyberspace* (Cambridge: The MIT Press, 2017), 24.

13 Henry Jenkins, *Fans, Bloggers, and Gamers: Exploring Participatory Culture* (New York: New York University Press, 2006), 137.

14 Craig Norris and Jason Bainbridge, 'Selling *Otaku*? Mapping the Relationship between Industry and Fandom in the Australian Cosplay Scene,' *Intersections: Gender and Sexuality in Asia and the Pacific* 20 (2009), para. 4.

15 Lucy Bennett, 'Tracing Textual Poachers: Reflections of the Development of Fan Studies and Digital Fandom,' *Journal of Fandom Studies* 2, no. 1 (2014), 8.

16 Nicolle Lamerichs, 'Stranger than Fiction: Fan Identity in Cosplay,' *Transformative Works and Cultures* 7, no. 3 (2011), para. 2.1–2.2.

17 Paul Booth, *Playing Fans: Negotiating Fandom and Media in the Digital Age* (Iowa City: University of Iowa Press, 2015), 151.

18 Scott Duchesne, 'Little Reckonings in Great Rooms: The Performance of Cosplay,' *Canadian Theatre Review* (2005), 17–26.

19 Jenkins, *Fans, Bloggers, and Gamers*, 137.

20 Jenkins, 'Afterword,' 357–64; Henry Jenkins, *Convergence Culture: Where Old and New Media Collide* (New York: New York University Press), 2006.

21 Brian Ashcraft and Luke Plunkett, *Cosplay World* (Munich: Prestel, 2014).

22 Anon, KamuiCosplay, accessed 1 January 2018, https://www.kamuicosplay.com/.

23 Yaya Han, Allison Deblasio and Joey Marsocci, *1000 Incredible Costume & Cosplay Ideas* (Singapore: Quarry Books, 2013), 6.

24 Jackie Cole, 'The Future of Cosplay, Today! Felicia Day Models 3D Printed Armor,' in Geek and Sundry (8 February 2016), accessed 1 January 2018, http://geekandsundry.com/the-future-of-cosplay-today-felicia-day-models-3d-printed-armor/.

25 Jenkins, *Fans, Bloggers, and Gamers*, 144.

26 Pierre Lévy, *Collective Intelligence* (Cambridge: Perseus Press, 1997), 28.

27 David Frayne, *The Refusal of Work: The Theory and Practice of Resistance to Work* (London: Zed Books, 2015), 52–53.

28 Han et al., *1000 Incredible Costume and Cosplay Ideas*, 7.

29 Samara Lynn, 'How to 3D Print Your Cosplay Costumes,' *PC Magazine* (14 October 2014), accessed 1 January 2018, http://au.pcmag.com/printers/25191/feature/how-to-3d-print-your-cosplay-costumes.

30 Zac Bertschy, '5 Things I Learned from SyFy's "Heroes of Cosplay,"' in *Anime News Network* (11 September 2013), accessed 1 January 2018, http://www.animenewsnetwork.com/feature/2013-09-10.

31 Suzanne Scott, '"Cosplay Is Serious Business": Gendering Material Fan Labor on *Heroes of Cosplay*,' *Cinema Journal* 54, no. 3 (Spring, 2015), 147.

32 The Futon Critic, 'Cosplayers Put Their Skills to the Test in Syfy's Newest Competition Series, "Cosplay Melee,"' accessed 1 January 2018, http://thefutoncritic.com/news/2017/02/16/cosplayers-put-their-skills-to-the-test-in-syfys-newest-competition-series-cosplay-melee-39110/20170216syfy01/.

33 Richard Schechner, *The Future of Ritual: Writings on Culture and Performance* (London and New York: Routledge, 1993), 36.

34 Rebecca Cullers, 'A Southern Chicken Chain Celebrates Anime Cosplay, but It's Not Mainstream Just Yet,' *Adweek* (8 March 2017), accessed 1 January 2018, http://www.adweek.com/creativity/a-southern-chicken-chain-celebrates-anime-cosplay-but-its-not-mainstream-just-yet/; Peter Ray Allison, 'Cosplay: "It Is Fun to be Someone Entirely Different,"' *Guardian Online* (13 May 2014), accessed 1 January 2018, https://www.theguardian.com/lifeandstyle/2014/may/13/cosplay-sci-fi-weekender-dressing-up-fantasy-characters; Paula Brehm-Heeger, Ann Conway, and Connie Vale, 'Cosplay, Gaming, and Conventions: The Amazing and Unexpected Places an Anime Club can lead Unsuspecting Librarians,' *Young Adult Library Services* 5, no. 2 (2007), 14–16.

35 Jenkins, 'Afterword,' 357–64; Nancy Baym, *Tune In, Log On: Soaps, Fandom, and Online Community* (Thousand Oaks: Sage, 2000), 157–58.

36 Paul Booth and Peter Kelly, 'The Changing Faces of *Doctor Who* Fandom: New Fans, New Technologies, Old Practices?,' *Participations* 10, no. 1 (2013), 68–69.

37 Lamerichs, 'Stranger than Fiction,' 246.

38 Kristina Busse, 'Capitalizing on the Fannish Labor of Love,' *Cinema Journal* 54, no. 3 (2015), 110–15.

39 Matthew Hale, 'Cosplay: Intertextuality, Public Texts, and the Body Fantastic,' *Western Folklore* 73, no. 1 (2014), 11.

40 Anne Peirson-Smith, 'Popular Culture as Content-Based Instruction in the Second Language Classroom to Enhance Critical Engagement,' in *Faces of English Education: Students, Teachers and Pedagogy*, eds. Ken Hyland and Lillian L. C. Wong (London: Routledge, 2017), 128.

41 Ernest Morrell, 'Toward a Critical Pedagogy of Popular Culture: Literacy Development Among Urban Youth,' *Journal of Adolescent and Adult Literacy* 46, no. 1 (2012), 77.

42 Henry Lee, 'As a Teenager I Was Struggling with Depression Which Left Me Feeling Suicidal—but Sewing Saved My Life (9 February 2017), *Belfast Telegraph*, accessed 1 January 2018, https://www.belfasttelegraph.co.uk/life/features/as-a-teenager-i-was-struggling-with-depression-which-left-me-feeling-suicidal-but-sewing-saved-my-life-35435429.html

43 *Rose of Versailles* (*Berusaiyu no Bara*), directed by Tadeo Nagahama and Osumu Dekazi (Tokyo: Tokyo Movie Shinsha, 1979–80), anime TV series.

44 James C. Davis, *Utopia and the Ideal Society: A Study of English Utopian Writing, 1516–1700* (Cambridge: Cambridge University Press, 1981), 12–13.

45 Julia Annas, *An Introduction to Plato's Republic* (Oxford: Oxford University Press, 1981); Thomas More, 'Utopia,' trans. John P. Dolan, in *The Essential Thomas More*, eds. James J. Greene and John P. Dolan (1516; New York: New American Library, 1967).

46 *Aria The Animation*, directed by Jun'ichi Sato (Tokyo: Hal Film Maker, 2005–15), Anime TV series.

47 *Time of Eve (Eve no Jikan)*, directed by Yashuhiro Yoshiura, (Tokyo: Studio Rikka, 2008–9), Anime TV series.

48 *The Hunger Games*, directed by Gary Ross (Los Angeles: Lionsgate Films, 2012), Film; Suzanne Collins, *The Hunger Games* (New York: Scholastic, 2008).

49 *Wolf's Rain (Urufuzu Rein)*, directed by Tensai Okamura (Tokyo: Madman Entertainment, 2003–04), Anime TV series.

50 Victor Witter Turner, 'Variations on a Theme of Liminality,' in *Secular Ritual*, eds. Sally F. Moore and Barbara G. Myerhoff (Assen, The Netherlands: Van Gorcum & Company, 1977), 48–49.

51 Talynn Kel, 'The World of Cosplay Is Filled with Black Joy,' in *The Huffington Post* (17 February 2017), accessed 1 January 2018, http://www.huffingtonpost.com/entry/the-world-of-cosplay-is-filled-with-black-joy_us_58b09e7be4b0658fc20f94e2.

52 Tom Mandrake, *Martian Manhunter* 2, no. 1,000,000 (New York: DC Comics: 2014), cartoon.

Index

CPSIA information can be obtained
at www.ICGtesting.com
Printed in the USA
FSHW021306230321
79755FS

SEP 0 4 2022

9 781789 381511